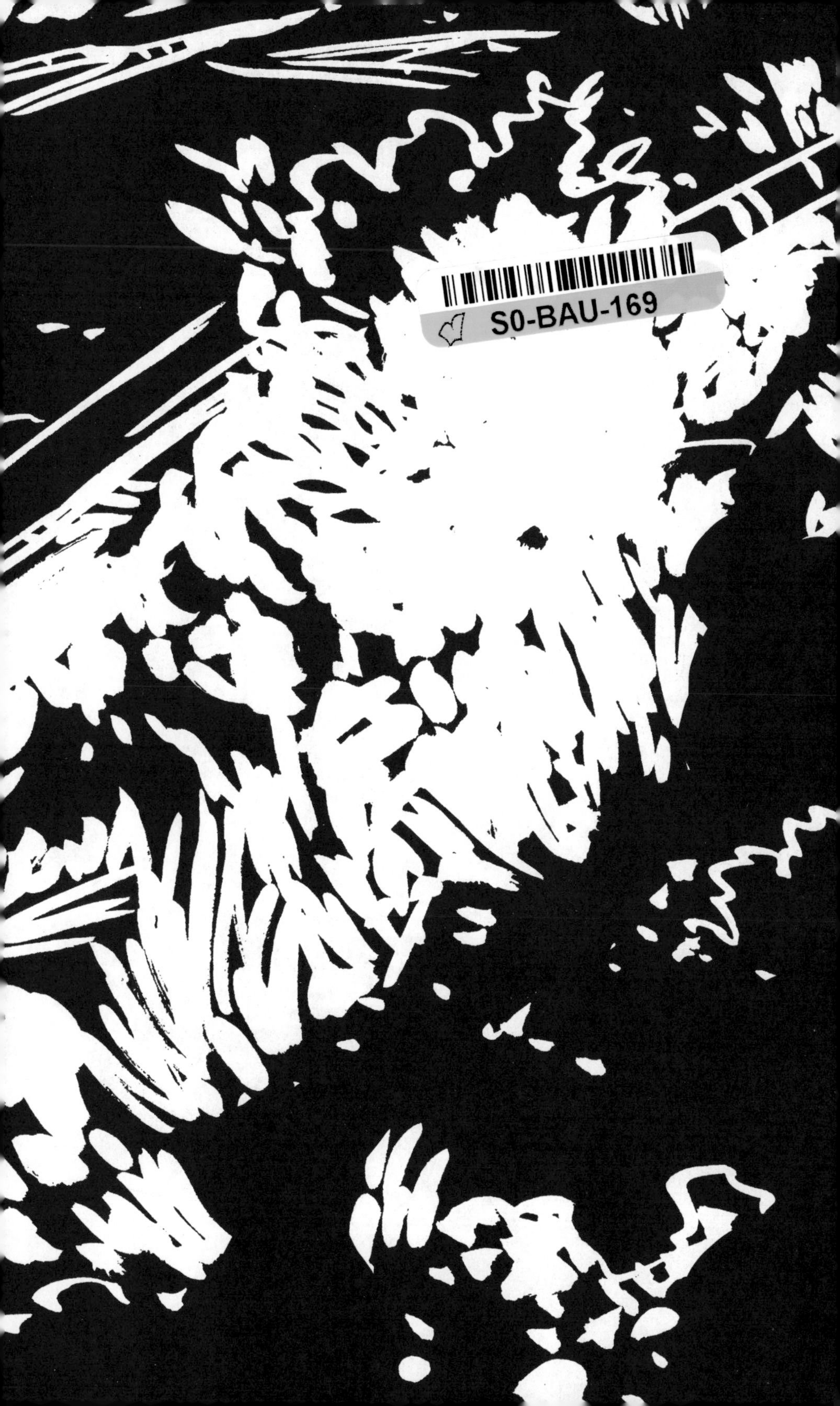

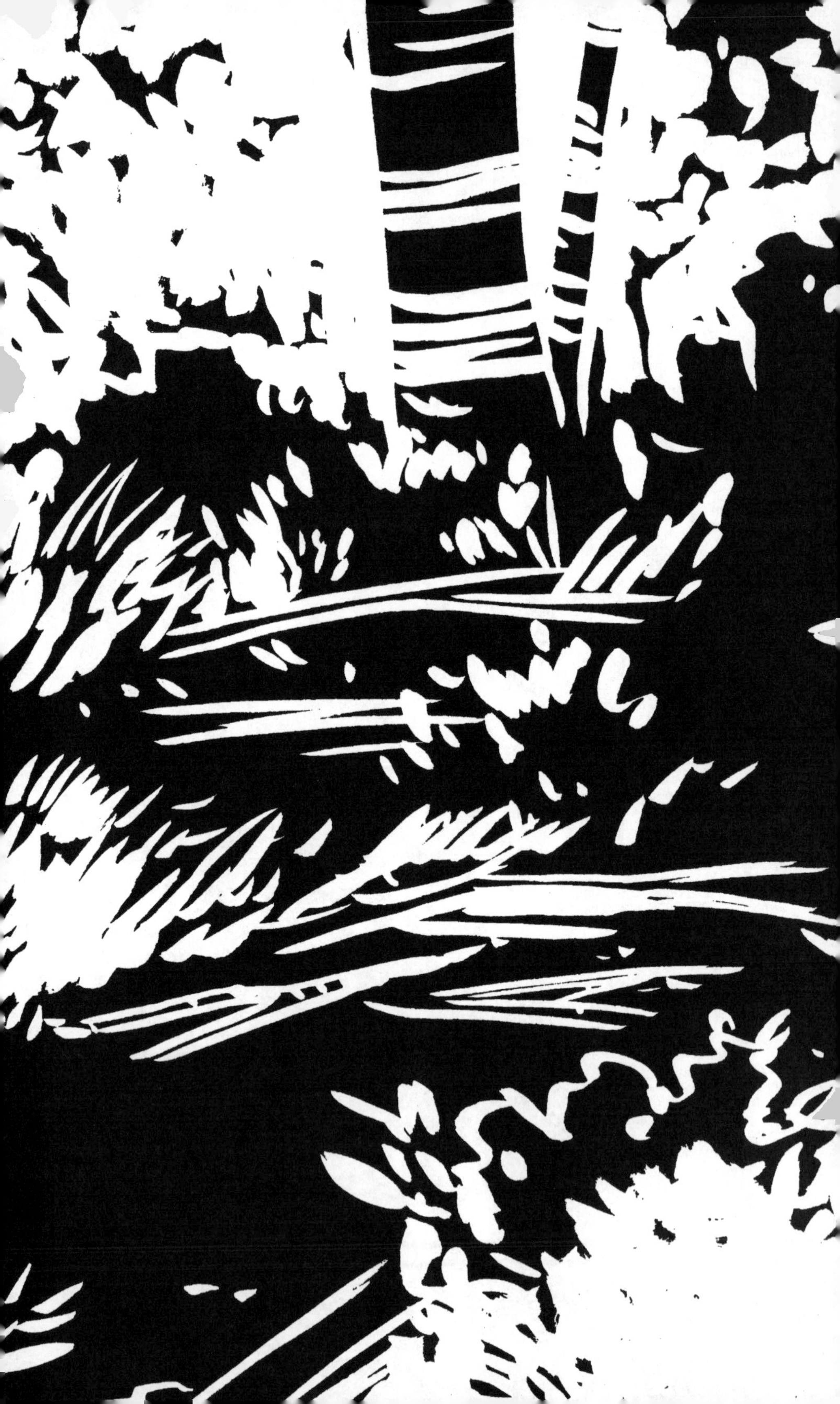

GREEN RIVER KILLER

A TRUE DETECTIVE STORY

writer **JEFF JENSEN**

artist **JONATHAN CASE**

letterer **NATE PIEKOS OF BLAMBOT**®

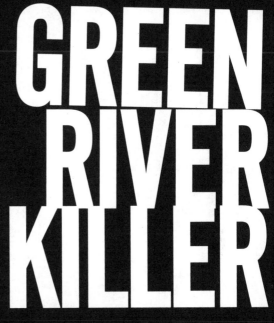

DARK HORSE BOOKS

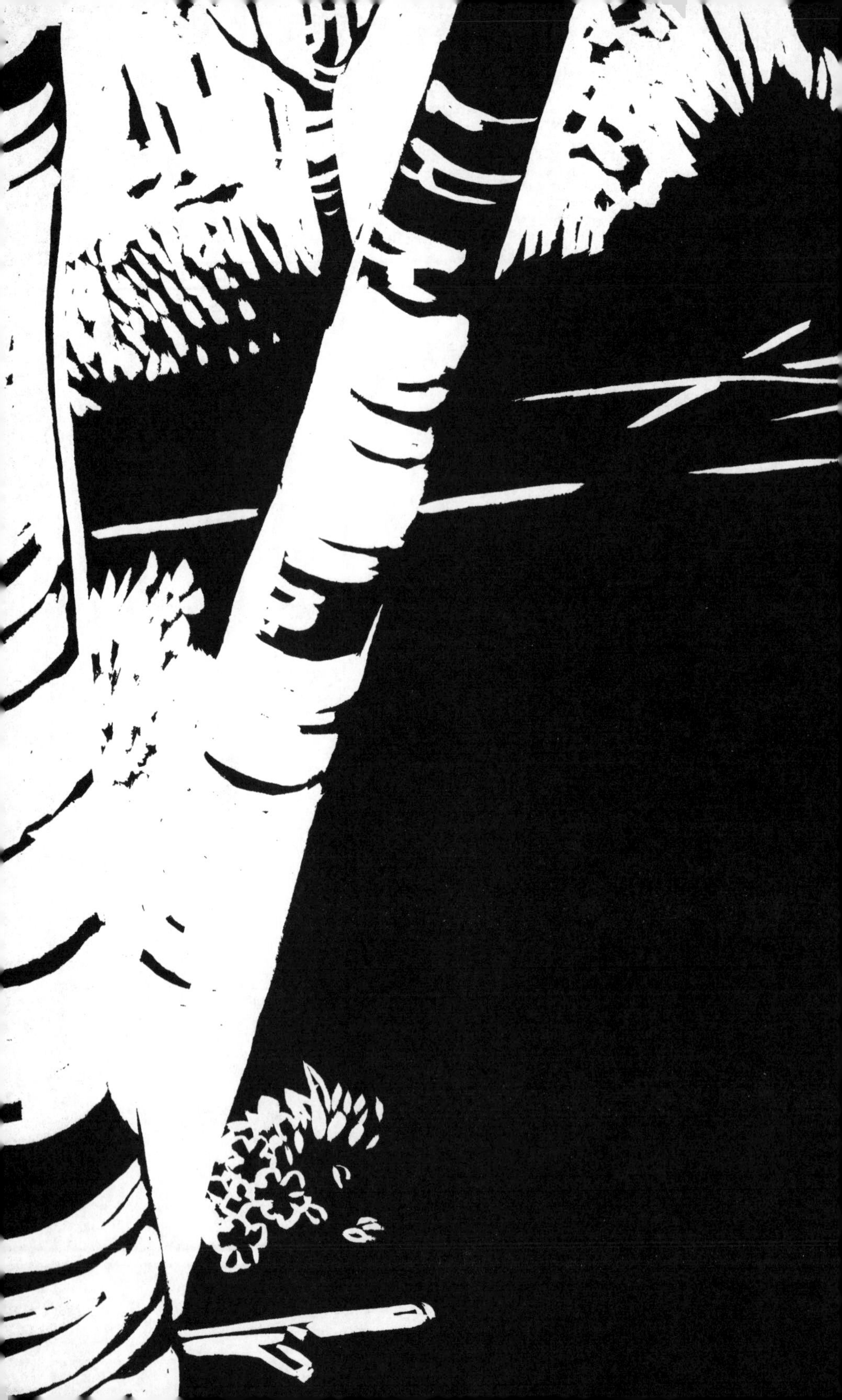

For my father, with love, admiration, and deep gratitude.
This is what you get for teaching me how to read with *Batman* comics.

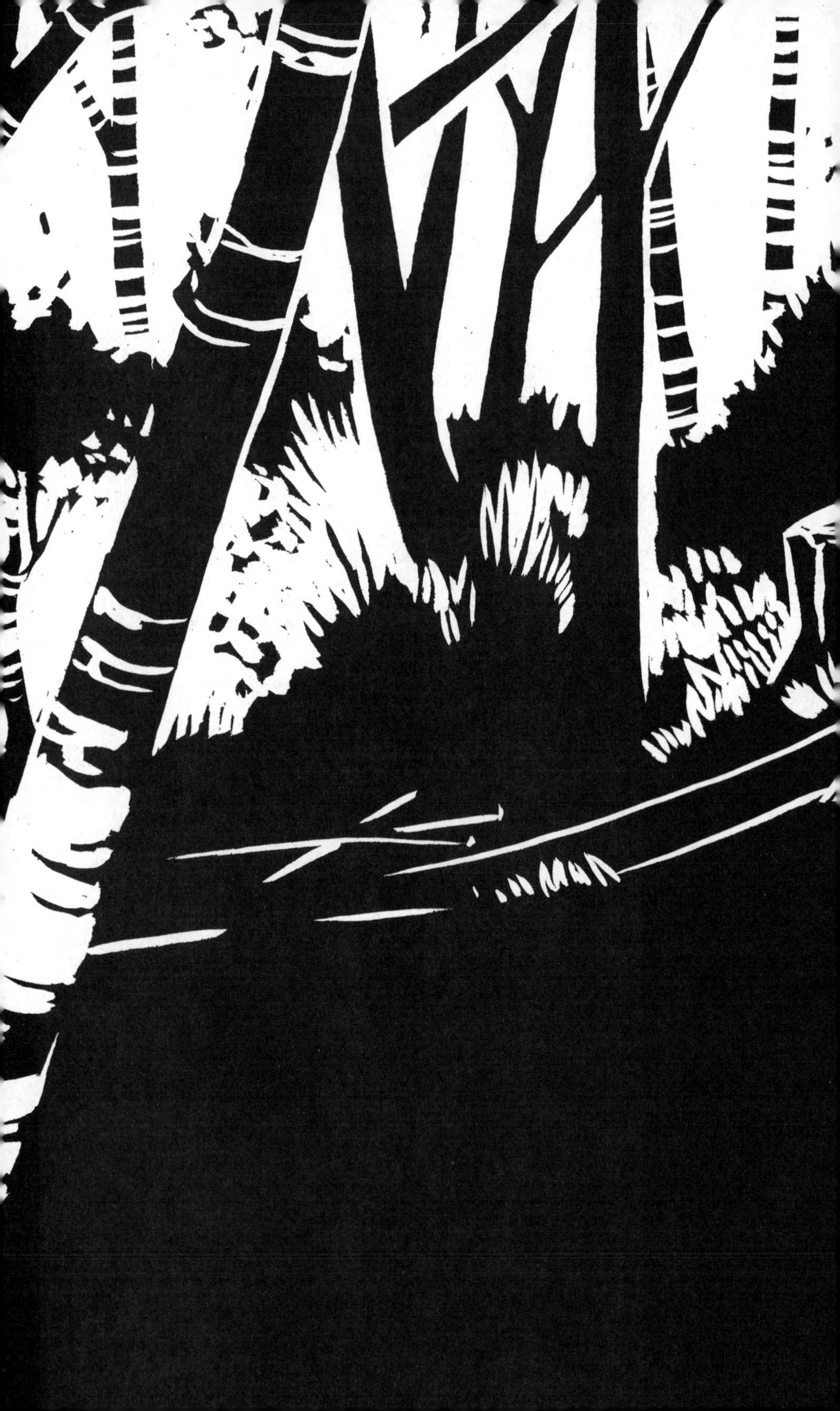

PROLOGUE: 1965

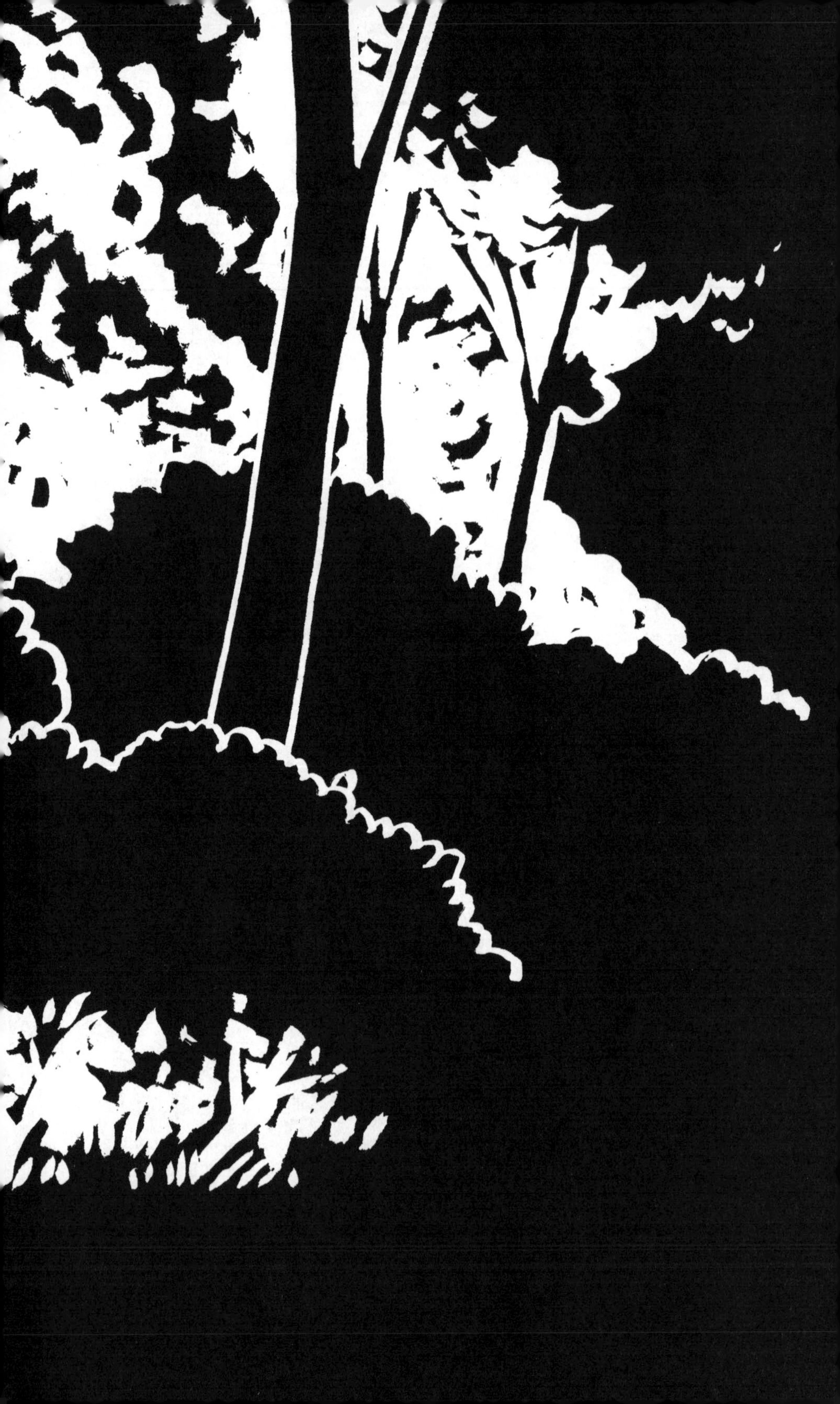

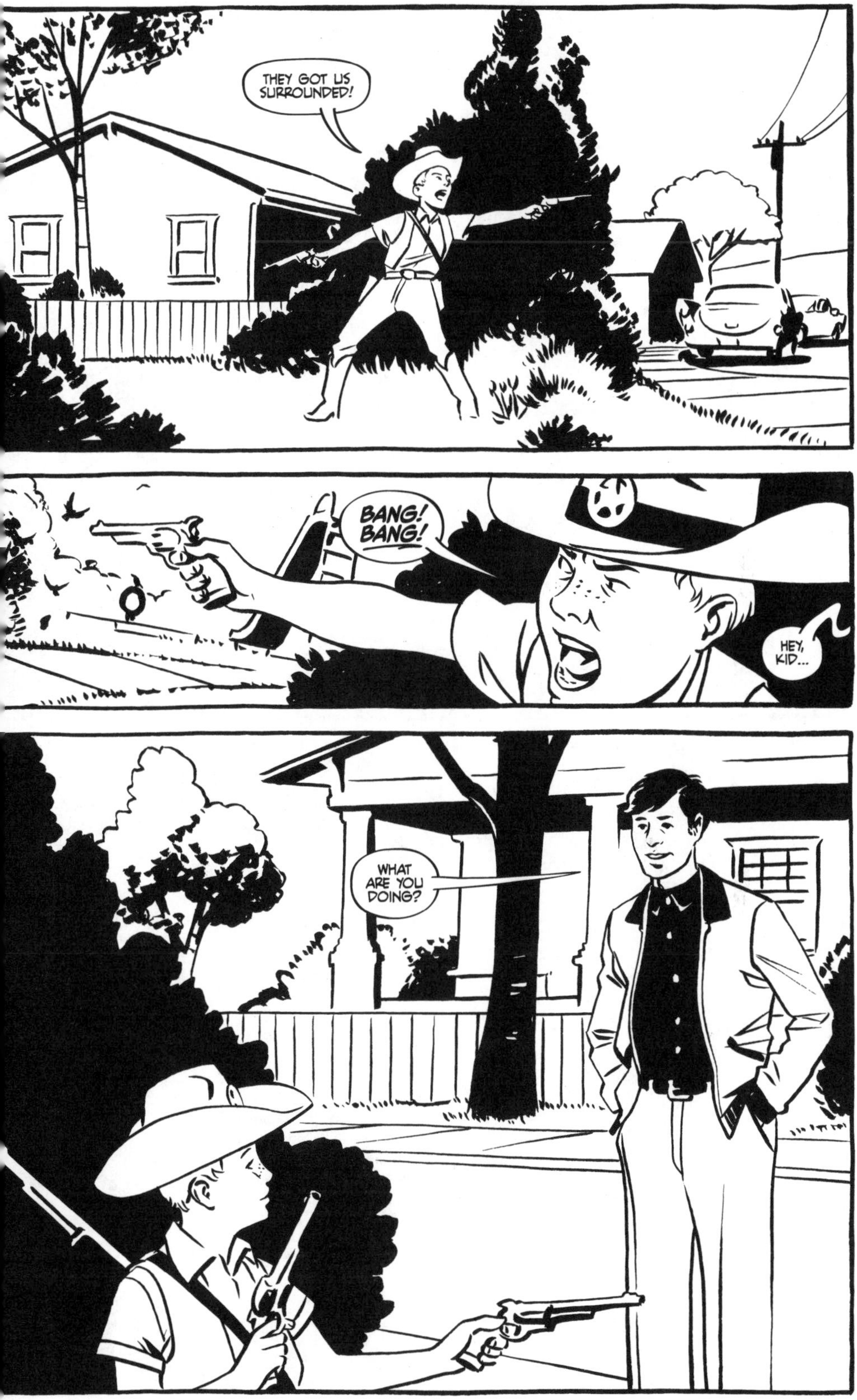
THEY GOT US SURROUNDED!
BANG! BANG!
HEY, KID...
WHAT ARE YOU DOING?

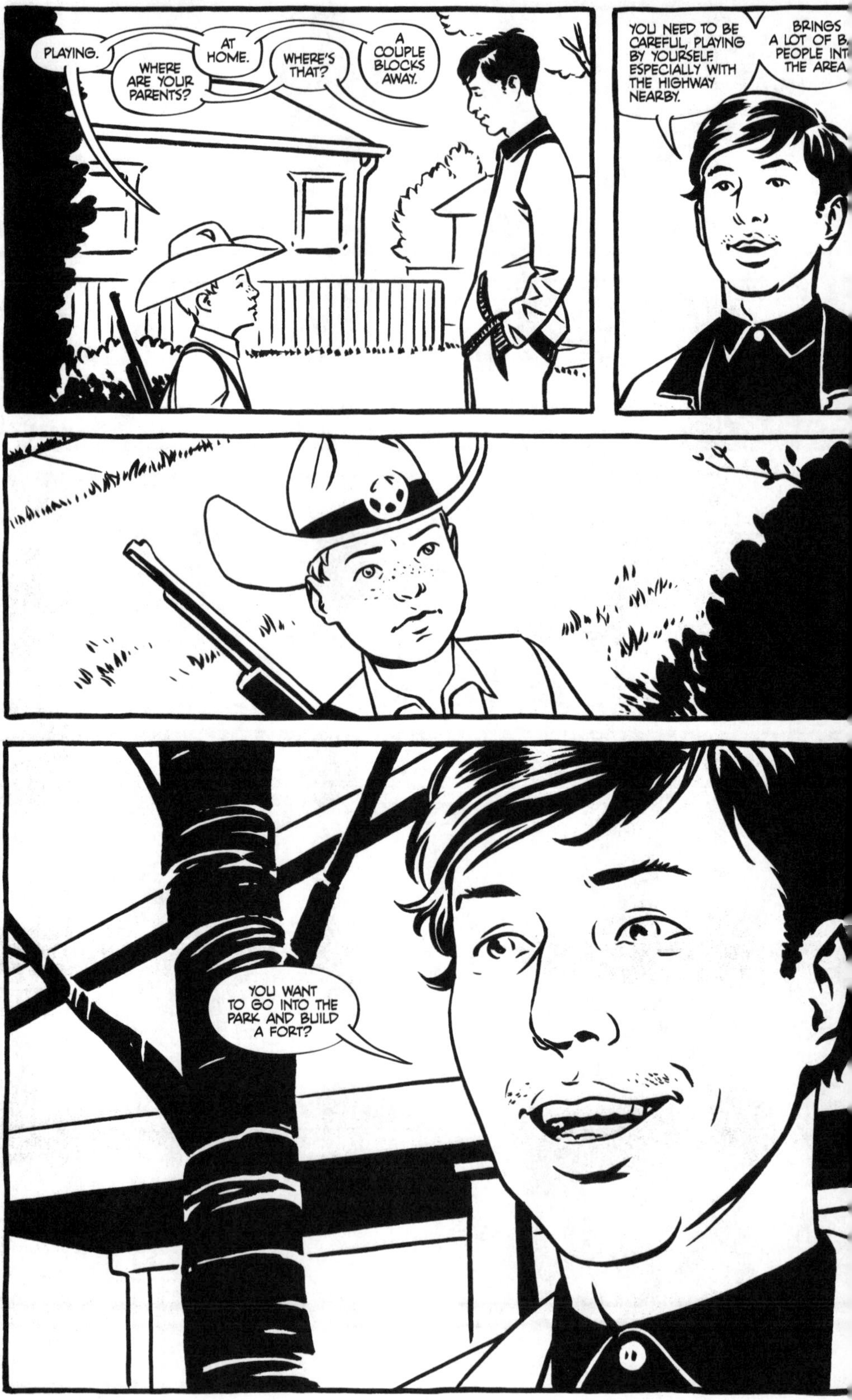
PLAYING.
WHERE ARE YOUR PARENTS?
AT HOME.
WHERE'S THAT?
A COUPLE BLOCKS AWAY.
YOU NEED TO BE CAREFUL, PLAYING BY YOURSELF. ESPECIALLY WITH THE HIGHWAY NEARBY.
BRINGS A LOT OF B
PEOPLE INT
THE AREA
YOU WANT TO GO INTO THE PARK AND BUILD A FORT?

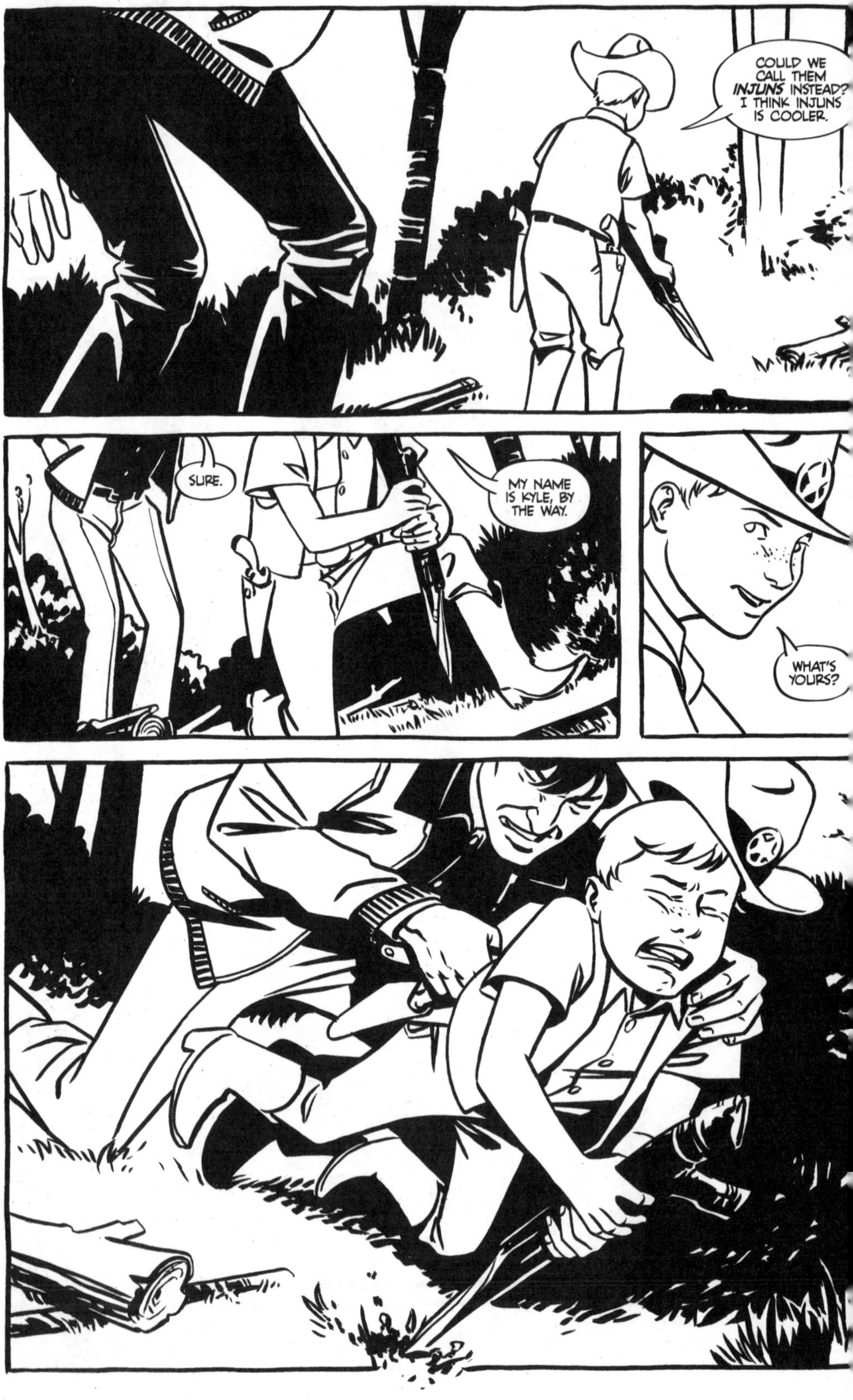
COULD WE CALL THEM INJUNS INSTEAD? I THINK INJUNS IS COOLER.
SURE.
MY NAME IS KYLE, BY THE WAY.
WHAT'S YOURS?

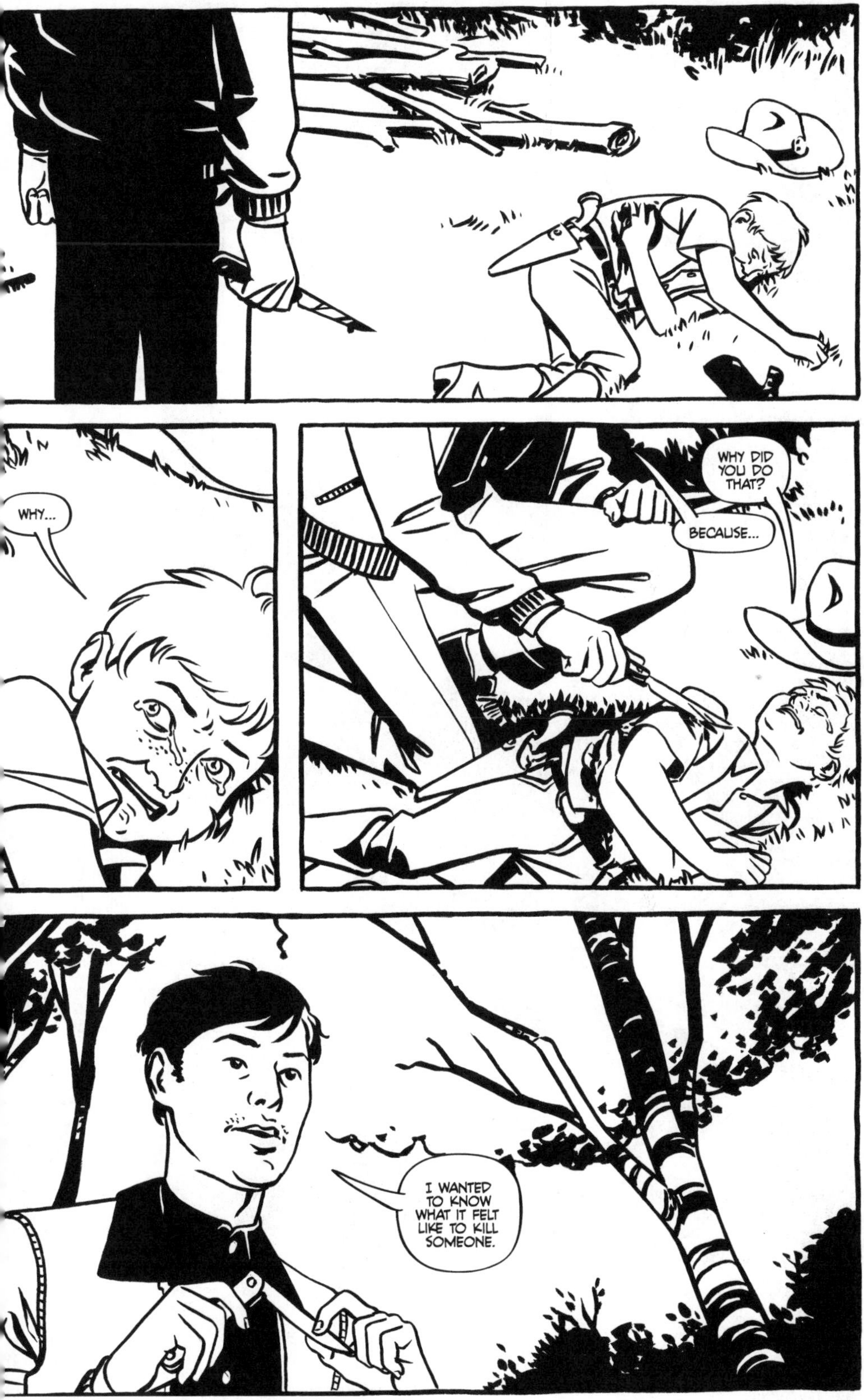
WHY...
WHY DID YOU DO THAT?
BECAUSE...
I WANTED TO KNOW WHAT IT FELT LIKE TO KILL SOMEONE.

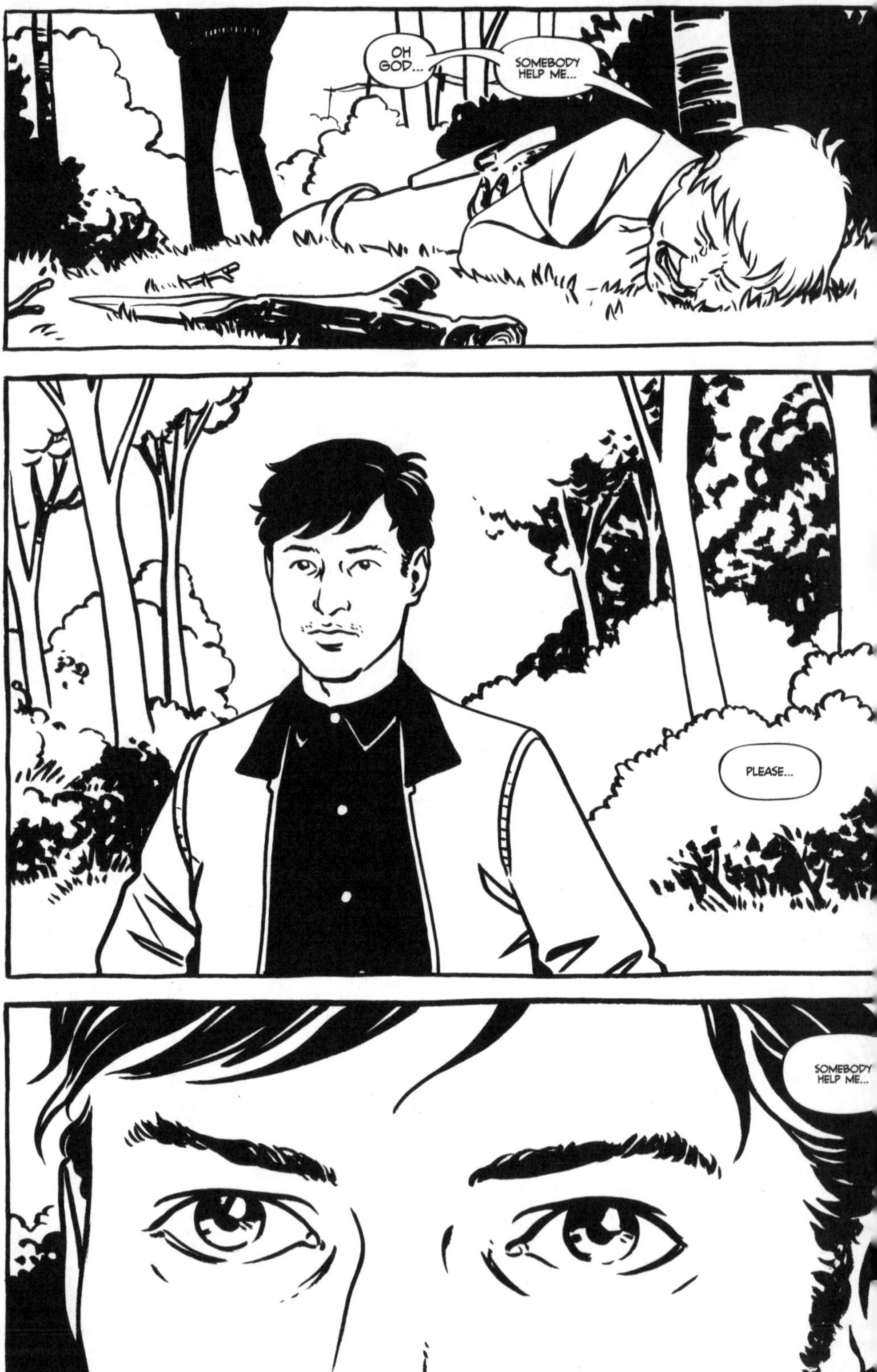
OH GOD...
SOMEBODY HELP ME...
PLEASE...
SOMEBODY HELP ME...

DAY ONE: ORIENTATION

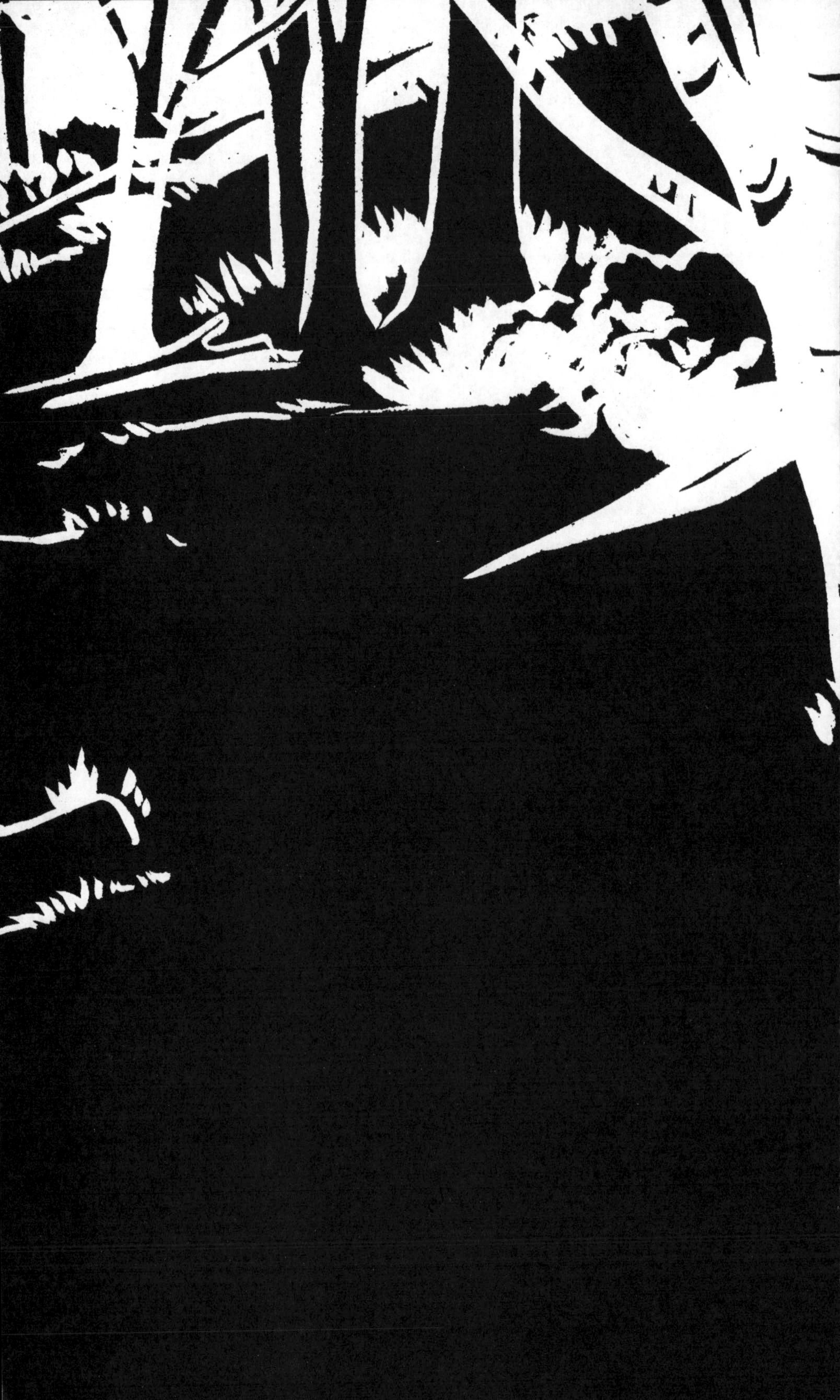

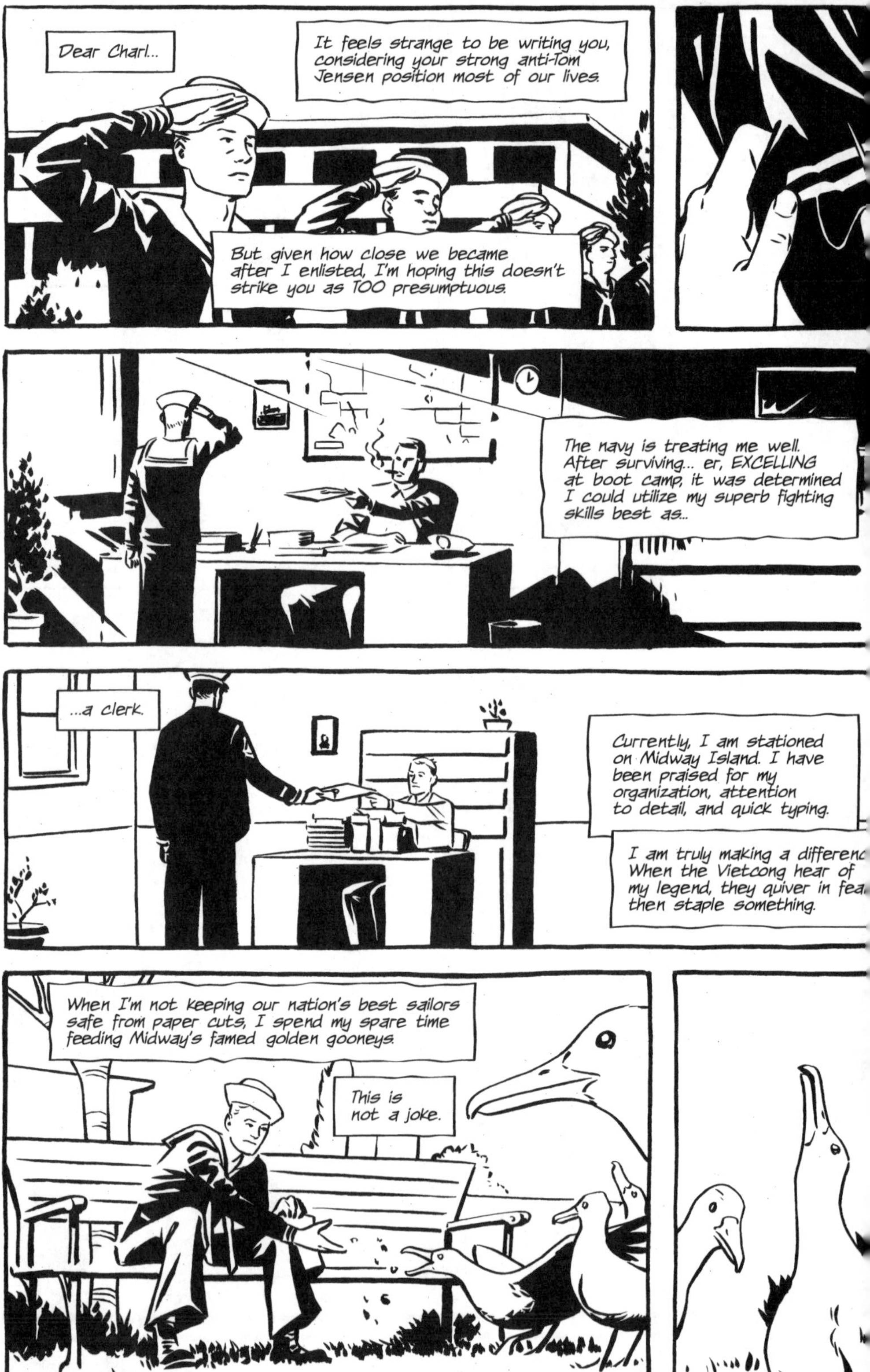
Dear Charl...
It feels strange to be writing you, considering your strong anti-Tom Jensen position most of our lives.
But given how close we became after I enlisted, I'm hoping this doesn't strike you as TOO presumptuous.
The navy is treating me well. After surviving... er, EXCELLING at boot camp, it was determined I could utilize my superb fighting skills best as...
...a clerk.
Currently, I am stationed on Midway Island. I have been praised for my organization, attention to detail, and quick typing.
I am truly making a differenc When the Vietcong hear of my legend, they quiver in fea then staple something.
When I'm not keeping our nation's best sailors safe from paper cuts, I spend my spare time feeding Midway's famed golden gooneys.
This is not a joke.

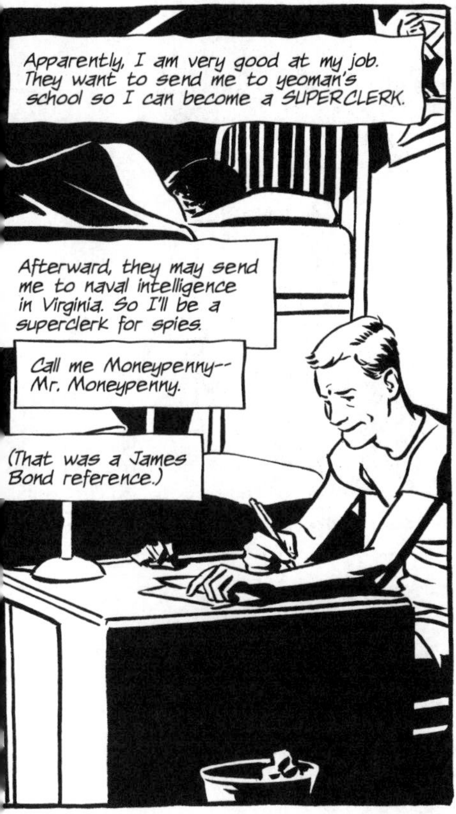
Apparently, I am very good at my job. They want to send me to yeoman's school so I can become a SUPERCLERK.
Afterward, they may send me to naval intelligence in Virginia. So I'll be a superclerk for spies.
Call me Moneypenny-- Mr. Moneypenny.
(That was a James Bond reference.)

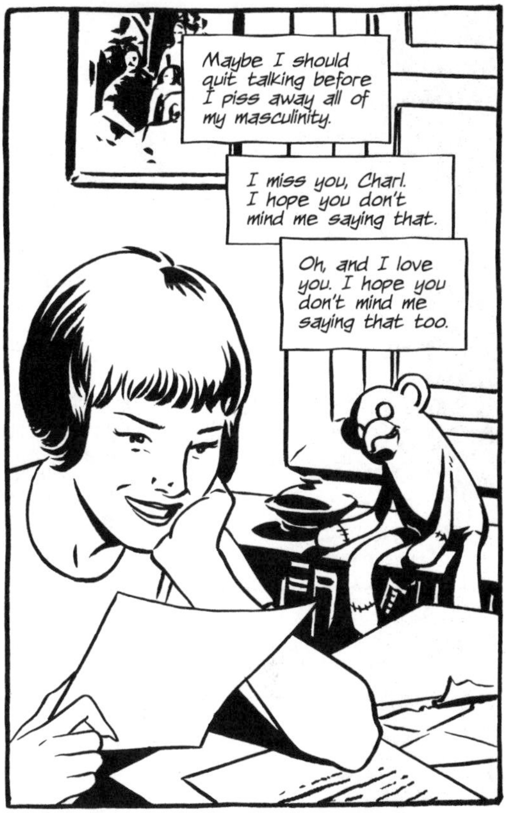
Maybe I should quit talking before I piss away all of my masculinity.
I miss you, Charl. I hope you don't mind me saying that.
Oh, and I love you. I hope you don't mind me saying that too.

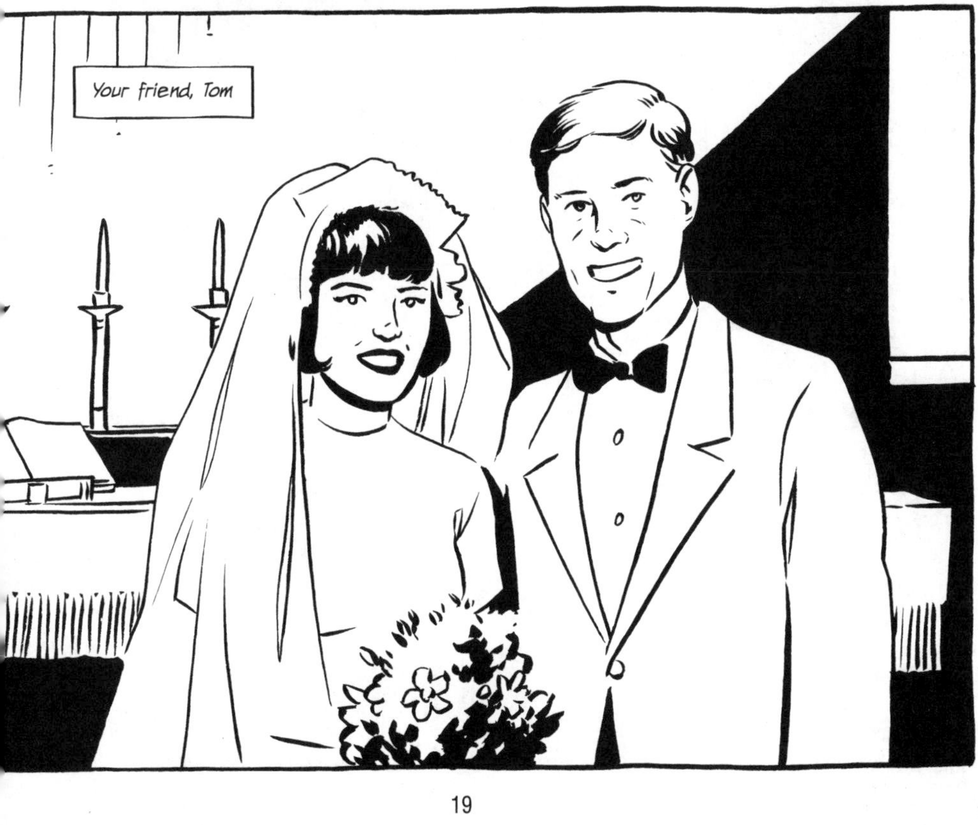
Your friend, Tom

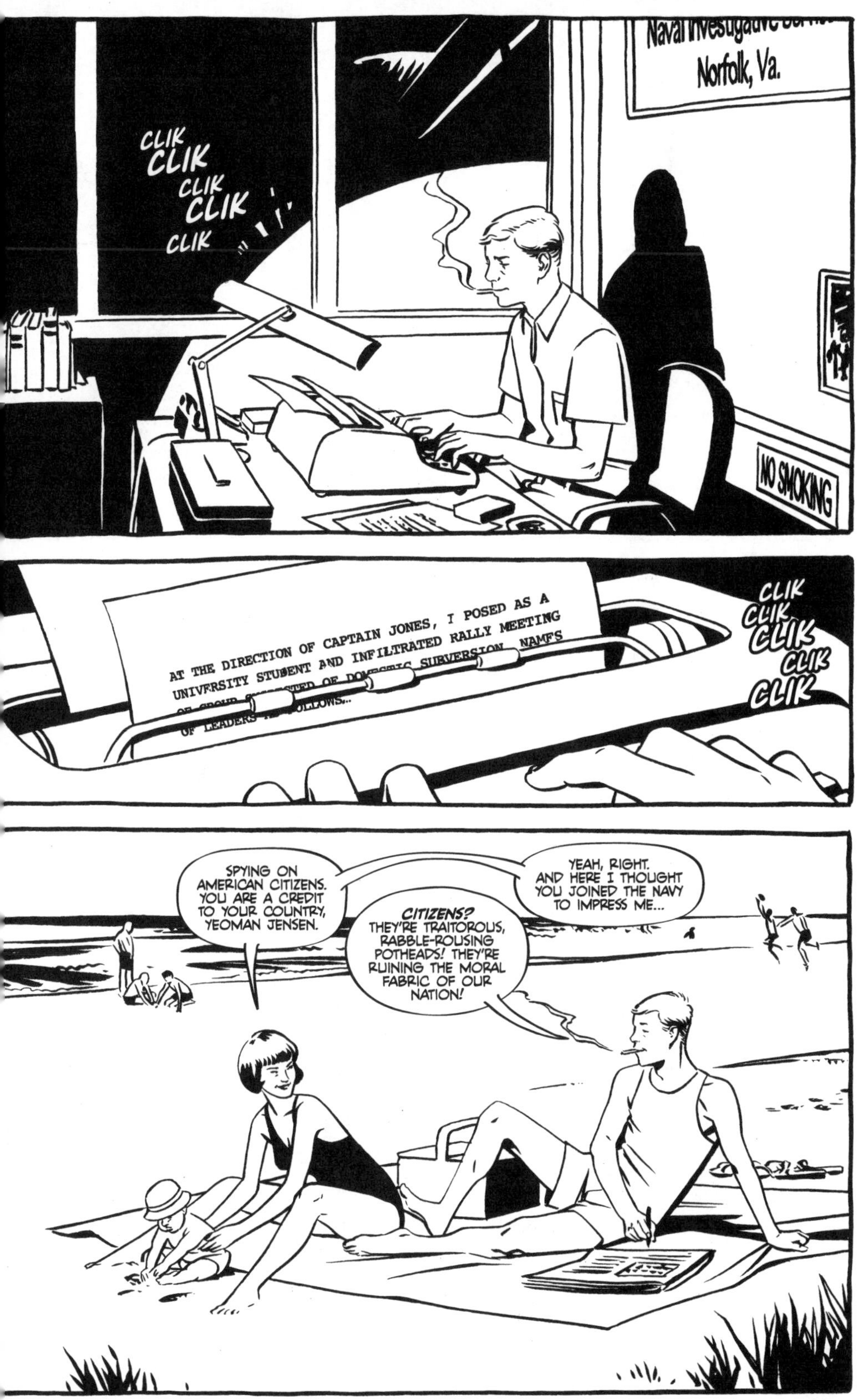

Norfolk, Va.
CLIK
CLIK
CLIK
CLIK
CLIK
NO SMOKING
AT THE DIRECTION OF CAPTAIN JONES, I POSED AS A
UNIVERSITY STUDENT AND INFILTRATED RALLY MEETING
CLIK
CLIK
CLIK
CLIK
CLIK
SPYING ON AMERICAN CITIZENS. YOU ARE A CREDIT TO YOUR COUNTRY, YEOMAN JENSEN.
CITIZENS? THEY'RE TRAITOROUS, RABBLE-ROUSING POTHEADS! THEY'RE RUINING THE MORAL FABRIC OF OUR NATION!
YEAH, RIGHT. AND HERE I THOUGHT YOU JOINED THE NAVY TO IMPRESS ME...

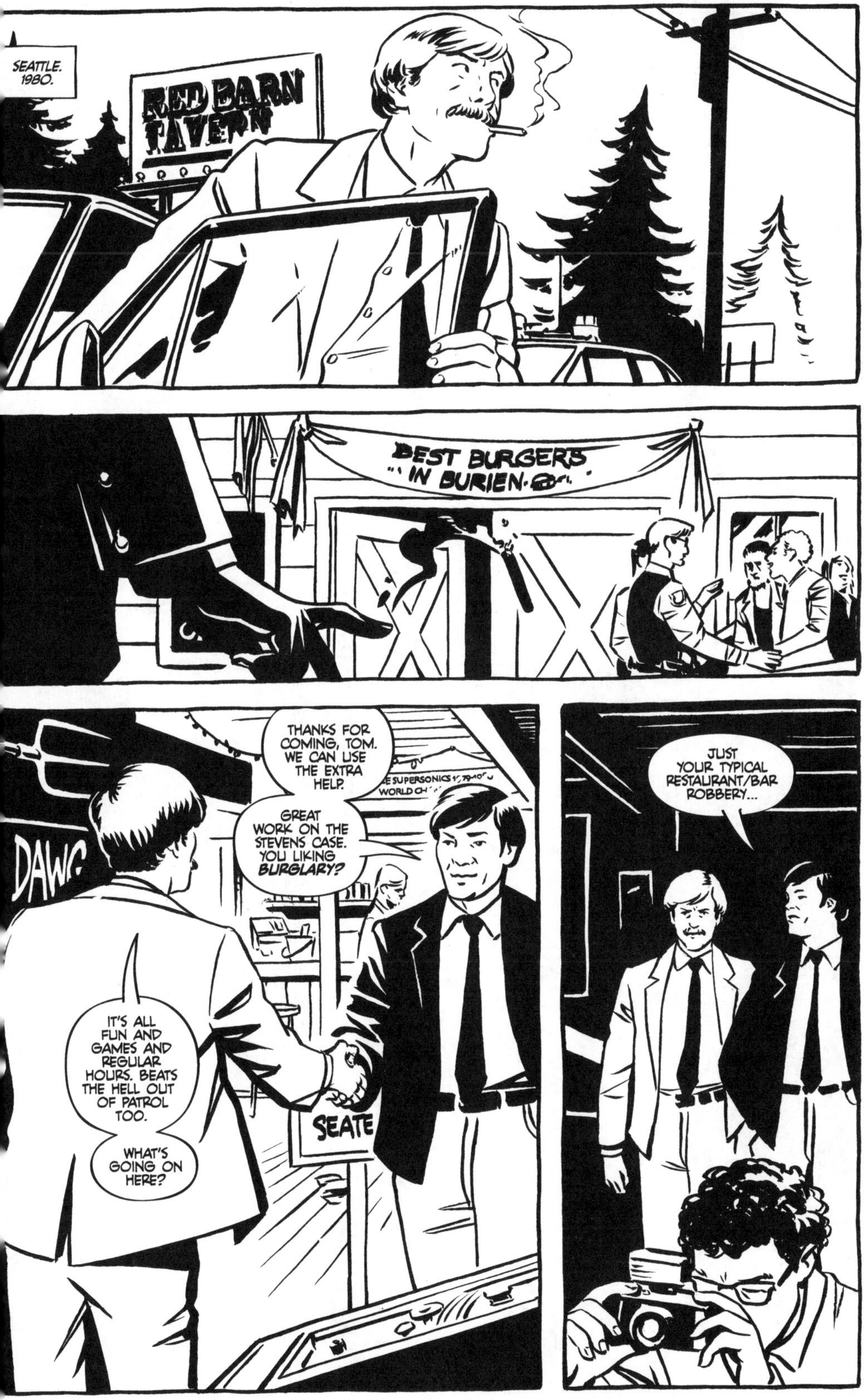
SEATTLE. 1980.
RED BARN TAVERN
BEST BURGERS IN BURIEN
THANKS FOR COMING, TOM. WE CAN USE THE EXTRA HELP.
GREAT WORK ON THE STEVENS CASE. YOU LIKING *BURGLARY?*
IT'S ALL FUN AND GAMES AND REGULAR HOURS. BEATS THE HELL OUT OF PATROL TOO.
WHAT'S GOING ON HERE?
JUST YOUR TYPICAL RESTAURANT/BAR ROBBERY...

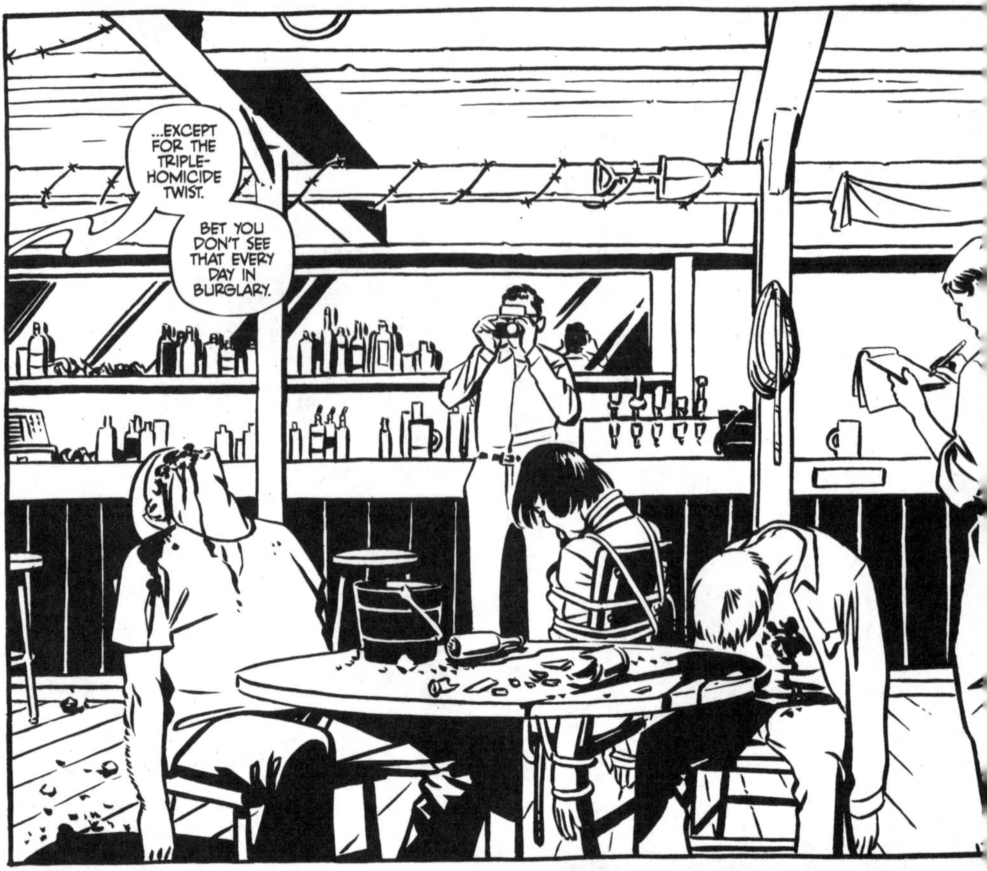
...EXCEPT FOR THE TRIPLE-HOMICIDE TWIST.
BET YOU DON'T SEE THAT EVERY DAY IN BURGLARY.

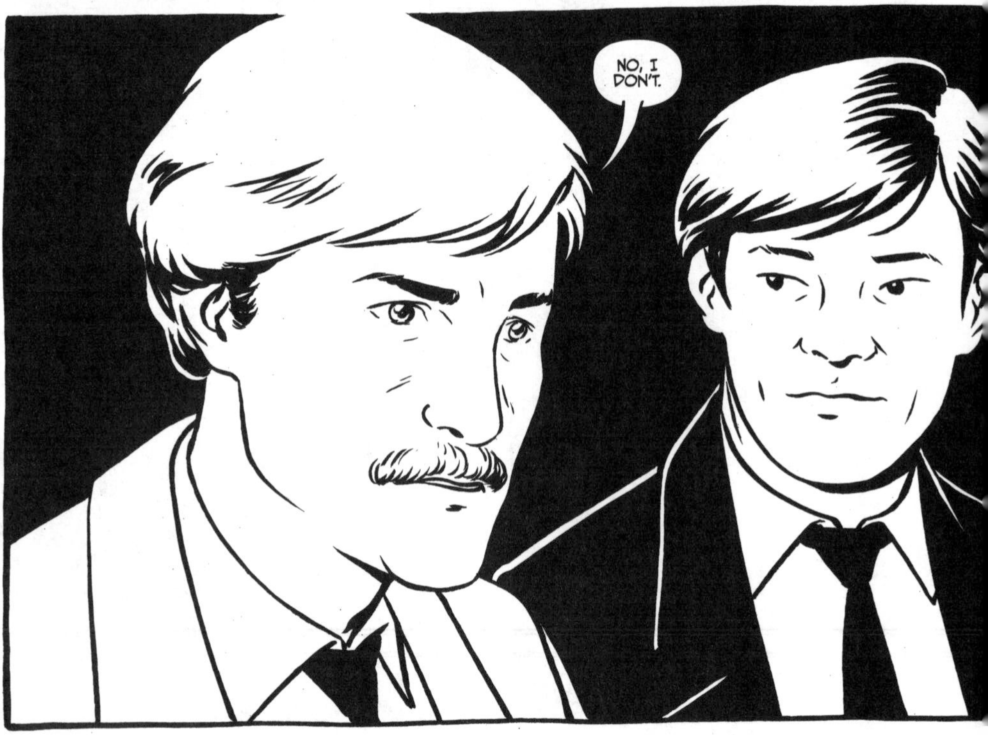
NO, I DON'T.

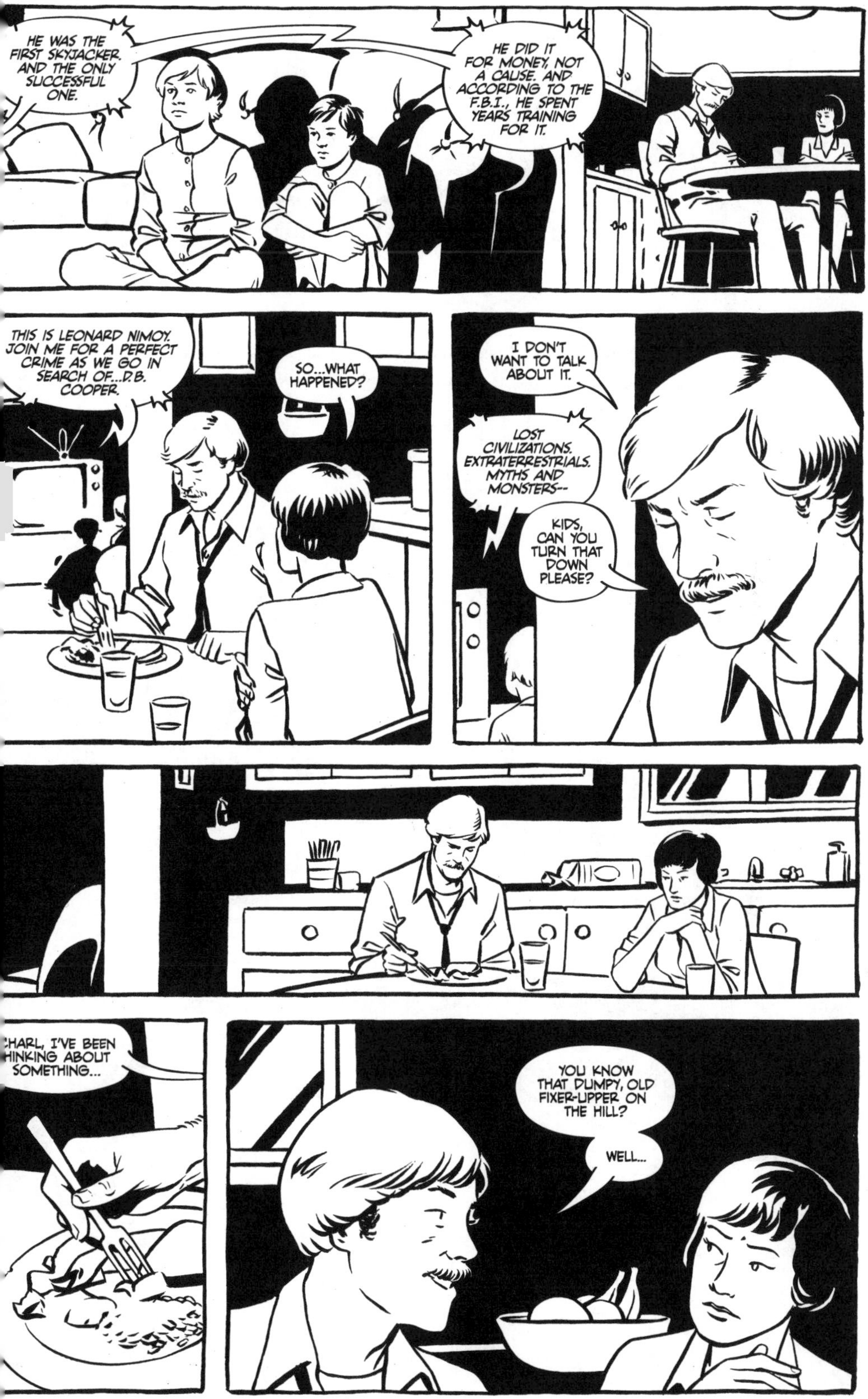

HE WAS THE FIRST SKYJACKER. AND THE ONLY SUCCESSFUL ONE.
HE DID IT FOR MONEY, NOT A CAUSE. AND ACCORDING TO THE F.B.I., HE SPENT YEARS TRAINING FOR IT.
THIS IS LEONARD NIMOY. JOIN ME FOR A PERFECT CRIME AS WE GO IN SEARCH OF...D.B. COOPER.
SO...WHAT HAPPENED?
I DON'T WANT TO TALK ABOUT IT.
LOST CIVILIZATIONS. EXTRATERRESTRIALS. MYTHS AND MONSTERS--
KIDS, CAN YOU TURN THAT DOWN PLEASE?
CHARL, I'VE BEEN THINKING ABOUT SOMETHING...
YOU KNOW THAT DUMPY, OLD FIXER-UPPER ON THE HILL?
WELL...

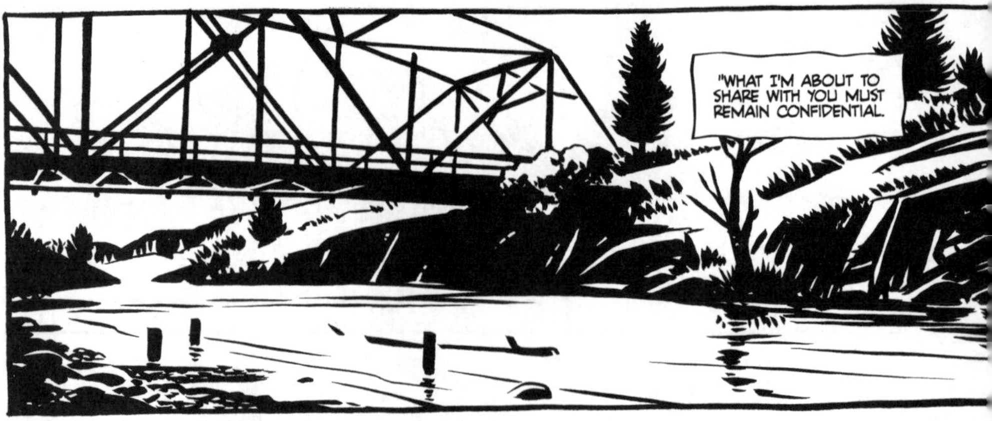
"WHAT I'M ABOUT TO SHARE WITH YOU MUST REMAIN CONFIDENTIAL.

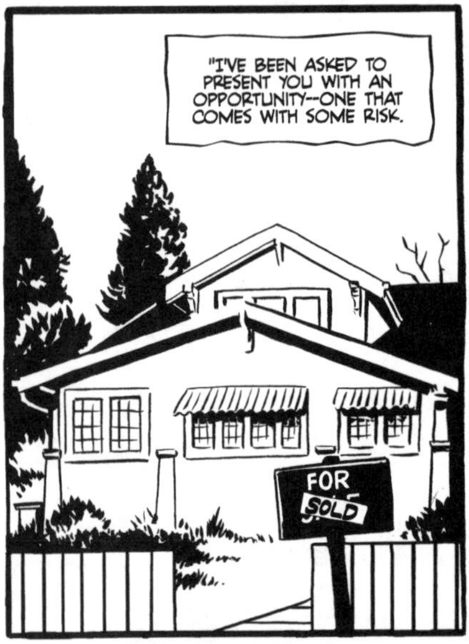
"I'VE BEEN ASKED TO PRESENT YOU WITH AN OPPORTUNITY--ONE THAT COMES WITH SOME RISK.
FOR
SOLD

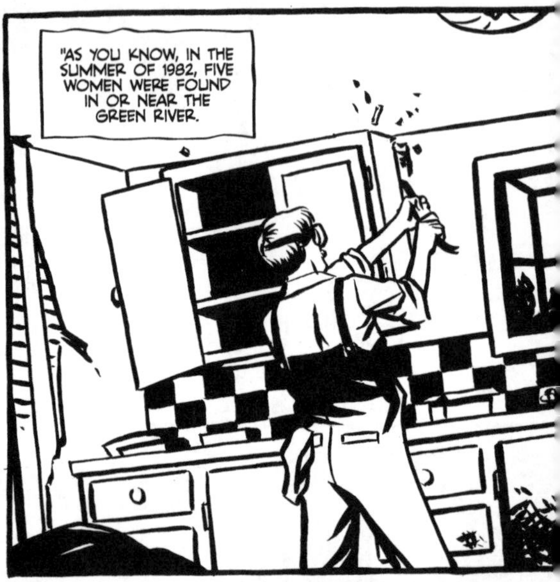
"AS YOU KNOW, IN THE SUMMER OF 1982, FIVE WOMEN WERE FOUND IN OR NEAR THE GREEN RIVER.

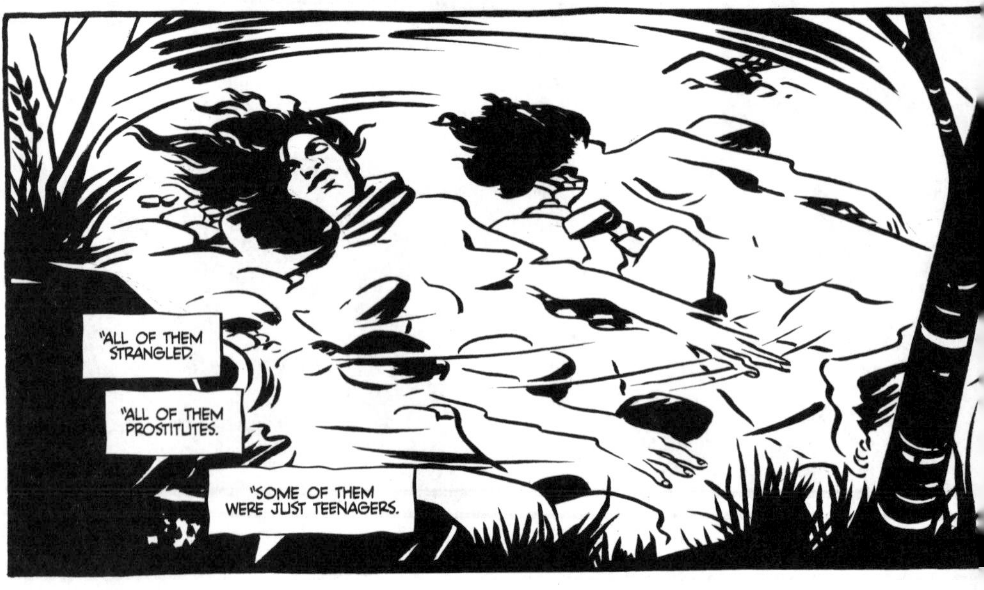
"ALL OF THEM STRANGLED.
"ALL OF THEM PROSTITUTES.
"SOME OF THEM WERE JUST TEENAGERS.

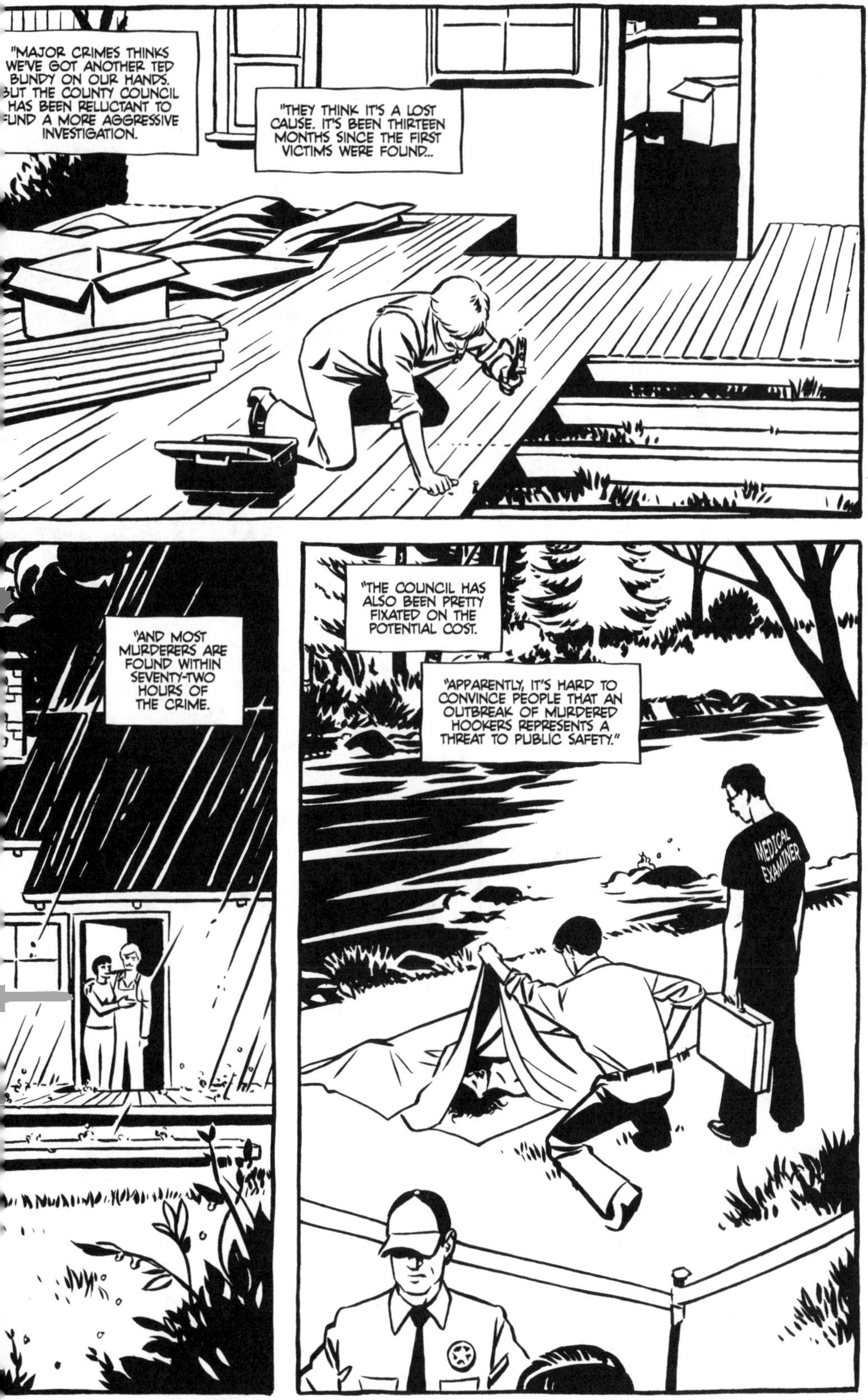
"MAJOR CRIMES THINKS WE'VE GOT ANOTHER TED BUNDY ON OUR HANDS. BUT THE COUNTY COUNCIL HAS BEEN RELUCTANT TO FUND A MORE AGGRESSIVE INVESTIGATION.
"THEY THINK IT'S A LOST CAUSE. IT'S BEEN THIRTEEN MONTHS SINCE THE FIRST VICTIMS WERE FOUND...
"AND MOST MURDERERS ARE FOUND WITHIN SEVENTY-TWO HOURS OF THE CRIME.
"THE COUNCIL HAS ALSO BEEN PRETTY FIXATED ON THE POTENTIAL COST.
"APPARENTLY, IT'S HARD TO CONVINCE PEOPLE THAT AN OUTBREAK OF MURDERED HOOKERS REPRESENTS A THREAT TO PUBLIC SAFETY."
MEDICAL EXAMINER

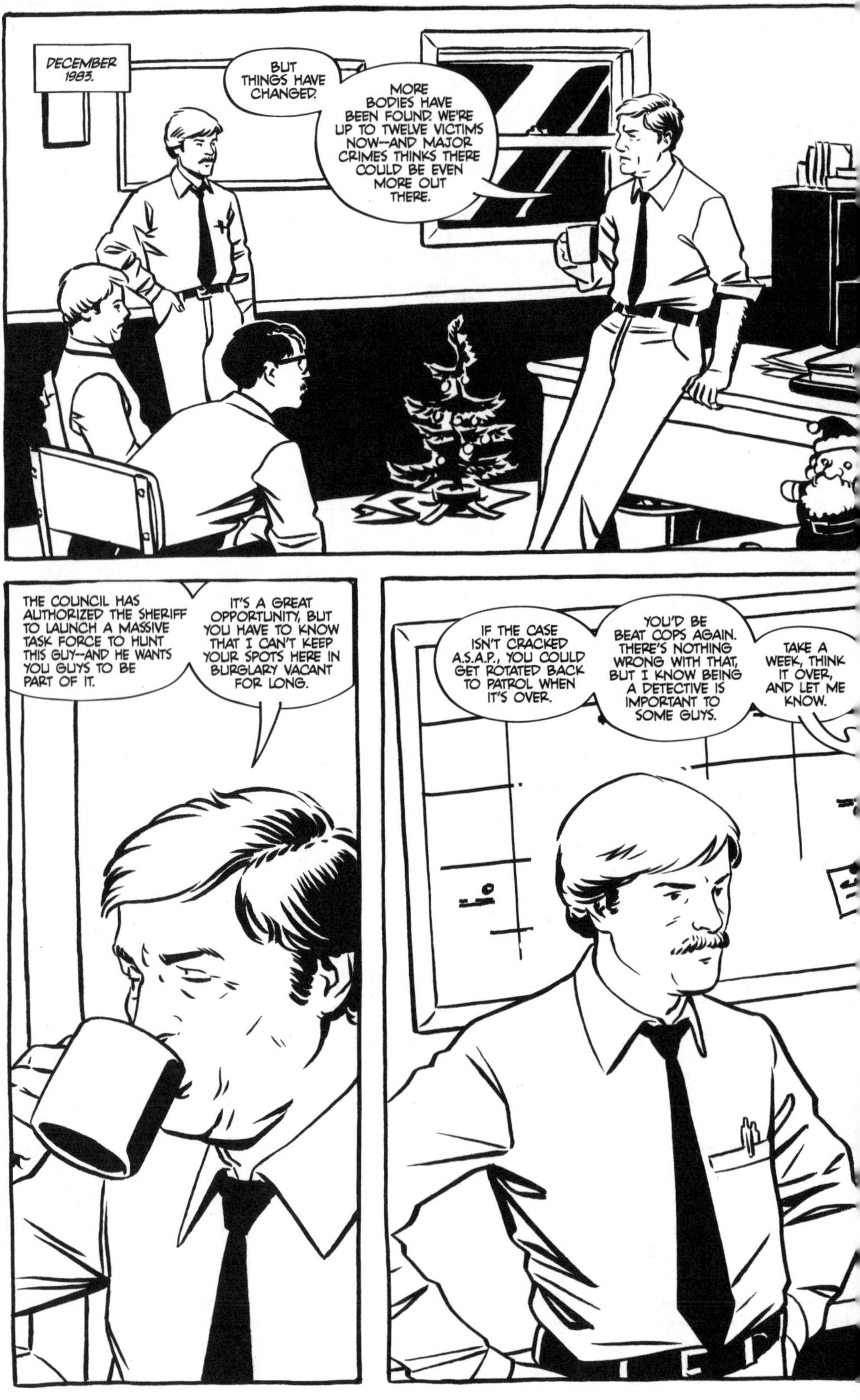
DECEMBER 1983.
BUT THINGS HAVE CHANGED.
MORE BODIES HAVE BEEN FOUND. WE'RE UP TO TWELVE VICTIMS NOW--AND MAJOR CRIMES THINKS THERE COULD BE EVEN MORE OUT THERE.
THE COUNCIL HAS AUTHORIZED THE SHERIFF TO LAUNCH A MASSIVE TASK FORCE TO HUNT THIS GUY--AND HE WANTS YOU GUYS TO BE PART OF IT.
IT'S A GREAT OPPORTUNITY, BUT YOU HAVE TO KNOW THAT I CAN'T KEEP YOUR SPOTS HERE IN BURGLARY VACANT FOR LONG.
IF THE CASE ISN'T CRACKED A.S.A.P., YOU COULD GET ROTATED BACK TO PATROL WHEN IT'S OVER.
YOU'D BE BEAT COPS AGAIN. THERE'S NOTHING WRONG WITH THAT, BUT I KNOW BEING A DETECTIVE IS IMPORTANT TO SOME GUYS.
TAKE A WEEK, THINK IT OVER, AND LET ME KNOW.

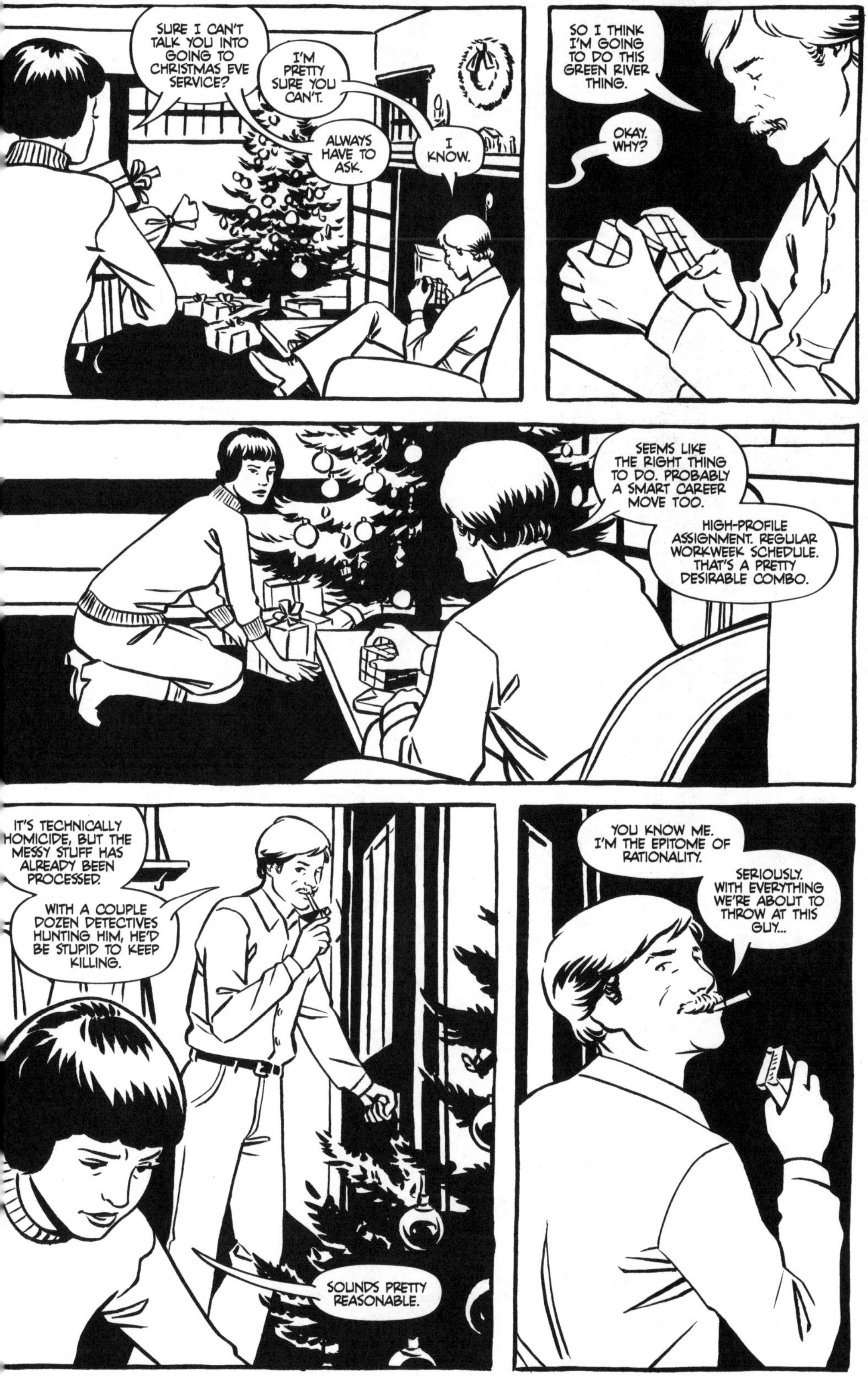
SURE I CAN'T TALK YOU INTO GOING TO CHRISTMAS EVE SERVICE?
I'M PRETTY SURE YOU CAN'T.
ALWAYS HAVE TO ASK.
I KNOW.
SO I THINK I'M GOING TO DO THIS GREEN RIVER THING.
OKAY. WHY?
SEEMS LIKE THE RIGHT THING TO DO. PROBABLY A SMART CAREER MOVE TOO.
HIGH-PROFILE ASSIGNMENT. REGULAR WORKWEEK SCHEDULE. THAT'S A PRETTY DESIRABLE COMBO.
IT'S TECHNICALLY HOMICIDE, BUT THE MESSY STUFF HAS ALREADY BEEN PROCESSED.
WITH A COUPLE DOZEN DETECTIVES HUNTING HIM, HE'D BE STUPID TO KEEP KILLING.
SOUNDS PRETTY REASONABLE.
YOU KNOW ME. I'M THE EPITOME OF RATIONALITY.
SERIOUSLY. WITH EVERYTHING WE'RE ABOUT TO THROW AT THIS GUY...

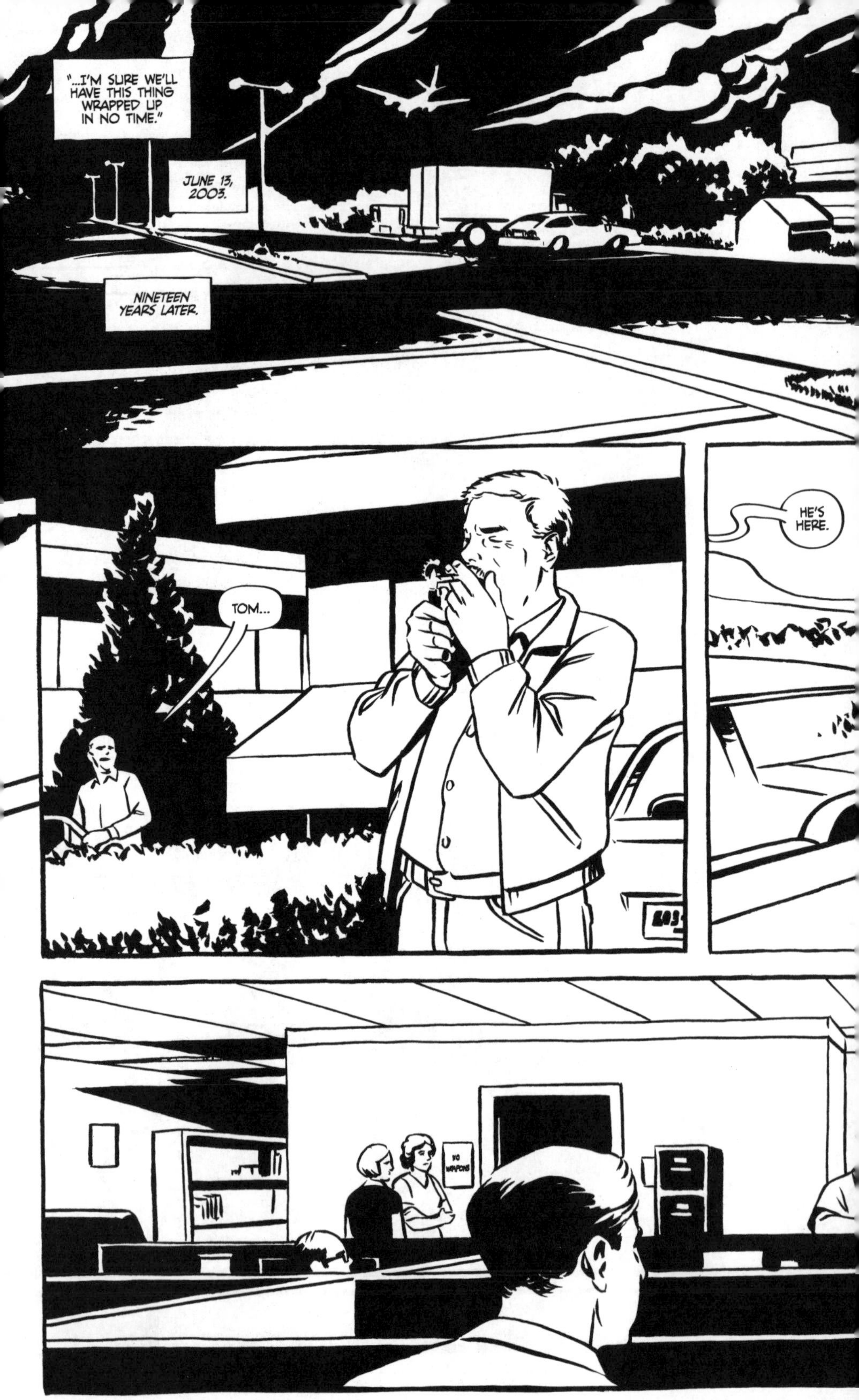
"...I'M SURE WE'LL HAVE THIS THING WRAPPED UP IN NO TIME."
JUNE 13, 2003.
NINETEEN YEARS LATER.
TOM...
HE'S HERE.
NO WEAPONS

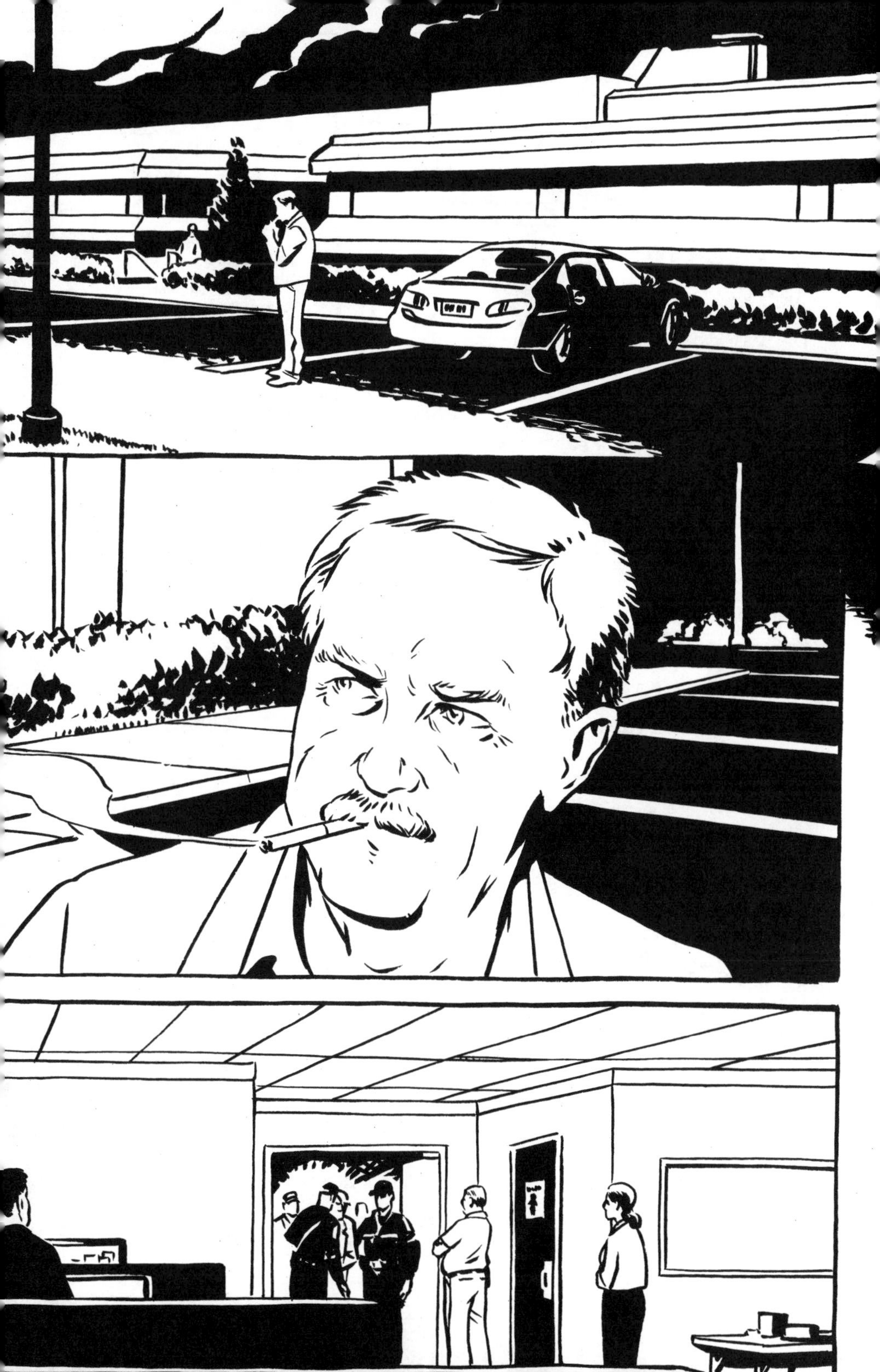

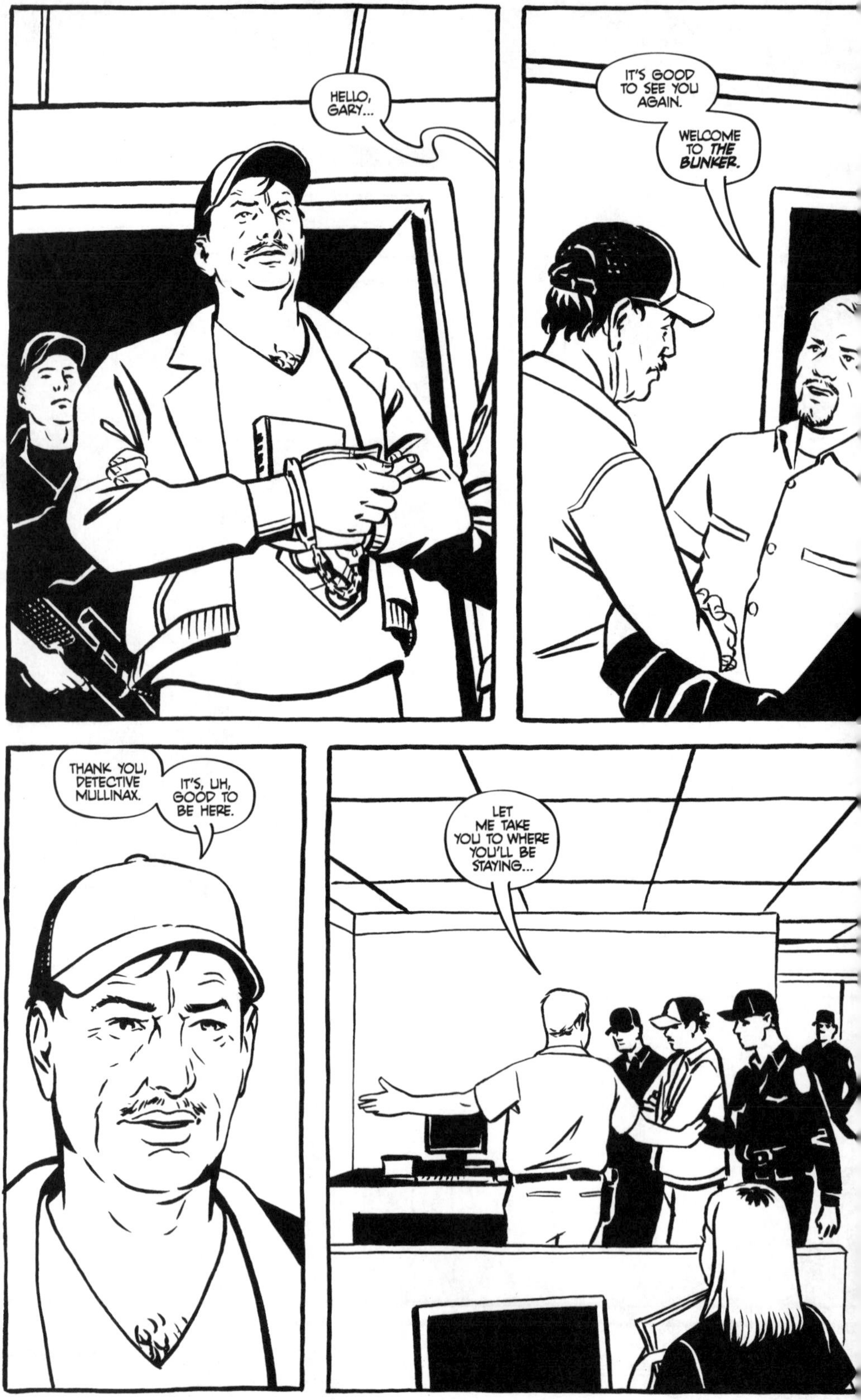
HELLO, GARY...
IT'S GOOD TO SEE YOU AGAIN.
WELCOME TO *THE BUNKER.*
THANK YOU, DETECTIVE MULLINAX.
IT'S, UH, GOOD TO BE HERE.
LET ME TAKE YOU TO WHERE YOU'LL BE STAYING...

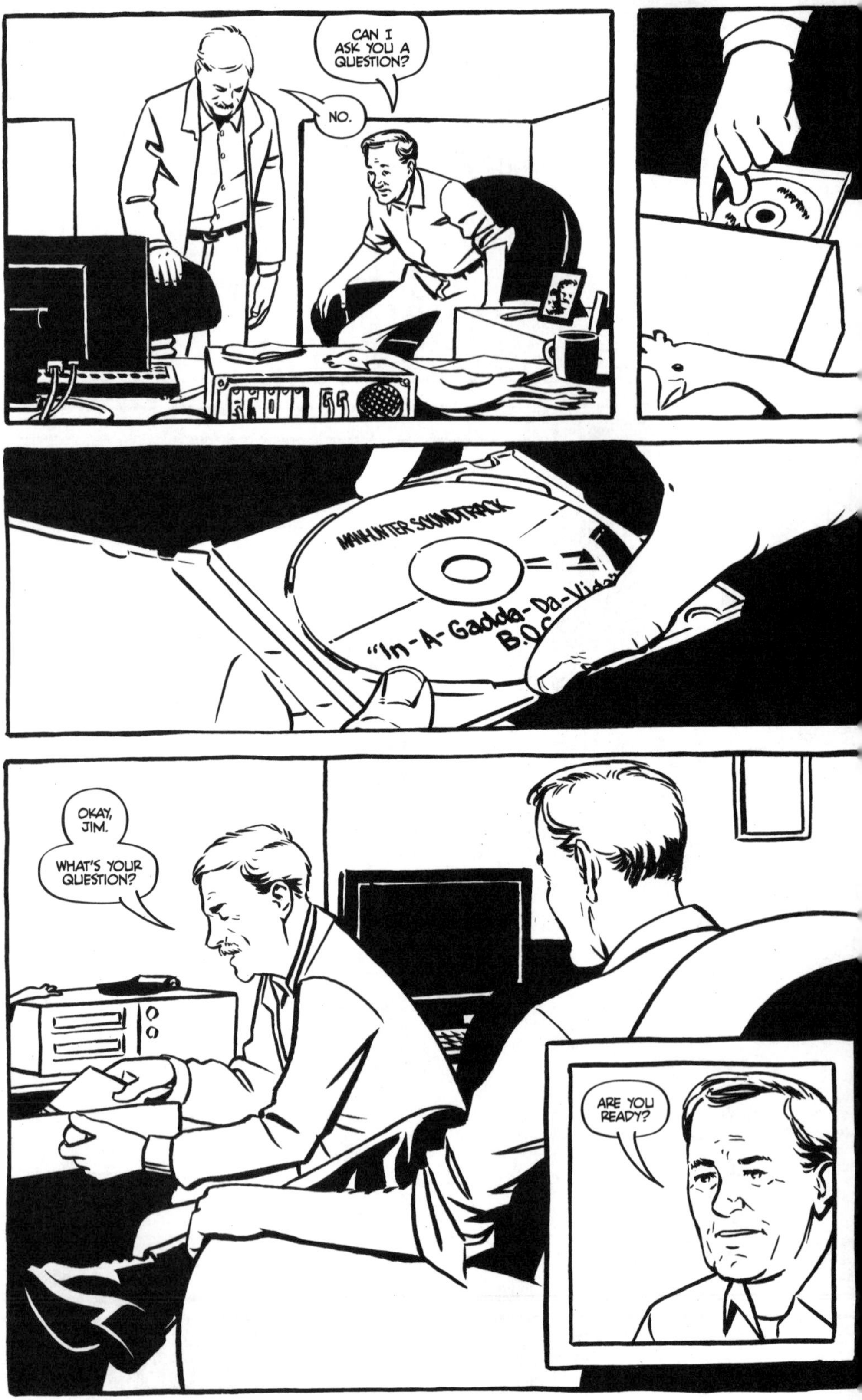
CAN I ASK YOU A QUESTION?
NO.
MANHUNTER SOUNDTRACK
"In-A-Gadda-Da-Vida"
OKAY, JIM.
WHAT'S YOUR QUESTION?
ARE YOU READY?

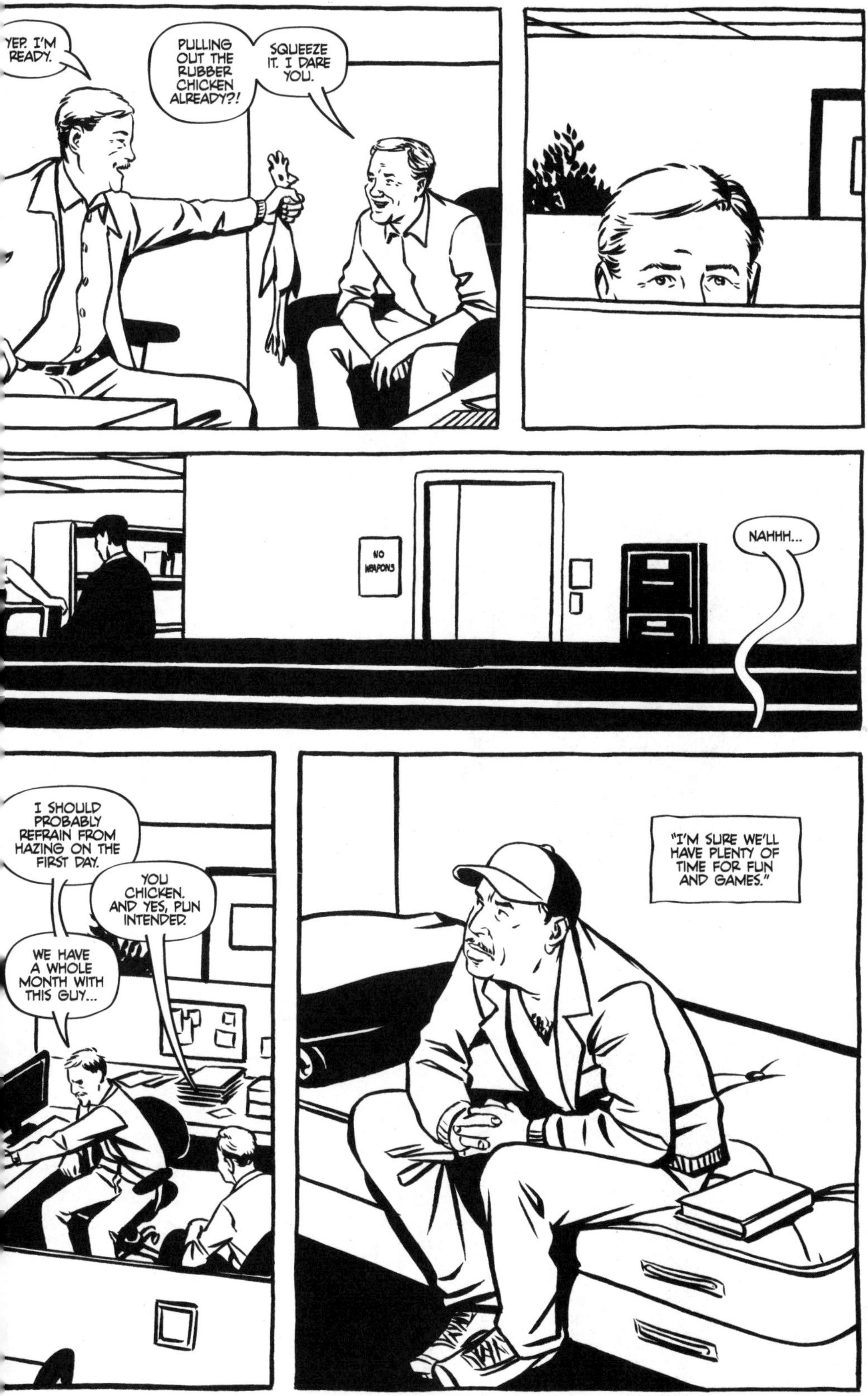
YEP. I'M READY.
PULLING OUT THE RUBBER CHICKEN ALREADY?!
SQUEEZE IT. I DARE YOU.
NO WEAPONS
NAHHH...
I SHOULD PROBABLY REFRAIN FROM HAZING ON THE FIRST DAY.
YOU CHICKEN. AND YES, PUN INTENDED.
WE HAVE A WHOLE MONTH WITH THIS GUY...
"I'M SURE WE'LL HAVE PLENTY OF TIME FOR FUN AND GAMES."

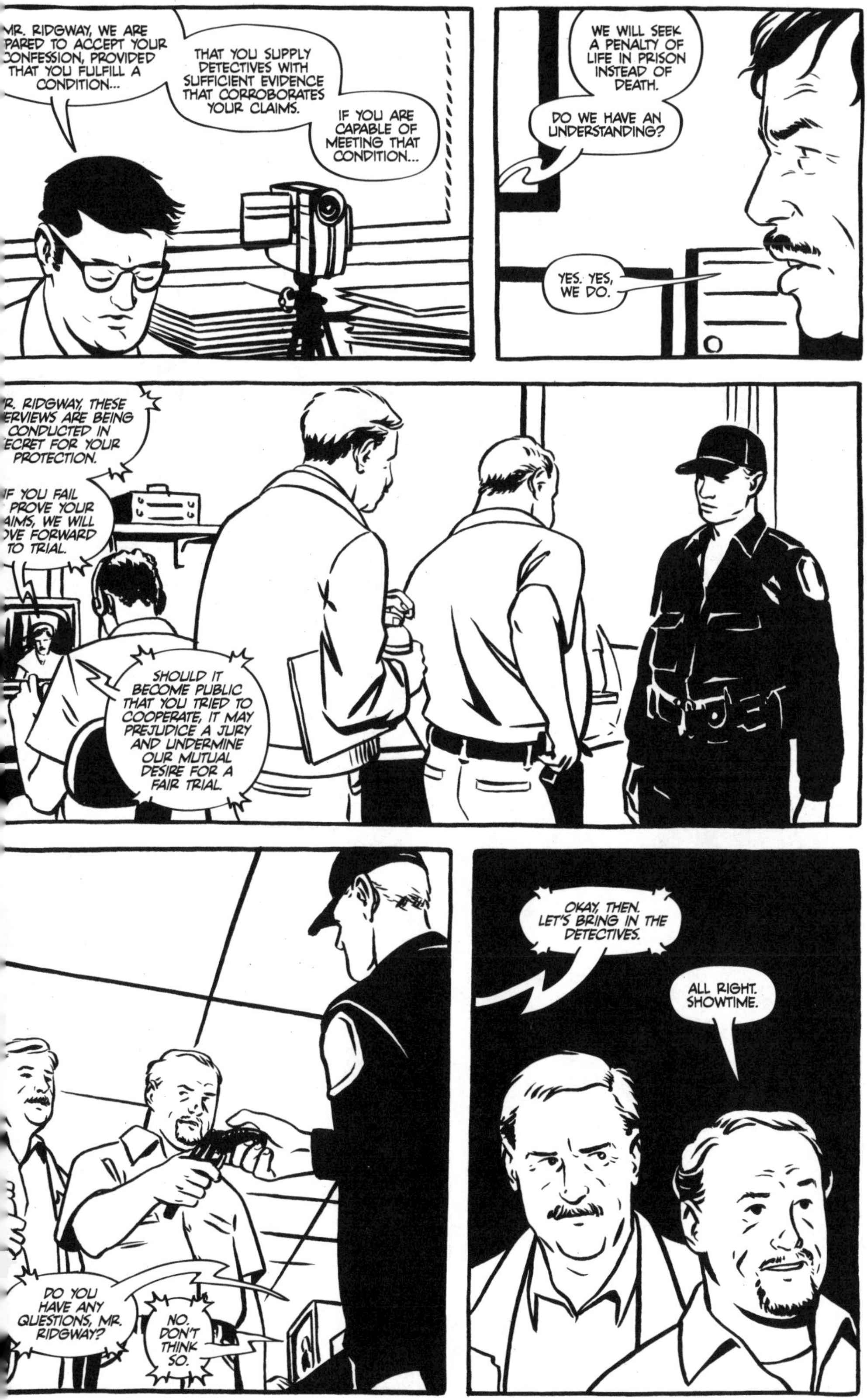

MR. RIDGWAY, WE ARE PARED TO ACCEPT YOUR CONFESSION, PROVIDED THAT YOU FULFILL A CONDITION...
THAT YOU SUPPLY DETECTIVES WITH SUFFICIENT EVIDENCE THAT CORROBORATES YOUR CLAIMS.
IF YOU ARE CAPABLE OF MEETING THAT CONDITION...
WE WILL SEEK A PENALTY OF LIFE IN PRISON INSTEAD OF DEATH.
DO WE HAVE AN UNDERSTANDING?
YES. YES, WE DO.
R. RIDGWAY, THESE ERVIEWS ARE BEING CONDUCTED IN ECRET FOR YOUR PROTECTION.
F YOU FAIL PROVE YOUR AIMS, WE WILL OVE FORWARD TO TRIAL.
SHOULD IT BECOME PUBLIC THAT YOU TRIED TO COOPERATE, IT MAY PREJUDICE A JURY AND UNDERMINE OUR MUTUAL DESIRE FOR A FAIR TRIAL.
DO YOU HAVE ANY QUESTIONS, MR. RIDGWAY?
NO. DON'T THINK SO.
OKAY, THEN. LET'S BRING IN THE DETECTIVES.
ALL RIGHT. SHOWTIME.

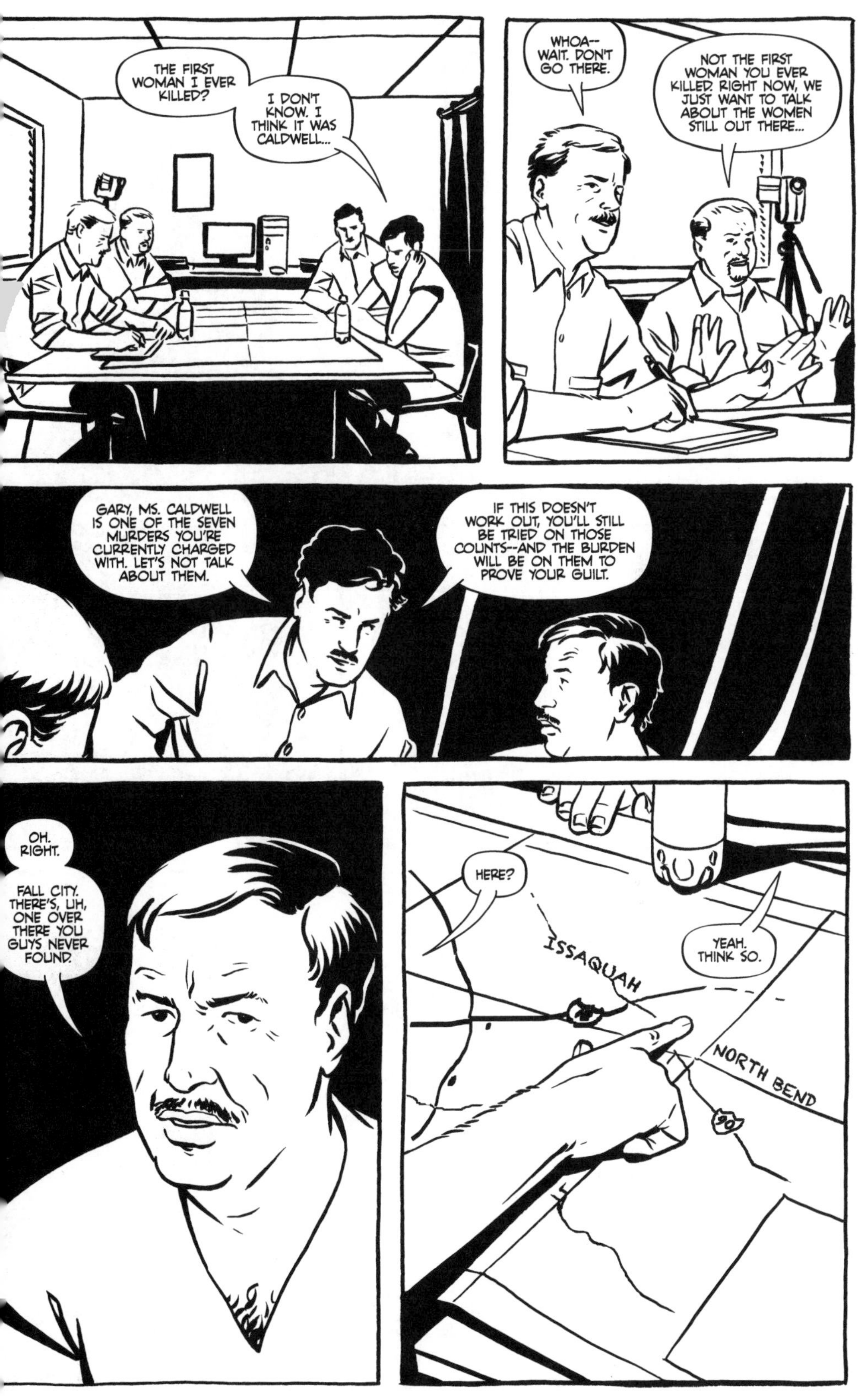
THE FIRST WOMAN I EVER KILLED?
I DON'T KNOW. I THINK IT WAS CALDWELL...
WHOA-- WAIT. DON'T GO THERE.
NOT THE FIRST WOMAN YOU EVER KILLED. RIGHT NOW, WE JUST WANT TO TALK ABOUT THE WOMEN STILL OUT THERE...
GARY, MS. CALDWELL IS ONE OF THE SEVEN MURDERS YOU'RE CURRENTLY CHARGED WITH. LET'S NOT TALK ABOUT THEM.
IF THIS DOESN'T WORK OUT, YOU'LL STILL BE TRIED ON THOSE COUNTS--AND THE BURDEN WILL BE ON THEM TO PROVE YOUR GUILT.
OH. RIGHT.
FALL CITY. THERE'S, UH, ONE OVER THERE YOU GUYS NEVER FOUND.
HERE?
ISSAQUAH
YEAH. THINK SO.
NORTH BEND
90

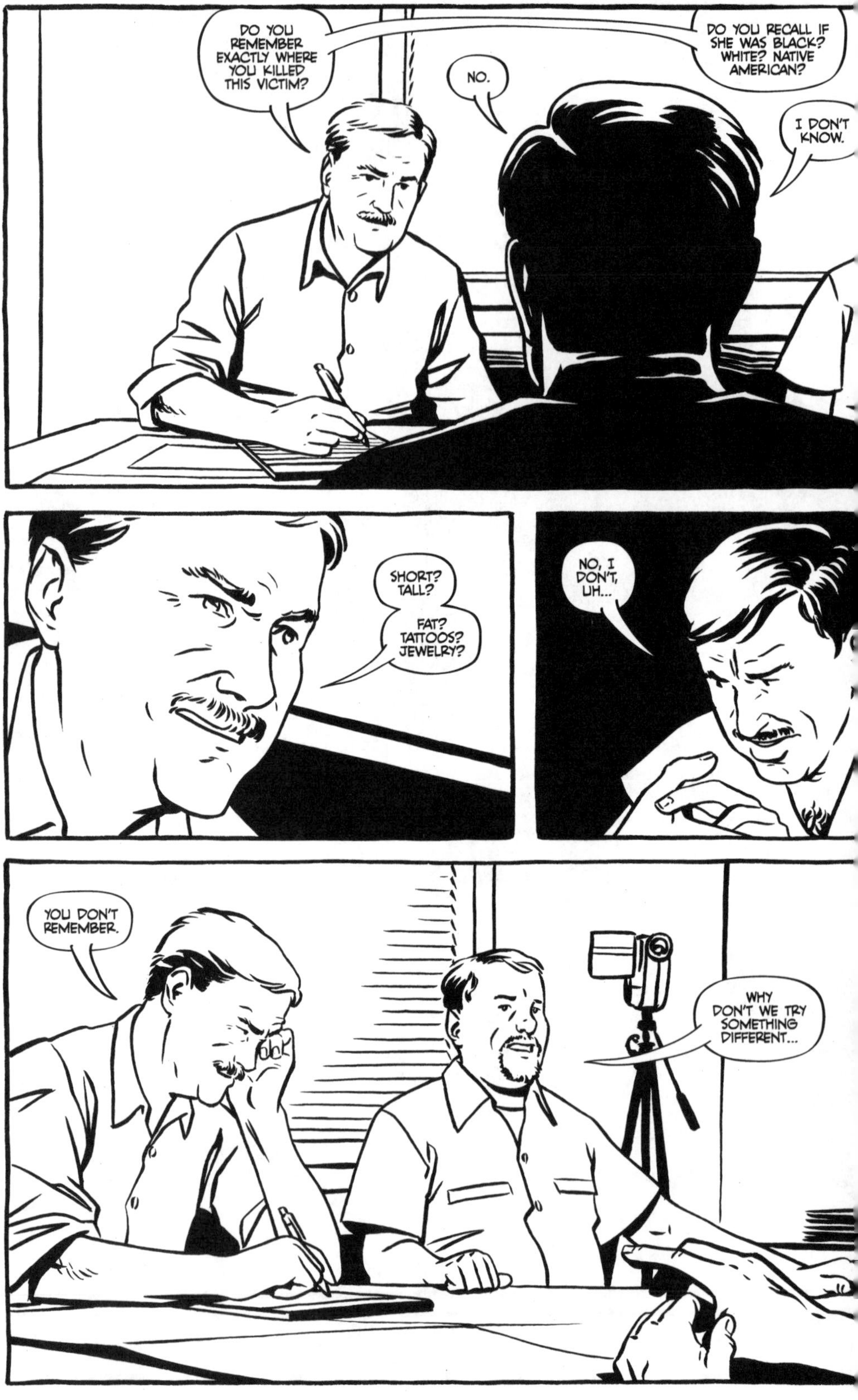
DO YOU REMEMBER EXACTLY WHERE YOU KILLED THIS VICTIM?
NO.
DO YOU RECALL IF SHE WAS BLACK? WHITE? NATIVE AMERICAN?
I DON'T KNOW.
SHORT? TALL?
FAT? TATTOOS? JEWELRY?
NO, I DON'T, UH...
YOU DON'T REMEMBER.
WHY DON'T WE TRY SOMETHING DIFFERENT...

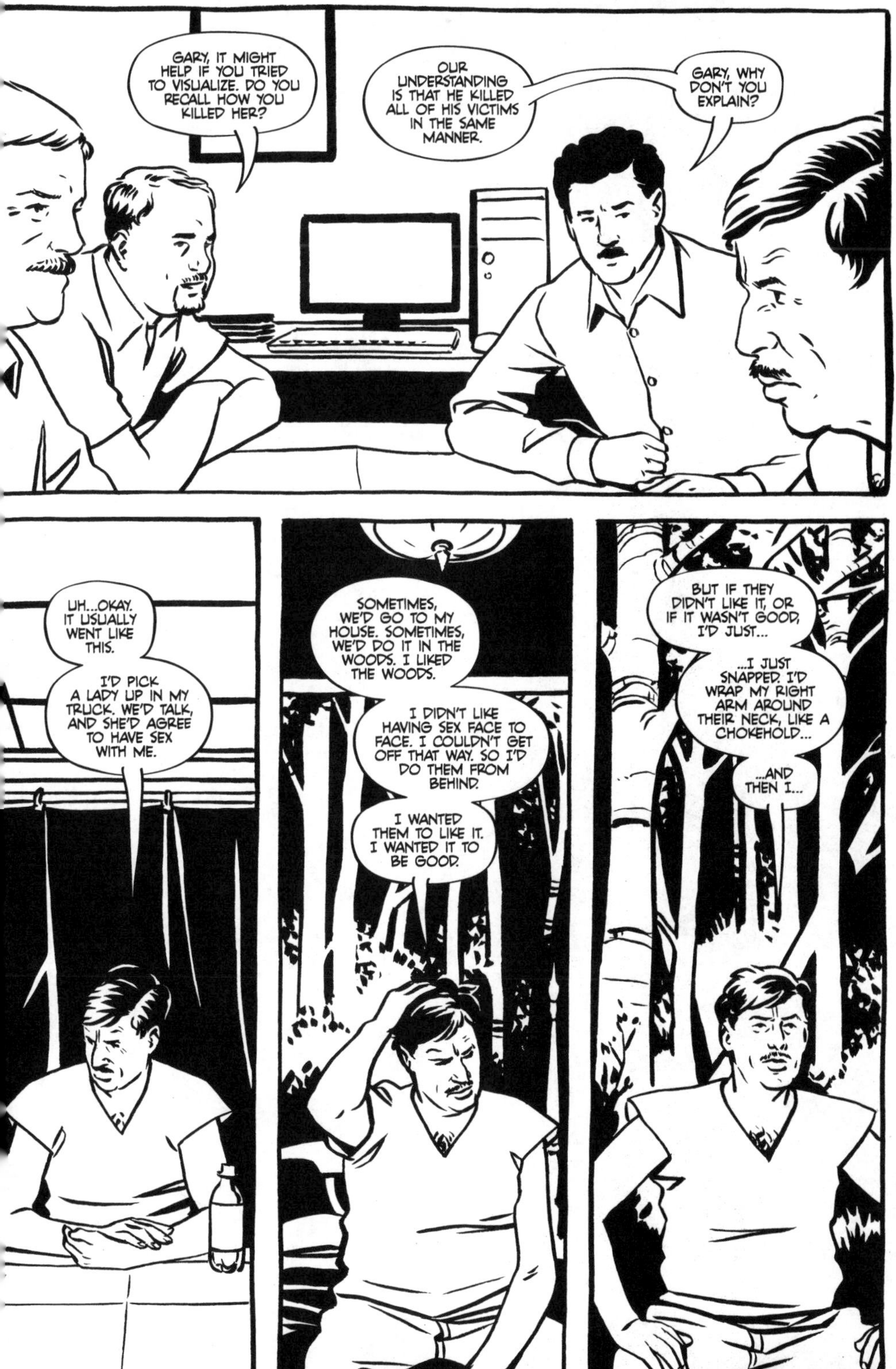
GARY, IT MIGHT HELP IF YOU TRIED TO VISUALIZE. DO YOU RECALL HOW YOU KILLED HER?
OUR UNDERSTANDING IS THAT HE KILLED ALL OF HIS VICTIMS IN THE SAME MANNER.
GARY, WHY DON'T YOU EXPLAIN?
UH...OKAY. IT USUALLY WENT LIKE THIS.
I'D PICK A LADY UP IN MY TRUCK. WE'D TALK, AND SHE'D AGREE TO HAVE SEX WITH ME.
SOMETIMES, WE'D GO TO MY HOUSE. SOMETIMES, WE'D DO IT IN THE WOODS. I LIKED THE WOODS.
I DIDN'T LIKE HAVING SEX FACE TO FACE. I COULDN'T GET OFF THAT WAY. SO I'D DO THEM FROM BEHIND.
I WANTED THEM TO LIKE IT. I WANTED IT TO BE GOOD.
BUT IF THEY DIDN'T LIKE IT, OR IF IT WASN'T GOOD, I'D JUST...
...I JUST SNAPPED. I'D WRAP MY RIGHT ARM AROUND THEIR NECK, LIKE A CHOKEHOLD...
...AND THEN I...

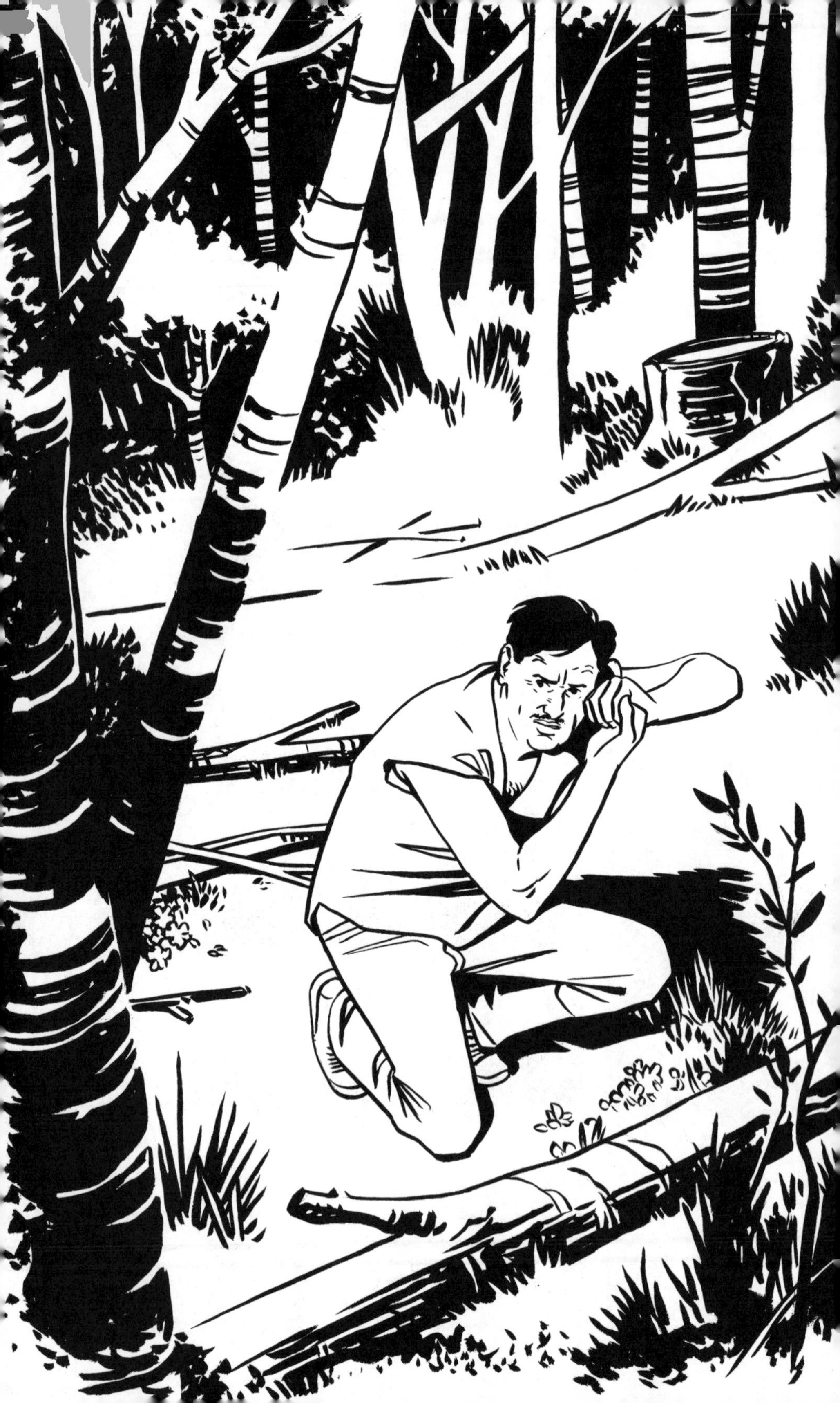

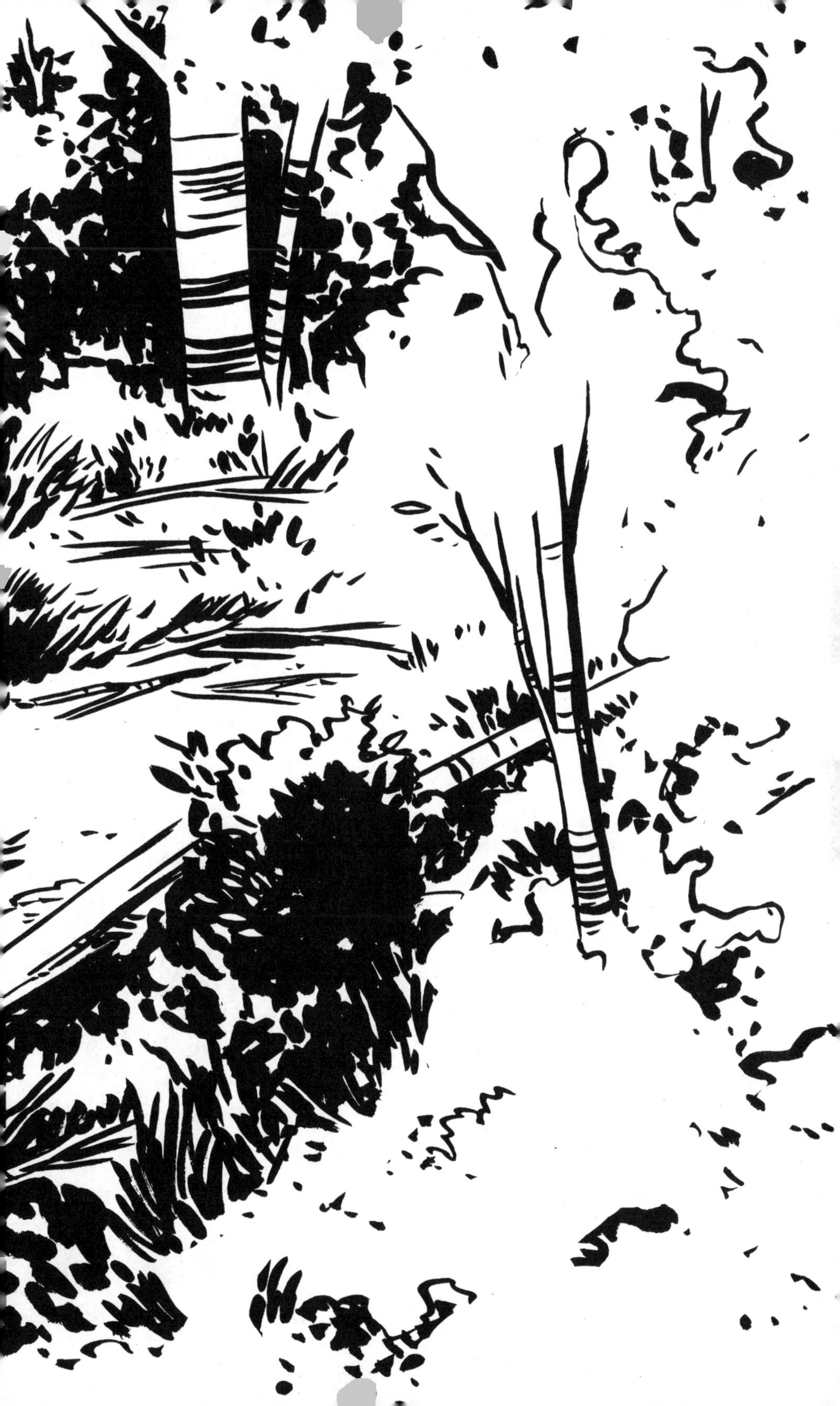

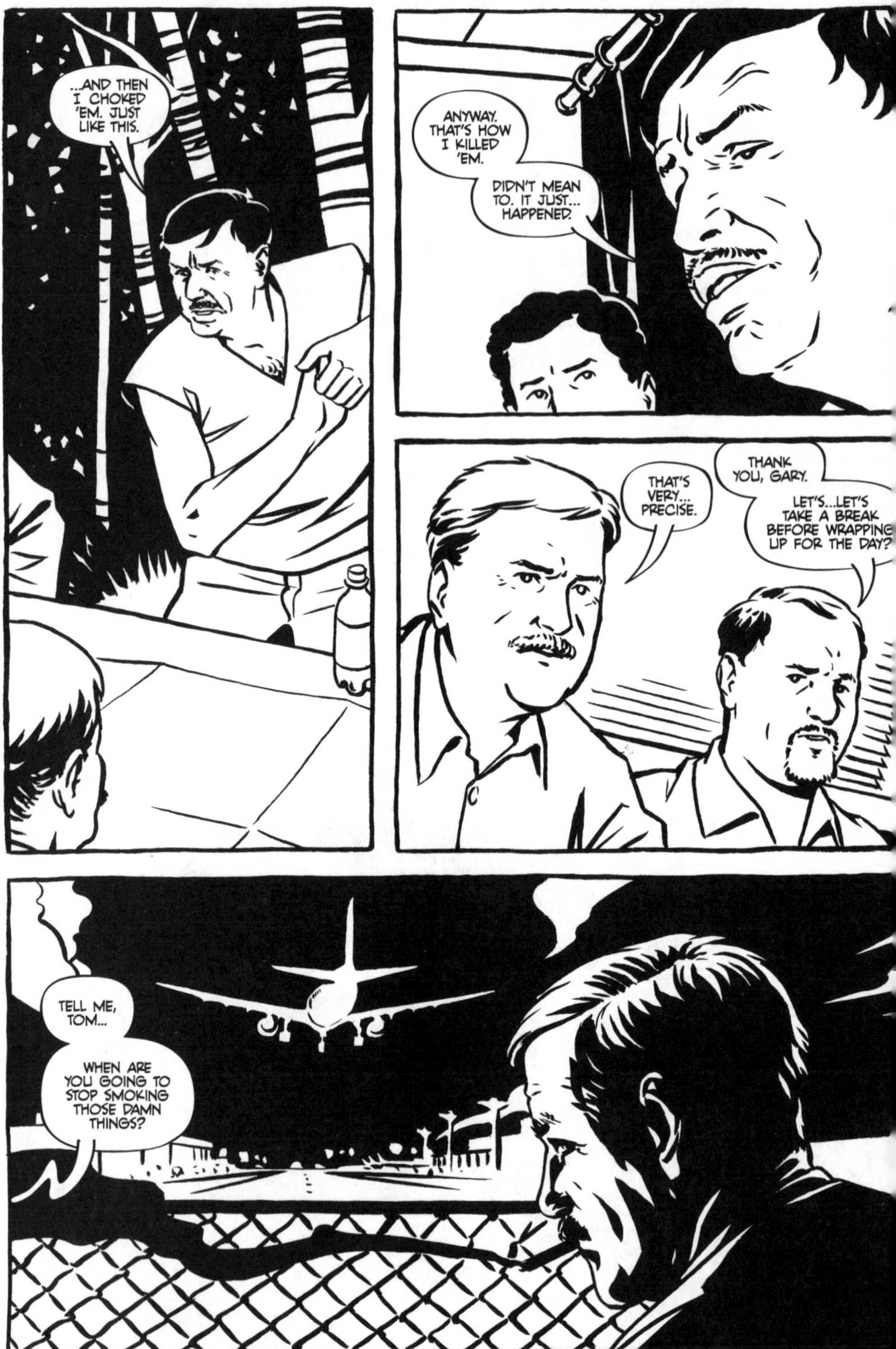
...AND THEN I CHOKED 'EM. JUST LIKE THIS.
ANYWAY. THAT'S HOW I KILLED 'EM.
DIDN'T MEAN TO. IT JUST... HAPPENED.
THAT'S VERY... PRECISE.
THANK YOU, GARY.
LET'S...LET'S TAKE A BREAK BEFORE WRAPPING UP FOR THE DAY?
TELL ME, TOM...
WHEN ARE YOU GOING TO STOP SMOKING THOSE DAMN THINGS?

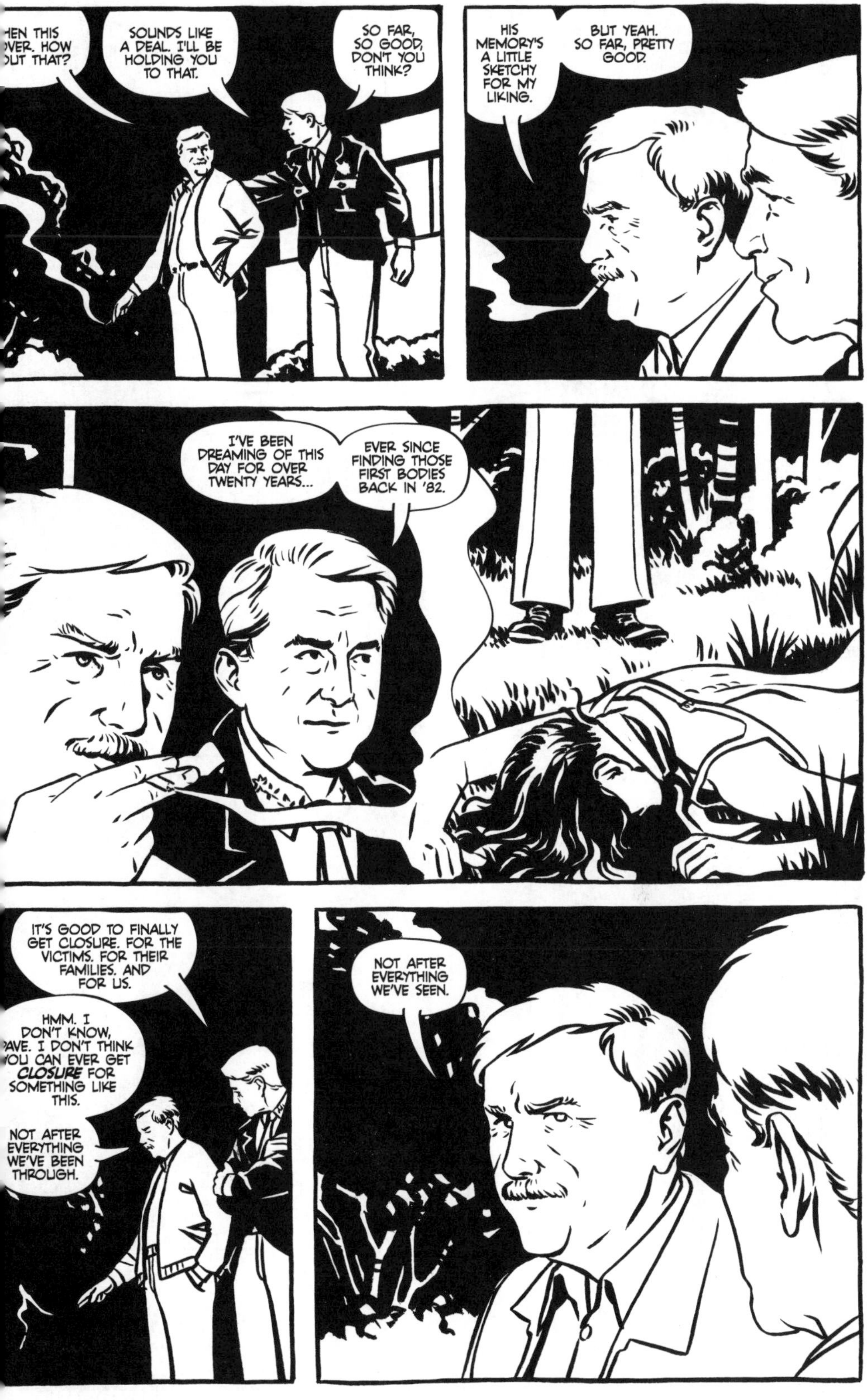
HEN THIS VER. HOW UT THAT?
SOUNDS LIKE A DEAL. I'LL BE HOLDING YOU TO THAT.
SO FAR, SO GOOD, DON'T YOU THINK?
HIS MEMORY'S A LITTLE SKETCHY FOR MY LIKING.
BUT YEAH. SO FAR, PRETTY GOOD.
I'VE BEEN DREAMING OF THIS DAY FOR OVER TWENTY YEARS...
EVER SINCE FINDING THOSE FIRST BODIES BACK IN '82.
IT'S GOOD TO FINALLY GET CLOSURE. FOR THE VICTIMS. FOR THEIR FAMILIES. AND FOR US.
HMM. I DON'T KNOW, AVE. I DON'T THINK OU CAN EVER GET *CLOSURE* FOR SOMETHING LIKE THIS.
NOT AFTER EVERYTHING WE'VE BEEN THROUGH.
NOT AFTER EVERYTHING WE'VE SEEN.

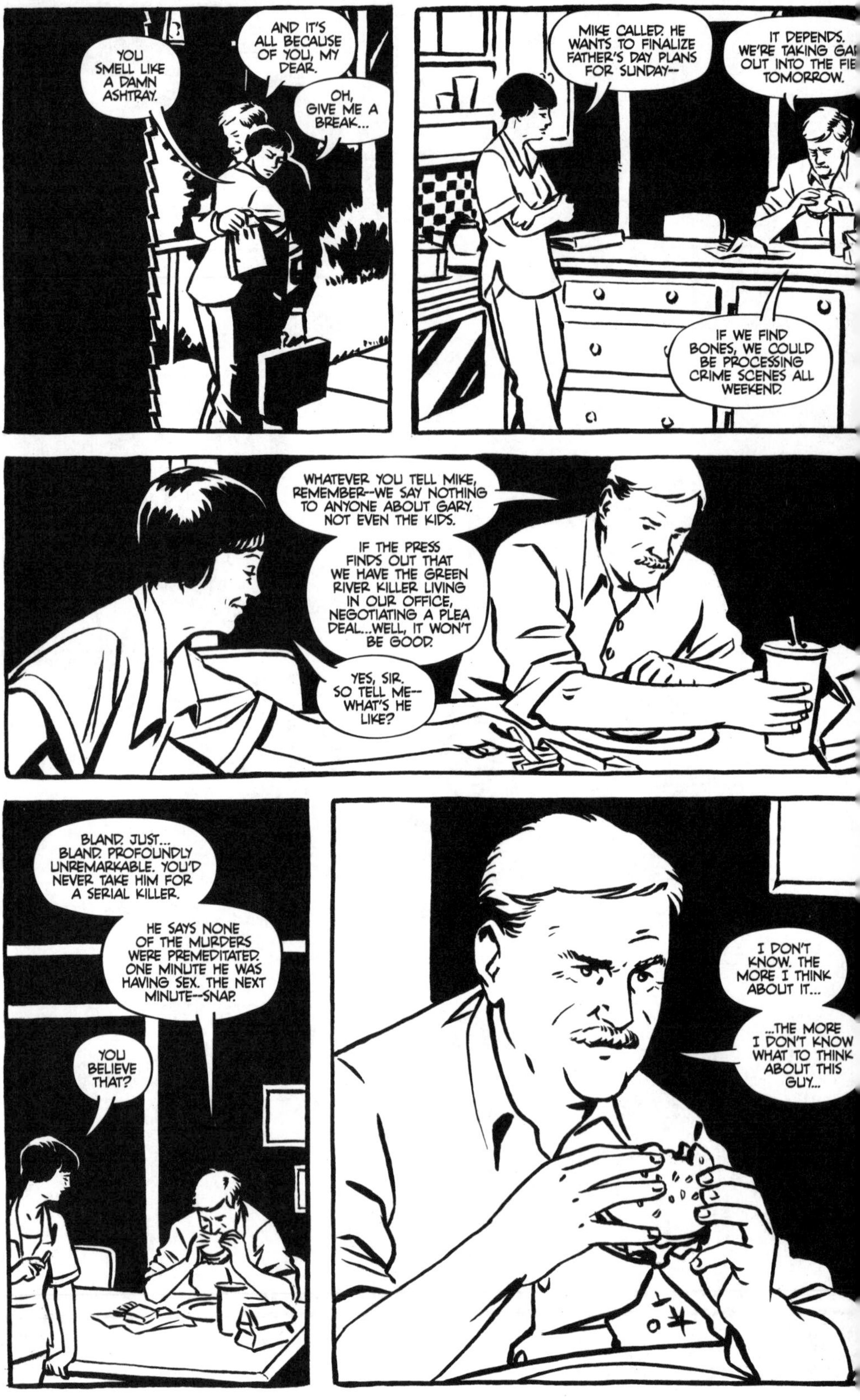
YOU SMELL LIKE A DAMN ASHTRAY.
AND IT'S ALL BECAUSE OF YOU, MY DEAR.
OH, GIVE ME A BREAK...
MIKE CALLED. HE WANTS TO FINALIZE FATHER'S DAY PLANS FOR SUNDAY--
IT DEPENDS. WE'RE TAKING GA OUT INTO THE FIE TOMORROW.
IF WE FIND BONES, WE COULD BE PROCESSING CRIME SCENES ALL WEEKEND.
WHATEVER YOU TELL MIKE, REMEMBER--WE SAY NOTHING TO ANYONE ABOUT GARY. NOT EVEN THE KIDS.
IF THE PRESS FINDS OUT THAT WE HAVE THE GREEN RIVER KILLER LIVING IN OUR OFFICE, NEGOTIATING A PLEA DEAL...WELL, IT WON'T BE GOOD.
YES, SIR. SO TELL ME-- WHAT'S HE LIKE?
BLAND. JUST... BLAND. PROFOUNDLY UNREMARKABLE. YOU'D NEVER TAKE HIM FOR A SERIAL KILLER.
HE SAYS NONE OF THE MURDERS WERE PREMEDITATED. ONE MINUTE HE WAS HAVING SEX. THE NEXT MINUTE--SNAP.
YOU BELIEVE THAT?
I DON'T KNOW. THE MORE I THINK ABOUT IT...
...THE MORE I DON'T KNOW WHAT TO THINK ABOUT THIS GUY...

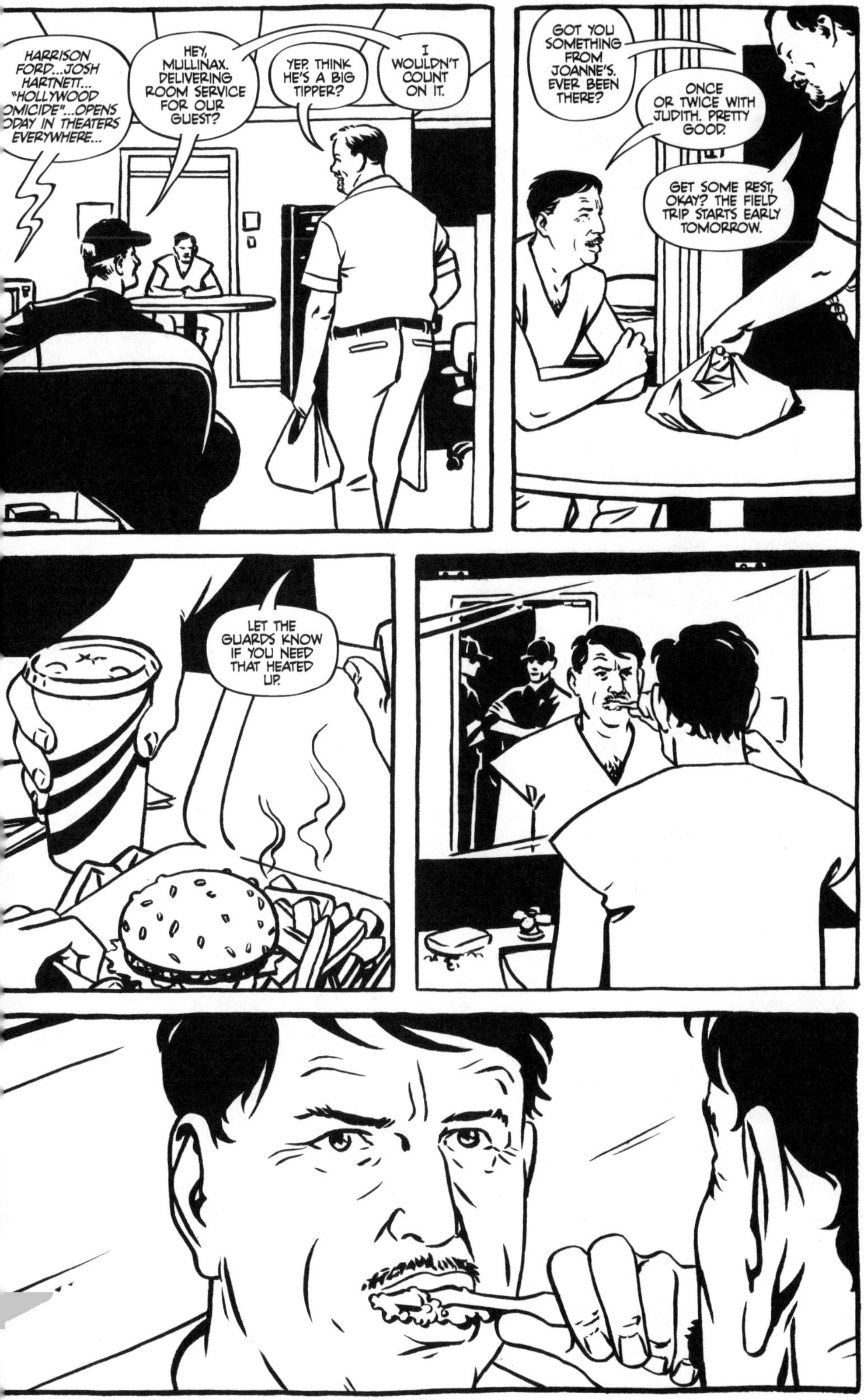

HARRISON FORD...JOSH HARTNETT... "HOLLYWOOD OMICIDE"...OPENS ODAY IN THEATERS EVERYWHERE...
HEY, MULLINAX. DELIVERING ROOM SERVICE FOR OUR GUEST?
YEP. THINK HE'S A BIG TIPPER?
I WOULDN'T COUNT ON IT.
GOT YOU SOMETHING FROM JOANNE'S. EVER BEEN THERE?
ONCE OR TWICE WITH JUDITH. PRETTY GOOD.
GET SOME REST, OKAY? THE FIELD TRIP STARTS EARLY TOMORROW.
LET THE GUARDS KNOW IF YOU NEED THAT HEATED UP.

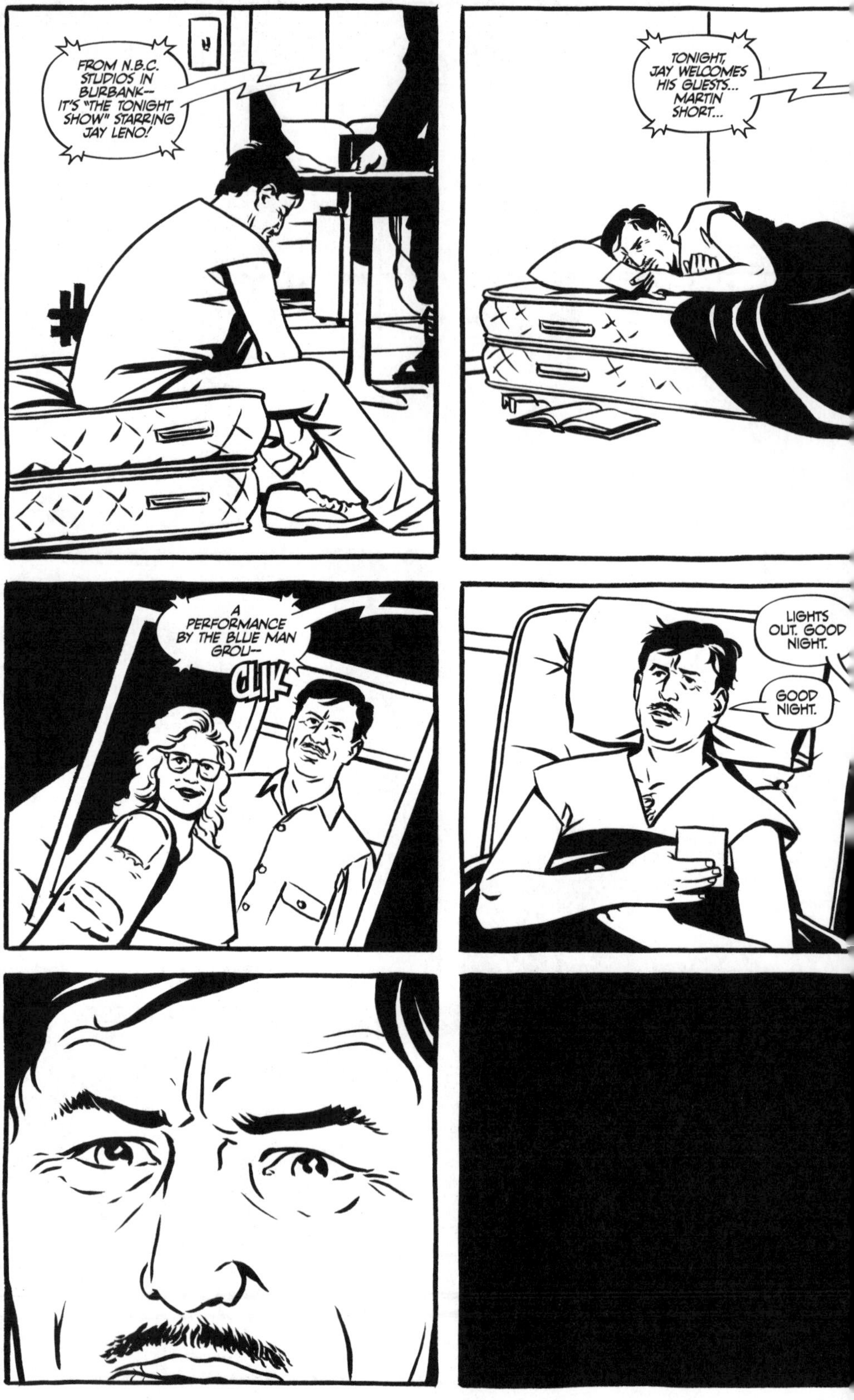
FROM N.B.C. STUDIOS IN BURBANK-- IT'S "THE TONIGHT SHOW" STARRING JAY LENO!
TONIGHT, JAY WELCOMES HIS GUESTS... MARTIN SHORT...
A PERFORMANCE BY THE BLUE MAN GROU--
CLIK
LIGHTS OUT. GOOD NIGHT.
GOOD NIGHT.

DAY TWO: FIELD TRIPS

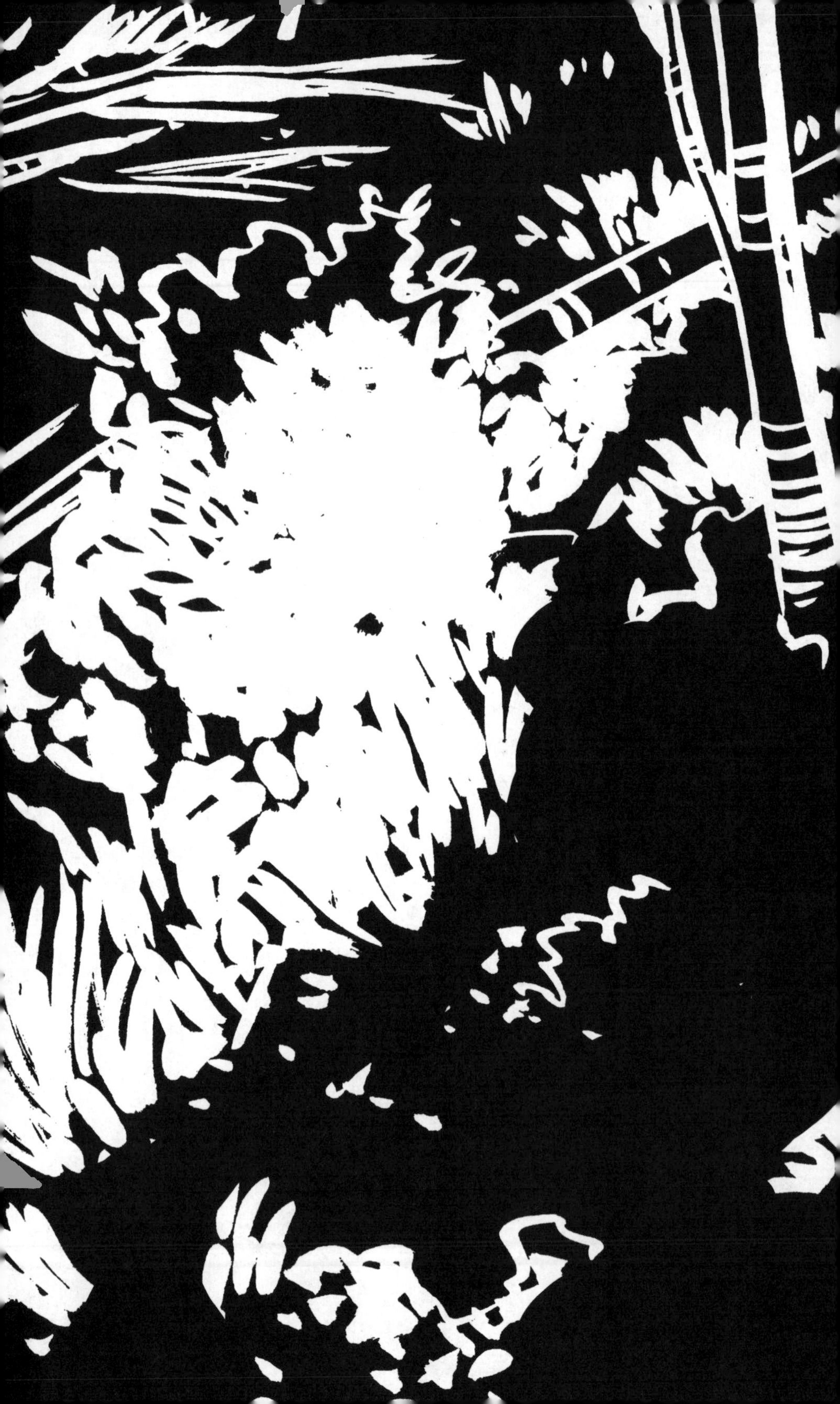

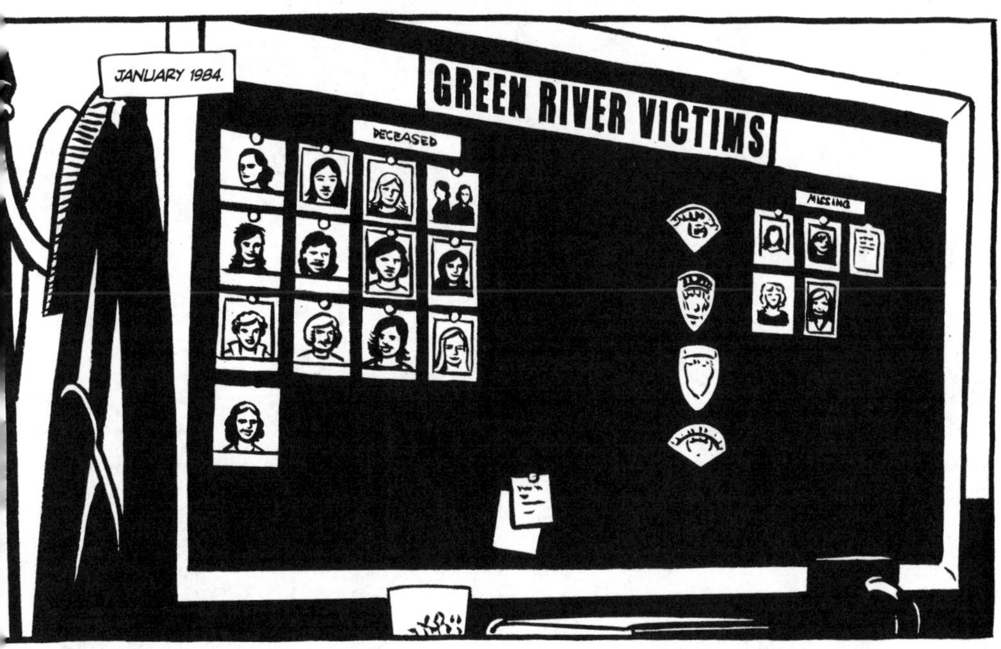
JANUARY 1984.
GREEN RIVER VICTIMS
DECEASED
MISSING

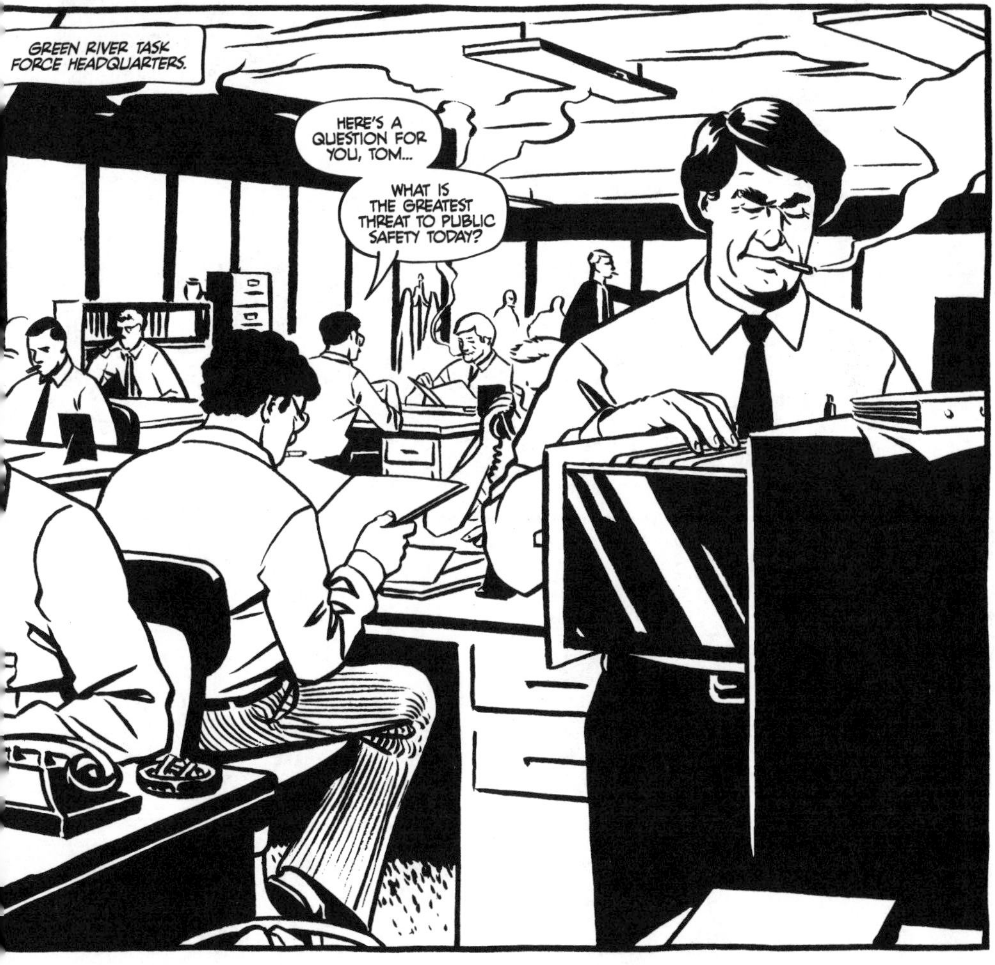
GREEN RIVER TASK FORCE HEADQUARTERS.
HERE'S A QUESTION FOR YOU, TOM...
WHAT IS THE GREATEST THREAT TO PUBLIC SAFETY TODAY?

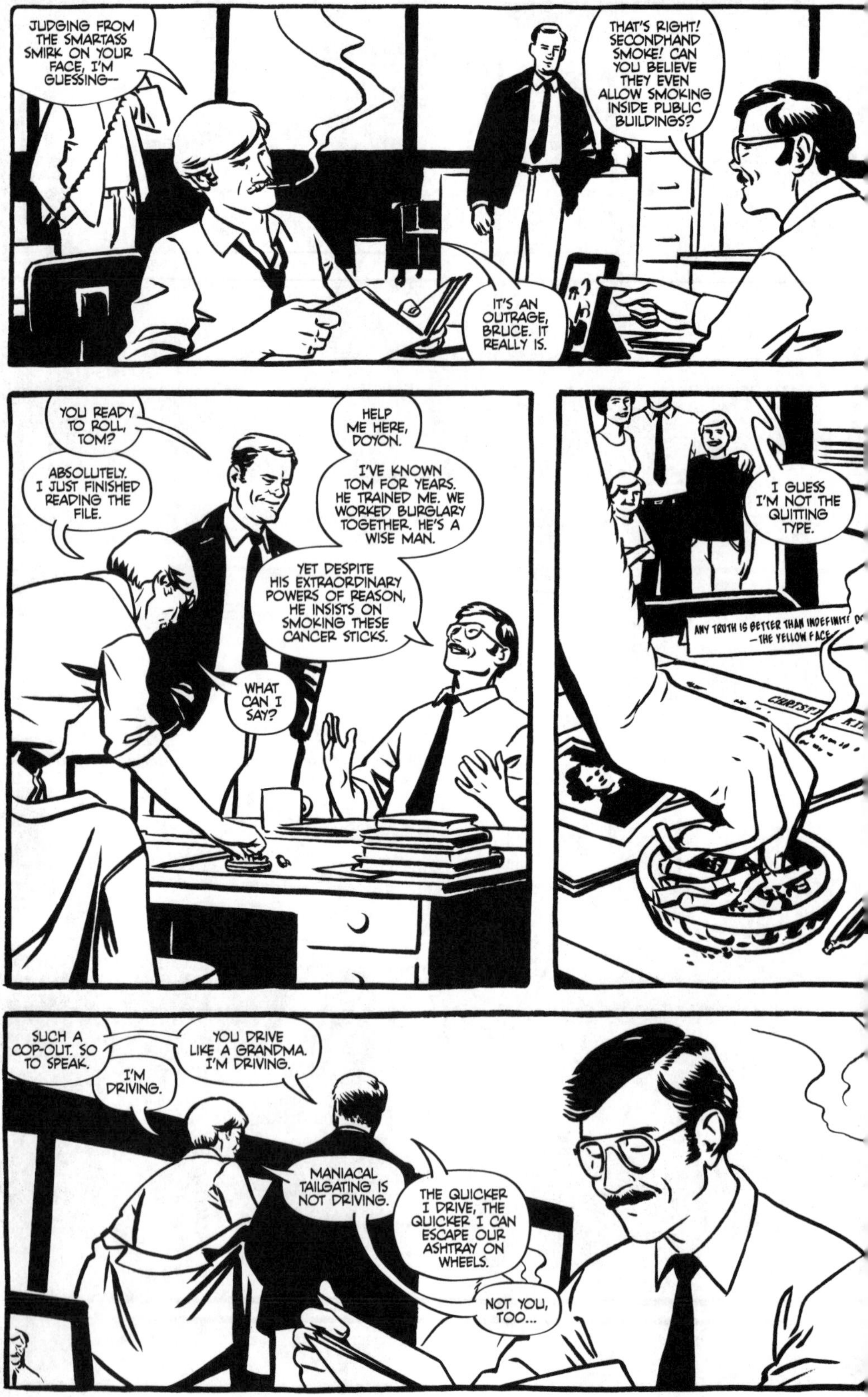
JUDGING FROM THE SMARTASS SMIRK ON YOUR FACE, I'M GUESSING--
THAT'S RIGHT! SECONDHAND SMOKE! CAN YOU BELIEVE THEY EVEN ALLOW SMOKING INSIDE PUBLIC BUILDINGS?
IT'S AN OUTRAGE, BRUCE. IT REALLY IS.
YOU READY TO ROLL, TOM?
ABSOLUTELY. I JUST FINISHED READING THE FILE.
HELP ME HERE, DOYON.
I'VE KNOWN TOM FOR YEARS. HE TRAINED ME. WE WORKED BURGLARY TOGETHER. HE'S A WISE MAN.
YET DESPITE HIS EXTRAORDINARY POWERS OF REASON, HE INSISTS ON SMOKING THESE CANCER STICKS.
WHAT CAN I SAY?
I GUESS I'M NOT THE QUITTING TYPE.
ANY TRUTH IS BETTER THAN INDEFINITE
—THE YELLOW FACE
SUCH A COP-OUT. SO TO SPEAK.
I'M DRIVING.
YOU DRIVE LIKE A GRANDMA. I'M DRIVING.
MANIACAL TAILGATING IS NOT DRIVING.
THE QUICKER I DRIVE, THE QUICKER I CAN ESCAPE OUR ASHTRAY ON WHEELS.
NOT YOU, TOO...

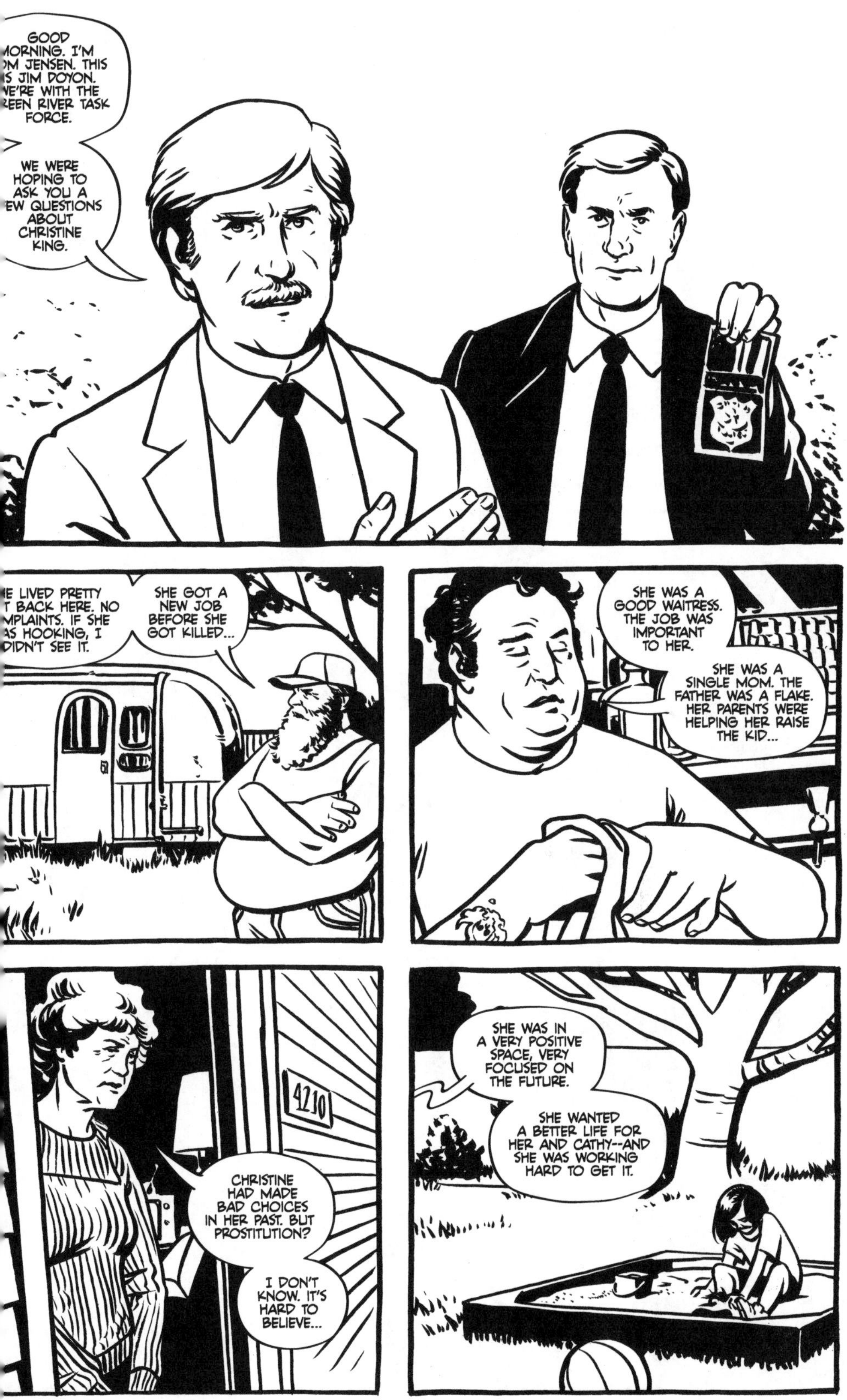
GOOD MORNING. I'M OM JENSEN. THIS S JIM DOYON. WE'RE WITH THE REEN RIVER TASK FORCE.
WE WERE HOPING TO ASK YOU A EW QUESTIONS ABOUT CHRISTINE KING.
E LIVED PRETTY T BACK HERE. NO MPLAINTS. IF SHE AS HOOKING, I DIDN'T SEE IT.
SHE GOT A NEW JOB BEFORE SHE GOT KILLED...
SHE WAS A GOOD WAITRESS. THE JOB WAS IMPORTANT TO HER.
SHE WAS A SINGLE MOM. THE FATHER WAS A FLAKE. HER PARENTS WERE HELPING HER RAISE THE KID...
4210
CHRISTINE HAD MADE BAD CHOICES IN HER PAST. BUT PROSTITUTION?
I DON'T KNOW. IT'S HARD TO BELIEVE...
SHE WAS IN A VERY POSITIVE SPACE, VERY FOCUSED ON THE FUTURE.
SHE WANTED A BETTER LIFE FOR HER AND CATHY--AND SHE WAS WORKING HARD TO GET IT.

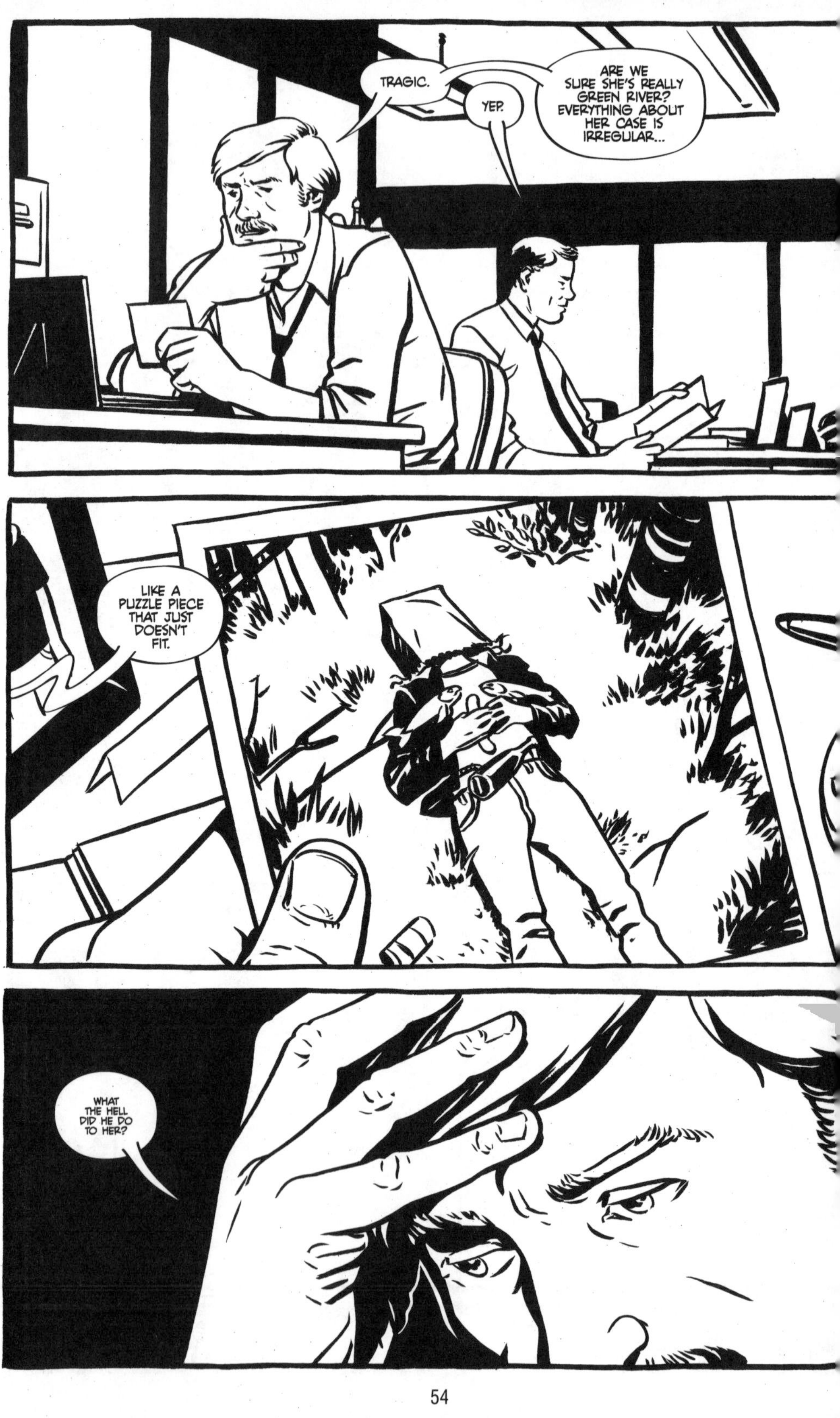
TRAGIC.
YEP.
ARE WE SURE SHE'S REALLY GREEN RIVER? EVERYTHING ABOUT HER CASE IS IRREGULAR...
LIKE A PUZZLE PIECE THAT JUST DOESN'T FIT.
WHAT THE HELL DID HE DO TO HER?

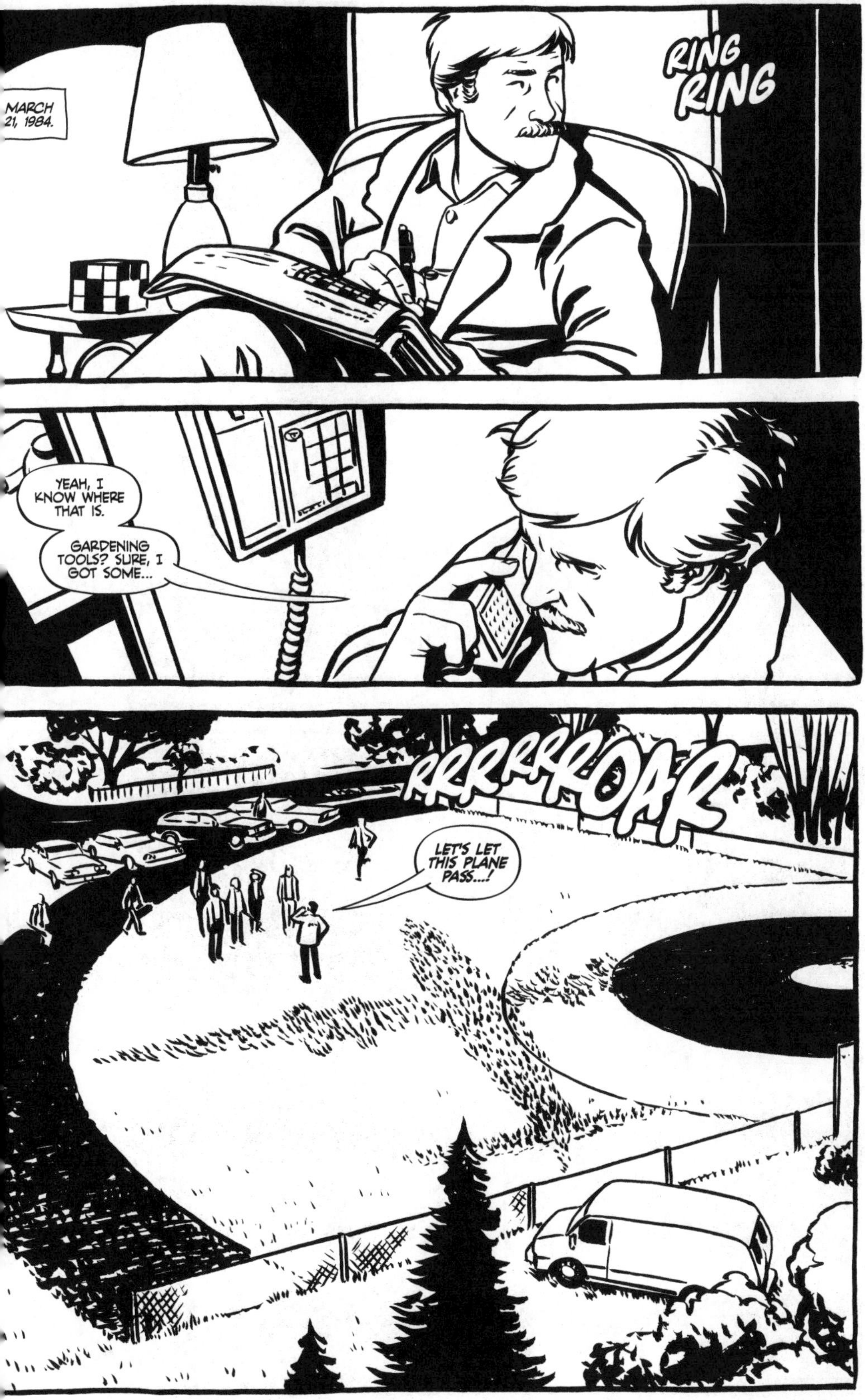
MARCH 21, 1984.
RING RING
YEAH, I KNOW WHERE THAT IS.
GARDENING TOOLS? SURE, I GOT SOME...
RRRRRROAR
LET'S LET THIS PLANE PASS...!

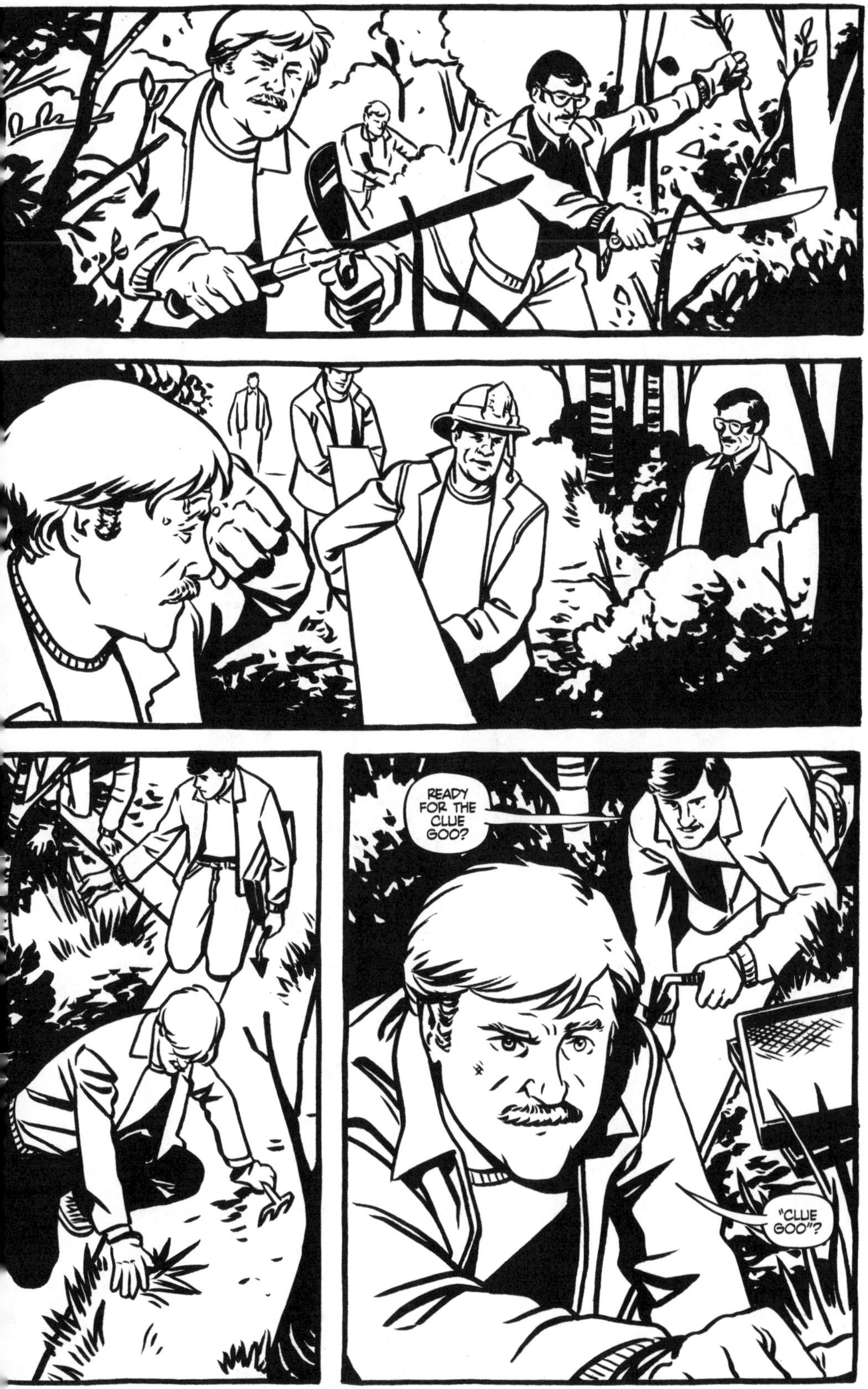
READY FOR THE CLUE GOO?
"CLUE GOO"?

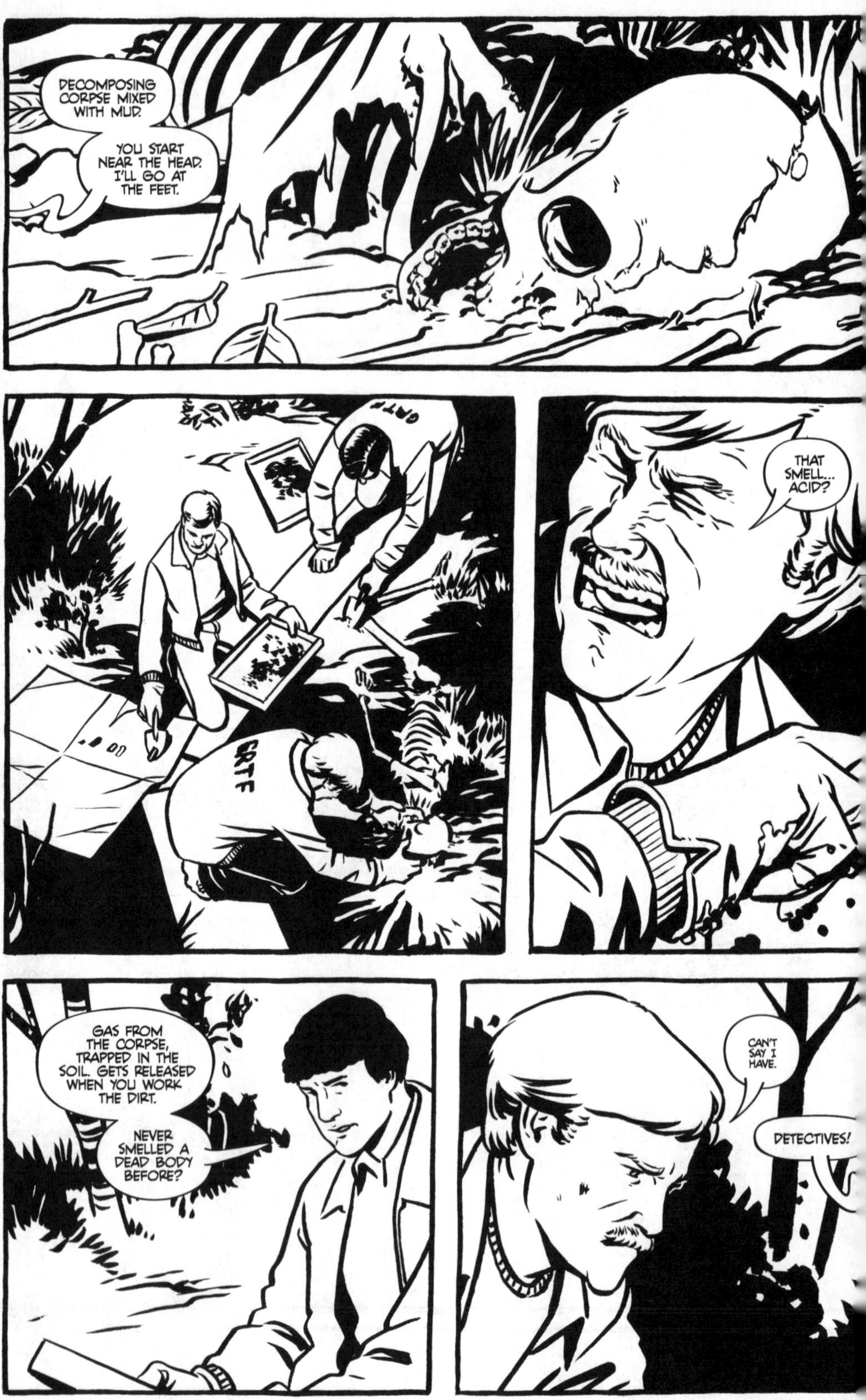

DECOMPOSING CORPSE MIXED WITH MUD.
YOU START NEAR THE HEAD. I'LL GO AT THE FEET.
GRTF
GRTF
THAT SMELL... ACID?
GAS FROM THE CORPSE, TRAPPED IN THE SOIL. GETS RELEASED WHEN YOU WORK THE DIRT.
NEVER SMELLED A DEAD BODY BEFORE?
CAN'T SAY I HAVE.
DETECTIVES!

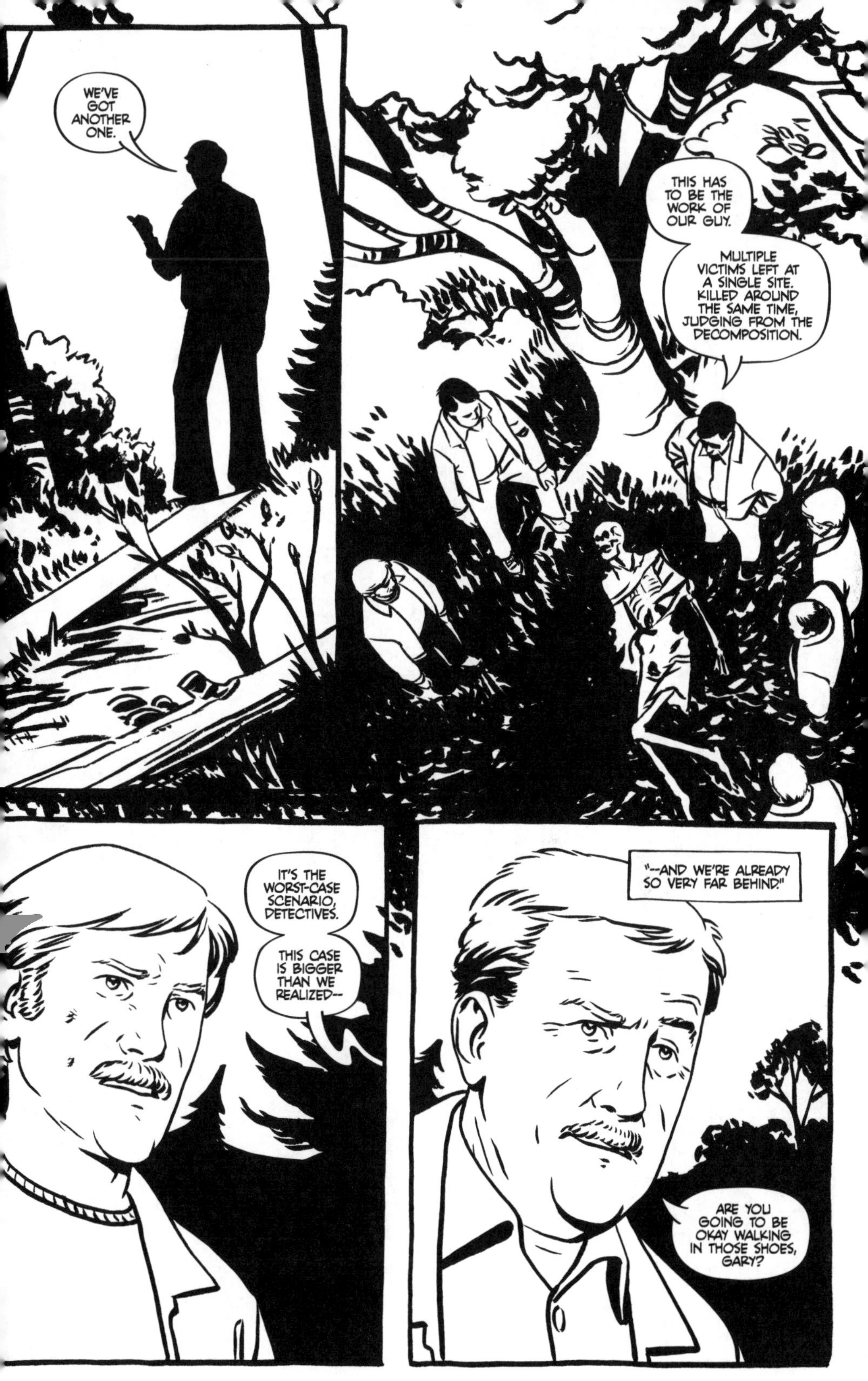
WE'VE GOT ANOTHER ONE.
THIS HAS TO BE THE WORK OF OUR GUY.
MULTIPLE VICTIMS LEFT AT A SINGLE SITE. KILLED AROUND THE SAME TIME, JUDGING FROM THE DECOMPOSITION.
IT'S THE WORST-CASE SCENARIO, DETECTIVES.
THIS CASE IS BIGGER THAN WE REALIZED--
"--AND WE'RE ALREADY SO VERY FAR BEHIND."
ARE YOU GOING TO BE OKAY WALKING IN THOSE SHOES, GARY?

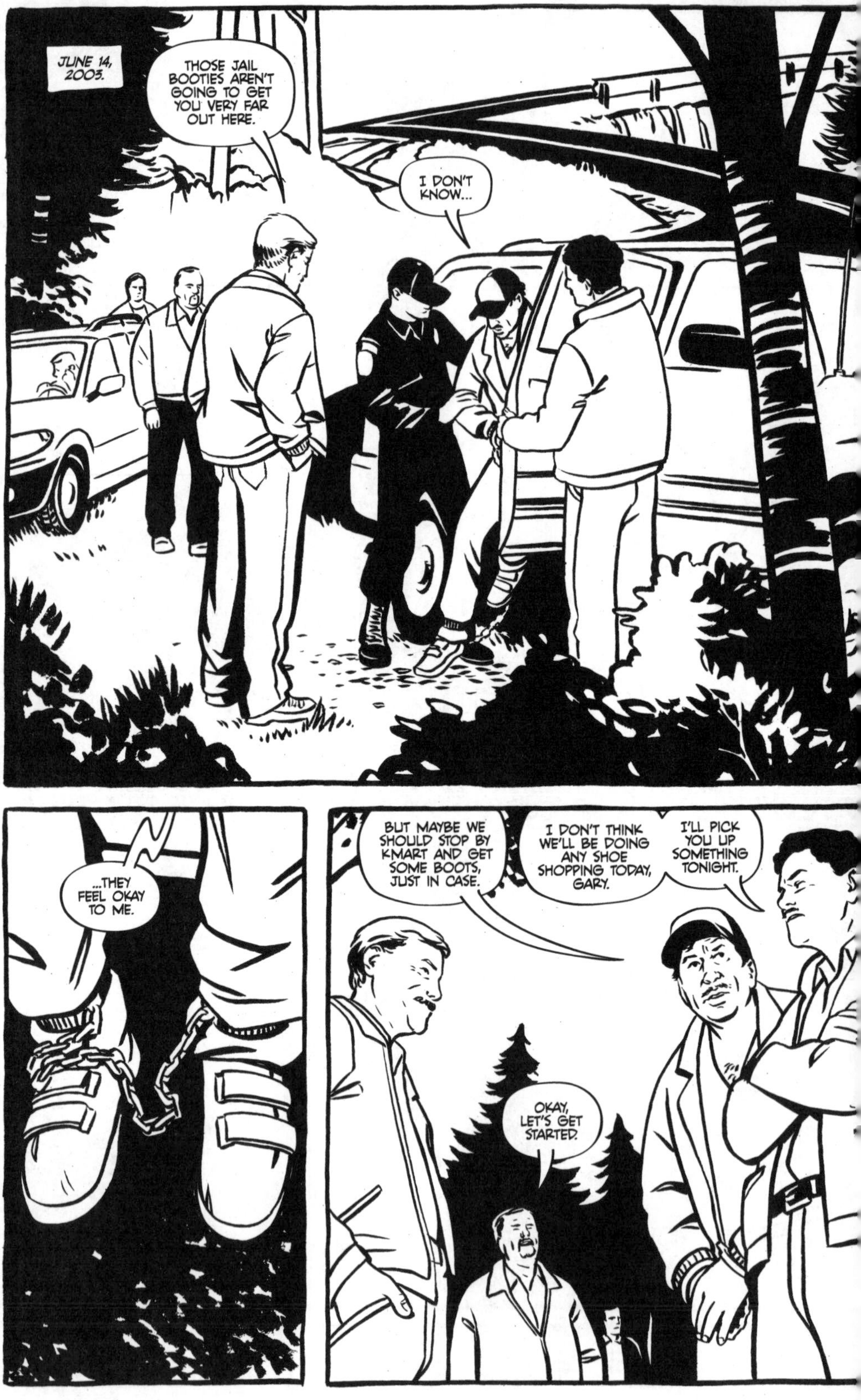
JUNE 14, 2003.
THOSE JAIL BOOTIES AREN'T GOING TO GET YOU VERY FAR OUT HERE.
I DON'T KNOW...
...THEY FEEL OKAY TO ME.
BUT MAYBE WE SHOULD STOP BY KMART AND GET SOME BOOTS, JUST IN CASE.
I DON'T THINK WE'LL BE DOING ANY SHOE SHOPPING TODAY, GARY.
I'LL PICK YOU UP SOMETHING TONIGHT.
OKAY, LET'S GET STARTED.

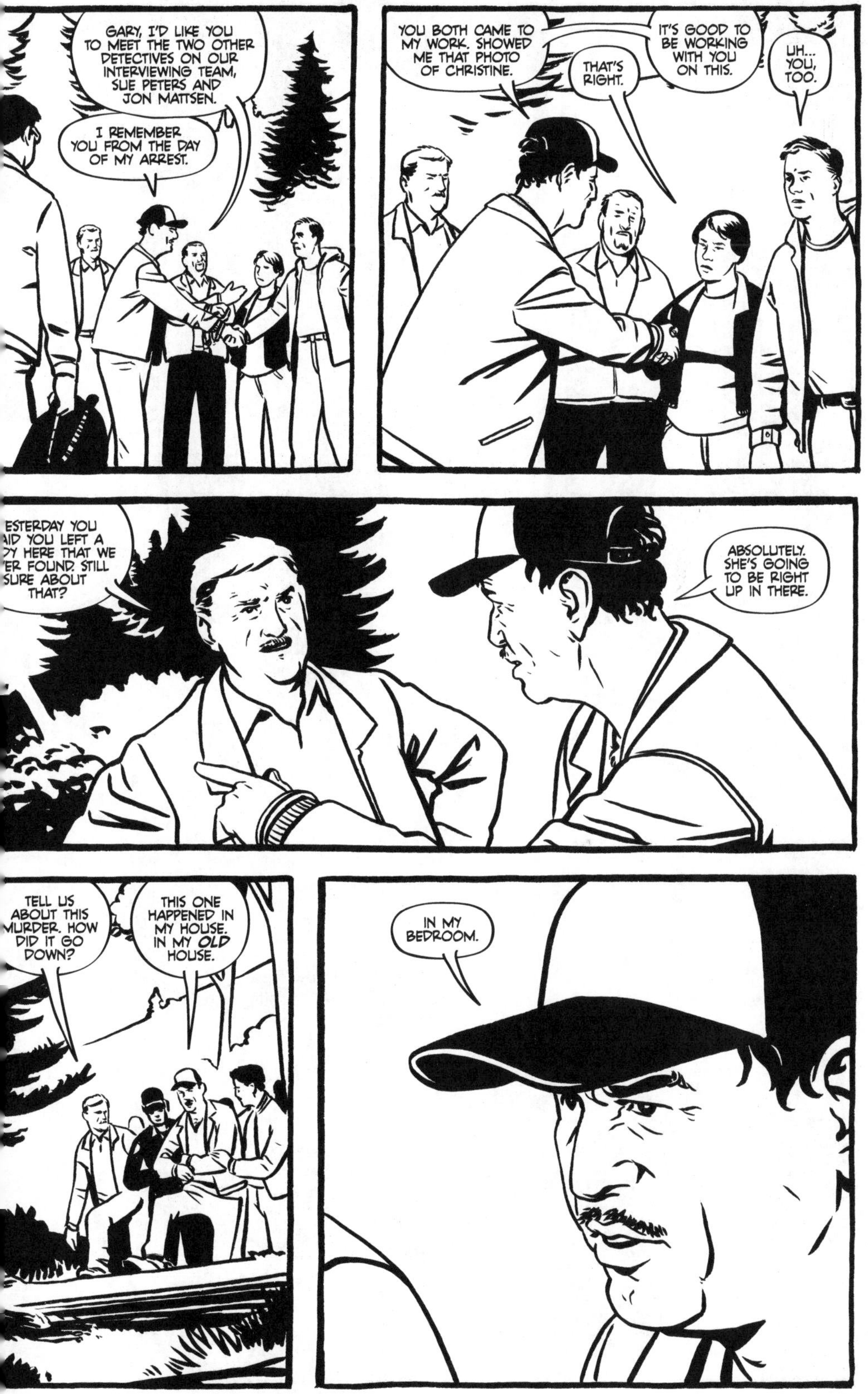
GARY, I'D LIKE YOU TO MEET THE TWO OTHER DETECTIVES ON OUR INTERVIEWING TEAM, SUE PETERS AND JON MATTSEN.
I REMEMBER YOU FROM THE DAY OF MY ARREST.
YOU BOTH CAME TO MY WORK. SHOWED ME THAT PHOTO OF CHRISTINE.
IT'S GOOD TO BE WORKING WITH YOU ON THIS.
THAT'S RIGHT.
UH... YOU, TOO.
ESTERDAY YOU AID YOU LEFT A DY HERE THAT WE ER FOUND. STILL SURE ABOUT THAT?
ABSOLUTELY. SHE'S GOING TO BE RIGHT UP IN THERE.
TELL US ABOUT THIS MURDER. HOW DID IT GO DOWN?
THIS ONE HAPPENED IN MY HOUSE. IN MY *OLD* HOUSE.
IN MY BEDROOM.

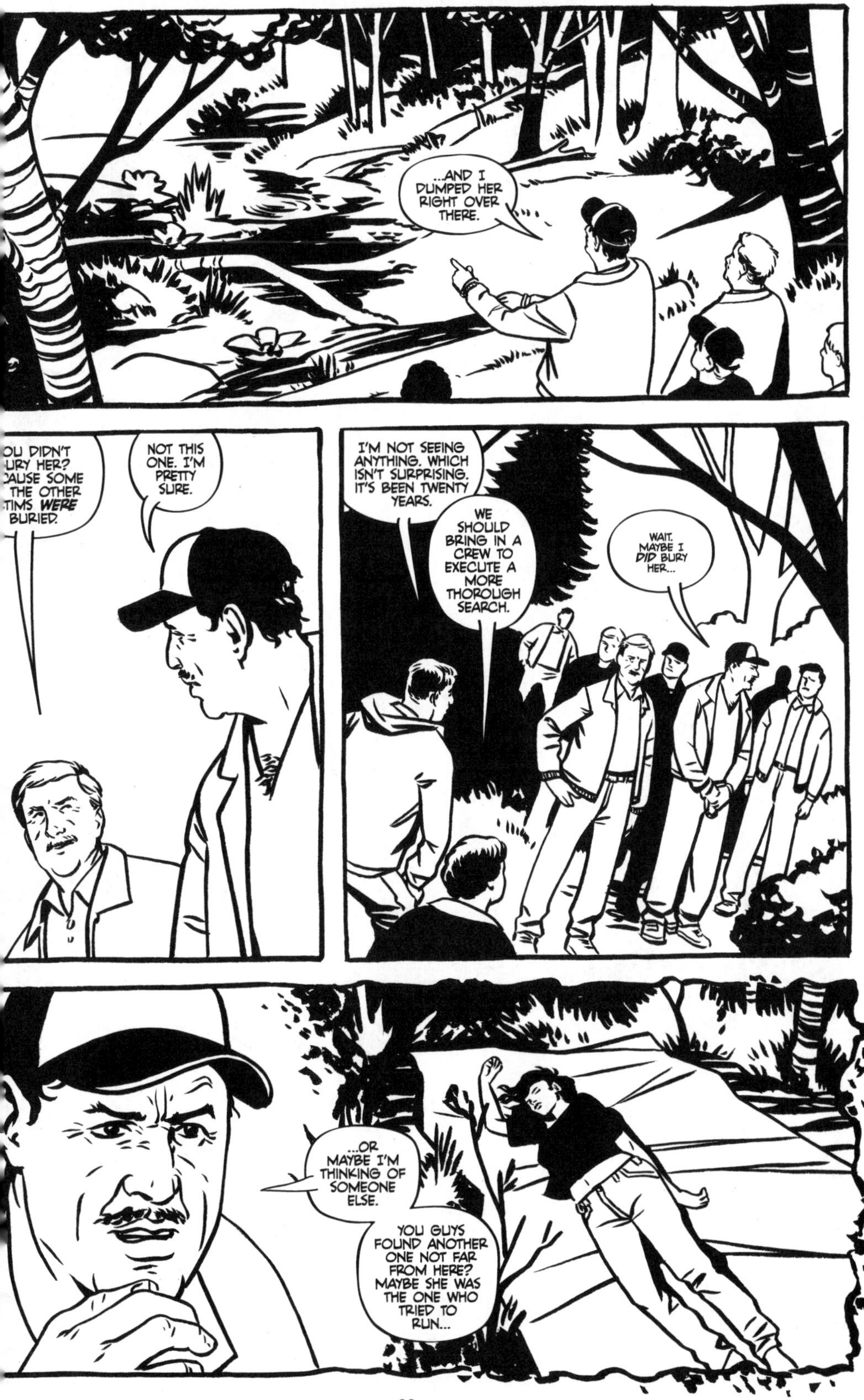
...AND I DUMPED HER RIGHT OVER THERE.
OU DIDN'T URY HER? CAUSE SOME THE OTHER TIMS WERE BURIED.
NOT THIS ONE. I'M PRETTY SURE.
I'M NOT SEEING ANYTHING. WHICH ISN'T SURPRISING. IT'S BEEN TWENTY YEARS.
WE SHOULD BRING IN A CREW TO EXECUTE A MORE THOROUGH SEARCH.
WAIT. MAYBE I DID BURY HER...
...OR MAYBE I'M THINKING OF SOMEONE ELSE.
YOU GUYS FOUND ANOTHER ONE NOT FAR FROM HERE? MAYBE SHE WAS THE ONE WHO TRIED TO RUN...

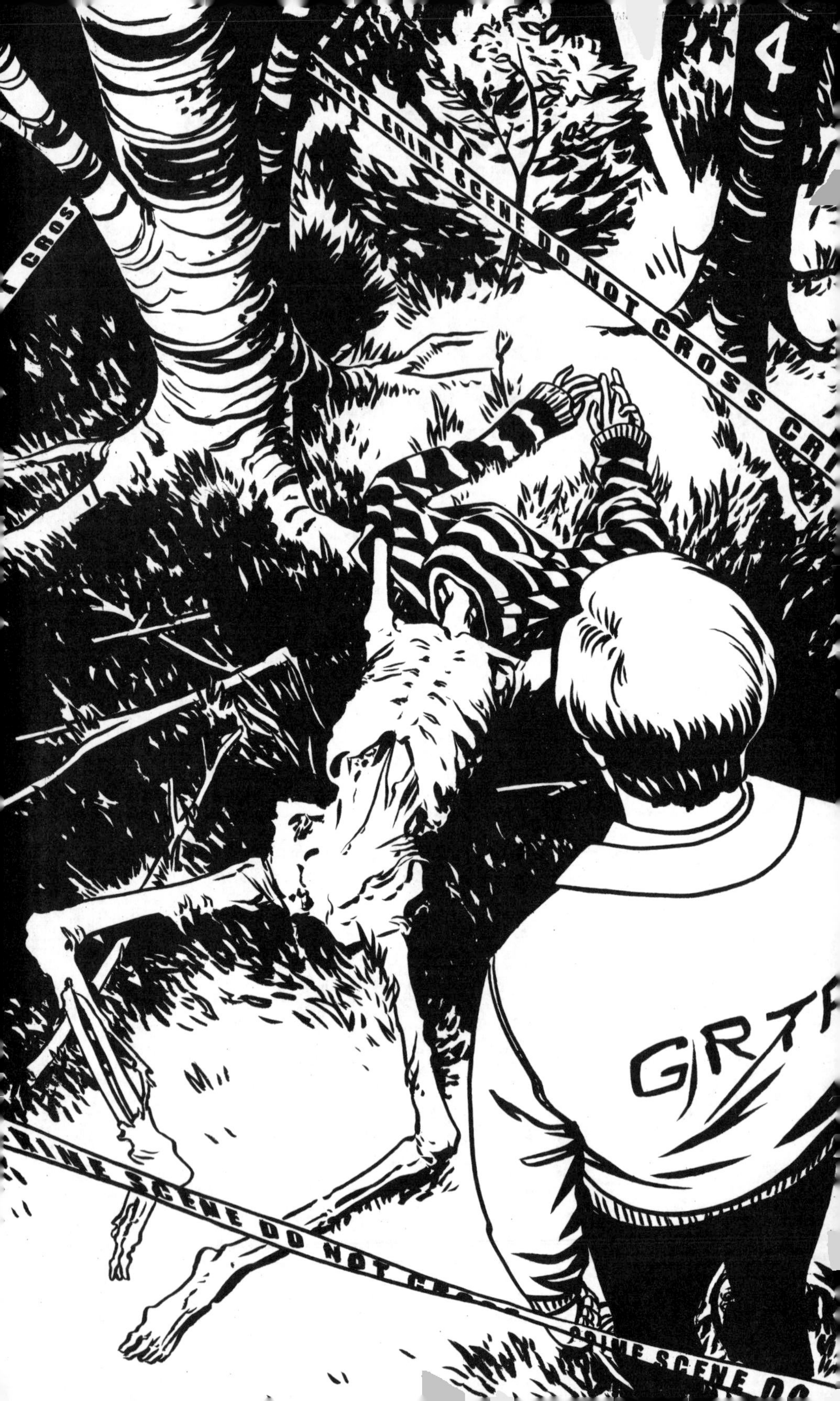
4
CRIME SCENE DO NOT CROSS
CROS
CRIME SCENE DO NOT
CRIME SCENE DO

THE COMMANDER WANTS TO SEE US TOPSIDE.

GRTF

OT CROSS

LET'S GO, TOM.

68

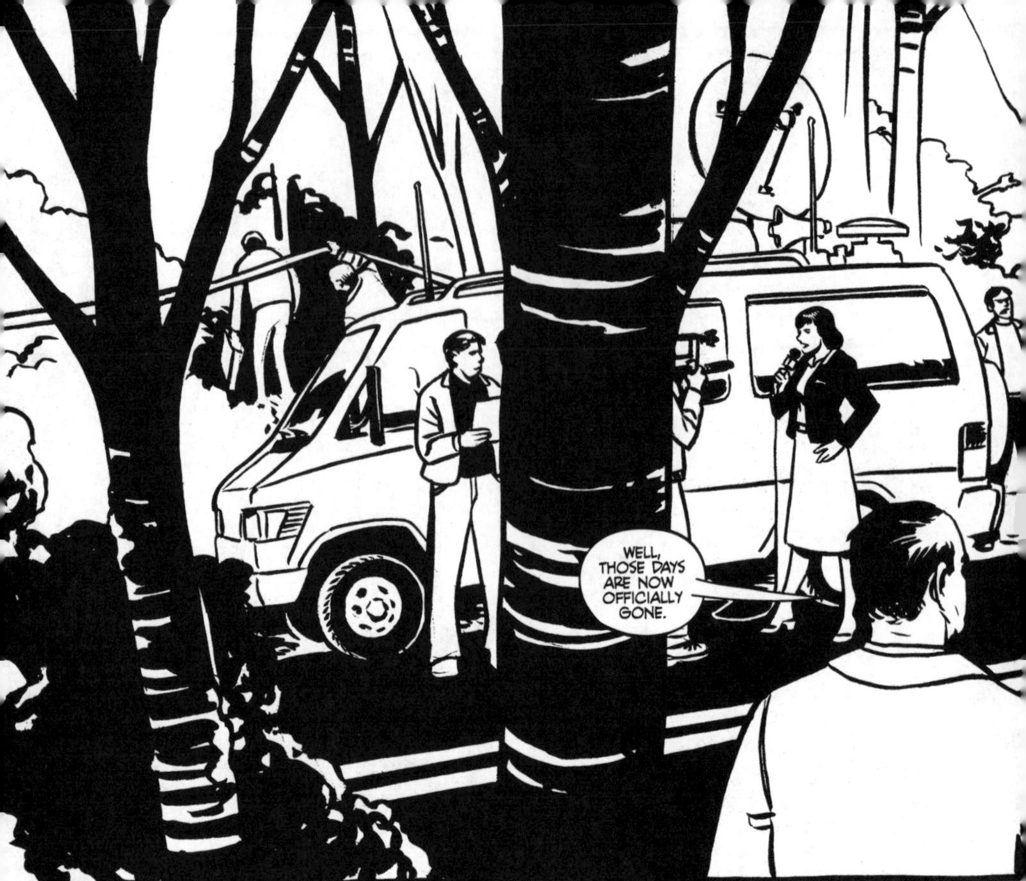
WELL, THOSE DAYS ARE NOW OFFICIALLY GONE.

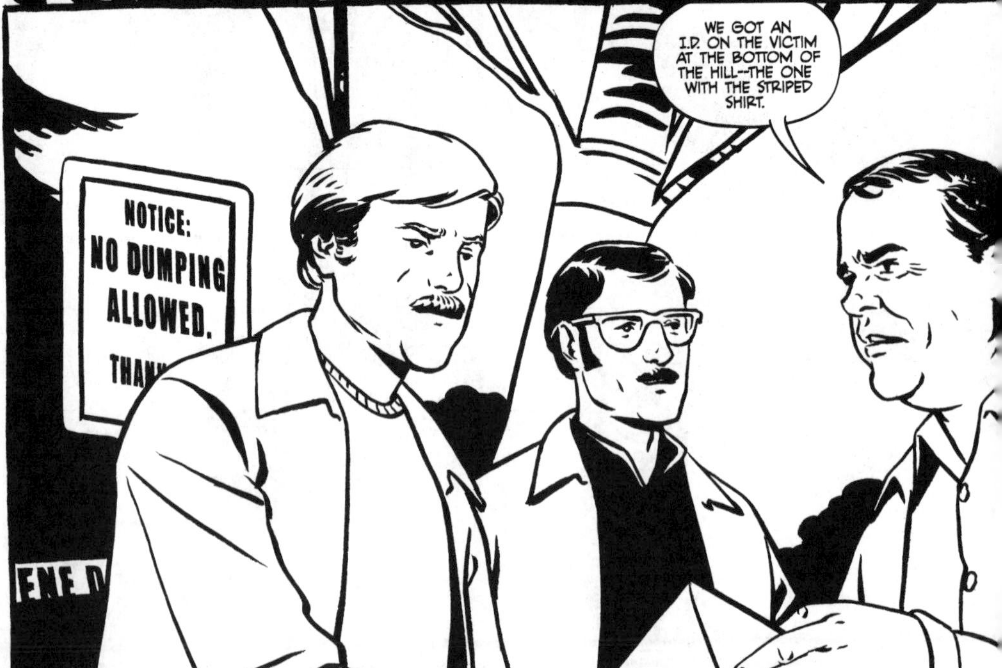
WE GOT AN I.D. ON THE VICTIM AT THE BOTTOM OF THE HILL--THE ONE WITH THE STRIPED SHIRT.
NOTICE:
NO DUMPING
ALLOWED.
THAN

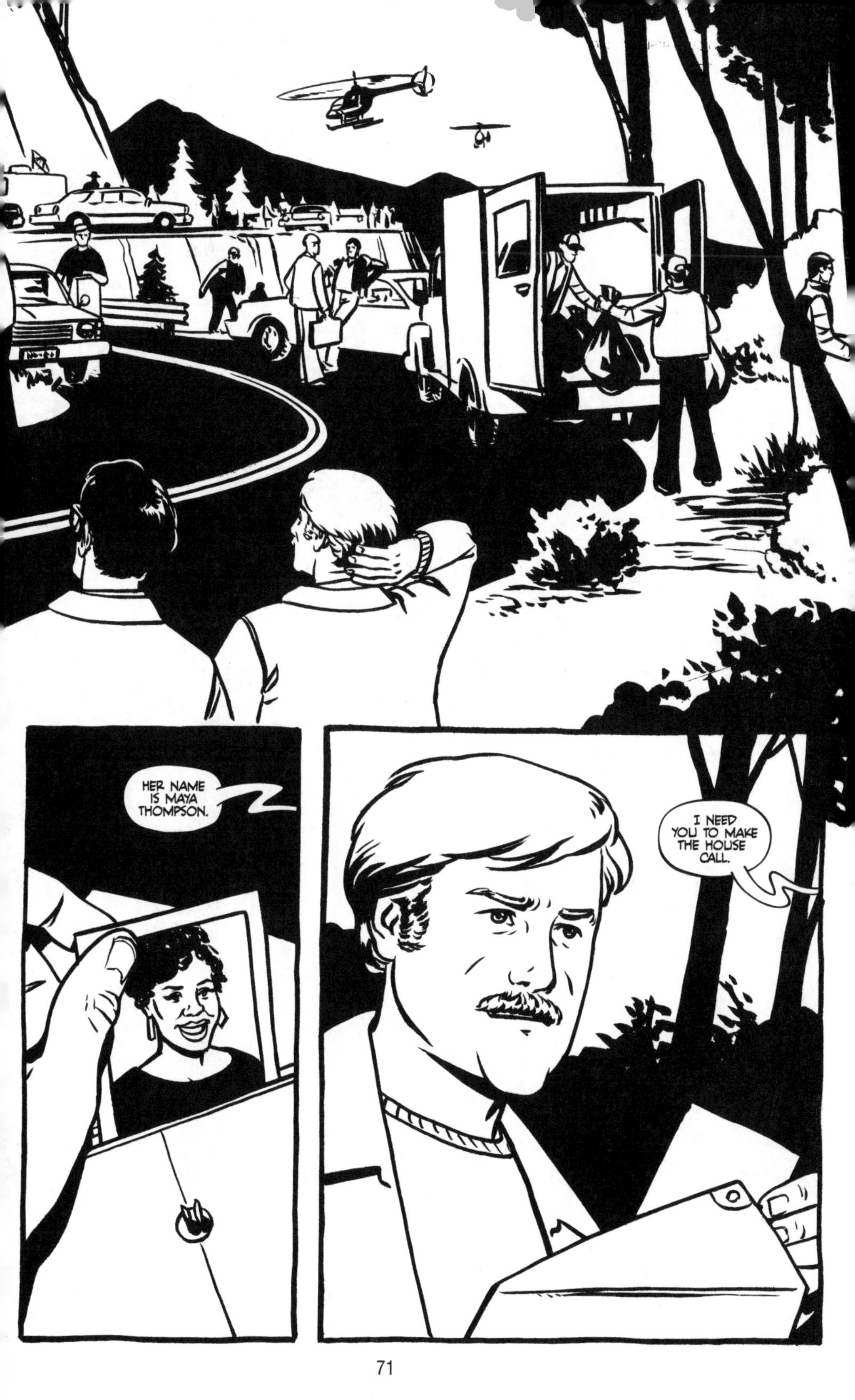
HER NAME IS MAYA THOMPSON.
I NEED YOU TO MAKE THE HOUSE CALL.

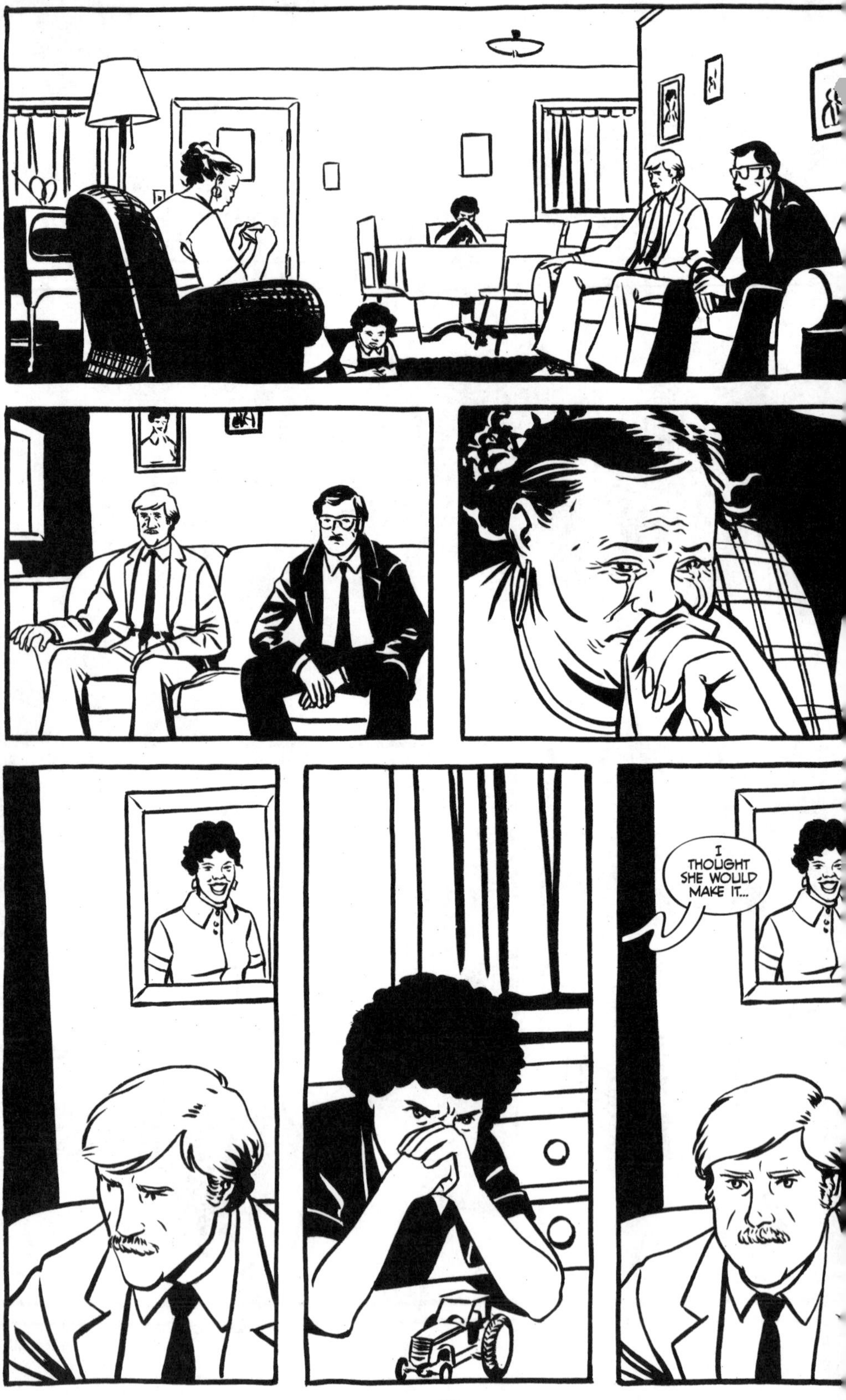
I THOUGHT SHE WOULD MAKE IT...

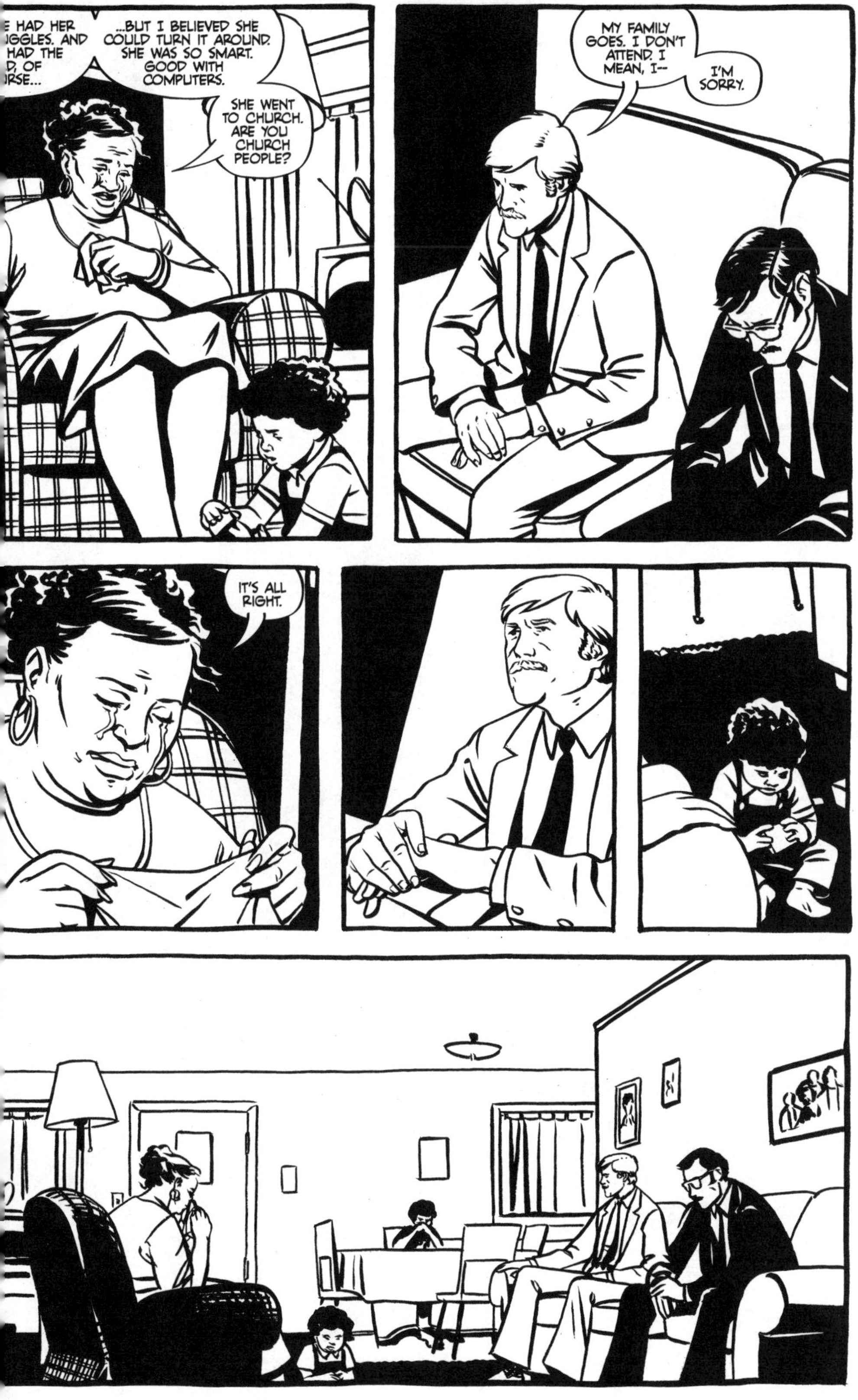

E HAD HER
UGGLES. AND
HAD THE
D, OF
RSE...
...BUT I BELIEVED SHE COULD TURN IT AROUND. SHE WAS SO SMART. GOOD WITH COMPUTERS.
SHE WENT TO CHURCH. ARE YOU CHURCH PEOPLE?
MY FAMILY GOES. I DON'T ATTEND. I MEAN, I--
I'M SORRY.
IT'S ALL RIGHT.

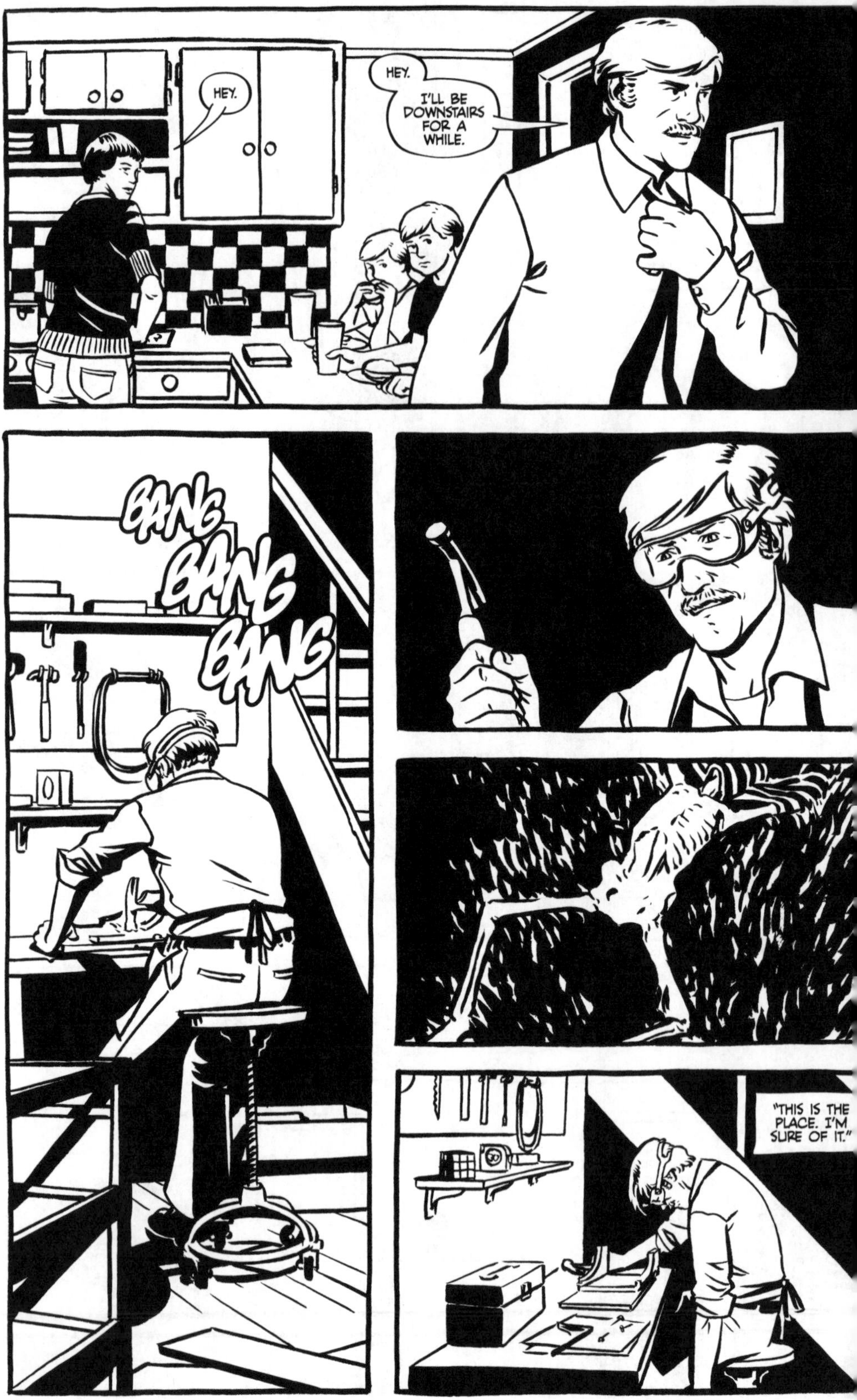
HEY.
HEY.
I'LL BE DOWNSTAIRS FOR A WHILE.
BANG
BANG
BANG
"THIS IS THE PLACE. I'M SURE OF IT."

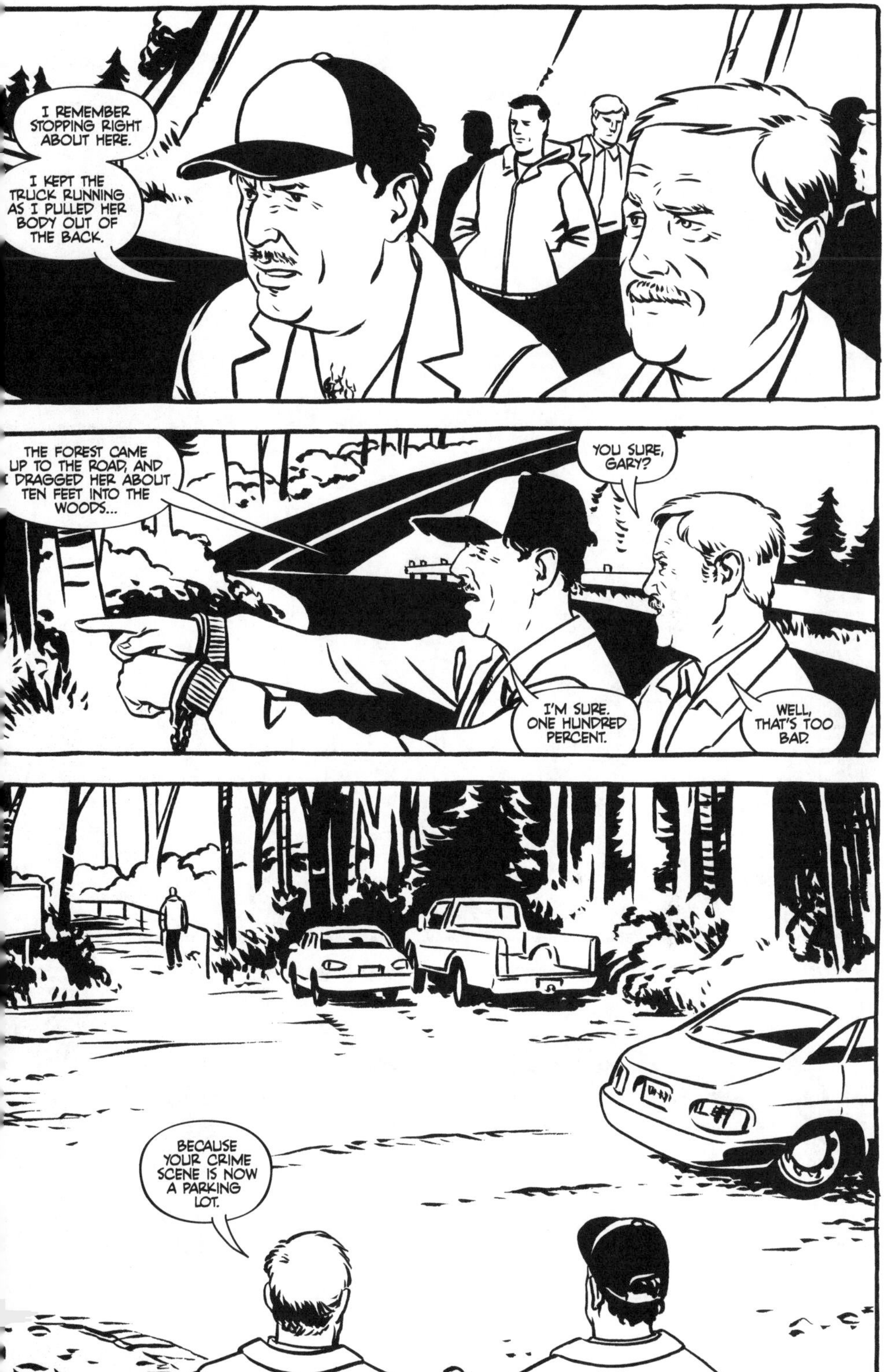
I REMEMBER STOPPING RIGHT ABOUT HERE.
I KEPT THE TRUCK RUNNING AS I PULLED HER BODY OUT OF THE BACK.
THE FOREST CAME UP TO THE ROAD, AND I DRAGGED HER ABOUT TEN FEET INTO THE WOODS...
YOU SURE, GARY?
I'M SURE. ONE HUNDRED PERCENT.
WELL, THAT'S TOO BAD.
BECAUSE YOUR CRIME SCENE IS NOW A PARKING LOT.

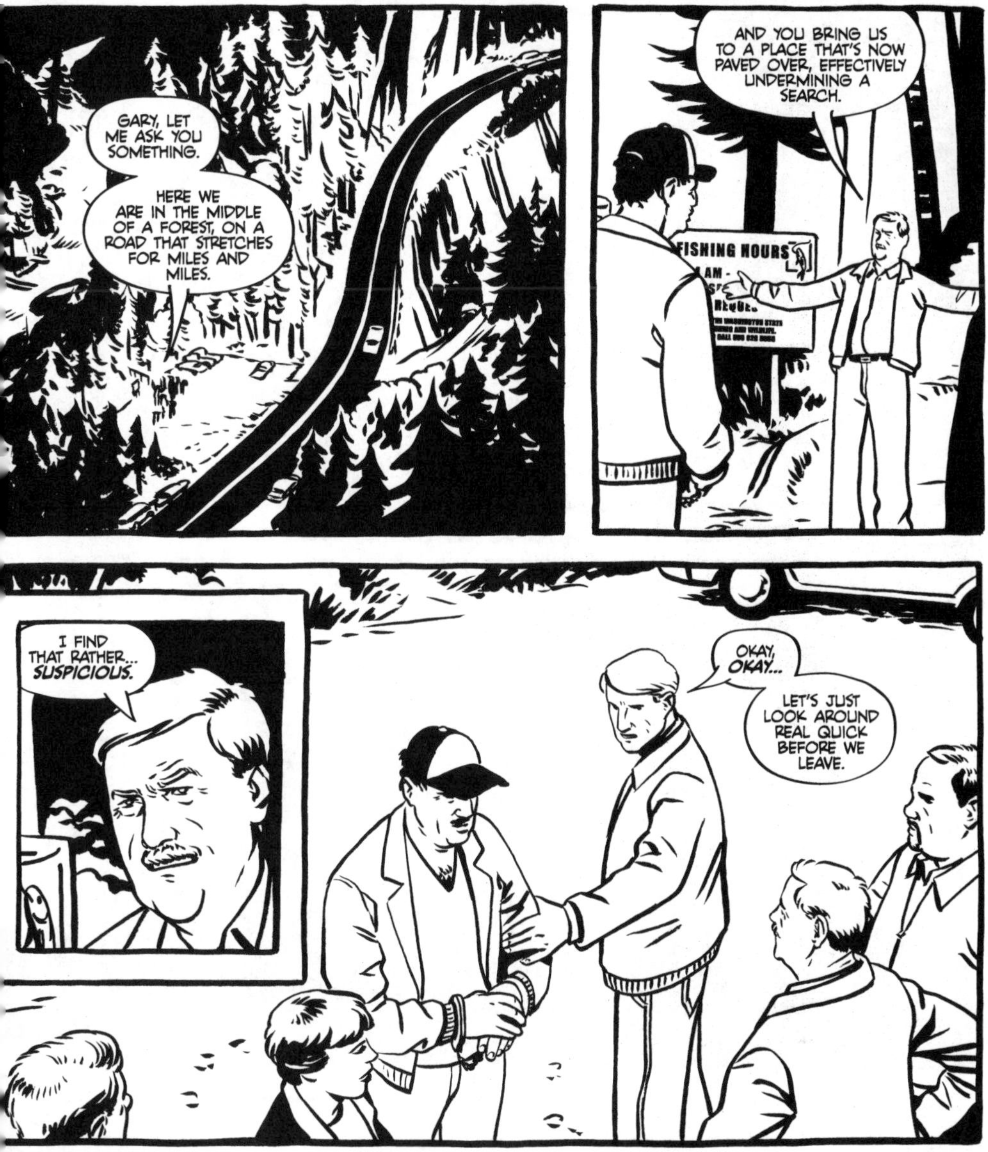
GARY, LET ME ASK YOU SOMETHING.
HERE WE ARE IN THE MIDDLE OF A FOREST, ON A ROAD THAT STRETCHES FOR MILES AND MILES.
AND YOU BRING US TO A PLACE THAT'S NOW PAVED OVER, EFFECTIVELY UNDERMINING A SEARCH.
FISHING HOURS
I FIND THAT RATHER... *SUSPICIOUS.*
OKAY, *OKAY...*
LET'S JUST LOOK AROUND REAL QUICK BEFORE WE LEAVE.
GO AHEAD.
I'M TAKING A CIGARETTE BREAK.

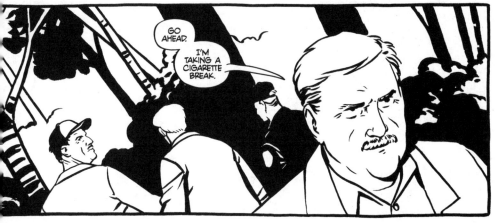

SUMMER 1984.

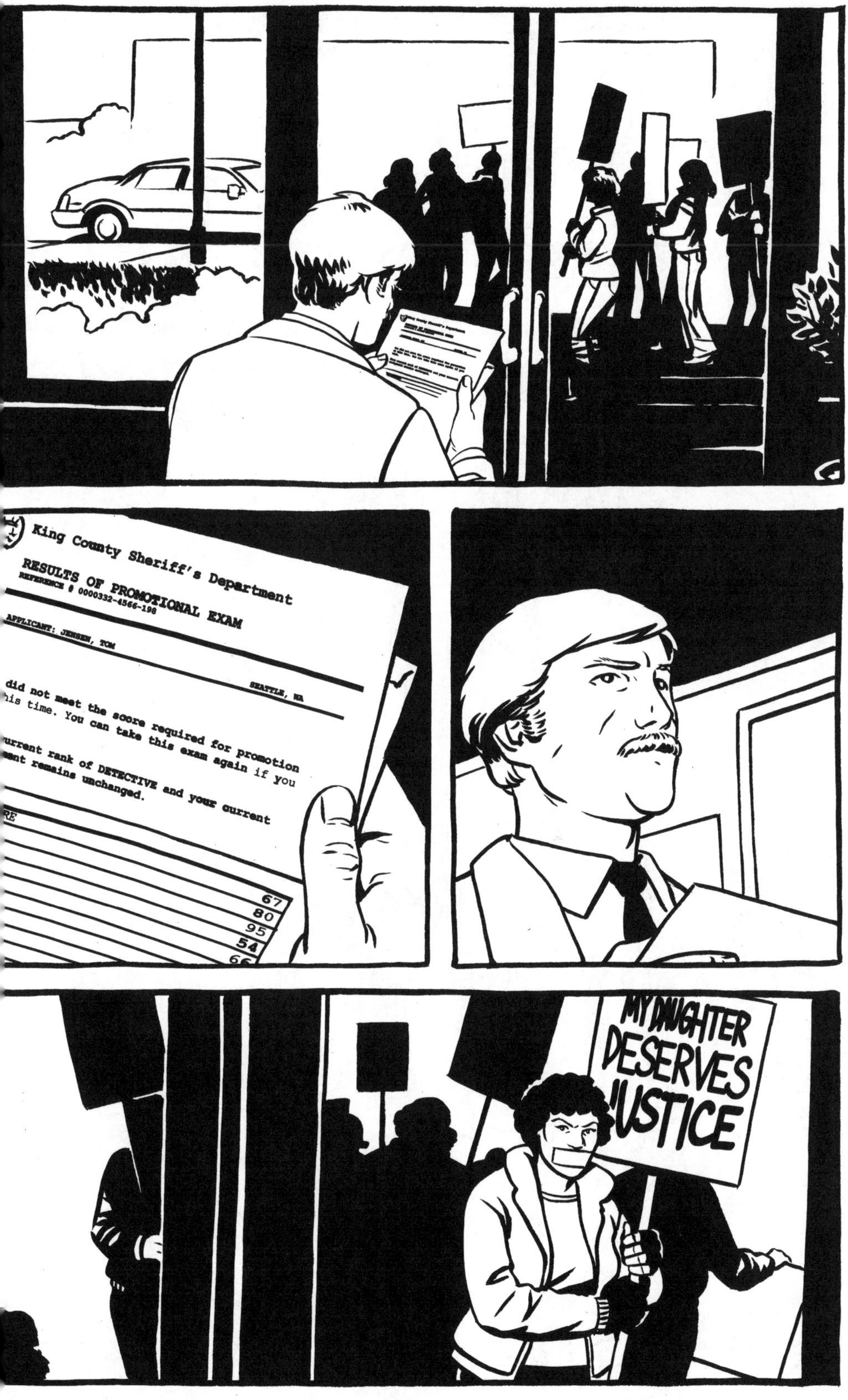
King County Sheriff's Department
RESULTS OF PROMOTIONAL EXAM
REFERENCE # 0000332-4566-198
APPLICANT: JENSEN, TOM
SEATTLE, WA
did not meet the score required for promotion
his time. You can take this exam again if you
urrent rank of DETECTIVE and your current
ent remains unchanged.
67
80
95
54
MY DAUGHTER DESERVES JUSTICE

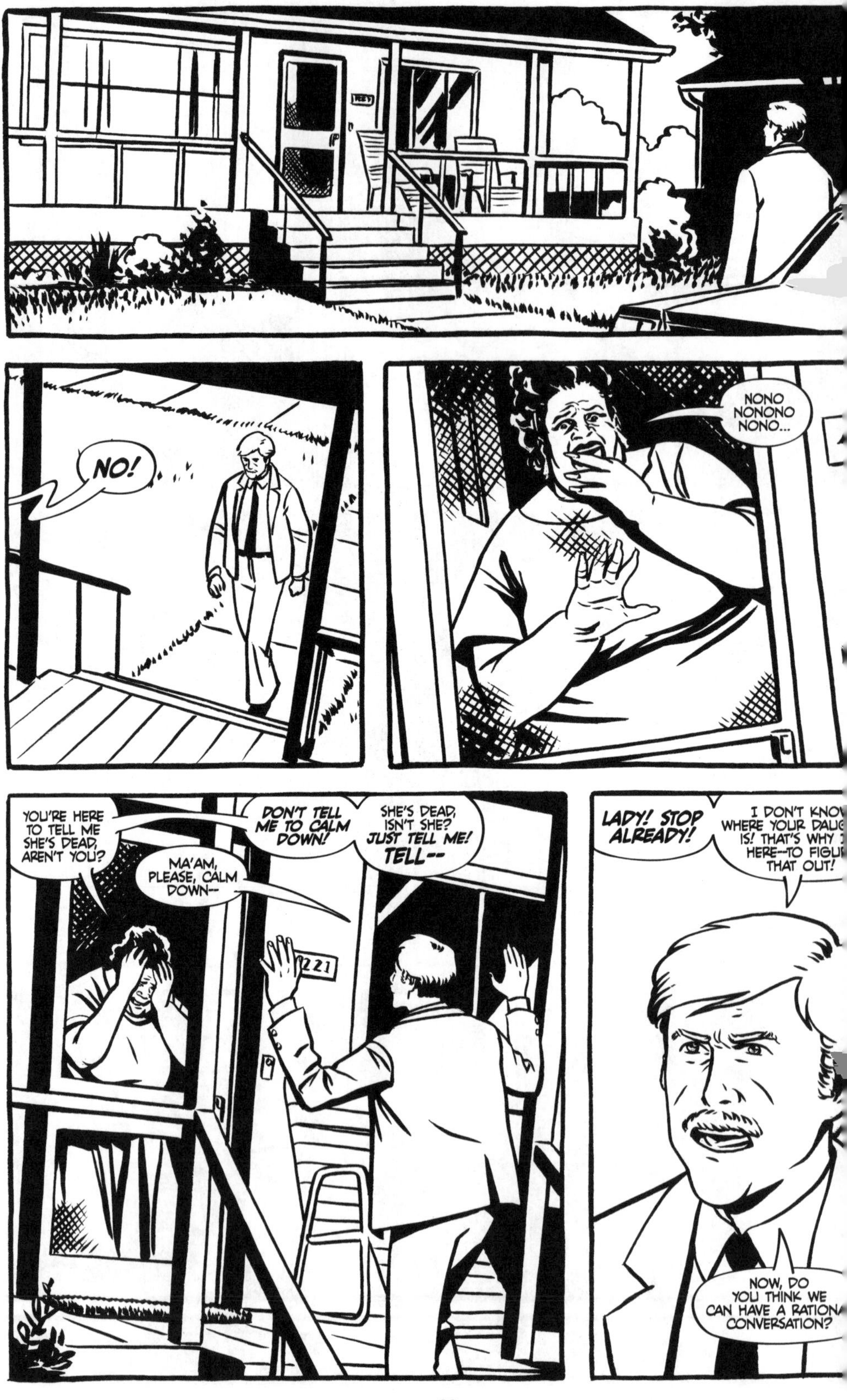

NO!
NONO
NONONO
NONO...
YOU'RE HERE
TO TELL ME
SHE'S DEAD,
AREN'T YOU?
MA'AM,
PLEASE, CALM
DOWN--
DON'T TELL
ME TO CALM
DOWN!
SHE'S DEAD,
ISN'T SHE?
JUST TELL ME!
TELL--
LADY! STOP
ALREADY!
I DON'T KNOW
WHERE YOUR DAUG
IS! THAT'S WHY I
HERE--TO FIGUR
THAT OUT!
NOW, DO
YOU THINK WE
CAN HAVE A RATION
CONVERSATION?

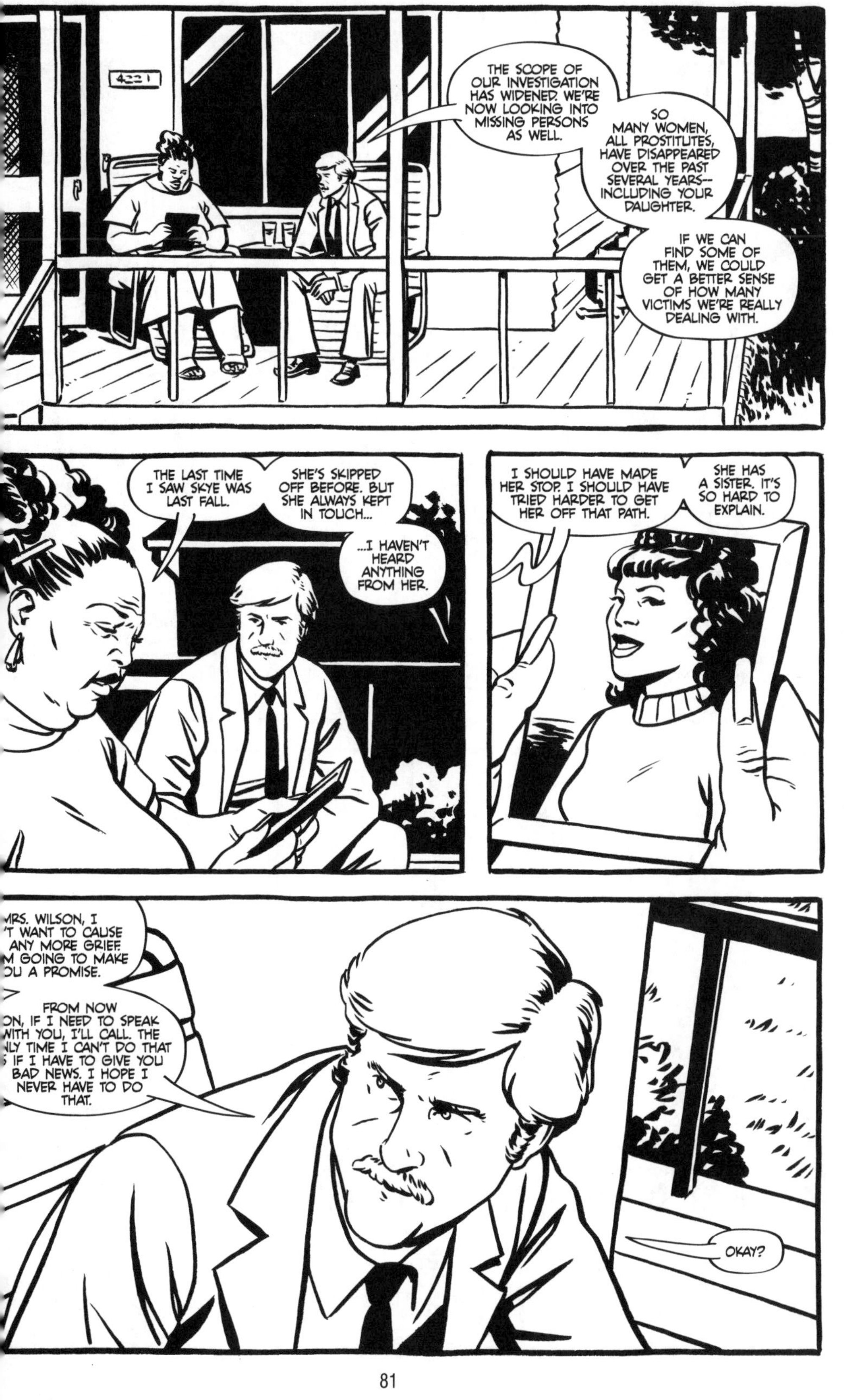
THE SCOPE OF OUR INVESTIGATION HAS WIDENED. WE'RE NOW LOOKING INTO MISSING PERSONS AS WELL.
SO MANY WOMEN, ALL PROSTITUTES, HAVE DISAPPEARED OVER THE PAST SEVERAL YEARS-- INCLUDING YOUR DAUGHTER.
IF WE CAN FIND SOME OF THEM, WE COULD GET A BETTER SENSE OF HOW MANY VICTIMS WE'RE REALLY DEALING WITH.
4221
THE LAST TIME I SAW SKYE WAS LAST FALL.
SHE'S SKIPPED OFF BEFORE. BUT SHE ALWAYS KEPT IN TOUCH...
...I HAVEN'T HEARD ANYTHING FROM HER.
I SHOULD HAVE MADE HER STOP. I SHOULD HAVE TRIED HARDER TO GET HER OFF THAT PATH.
SHE HAS A SISTER. IT'S SO HARD TO EXPLAIN.
MRS. WILSON, I 'T WANT TO CAUSE ANY MORE GRIEF. M GOING TO MAKE OU A PROMISE.
FROM NOW ON, IF I NEED TO SPEAK WITH YOU, I'LL CALL. THE NLY TIME I CAN'T DO THAT IF I HAVE TO GIVE YOU BAD NEWS. I HOPE I NEVER HAVE TO DO THAT.
OKAY?

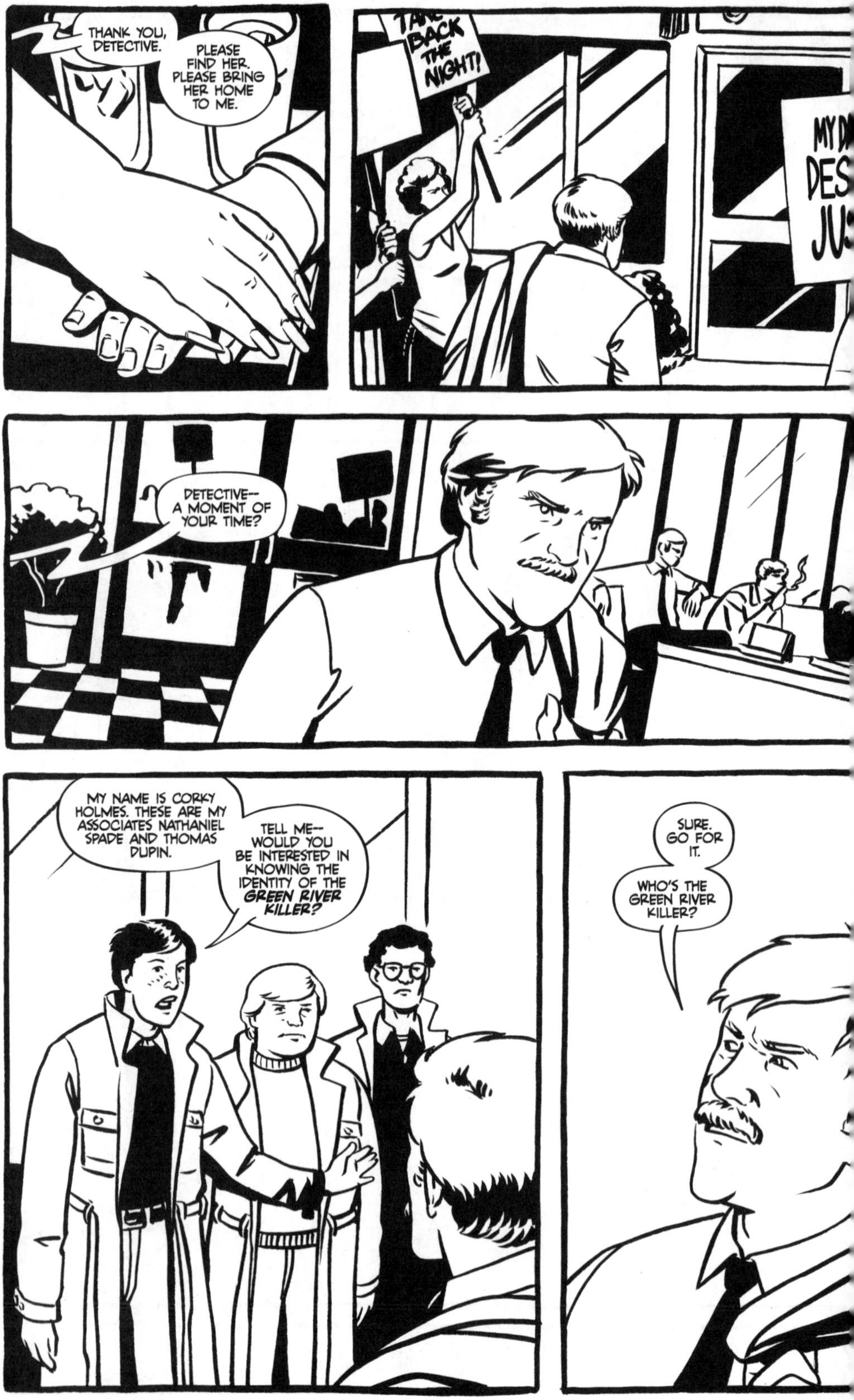
THANK YOU, DETECTIVE.
PLEASE FIND HER. PLEASE BRING HER HOME TO ME.
TAKE BACK THE NIGHT!
DETECTIVE-- A MOMENT OF YOUR TIME?
MY NAME IS CORKY HOLMES. THESE ARE MY ASSOCIATES NATHANIEL SPADE AND THOMAS DUPIN.
TELL ME-- WOULD YOU BE INTERESTED IN KNOWING THE IDENTITY OF THE *GREEN RIVER KILLER?*
SURE. GO FOR IT.
WHO'S THE GREEN RIVER KILLER?

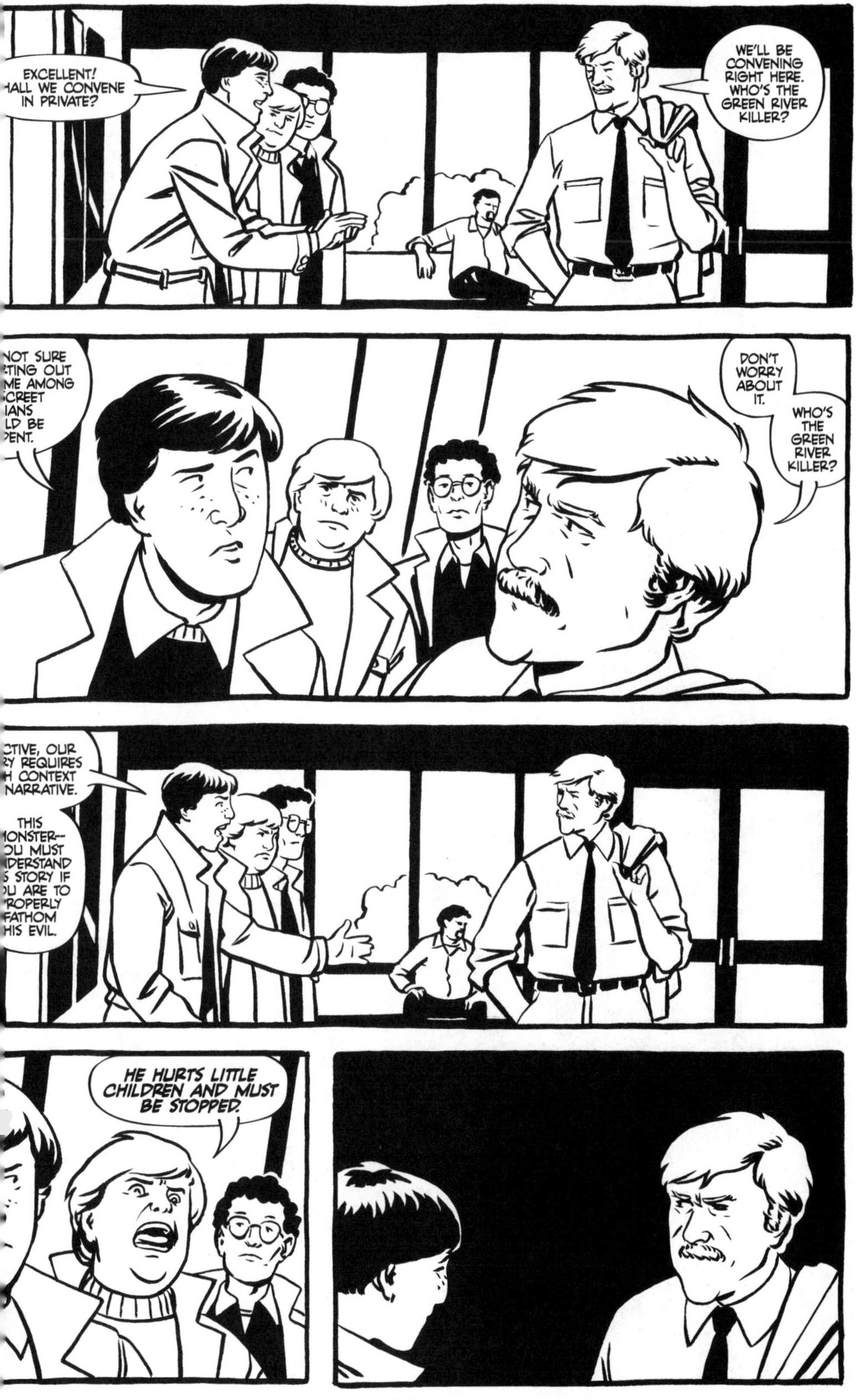

EXCELLENT! HALL WE CONVENE IN PRIVATE?
WE'LL BE CONVENING RIGHT HERE. WHO'S THE GREEN RIVER KILLER?
NOT SURE TING OUT ME AMONG CREET IANS LD BE PENT.
DON'T WORRY ABOUT IT.
WHO'S THE GREEN RIVER KILLER?
CTIVE, OUR Y REQUIRES H CONTEXT NARRATIVE.
THIS ONSTER-- OU MUST DERSTAND S STORY IF U ARE TO ROPERLY FATHOM HIS EVIL.
HE HURTS LITTLE CHILDREN AND MUST BE STOPPED.

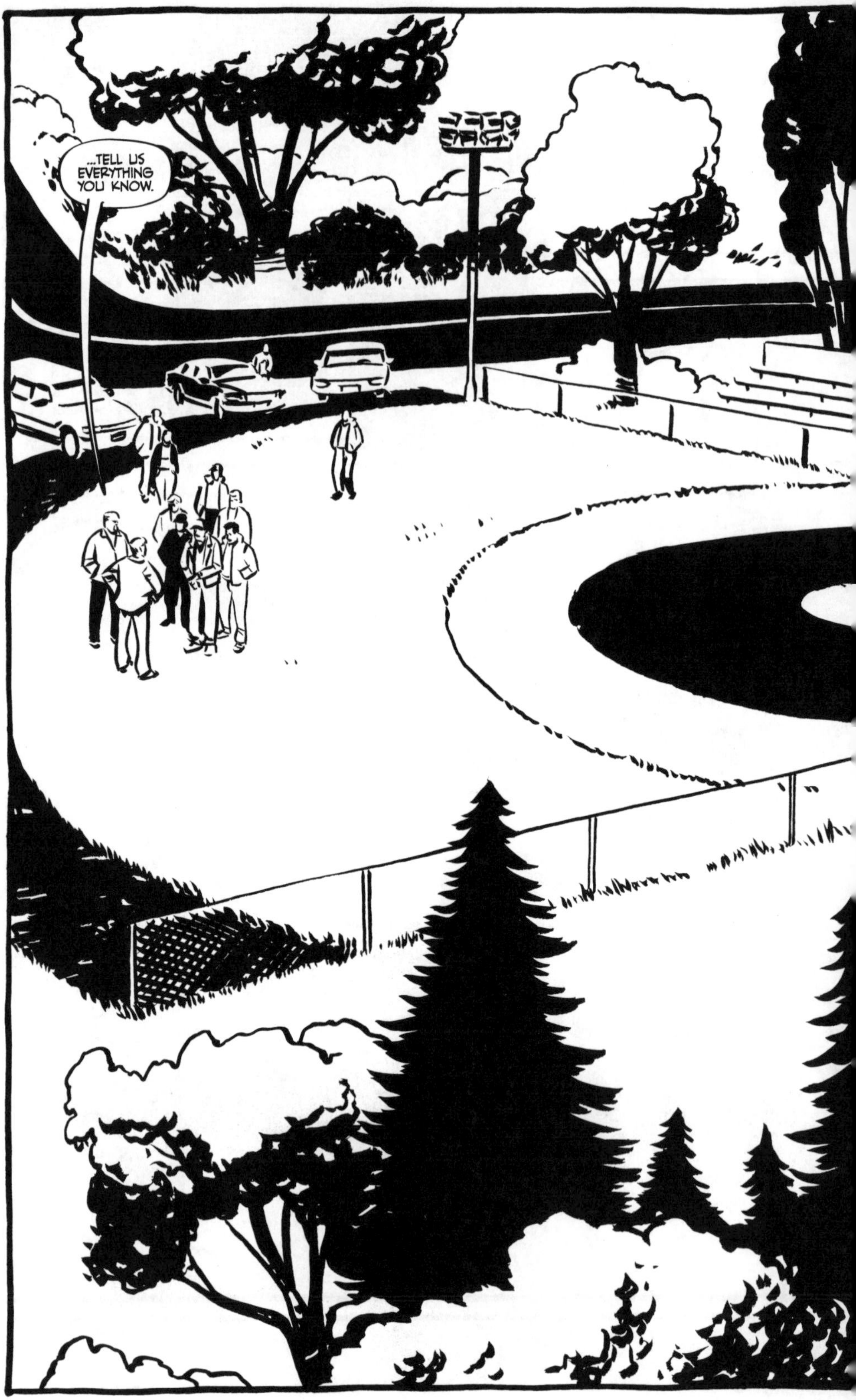
...TELL US EVERYTHING YOU KNOW.

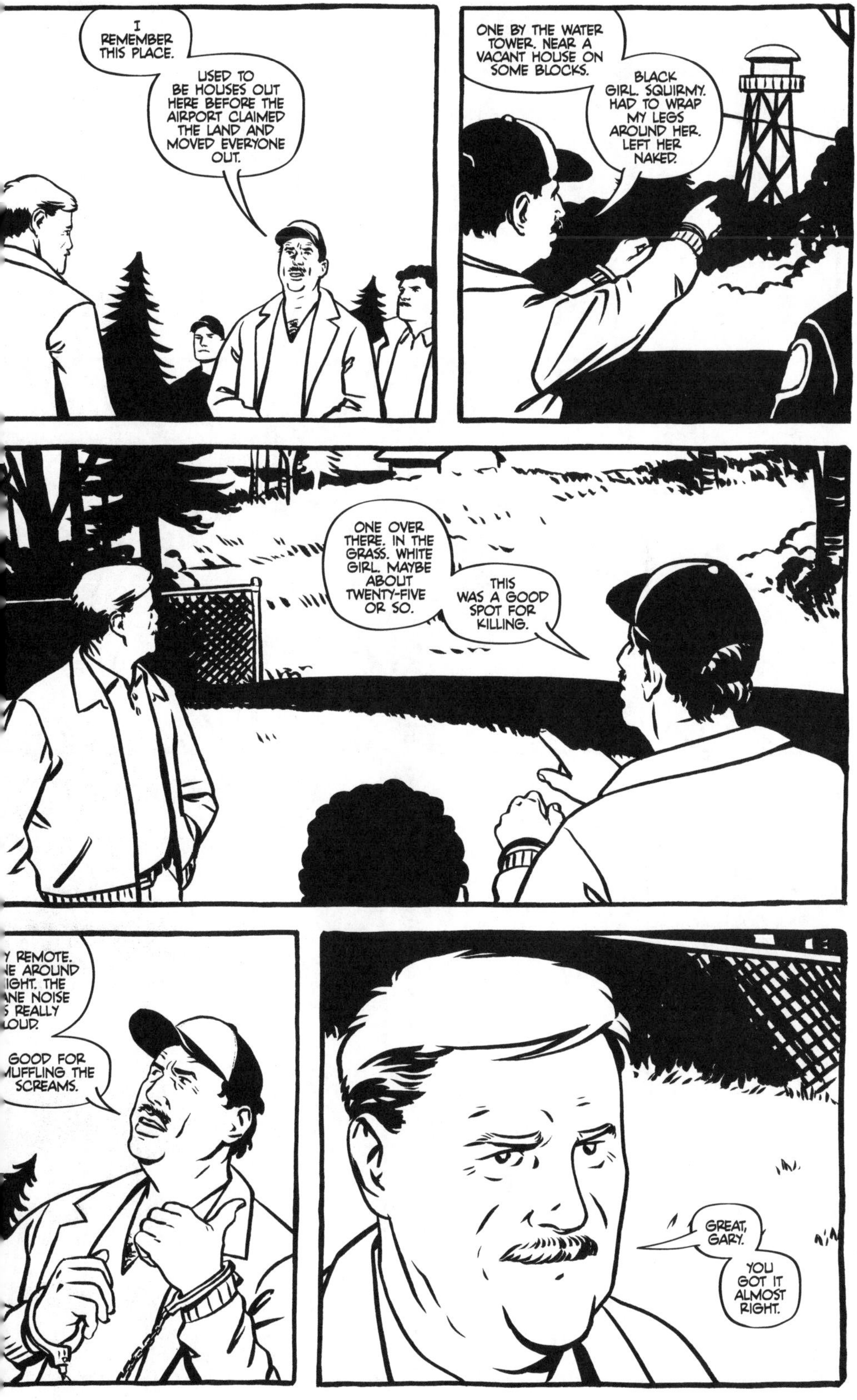
I REMEMBER THIS PLACE.
USED TO BE HOUSES OUT HERE BEFORE THE AIRPORT CLAIMED THE LAND AND MOVED EVERYONE OUT.
ONE BY THE WATER TOWER. NEAR A VACANT HOUSE ON SOME BLOCKS.
BLACK GIRL. SQUIRMY. HAD TO WRAP MY LEGS AROUND HER. LEFT HER NAKED.
ONE OVER THERE. IN THE GRASS. WHITE GIRL. MAYBE ABOUT TWENTY-FIVE OR SO.
THIS WAS A GOOD SPOT FOR KILLING.
Y REMOTE. NE AROUND IGHT. THE ANE NOISE S REALLY LOUD.
GOOD FOR MUFFLING THE SCREAMS.
GREAT, GARY.
YOU GOT IT ALMOST RIGHT.

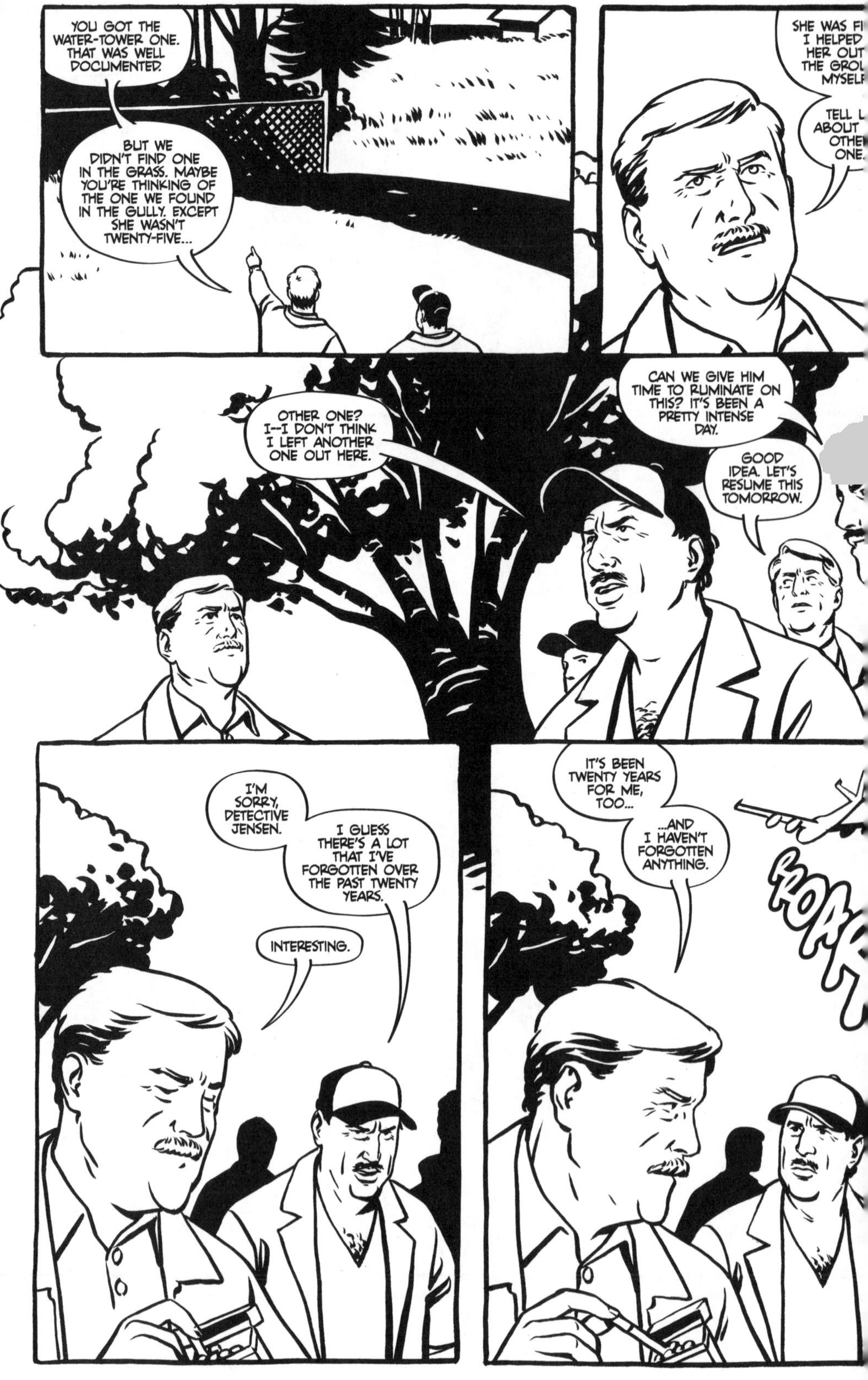
YOU GOT THE WATER-TOWER ONE. THAT WAS WELL DOCUMENTED.
BUT WE DIDN'T FIND ONE IN THE GRASS. MAYBE YOU'RE THINKING OF THE ONE WE FOUND IN THE GULLY. EXCEPT SHE WASN'T TWENTY-FIVE...
OTHER ONE? I--I DON'T THINK I LEFT ANOTHER ONE OUT HERE.
CAN WE GIVE HIM TIME TO RUMINATE ON THIS? IT'S BEEN A PRETTY INTENSE DAY.
GOOD IDEA. LET'S RESUME THIS TOMORROW.
I'M SORRY, DETECTIVE JENSEN.
I GUESS THERE'S A LOT THAT I'VE FORGOTTEN OVER THE PAST TWENTY YEARS.
INTERESTING.
IT'S BEEN TWENTY YEARS FOR ME, TOO...
...AND I HAVEN'T FORGOTTEN ANYTHING.

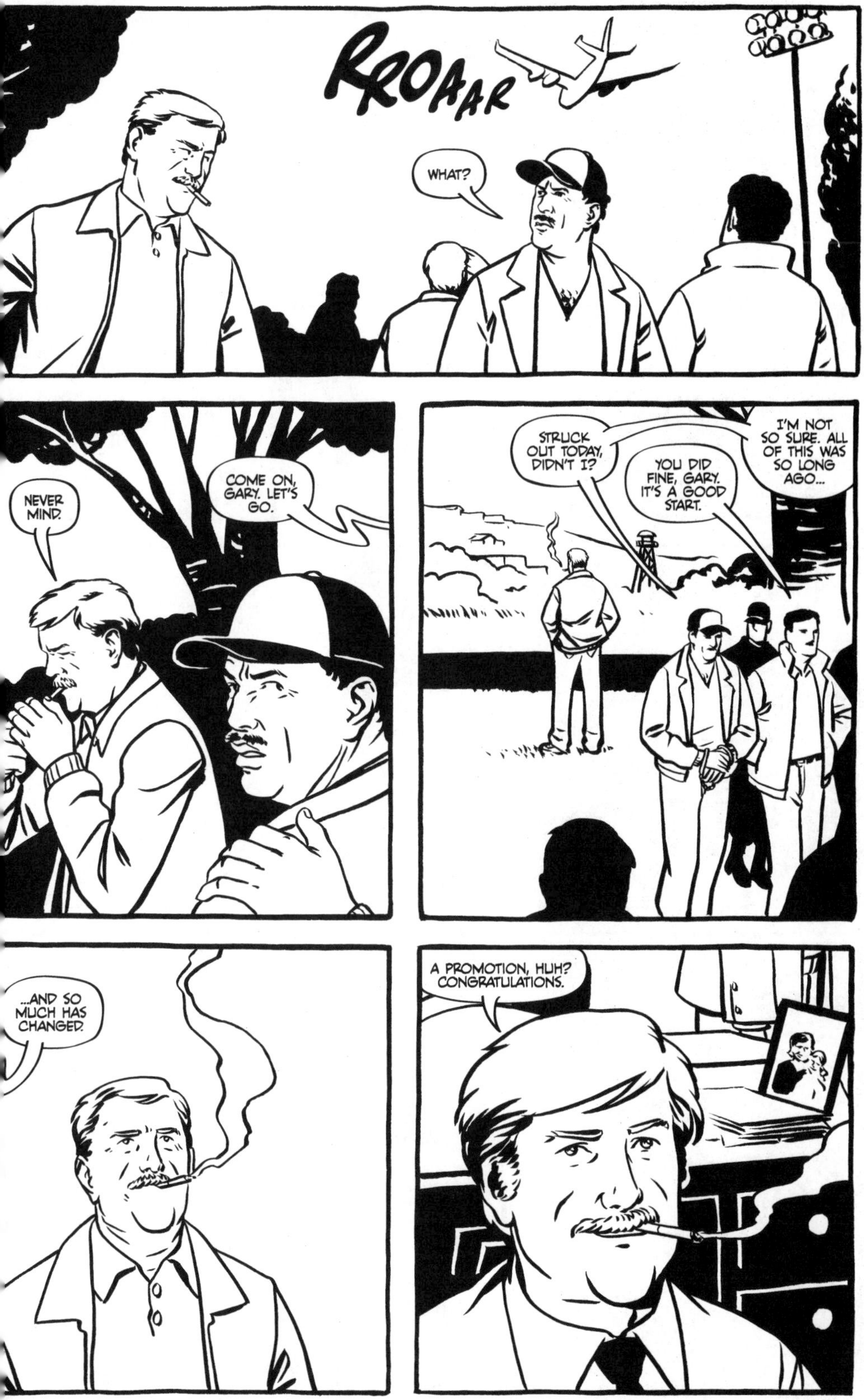
RROAAAR
WHAT?
NEVER MIND.
COME ON, GARY. LET'S GO.
STRUCK OUT TODAY, DIDN'T I?
YOU DID FINE, GARY. IT'S A GOOD START.
I'M NOT SO SURE. ALL OF THIS WAS SO LONG AGO...
...AND SO MUCH HAS CHANGED.
A PROMOTION, HUH? CONGRATULATIONS.

DON'T FORGET ABOUT US LITTLE PEOPLE, BRUCE.

ARSON. IT'S A GOOD FIT FOR ME.

WHERE THEY PUTTING YOU?

HEY, DID YOU KNOW CIGARETTES ARE A LEADING CAUSE OF HOUSE FIRES?

DULY NOTED, ASSHOLE.

ANY TRUTH IS BETTER THAN INDEFINITE — THE YELLOW FACE

HAVE YOU THOUGHT ABOUT TAKING THE PROMOTIONAL EXAM?

I HAVE. AND I DI AND I DID PASS.

TAKE IT AGAIN! THAT'S WHAT YOU'RE SUPPOSED TO DO. TAKE IT AND FAIL IT. TAKE IT AGAIN AND ACE IT.

MAYBE. BUT NOT NOW.

"THERE IS NOTHING MORE STIMULATING THAN A CASE WHERE EVERYTHING GOES AGAINST YOU."

"A STUDY IN SCARLET"?

"HOUND OF THE BASKERVILLES."

NERD?

ALL RIGHT, FOLKS. LISTEN UP!

EVERY PIECE OF INFORMATION WE HAVE NEEDS TO BE INPUTED INTO THIS THING.

IT WILL BE TEDIOUS WORK. NOT ALL OF YOU ACTION-HERO COPS WILL BE INTERESTED IN IT, I'M SURE.

BUT IT COULD ULTIMATELY BRING US THE BREAKTHROUGH WE NEED.

WHO KNOWS? IF WE ASK THE RIGHT QUESTION, MAYBE IT COULD EVEN SPIT OUT THE NAME OF THE KILLER.

ANY VOLUNTEERS?

DAY THREE: FATHER'S DAY

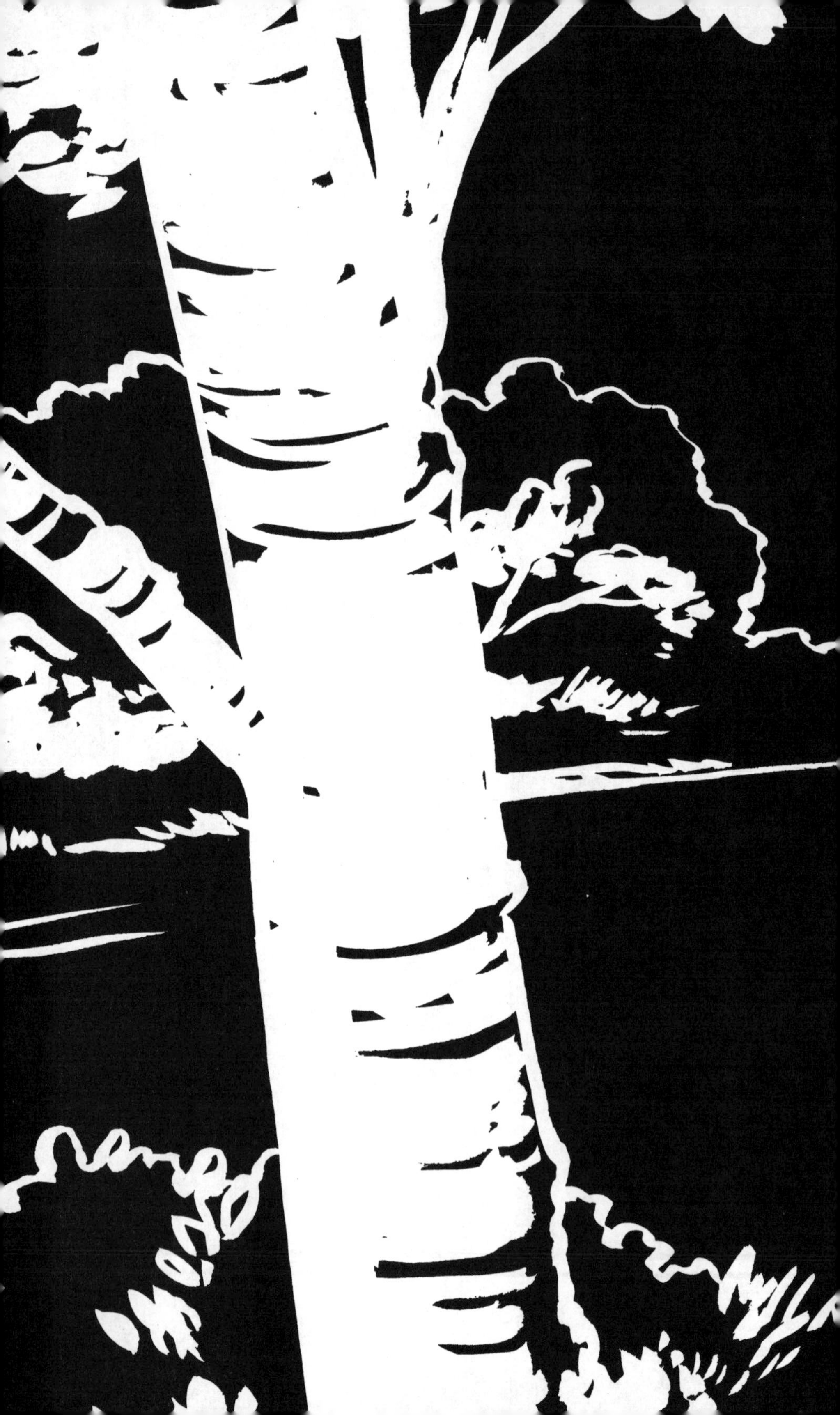

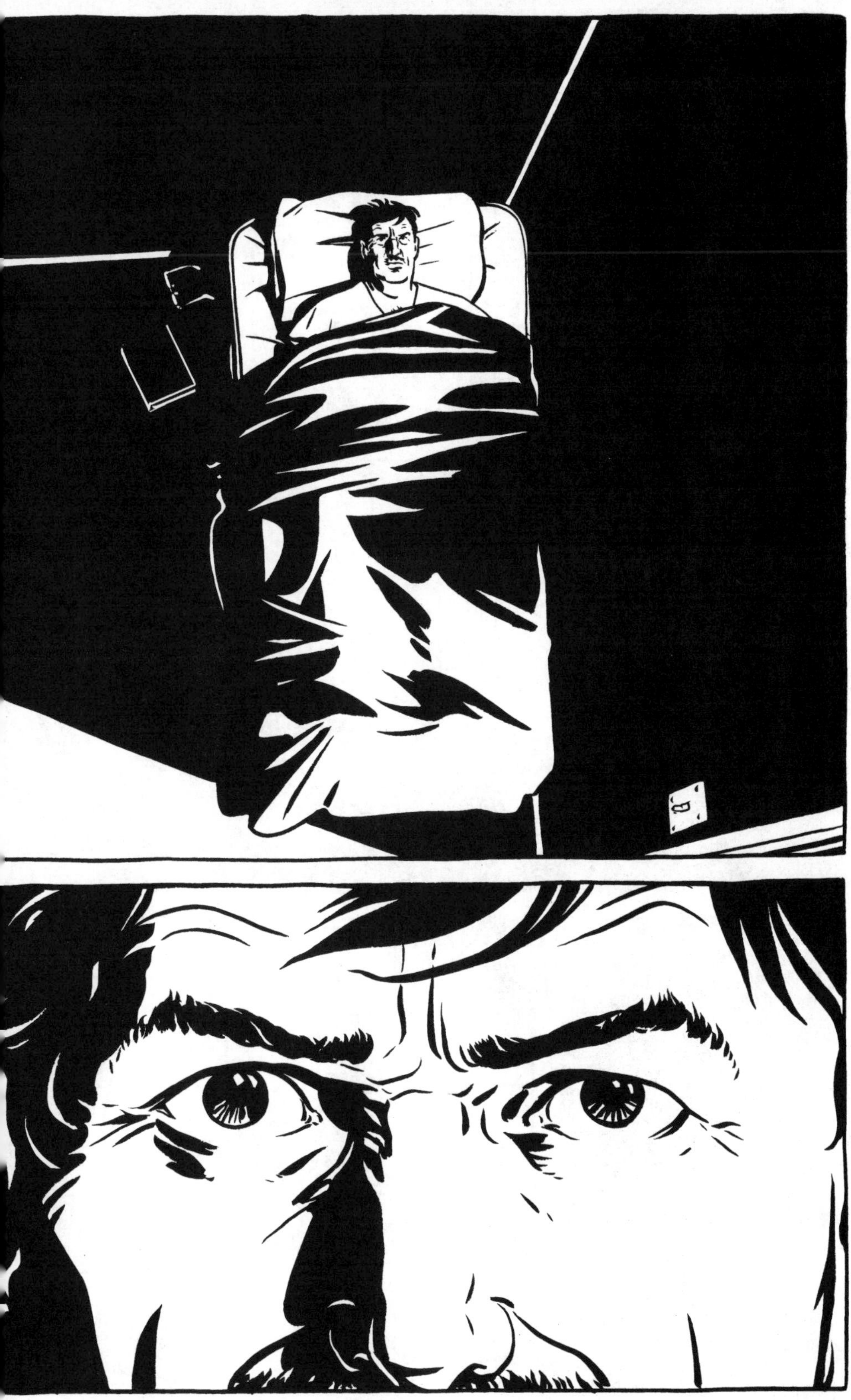

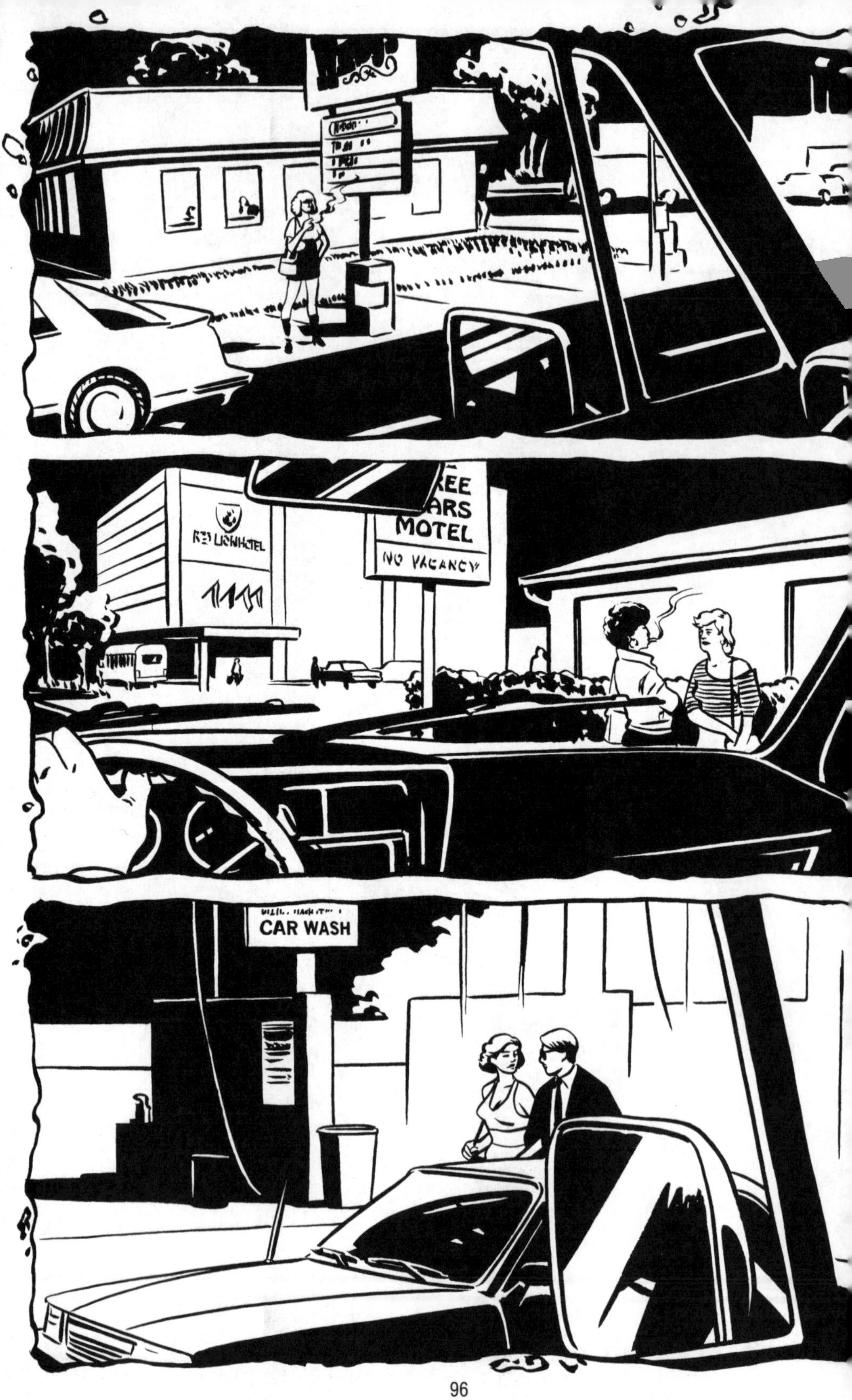
RED LION HOTEL
MOTEL
NO VACANCY
CAR WASH

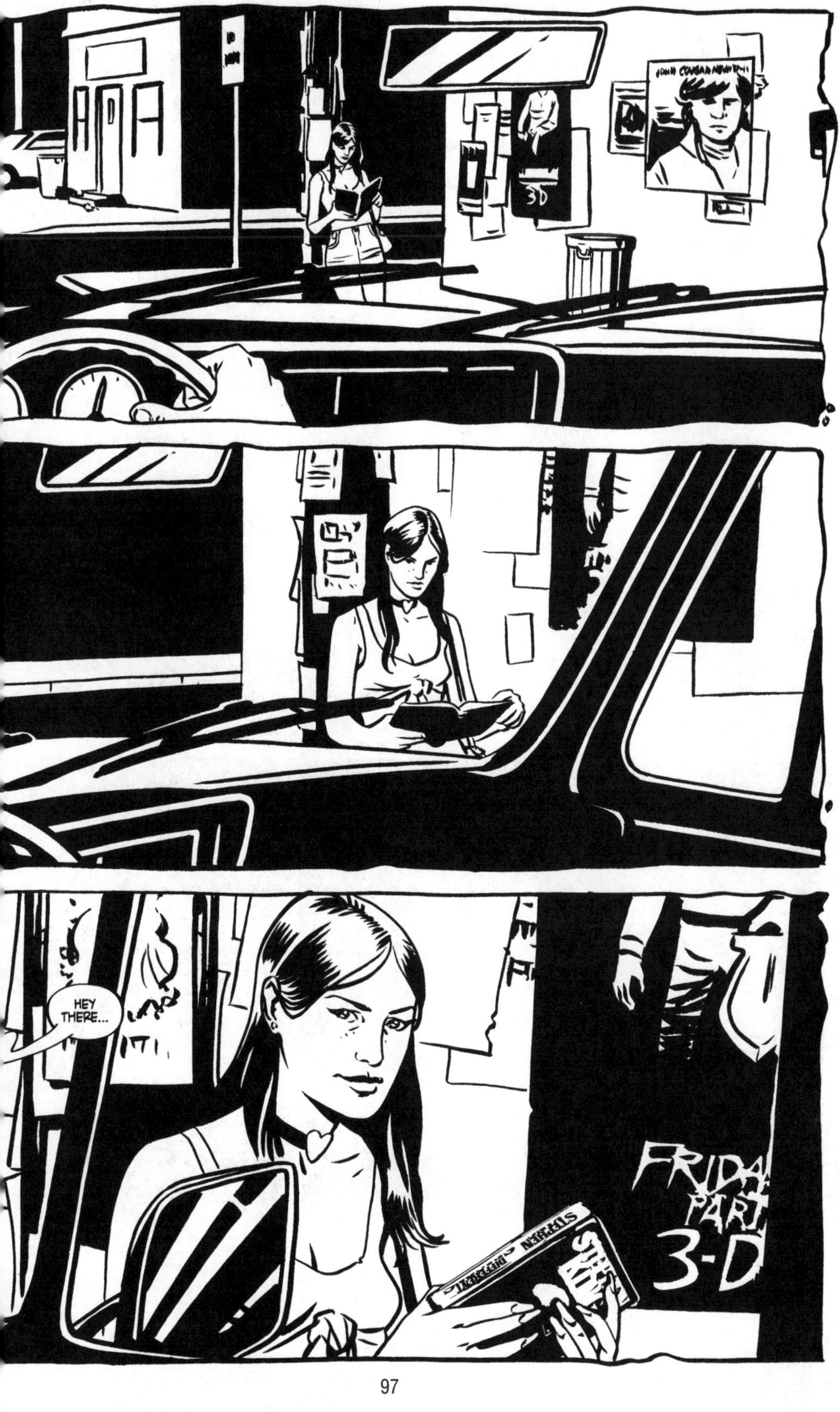
HEY THERE...
3-D

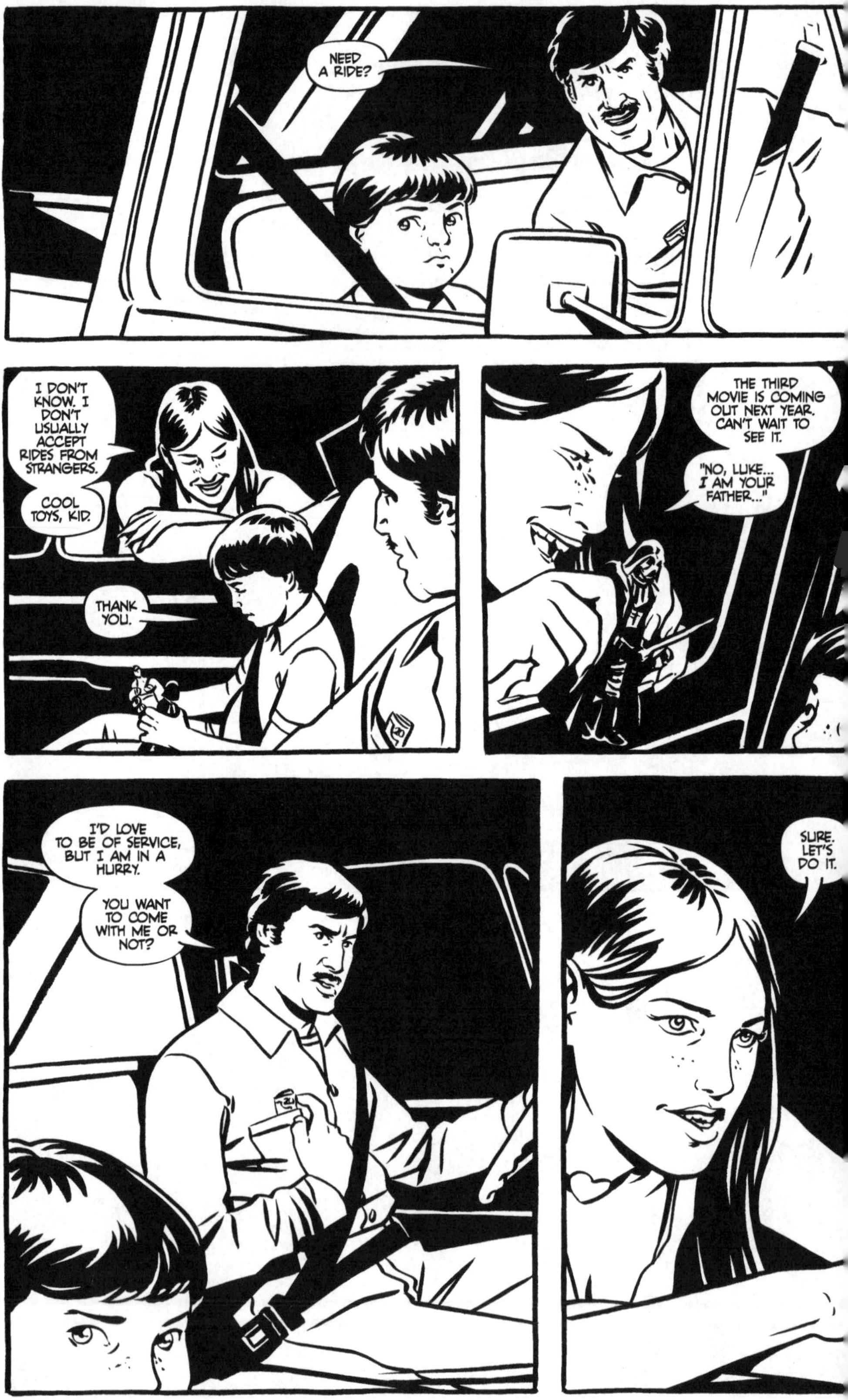
NEED A RIDE?
I DON'T KNOW. I DON'T USUALLY ACCEPT RIDES FROM STRANGERS.
COOL TOYS, KID.
THANK YOU.
THE THIRD MOVIE IS COMING OUT NEXT YEAR. CAN'T WAIT TO SEE IT.
"NO, LUKE... I AM YOUR FATHER..."
I'D LOVE TO BE OF SERVICE, BUT I AM IN A HURRY.
YOU WANT TO COME WITH ME OR NOT?
SURE. LET'S DO IT.

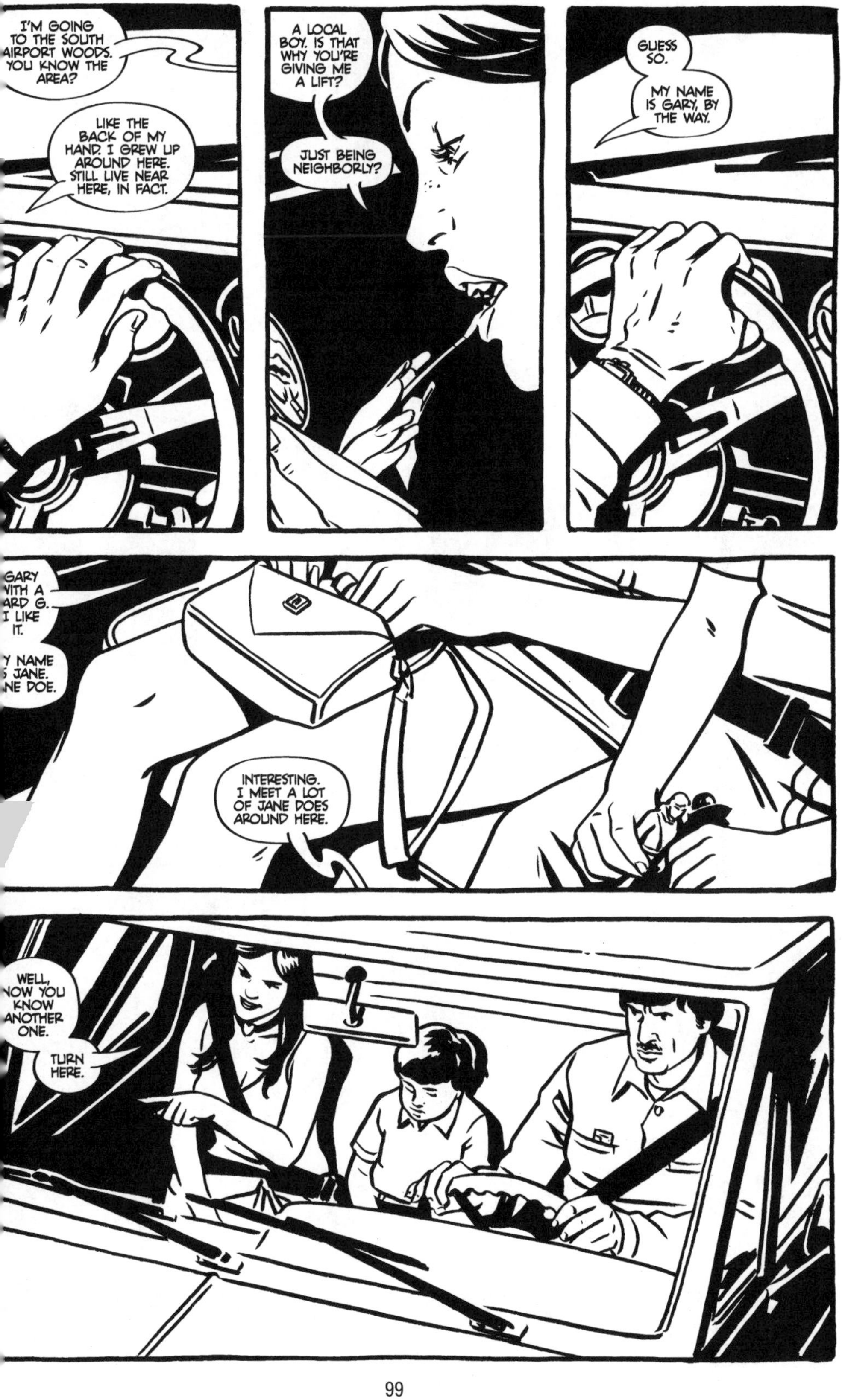
I'M GOING TO THE SOUTH AIRPORT WOODS. YOU KNOW THE AREA?
LIKE THE BACK OF MY HAND. I GREW UP AROUND HERE. STILL LIVE NEAR HERE, IN FACT.
A LOCAL BOY. IS THAT WHY YOU'RE GIVING ME A LIFT?
JUST BEING NEIGHBORLY?
GUESS SO.
MY NAME IS GARY, BY THE WAY.
GARY WITH A ARD G. I LIKE IT.
Y NAME S JANE. NE DOE.
INTERESTING. I MEET A LOT OF JANE DOES AROUND HERE.
WELL, NOW YOU KNOW ANOTHER ONE.
TURN HERE.

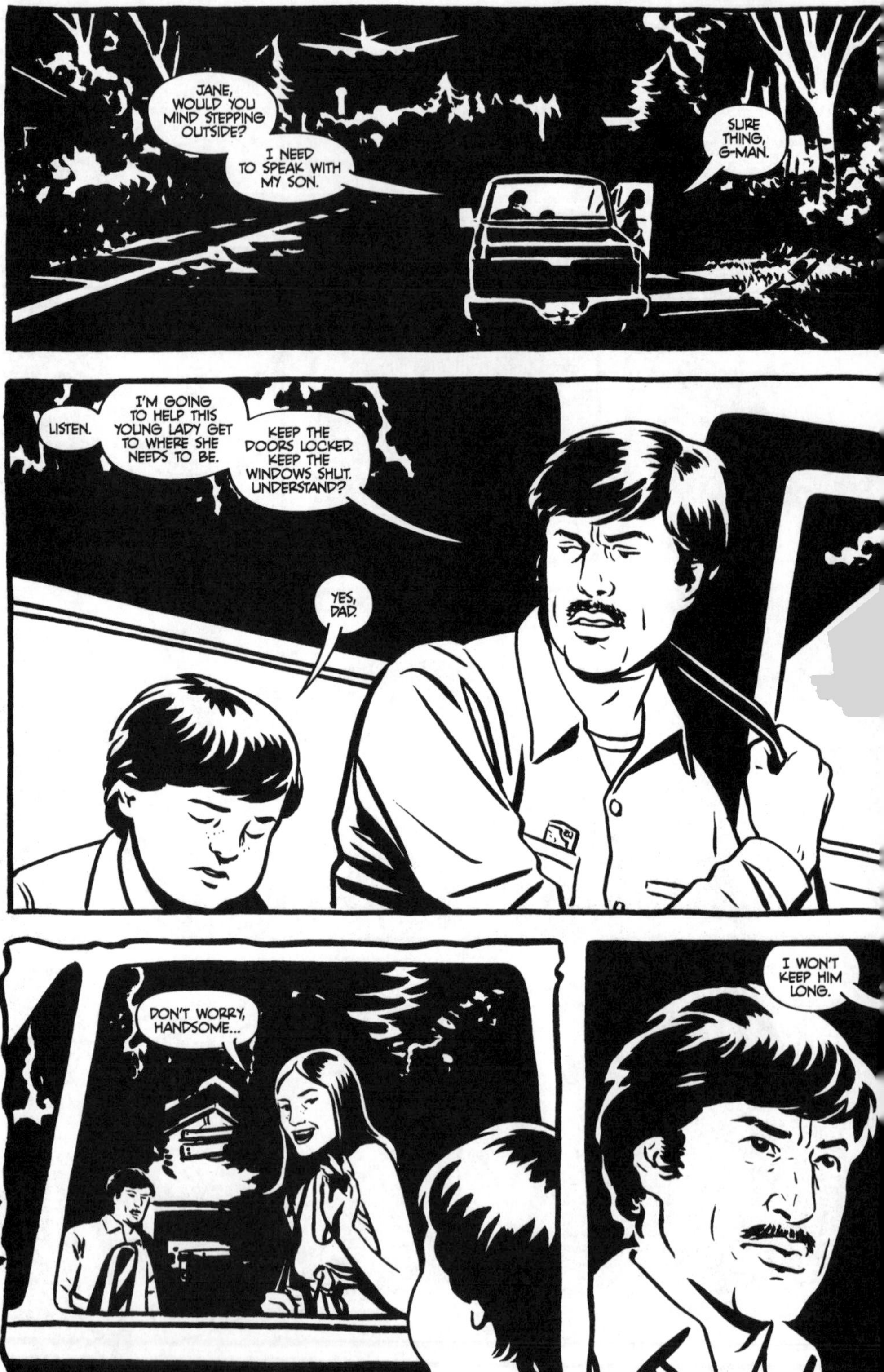
JANE, WOULD YOU MIND STEPPING OUTSIDE?
I NEED TO SPEAK WITH MY SON.
SURE THING, G-MAN.
LISTEN.
I'M GOING TO HELP THIS YOUNG LADY GET TO WHERE SHE NEEDS TO BE.
KEEP THE DOORS LOCKED. KEEP THE WINDOWS SHUT. UNDERSTAND?
YES, DAD.
DON'T WORRY, HANDSOME...
I WON'T KEEP HIM LONG.

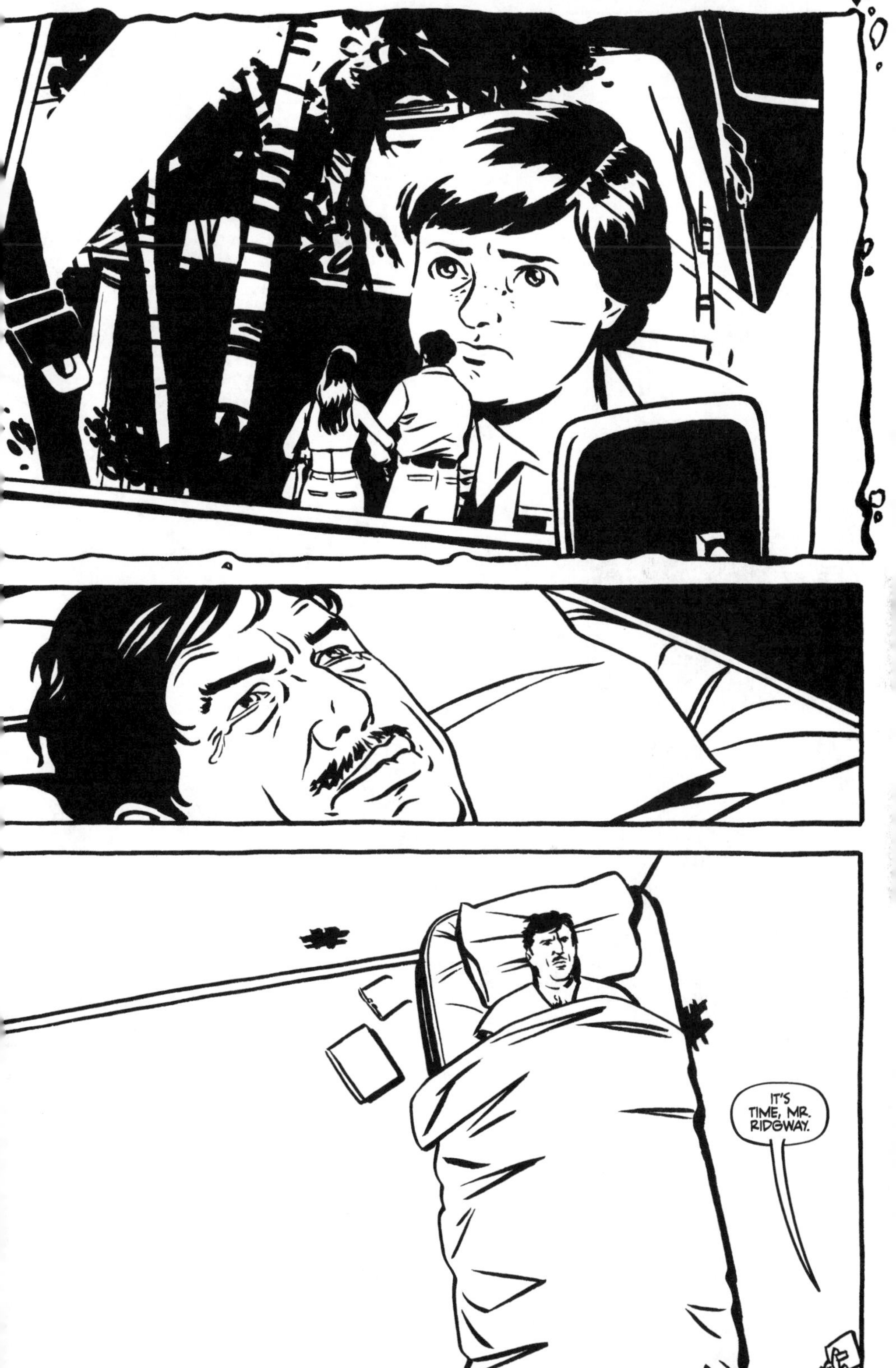
IT'S TIME, MR. RIDGWAY.

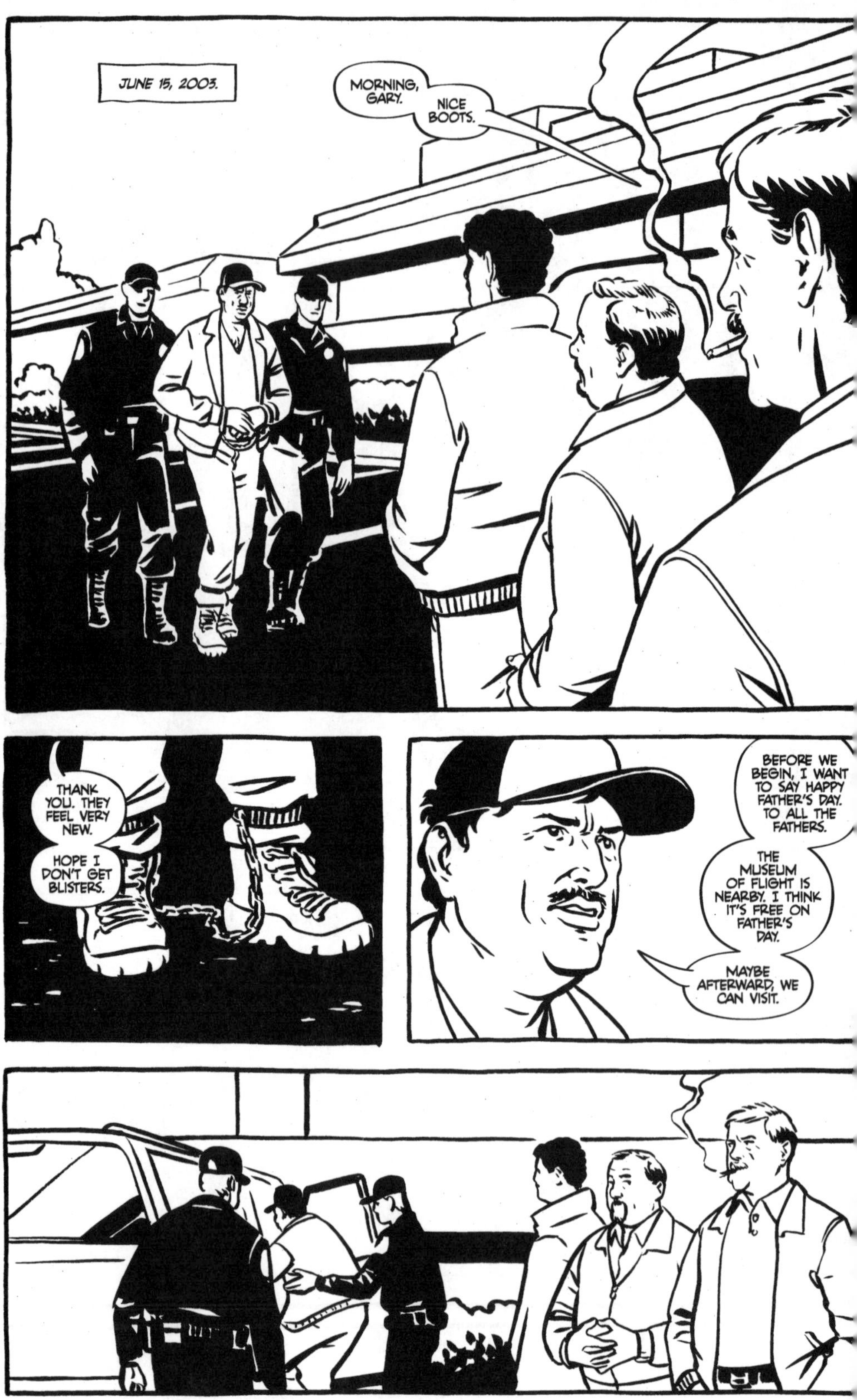
JUNE 15, 2003.
MORNING, GARY.
NICE BOOTS.
THANK YOU. THEY FEEL VERY NEW.
HOPE I DON'T GET BLISTERS.
BEFORE WE BEGIN, I WANT TO SAY HAPPY FATHER'S DAY. TO ALL THE FATHERS.
THE MUSEUM OF FLIGHT IS NEARBY. I THINK IT'S FREE ON FATHER'S DAY.
MAYBE AFTERWARD, WE CAN VISIT.

CRUNCH

105

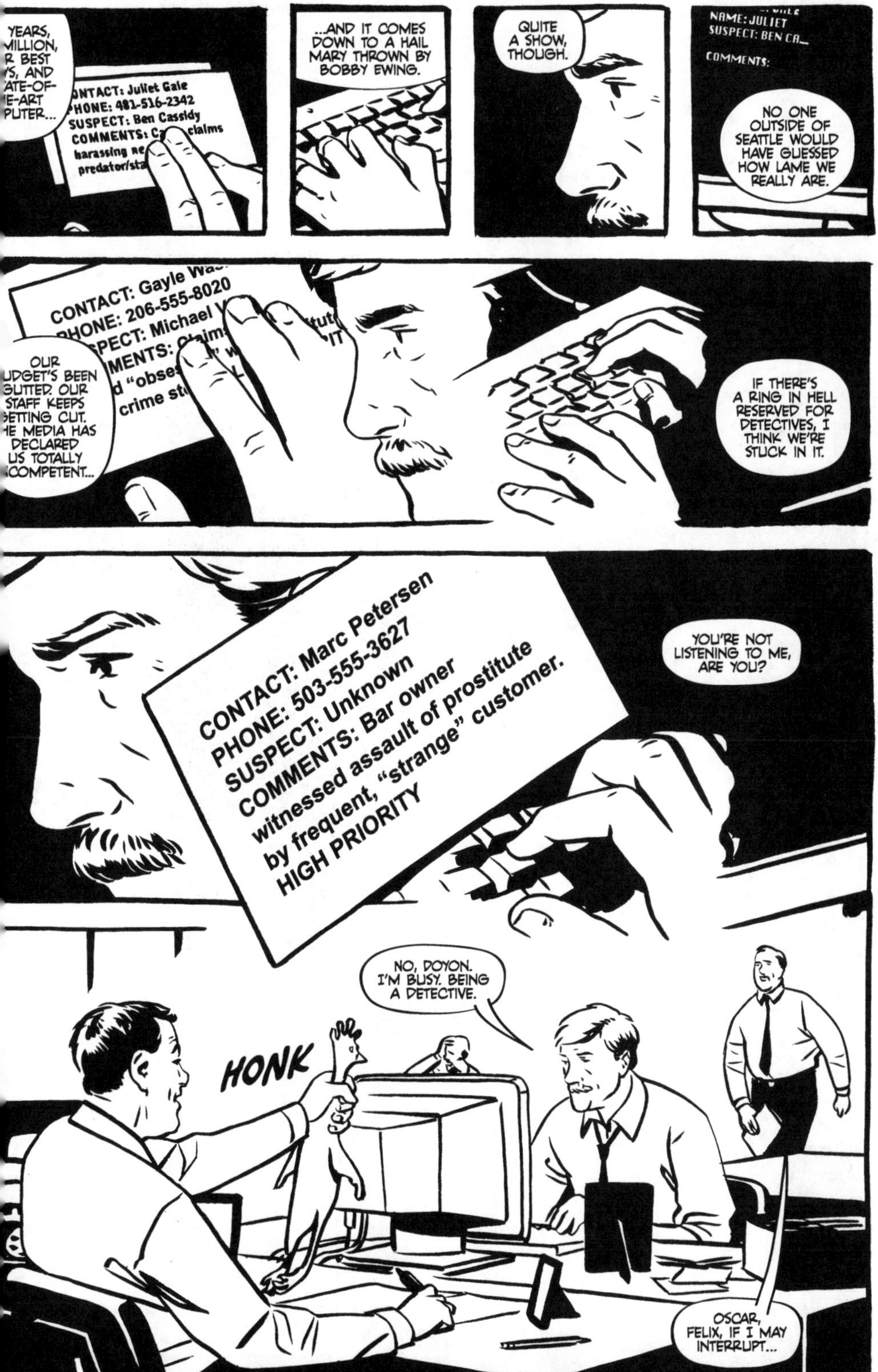

YEARS, MILLION, R BEST 'S, AND TATE-OF-HE-ART PUTER...
ONTACT: Juliet Gale
HONE: 481-516-2342
SUSPECT: Ben Cassidy
COMMENTS: C claims
harassing ne
predator/sta
...AND IT COMES DOWN TO A HAIL MARY THROWN BY BOBBY EWING.
QUITE A SHOW, THOUGH.
NAME: JULIET
SUSPECT: BEN CA_
COMMENTS:
NO ONE OUTSIDE OF SEATTLE WOULD HAVE GUESSED HOW LAME WE REALLY ARE.
CONTACT: Gayle Wa
PHONE: 206-555-8020
SPECT: Michael
MENTS:
d "obses
crime st
OUR UDGET'S BEEN GUTTED. OUR STAFF KEEPS GETTING CUT. HE MEDIA HAS DECLARED US TOTALLY NCOMPETENT...
IF THERE'S A RING IN HELL RESERVED FOR DETECTIVES, I THINK WE'RE STUCK IN IT.
CONTACT: Marc Petersen
PHONE: 503-555-3627
SUSPECT: Unknown
COMMENTS: Bar owner
witnessed assault of prostitute
by frequent, "strange" customer.
HIGH PRIORITY
YOU'RE NOT LISTENING TO ME, ARE YOU?
NO, DOYON. I'M BUSY. BEING A DETECTIVE.
HONK
OSCAR, FELIX, IF I MAY INTERRUPT...

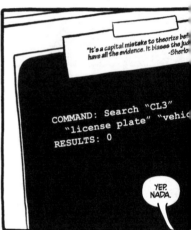

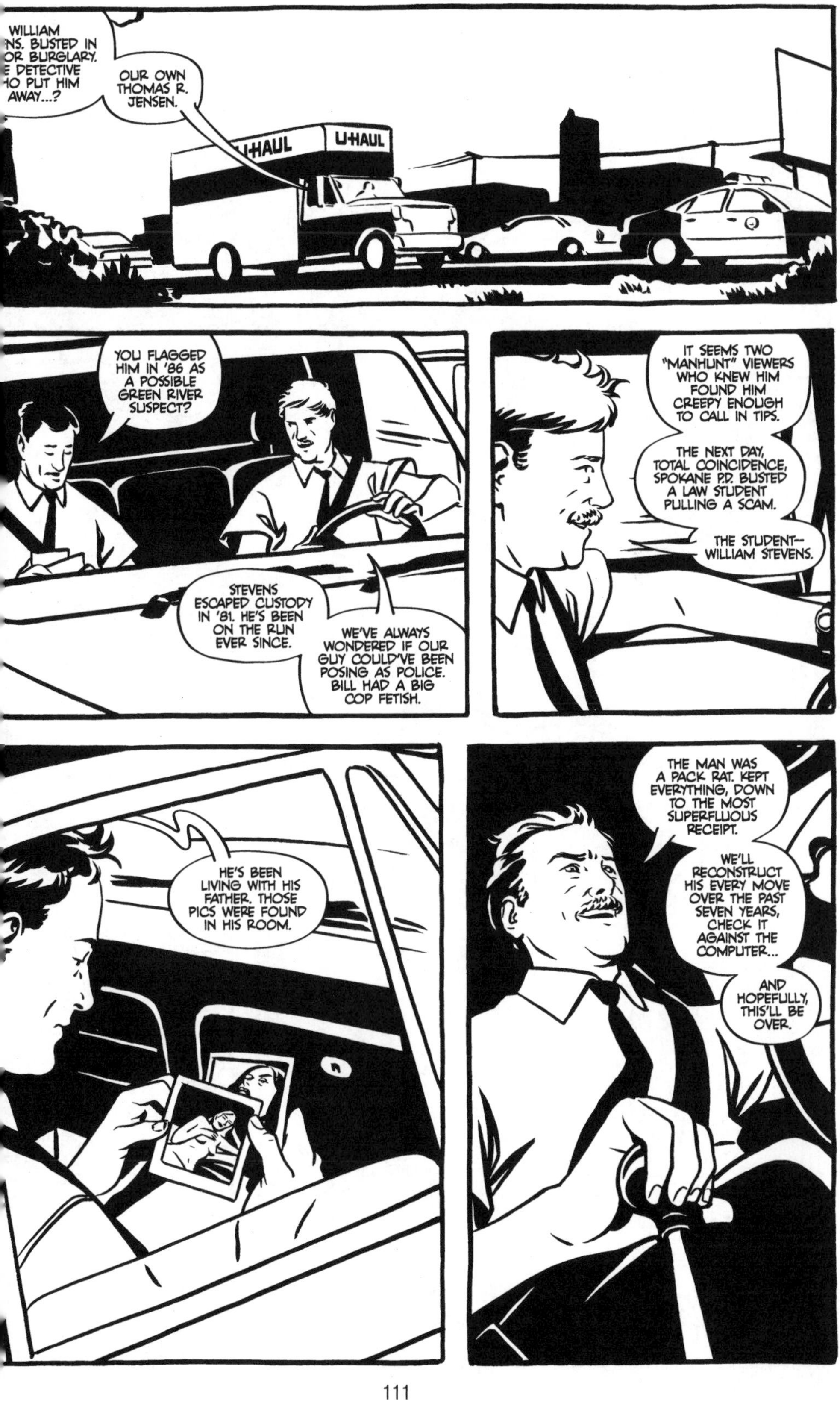
WILLIAM ‑NS. BUSTED IN ‑OR BURGLARY. ‑E DETECTIVE ‑HO PUT HIM AWAY...?
OUR OWN THOMAS R. JENSEN.
U-HAUL
U-HAUL
YOU FLAGGED HIM IN '86 AS A POSSIBLE GREEN RIVER SUSPECT?
STEVENS ESCAPED CUSTODY IN '81. HE'S BEEN ON THE RUN EVER SINCE.
WE'VE ALWAYS WONDERED IF OUR GUY COULD'VE BEEN POSING AS POLICE. BILL HAD A BIG COP FETISH.
IT SEEMS TWO "MANHUNT" VIEWERS WHO KNEW HIM FOUND HIM CREEPY ENOUGH TO CALL IN TIPS.
THE NEXT DAY, TOTAL COINCIDENCE, SPOKANE P.D. BUSTED A LAW STUDENT PULLING A SCAM.
THE STUDENT-- WILLIAM STEVENS.
HE'S BEEN LIVING WITH HIS FATHER. THOSE PICS WERE FOUND IN HIS ROOM.
THE MAN WAS A PACK RAT. KEPT EVERYTHING, DOWN TO THE MOST SUPERFLUOUS RECEIPT.
WE'LL RECONSTRUCT HIS EVERY MOVE OVER THE PAST SEVEN YEARS, CHECK IT AGAINST THE COMPUTER...
AND HOPEFULLY, THIS'LL BE OVER.

AFTER YOU FIGURE OUT YOU'RE WRONG ABOUT MY SON...

YOU WILL BE GIVING HIM EVERYTHING BACK, RIGHT?

I DON'T KNOW.

WE'LL SEE.

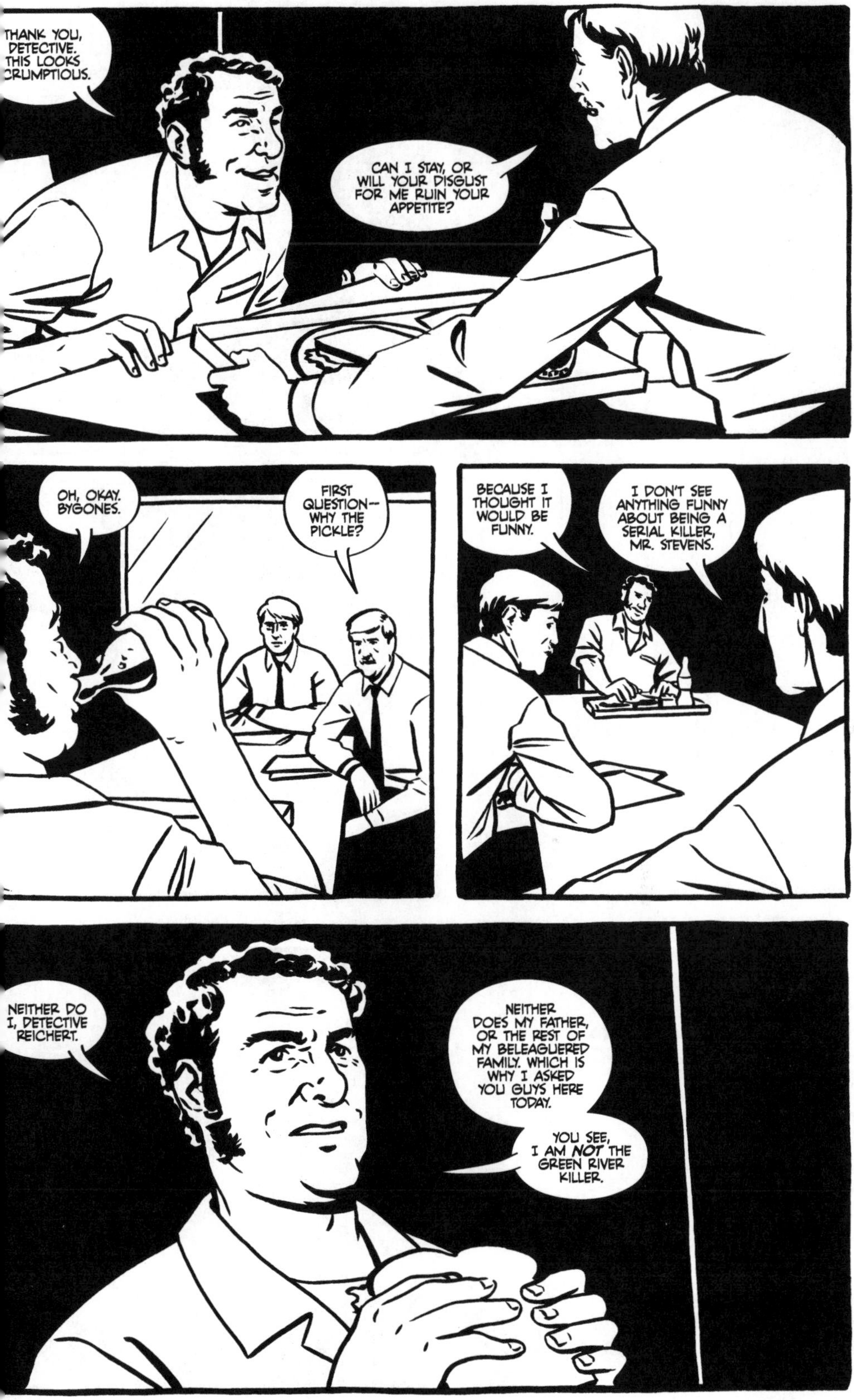
THANK YOU, DETECTIVE. THIS LOOKS CRUMPTIOUS.
CAN I STAY, OR WILL YOUR DISGUST FOR ME RUIN YOUR APPETITE?
OH, OKAY. BYGONES.
FIRST QUESTION-- WHY THE PICKLE?
BECAUSE I THOUGHT IT WOULD BE FUNNY.
I DON'T SEE ANYTHING FUNNY ABOUT BEING A SERIAL KILLER, MR. STEVENS.
NEITHER DO I, DETECTIVE REICHERT.
NEITHER DOES MY FATHER, OR THE REST OF MY BELEAGUERED FAMILY. WHICH IS WHY I ASKED YOU GUYS HERE TODAY.
YOU SEE, I AM ***NOT*** THE GREEN RIVER KILLER.

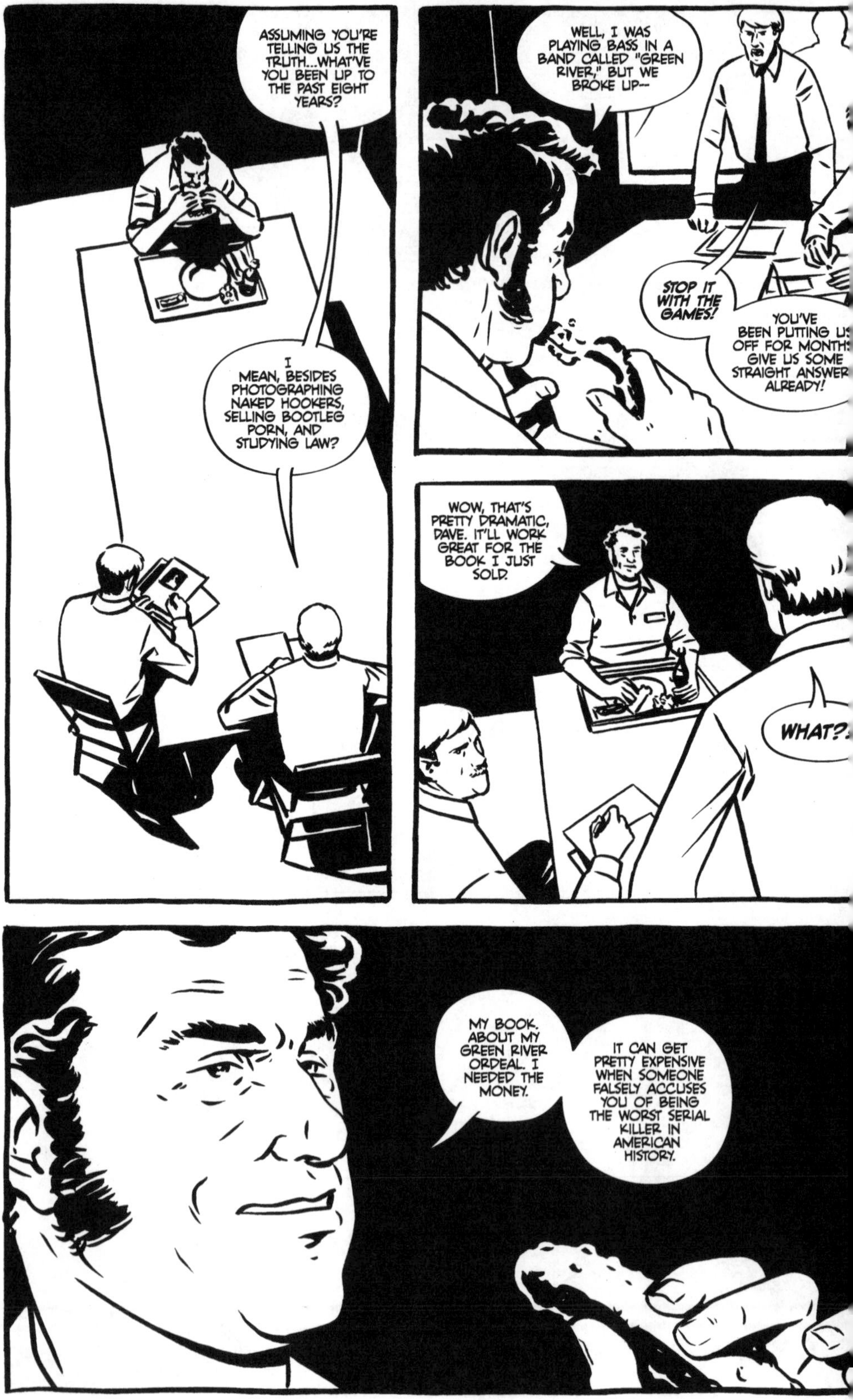
ASSUMING YOU'RE TELLING US THE TRUTH...WHAT'VE YOU BEEN UP TO THE PAST EIGHT YEARS?
I MEAN, BESIDES PHOTOGRAPHING NAKED HOOKERS, SELLING BOOTLEG PORN, AND STUDYING LAW?
WELL, I WAS PLAYING BASS IN A BAND CALLED "GREEN RIVER," BUT WE BROKE UP--
STOP IT WITH THE GAMES!
YOU'VE BEEN PUTTING US OFF FOR MONTHS GIVE US SOME STRAIGHT ANSWER ALREADY!
WOW, THAT'S PRETTY DRAMATIC, DAVE. IT'LL WORK GREAT FOR THE BOOK I JUST SOLD.
WHAT?
MY BOOK. ABOUT MY GREEN RIVER ORDEAL. I NEEDED THE MONEY.
IT CAN GET PRETTY EXPENSIVE WHEN SOMEONE FALSELY ACCUSES YOU OF BEING THE WORST SERIAL KILLER IN AMERICAN HISTORY.

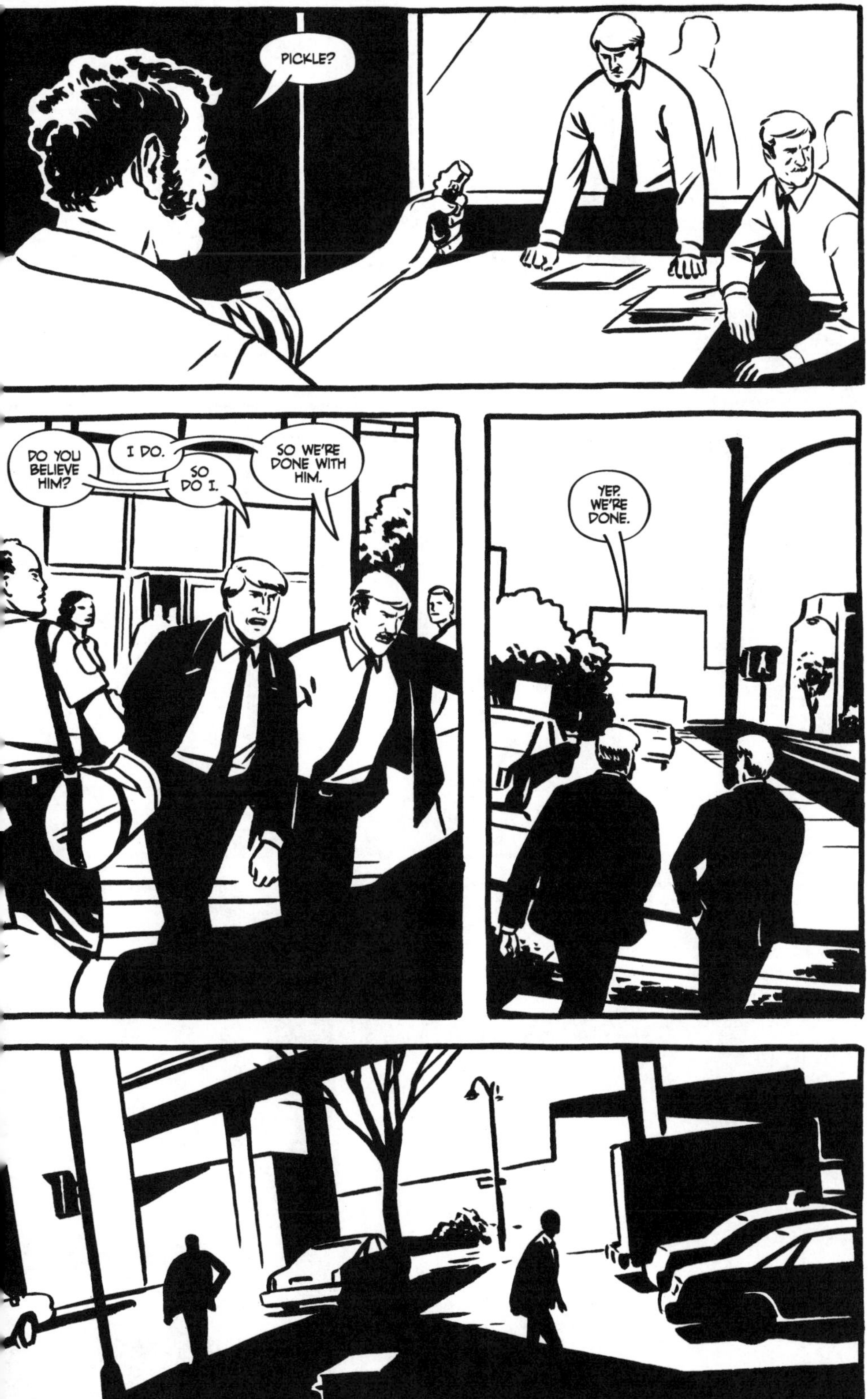
PICKLE?
DO YOU BELIEVE HIM?
I DO.
SO DO I.
SO WE'RE DONE WITH HIM.
YEP. WE'RE DONE.

118

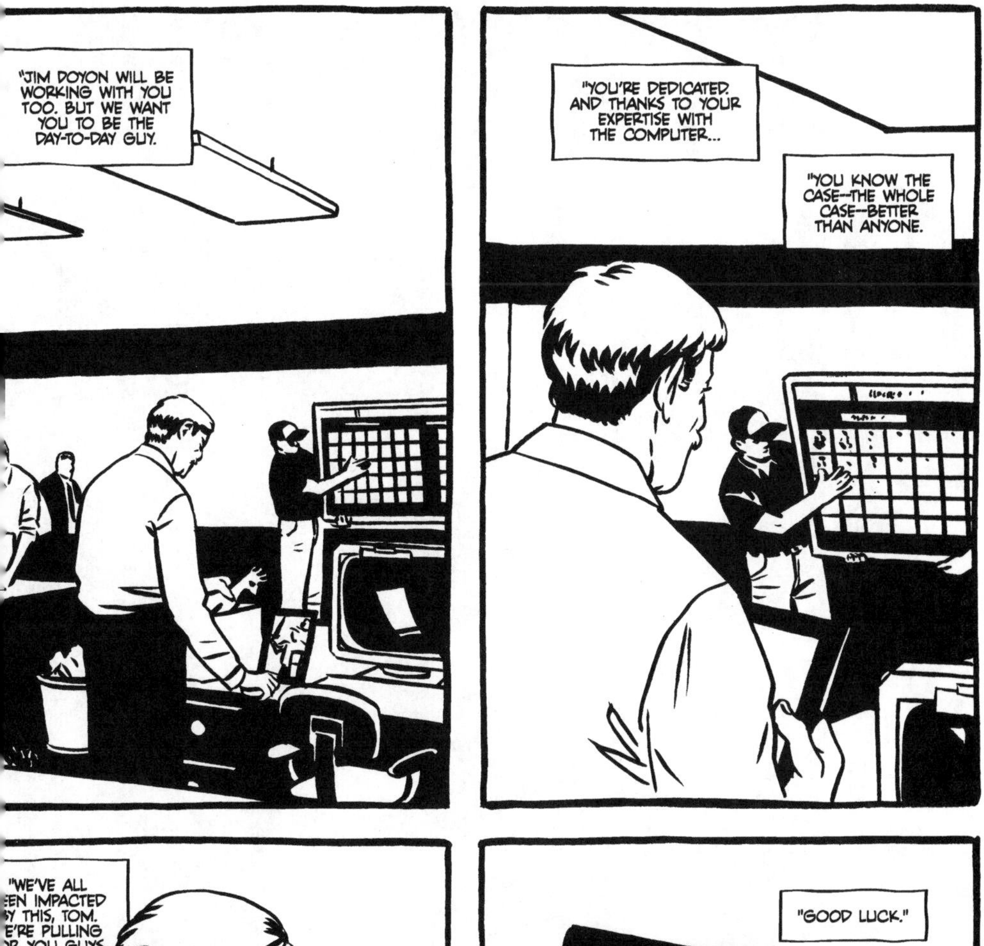
"JIM DOYON WILL BE WORKING WITH YOU TOO. BUT WE WANT YOU TO BE THE DAY-TO-DAY GUY.
"YOU'RE DEDICATED. AND THANKS TO YOUR EXPERTISE WITH THE COMPUTER...
"YOU KNOW THE CASE--THE WHOLE CASE--BETTER THAN ANYONE.
"WE'VE ALL
EEN IMPACTED
SY THIS, TOM.
E'RE PULLING
OR YOU GUYS.
"GOOD LUCK."

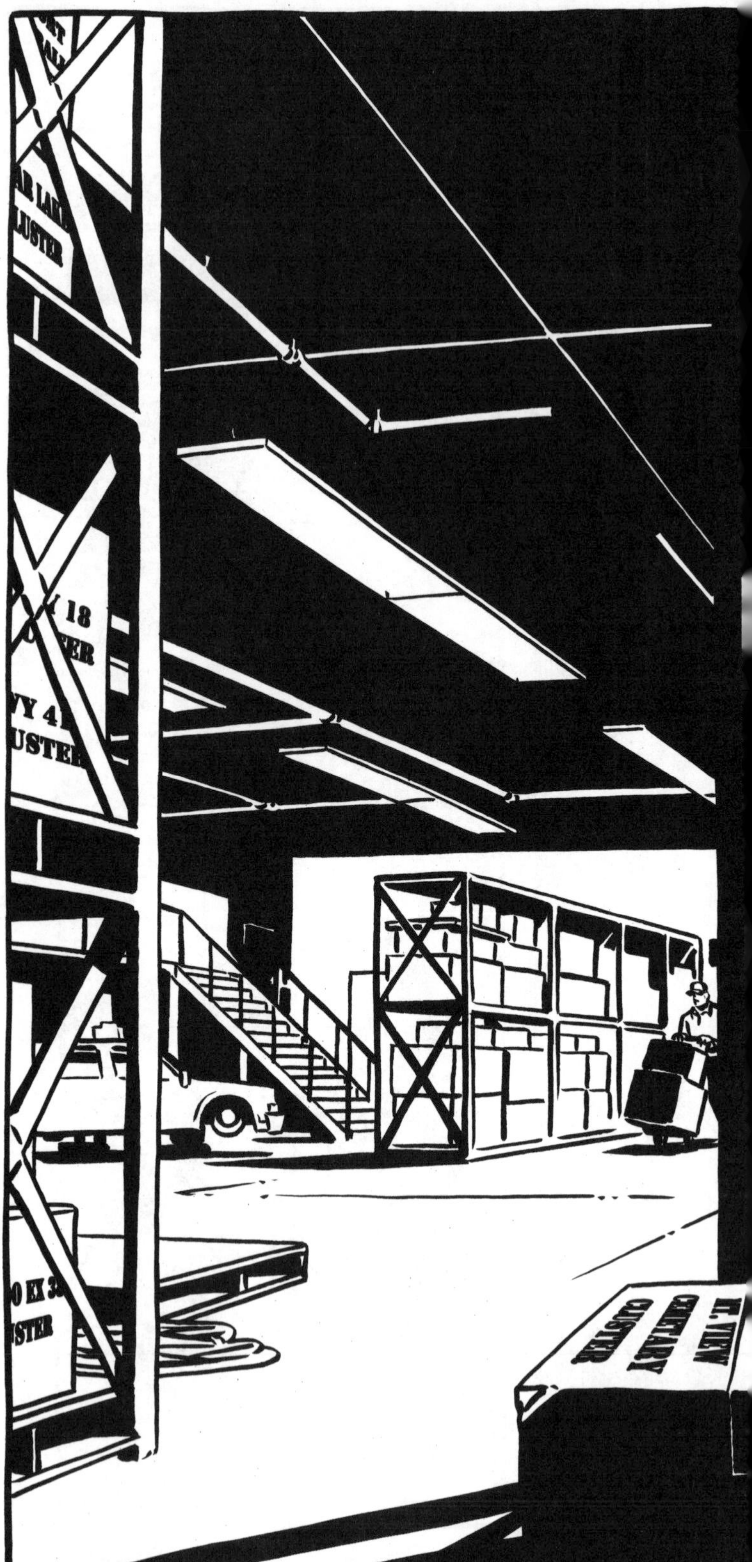
T. VIEW
CEMETARY
CLUSTER

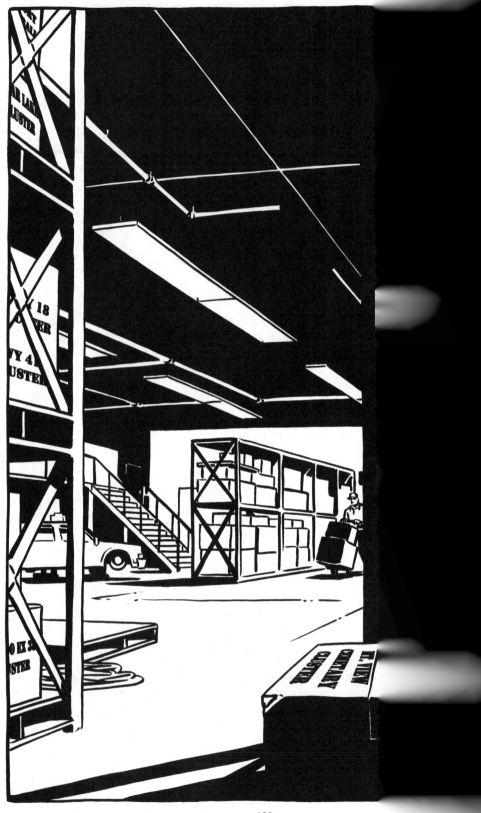

REFRIGERATION UNIT

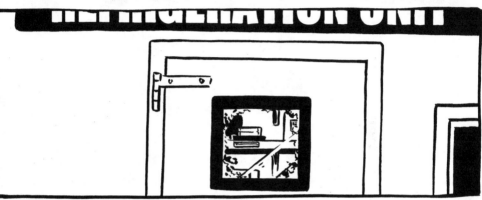

RIDGWAY, GARY LEON — SALIVA SAMPLE
04/08/87

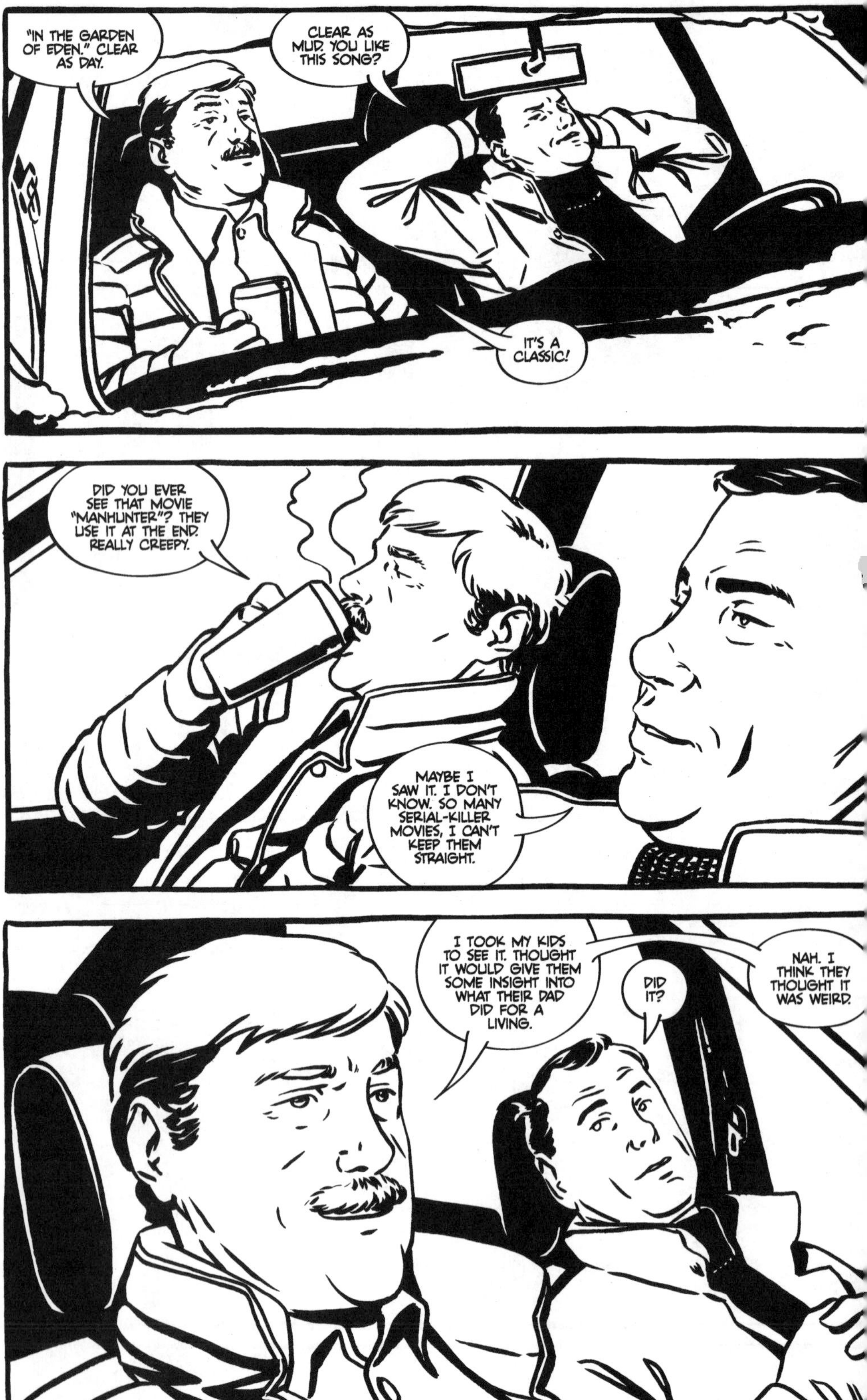
"IN THE GARDEN OF EDEN." CLEAR AS DAY.
CLEAR AS MUD. YOU LIKE THIS SONG?
IT'S A CLASSIC!
DID YOU EVER SEE THAT MOVIE "MANHUNTER"? THEY USE IT AT THE END. REALLY CREEPY.
MAYBE I SAW IT. I DON'T KNOW. SO MANY SERIAL-KILLER MOVIES, I CAN'T KEEP THEM STRAIGHT.
I TOOK MY KIDS TO SEE IT. THOUGHT IT WOULD GIVE THEM SOME INSIGHT INTO WHAT THEIR DAD DID FOR A LIVING.
DID IT?
NAH. I THINK THEY THOUGHT IT WAS WEIRD.

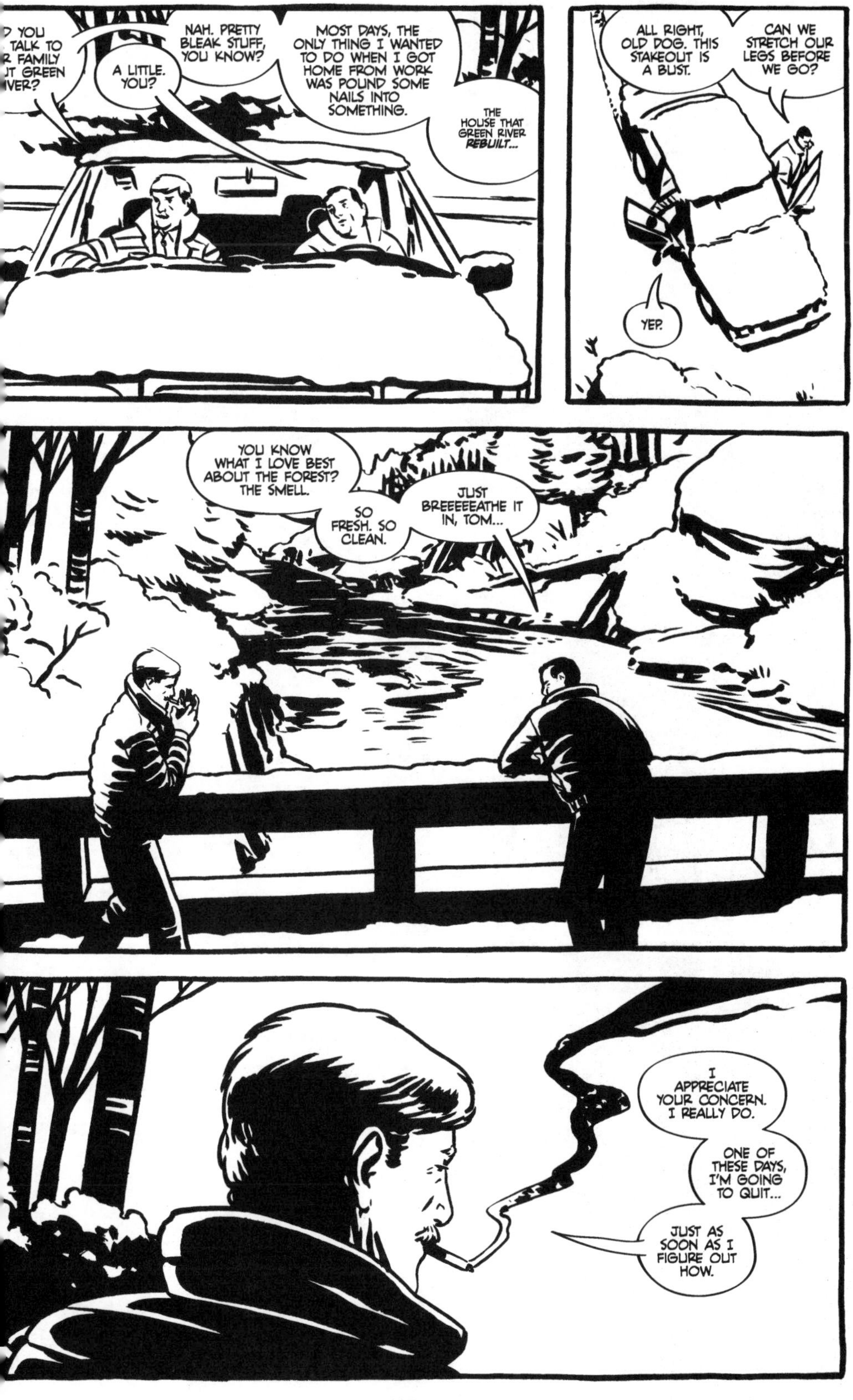
D YOU TALK TO R FAMILY UT GREEN IVER?
A LITTLE. YOU?
NAH. PRETTY BLEAK STUFF, YOU KNOW?
MOST DAYS, THE ONLY THING I WANTED TO DO WHEN I GOT HOME FROM WORK WAS POUND SOME NAILS INTO SOMETHING.
THE HOUSE THAT GREEN RIVER REBUILT...
ALL RIGHT, OLD DOG. THIS STAKEOUT IS A BUST.
CAN WE STRETCH OUR LEGS BEFORE WE GO?
YEP.
YOU KNOW WHAT I LOVE BEST ABOUT THE FOREST? THE SMELL.
SO FRESH. SO CLEAN.
JUST BREEEEEATHE IT IN, TOM...
I APPRECIATE YOUR CONCERN. I REALLY DO.
ONE OF THESE DAYS, I'M GOING TO QUIT...
JUST AS SOON AS I FIGURE OUT HOW.

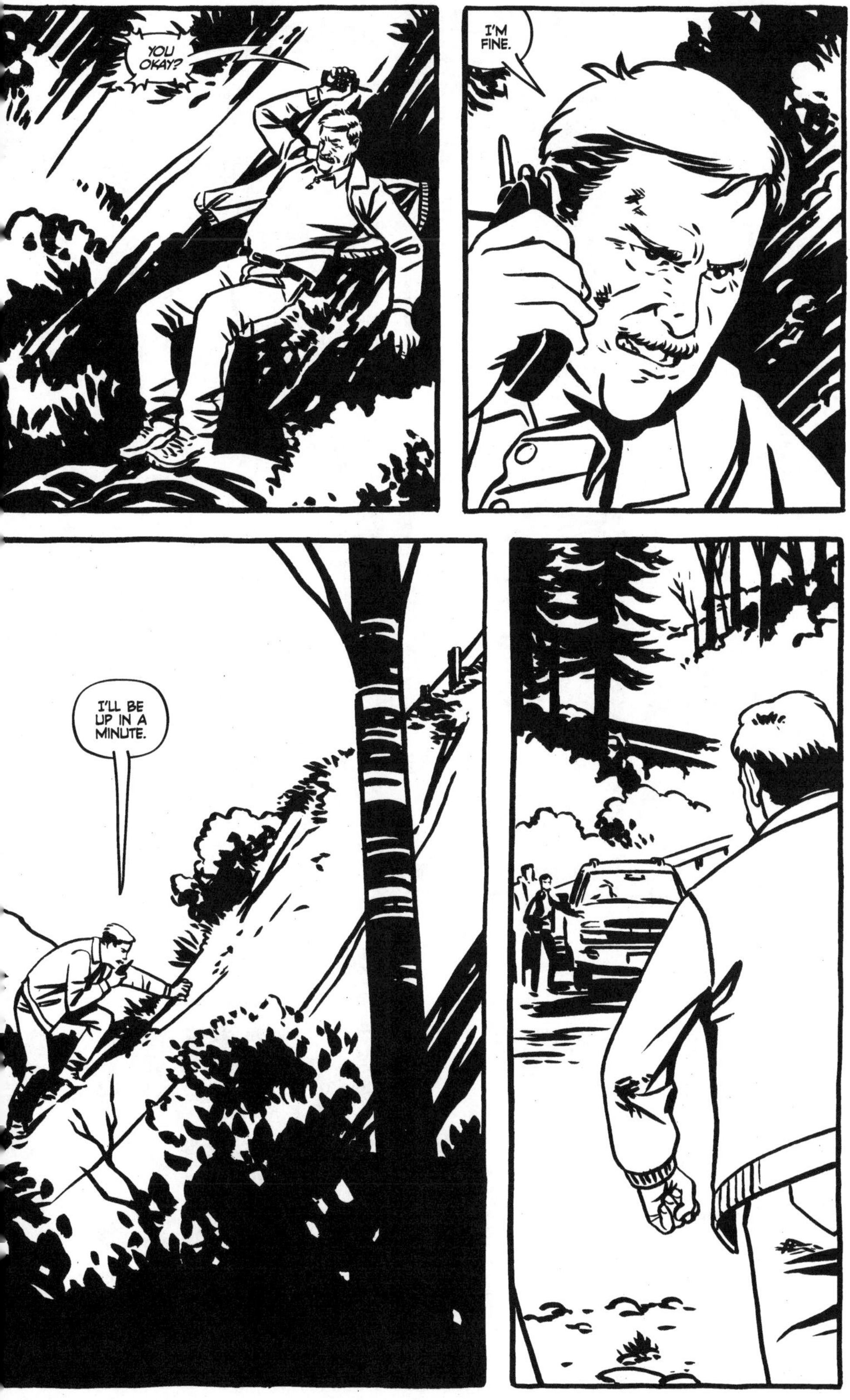
YOU OKAY?
I'M FINE.
I'LL BE UP IN A MINUTE.

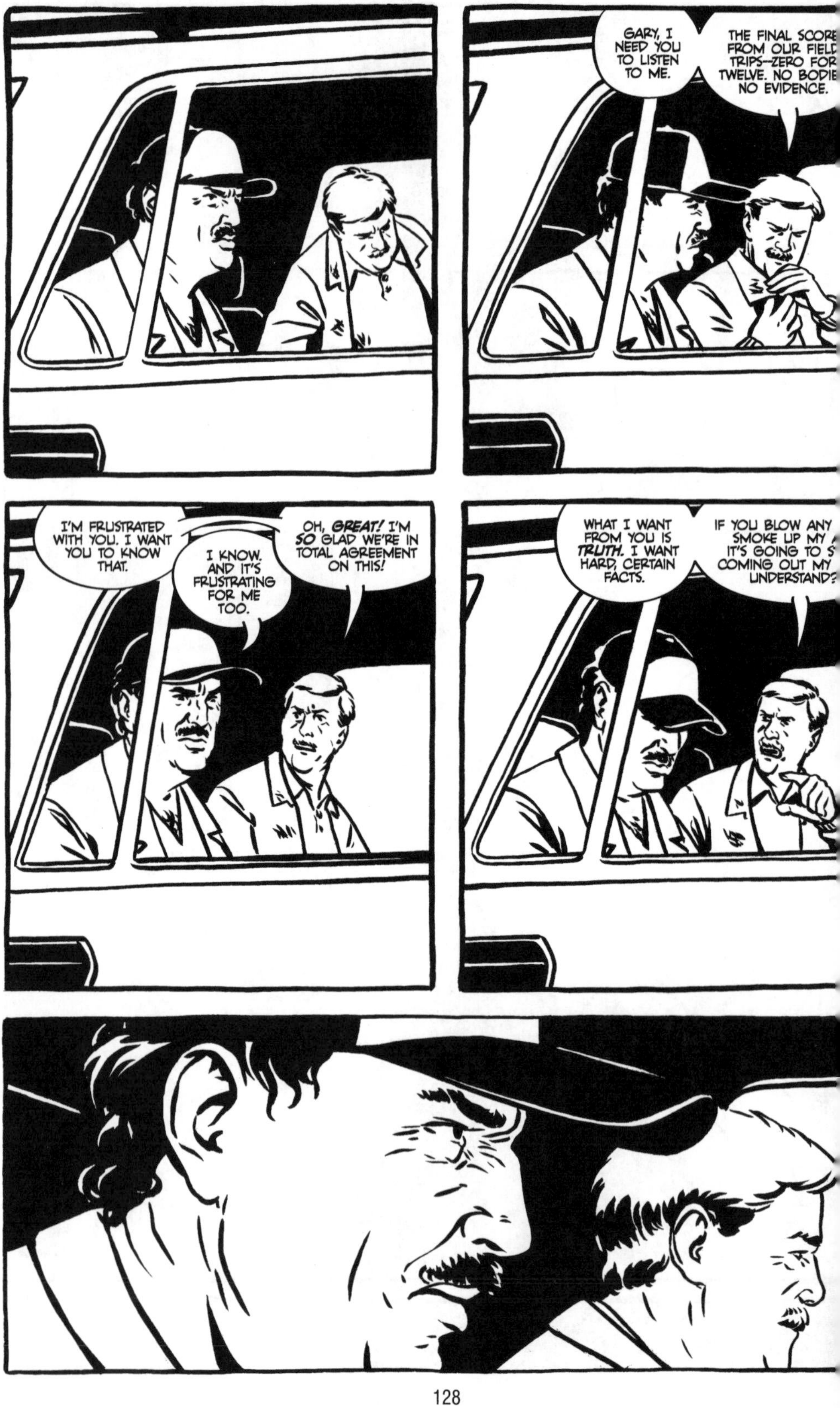
GARY, I NEED YOU TO LISTEN TO ME.
THE FINAL SCORE FROM OUR FIELD TRIPS--ZERO FOR TWELVE. NO BODIE NO EVIDENCE.
I'M FRUSTRATED WITH YOU. I WANT YOU TO KNOW THAT.
I KNOW. AND IT'S FRUSTRATING FOR ME TOO.
OH, GREAT! I'M SO GLAD WE'RE IN TOTAL AGREEMENT ON THIS!
WHAT I WANT FROM YOU IS TRUTH. I WANT HARD, CERTAIN FACTS.
IF YOU BLOW ANY SMOKE UP MY IT'S GOING TO COMING OUT MY UNDERSTAND?

UP YOUR ASS AND OUT YOUR EARS, HUH?

IS THAT ONE OF YOUR SHERLOCK HOLMES QUOTES?

I GET POETIC WHEN I'M PISSED.

DON'T WORRY. I HAVE IT UNDER CONTROL.

...OUSLY, ...S NOT ...G THE ...PED.

HE PROMISED US PROOF. HE PROMISED US BODIES. BUT WE'RE NOT GETTING WHAT WE NEED.

THE QUESTION, THOUGH, IS WHY?

SO THE FUZZY-MEMORY THING REALLY DOESN'T FLY WITH YOU GUYS? ALL OF YOU HAVE PERFECT RECALL OF EVERYTHING YOU DID TWENTY YEARS AGO?

IF IT INVOLVED THE EXTRAORDINARY ACTIVITY OF MURDERING WOMEN AND DISPOSING OF THEIR CORPSES? YES. I THINK I'D REMEMBER EVERY BIT OF THAT.

...AREN'T ...NG WHAT ...ED FROM ...IN THE ...RVIEWS ...THER.

THIS GUY'S BEEN LYING SO LONG, I'M NOT SURE HE KNOWS *HOW* TO TELL THE TRUTH.

IT FEELS MORE LIKE RELUCTANCE AND MINIMIZING-- LIKE HE'S AFRAID OF WHAT PEOPLE MAY THINK OF HIM.

CONFESSING TO BEING A SERIAL KILLER IS ONE THING. DETAILING THE EXTENT OF YOUR DEPRAVITY IS ANOTHER.

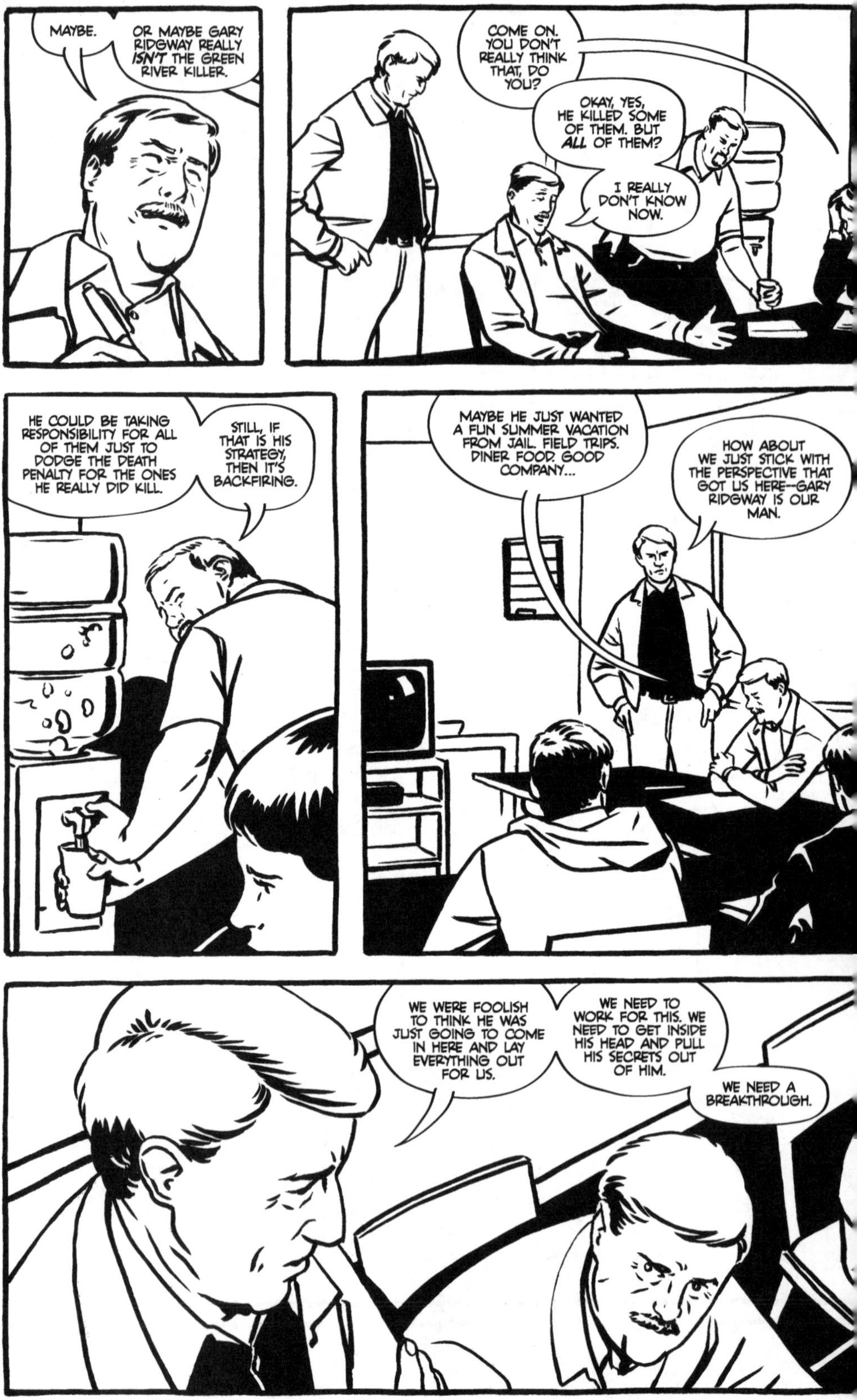
MAYBE.
OR MAYBE GARY RIDGWAY REALLY *ISN'T* THE GREEN RIVER KILLER.
COME ON. YOU DON'T REALLY THINK THAT, DO YOU?
OKAY, YES, HE KILLED SOME OF THEM. BUT *ALL* OF THEM?
I REALLY DON'T KNOW NOW.
HE COULD BE TAKING RESPONSIBILITY FOR ALL OF THEM JUST TO DODGE THE DEATH PENALTY FOR THE ONES HE REALLY DID KILL.
STILL, IF THAT IS HIS STRATEGY, THEN IT'S BACKFIRING.
MAYBE HE JUST WANTED A FUN SUMMER VACATION FROM JAIL. FIELD TRIPS. DINER FOOD. GOOD COMPANY...
HOW ABOUT WE JUST STICK WITH THE PERSPECTIVE THAT GOT US HERE--GARY RIDGWAY IS OUR MAN.
WE WERE FOOLISH TO THINK HE WAS JUST GOING TO COME IN HERE AND LAY EVERYTHING OUT FOR US.
WE NEED TO WORK FOR THIS. WE NEED TO GET INSIDE HIS HEAD AND PULL HIS SECRETS OUT OF HIM.
WE NEED A BREAKTHROUGH.

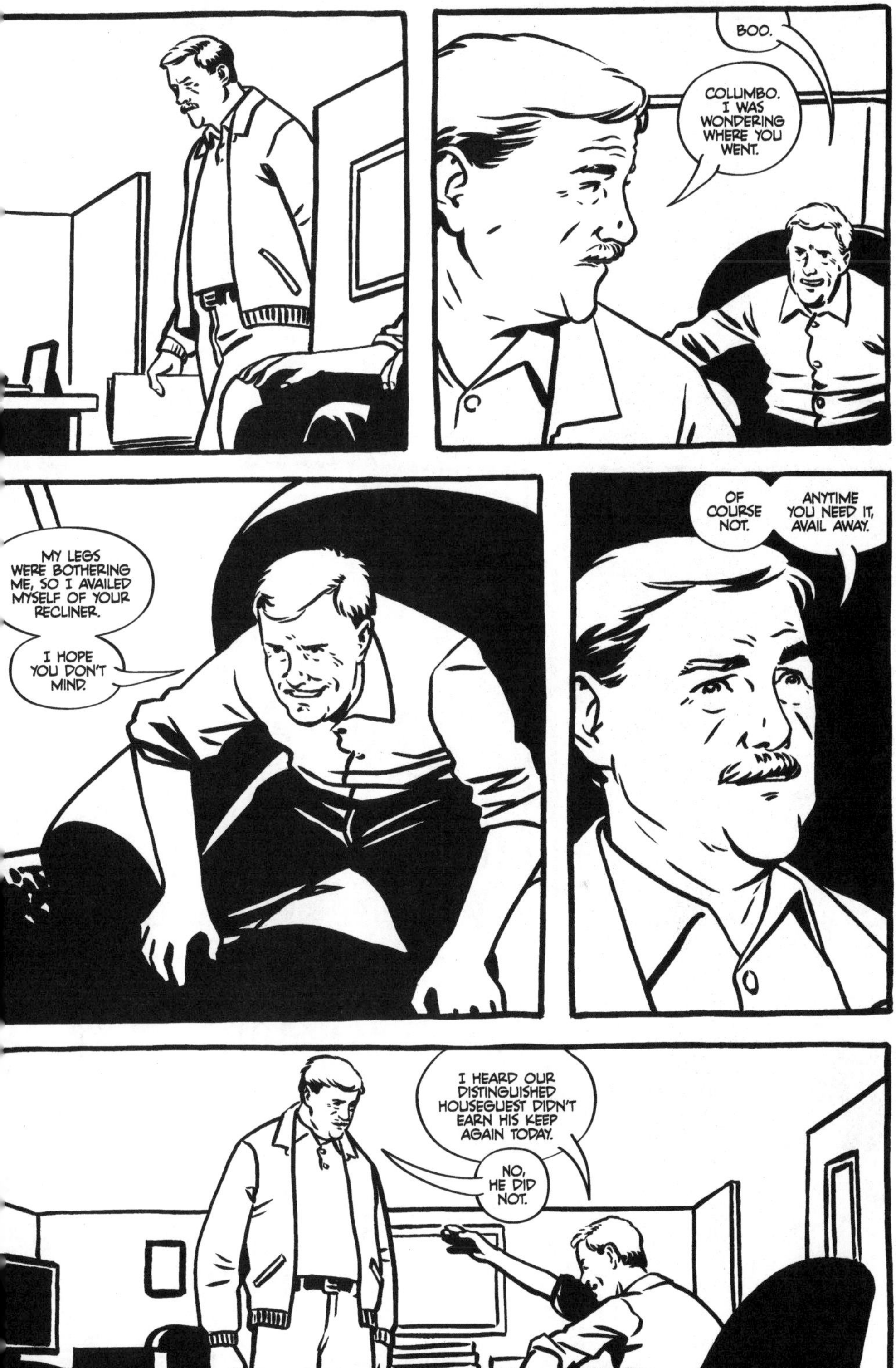
BOO.
COLUMBO. I WAS WONDERING WHERE YOU WENT.
MY LEGS WERE BOTHERING ME, SO I AVAILED MYSELF OF YOUR RECLINER.
I HOPE YOU DON'T MIND.
OF COURSE NOT.
ANYTIME YOU NEED IT, AVAIL AWAY.
I HEARD OUR DISTINGUISHED HOUSEGUEST DIDN'T EARN HIS KEEP AGAIN TODAY.
NO, HE DID NOT.

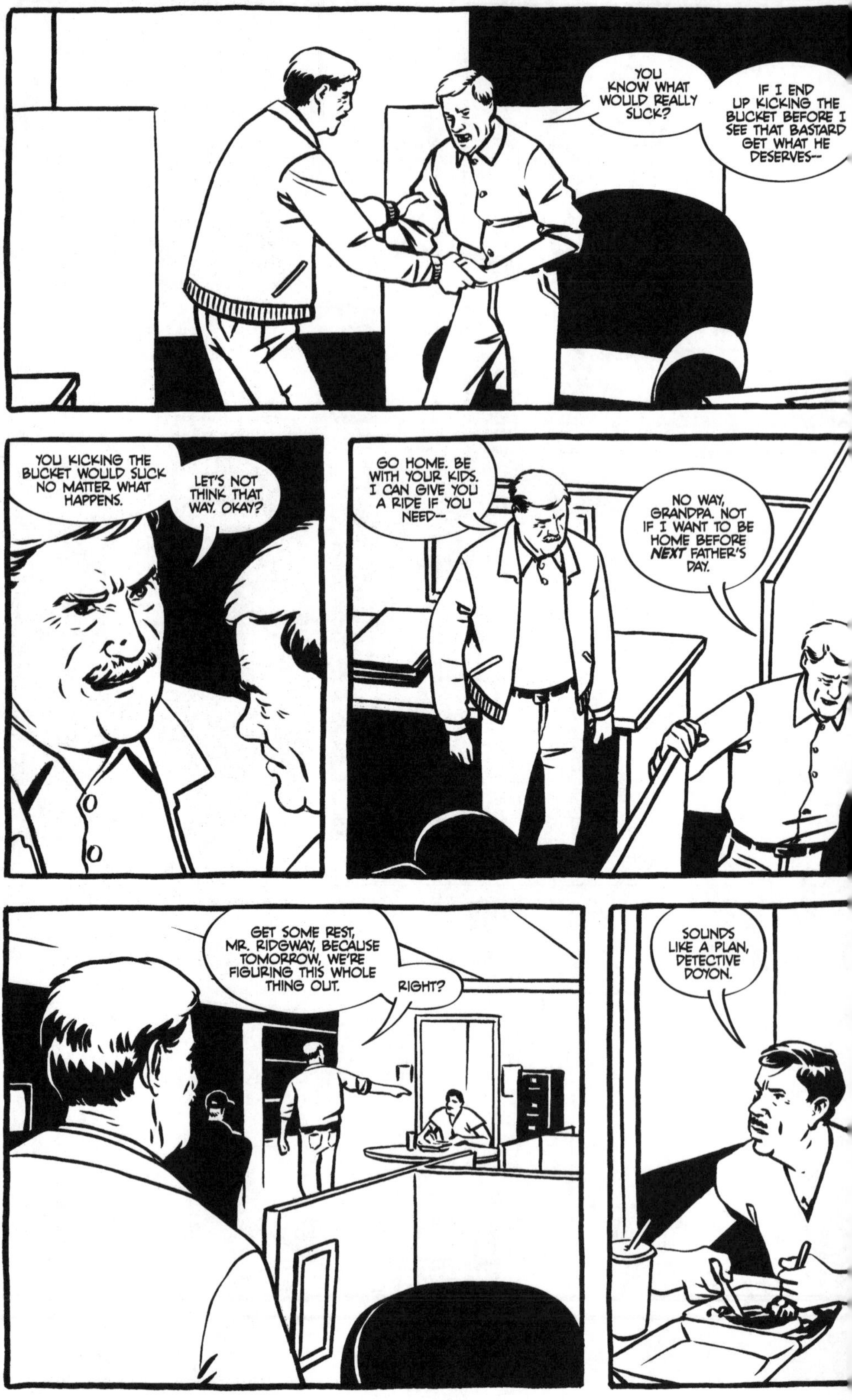
YOU KNOW WHAT WOULD REALLY SUCK?
IF I END UP KICKING THE BUCKET BEFORE I SEE THAT BASTARD GET WHAT HE DESERVES--
YOU KICKING THE BUCKET WOULD SUCK NO MATTER WHAT HAPPENS.
LET'S NOT THINK THAT WAY. OKAY?
GO HOME. BE WITH YOUR KIDS. I CAN GIVE YOU A RIDE IF YOU NEED--
NO WAY, GRANDPA. NOT IF I WANT TO BE HOME BEFORE *NEXT* FATHER'S DAY.
GET SOME REST, MR. RIDGWAY, BECAUSE TOMORROW, WE'RE FIGURING THIS WHOLE THING OUT.
RIGHT?
SOUNDS LIKE A PLAN, DETECTIVE DOYON.

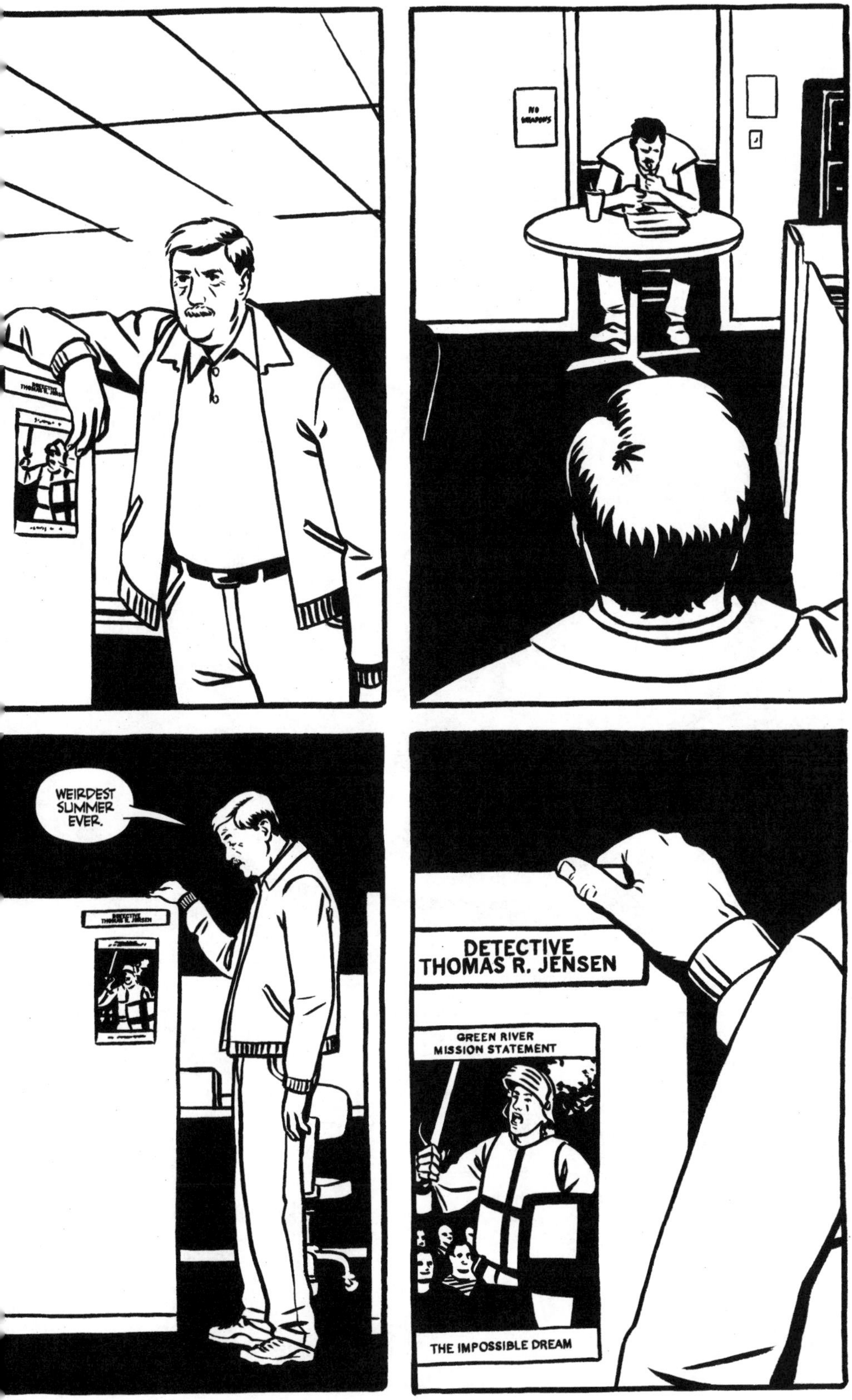
NO WEAPONS
WEIRDEST SUMMER EVER.
DETECTIVE THOMAS R. JENSEN
GREEN RIVER MISSION STATEMENT
THE IMPOSSIBLE DREAM

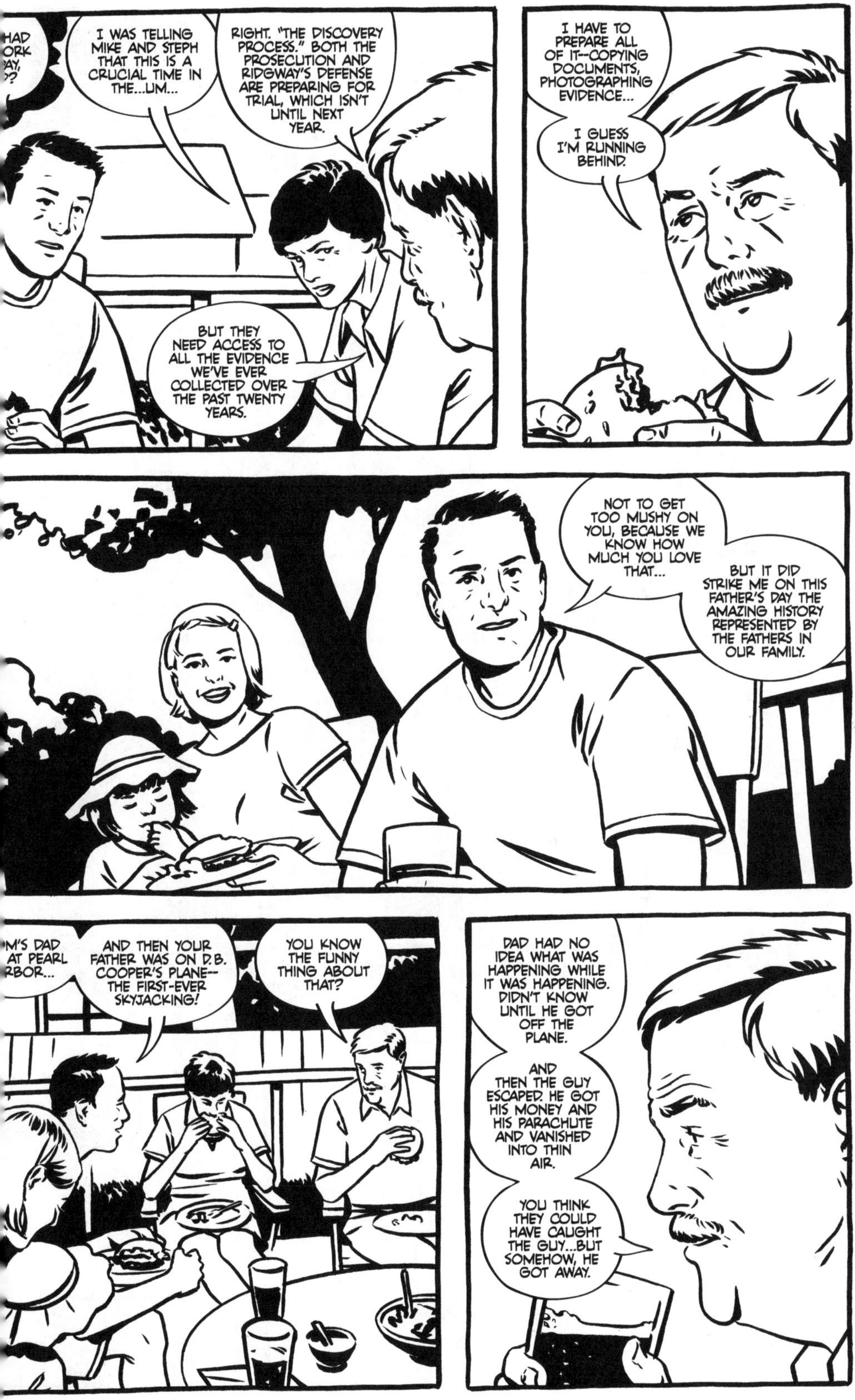
HAD
ORK
AY,
?
I WAS TELLING MIKE AND STEPH THAT THIS IS A CRUCIAL TIME IN THE...UM...
RIGHT. "THE DISCOVERY PROCESS." BOTH THE PROSECUTION AND RIDGWAY'S DEFENSE ARE PREPARING FOR TRIAL, WHICH ISN'T UNTIL NEXT YEAR.
BUT THEY NEED ACCESS TO ALL THE EVIDENCE WE'VE EVER COLLECTED OVER THE PAST TWENTY YEARS.
I HAVE TO PREPARE ALL OF IT--COPYING DOCUMENTS, PHOTOGRAPHING EVIDENCE...
I GUESS I'M RUNNING BEHIND.
NOT TO GET TOO MUSHY ON YOU, BECAUSE WE KNOW HOW MUCH YOU LOVE THAT...
BUT IT DID STRIKE ME ON THIS FATHER'S DAY THE AMAZING HISTORY REPRESENTED BY THE FATHERS IN OUR FAMILY.
M'S DAD AT PEARL RBOR...
AND THEN YOUR FATHER WAS ON D.B. COOPER'S PLANE-- THE FIRST-EVER SKYJACKING!
YOU KNOW THE FUNNY THING ABOUT THAT?
DAD HAD NO IDEA WHAT WAS HAPPENING WHILE IT WAS HAPPENING. DIDN'T KNOW UNTIL HE GOT OFF THE PLANE.
AND THEN THE GUY ESCAPED. HE GOT HIS MONEY AND HIS PARACHUTE AND VANISHED INTO THIN AIR.
YOU THINK THEY COULD HAVE CAUGHT THE GUY...BUT SOMEHOW, HE GOT AWAY.

DAY FOUR: BURDEN OF PROOF

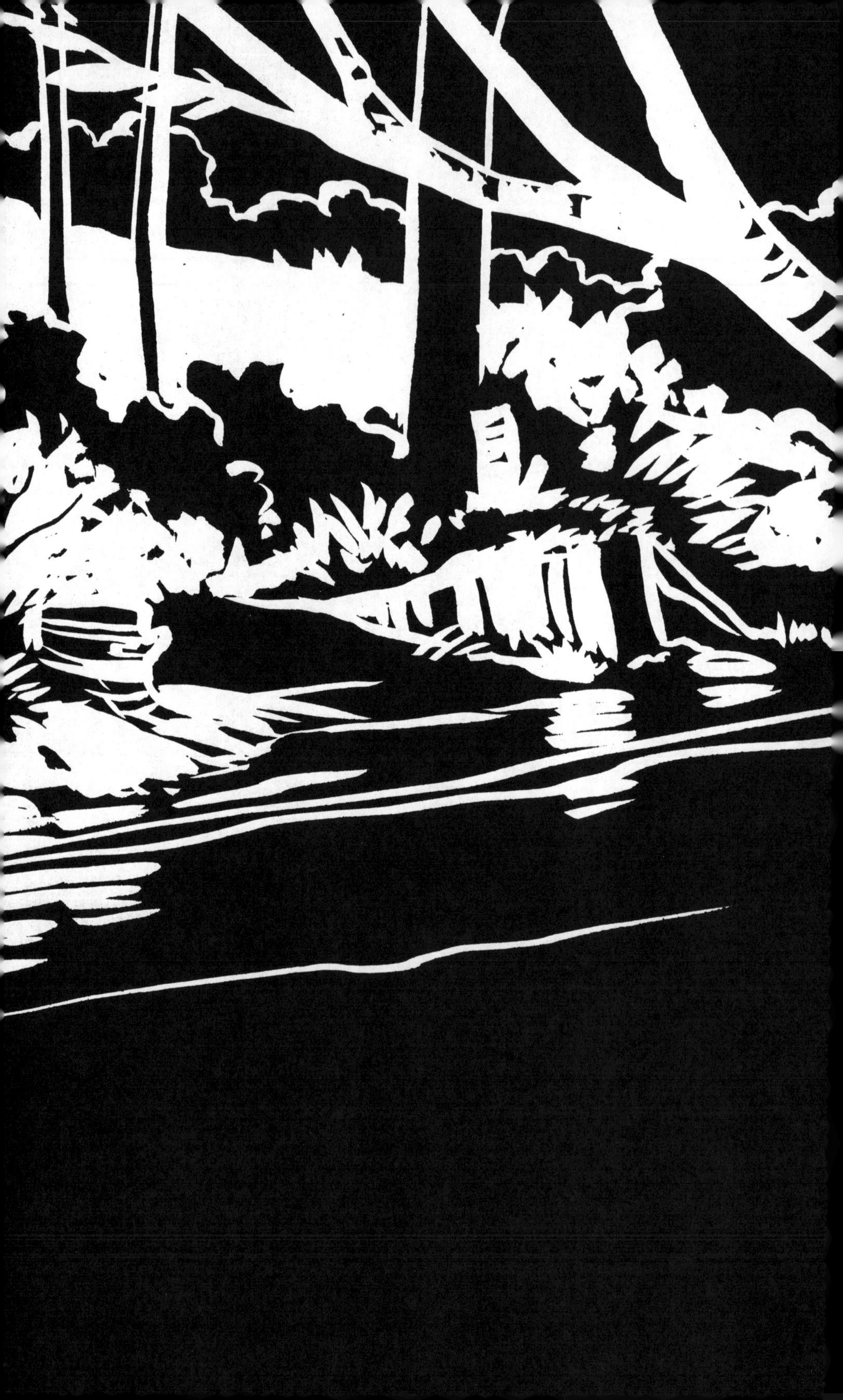

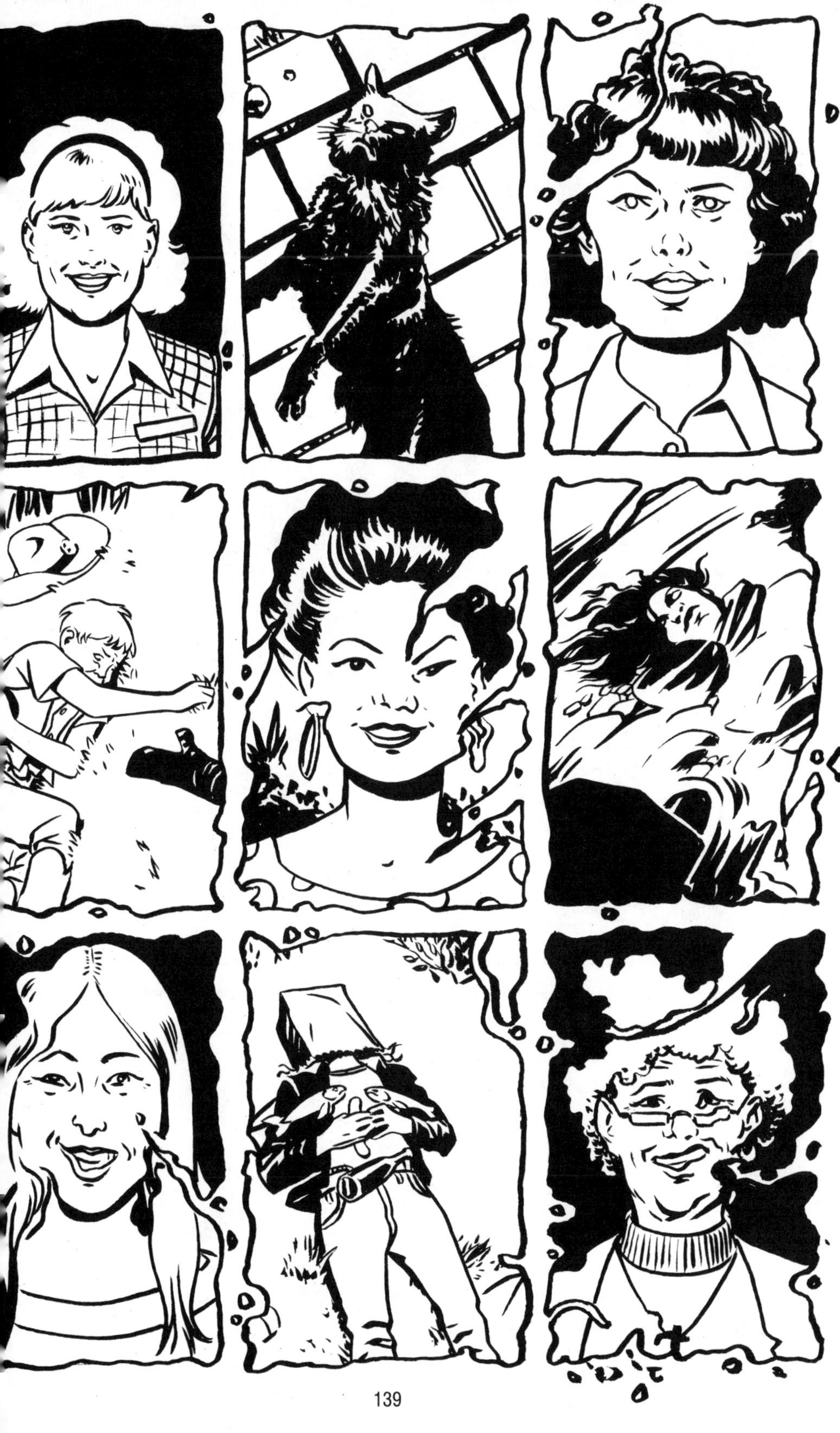

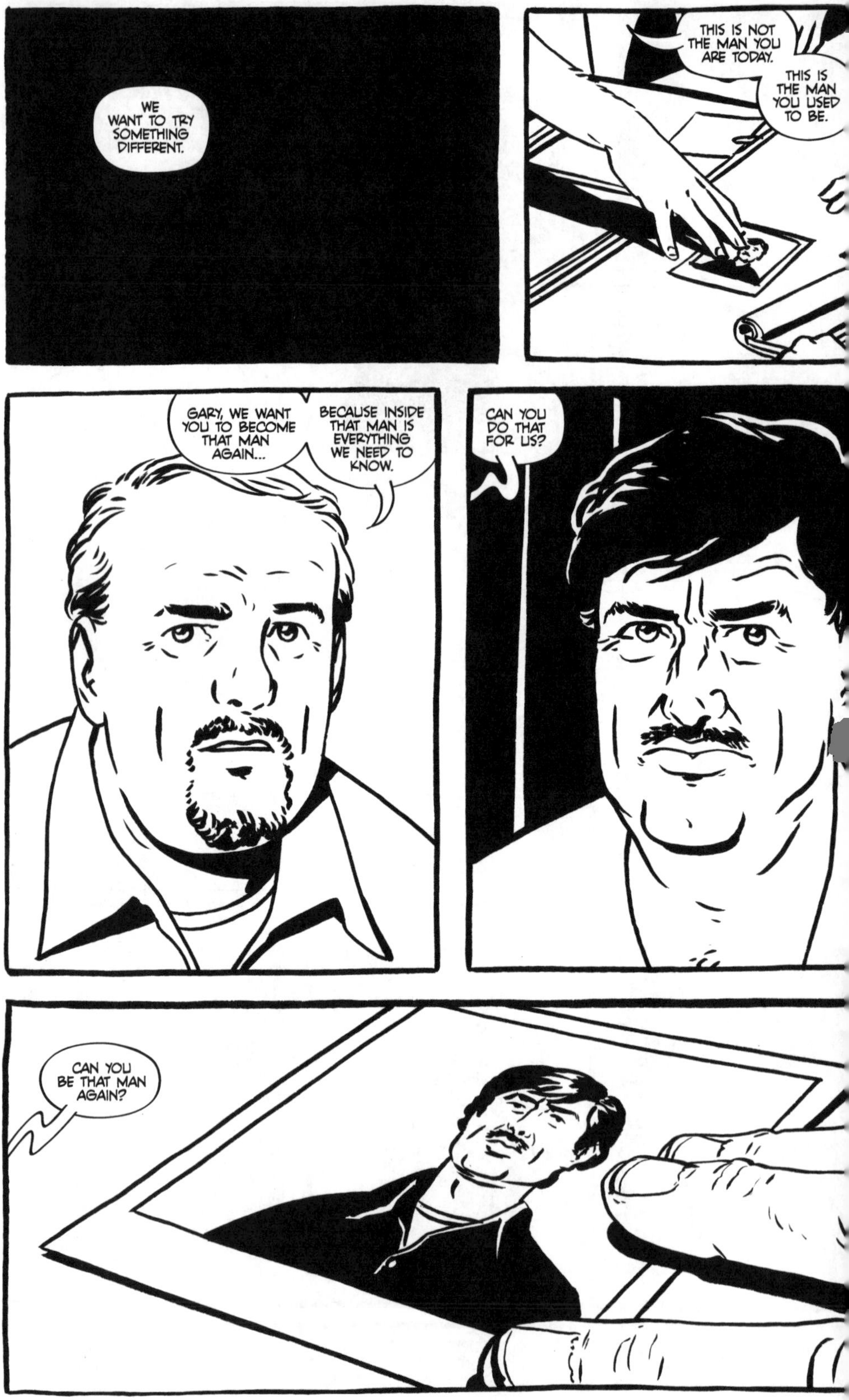
WE WANT TO TRY SOMETHING DIFFERENT.
THIS IS NOT THE MAN YOU ARE TODAY.
THIS IS THE MAN YOU USED TO BE.
GARY, WE WANT YOU TO BECOME THAT MAN AGAIN...
BECAUSE INSIDE THAT MAN IS EVERYTHING WE NEED TO KNOW.
CAN YOU DO THAT FOR US?
CAN YOU BE THAT MAN AGAIN?

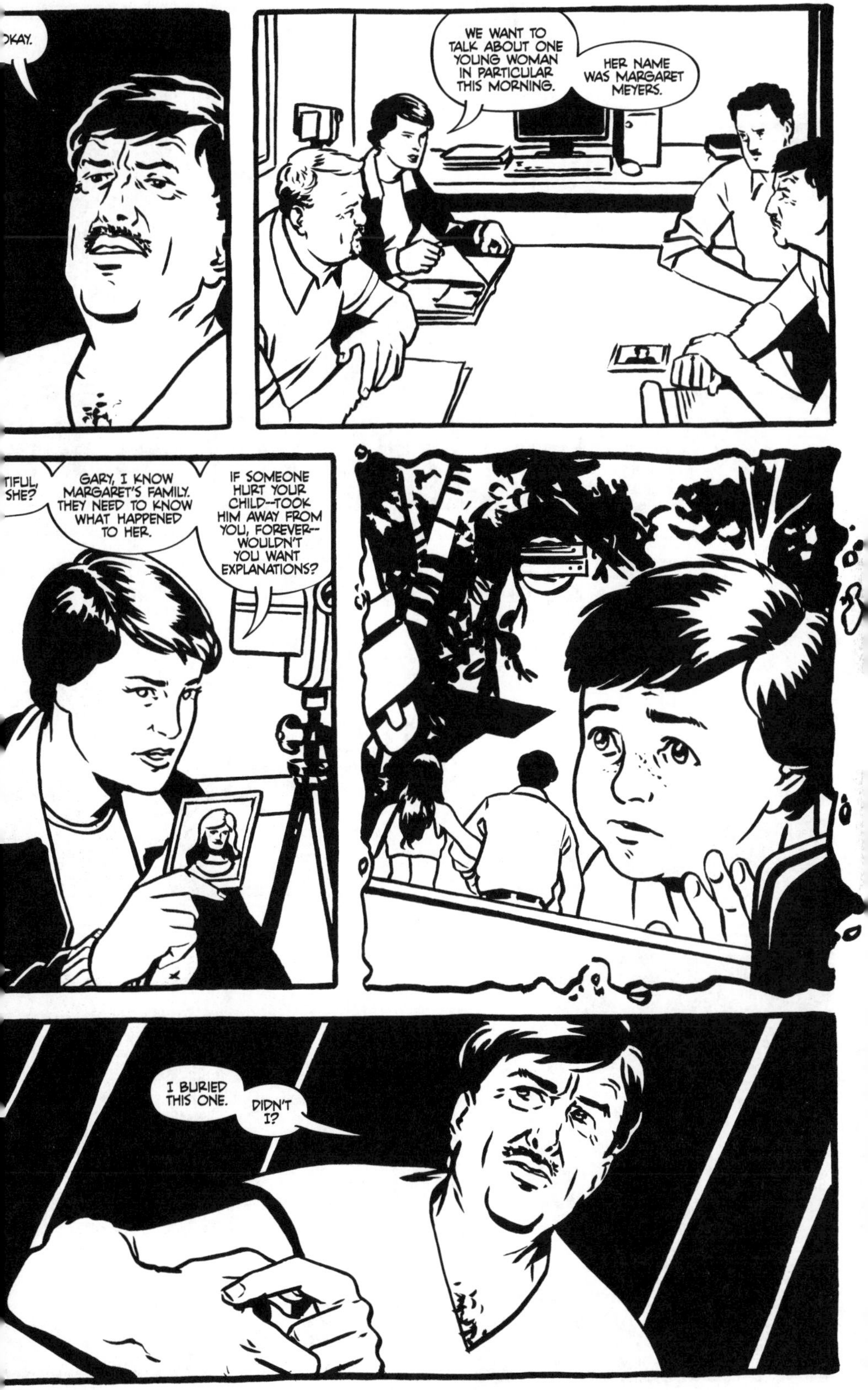
OKAY.
WE WANT TO TALK ABOUT ONE YOUNG WOMAN IN PARTICULAR THIS MORNING.
HER NAME WAS MARGARET MEYERS.
TIFUL, SHE?
GARY, I KNOW MARGARET'S FAMILY. THEY NEED TO KNOW WHAT HAPPENED TO HER.
IF SOMEONE HURT YOUR CHILD--TOOK HIM AWAY FROM YOU, FOREVER--WOULDN'T YOU WANT EXPLANATIONS?
I BURIED THIS ONE.
DIDN'T I?

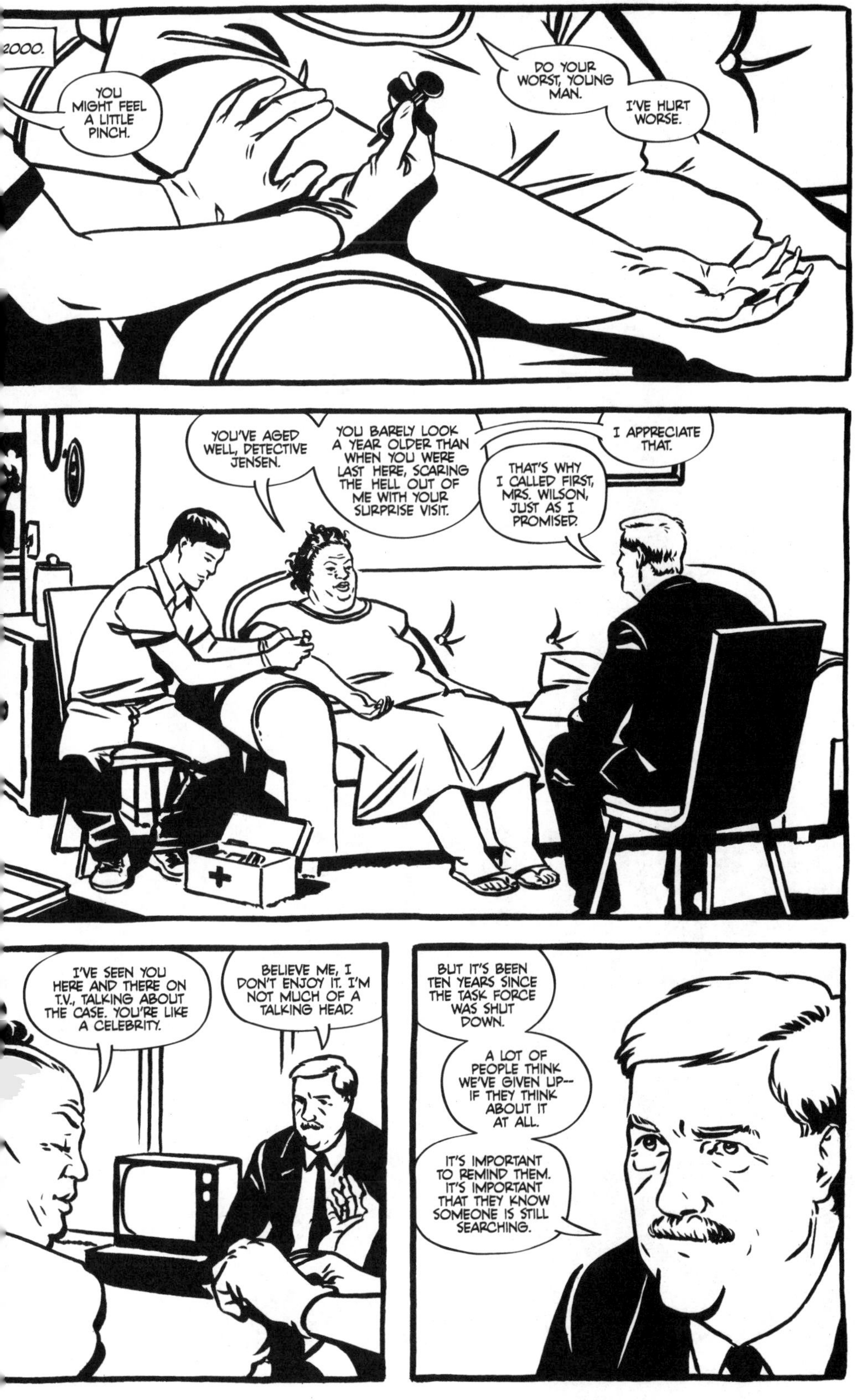
2000.
YOU MIGHT FEEL A LITTLE PINCH.
DO YOUR WORST, YOUNG MAN.
I'VE HURT WORSE.
YOU'VE AGED WELL, DETECTIVE JENSEN.
YOU BARELY LOOK A YEAR OLDER THAN WHEN YOU WERE LAST HERE, SCARING THE HELL OUT OF ME WITH YOUR SURPRISE VISIT.
I APPRECIATE THAT.
THAT'S WHY I CALLED FIRST, MRS. WILSON, JUST AS I PROMISED.
I'VE SEEN YOU HERE AND THERE ON T.V., TALKING ABOUT THE CASE. YOU'RE LIKE A CELEBRITY.
BELIEVE ME, I DON'T ENJOY IT. I'M NOT MUCH OF A TALKING HEAD.
BUT IT'S BEEN TEN YEARS SINCE THE TASK FORCE WAS SHUT DOWN.
A LOT OF PEOPLE THINK WE'VE GIVEN UP-- IF THEY THINK ABOUT IT AT ALL.
IT'S IMPORTANT TO REMIND THEM. IT'S IMPORTANT THAT THEY KNOW SOMEONE IS STILL SEARCHING.

144

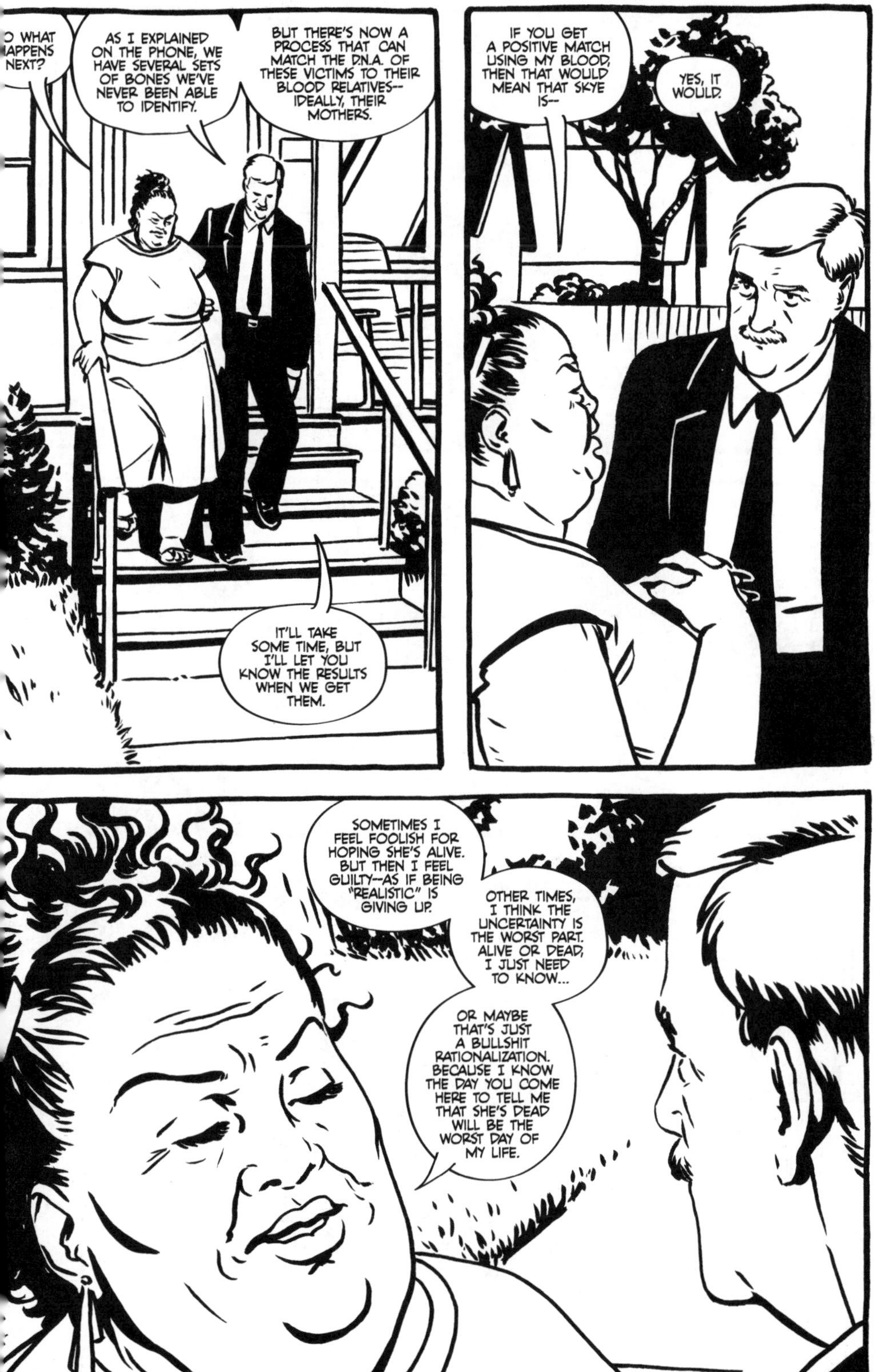
O WHAT
APPENS
NEXT?
AS I EXPLAINED ON THE PHONE, WE HAVE SEVERAL SETS OF BONES WE'VE NEVER BEEN ABLE TO IDENTIFY.
BUT THERE'S NOW A PROCESS THAT CAN MATCH THE D.N.A. OF THESE VICTIMS TO THEIR BLOOD RELATIVES--IDEALLY, THEIR MOTHERS.
IT'LL TAKE SOME TIME, BUT I'LL LET YOU KNOW THE RESULTS WHEN WE GET THEM.
IF YOU GET A POSITIVE MATCH USING MY BLOOD, THEN THAT WOULD MEAN THAT SKYE IS--
YES, IT WOULD.
SOMETIMES I FEEL FOOLISH FOR HOPING SHE'S ALIVE. BUT THEN I FEEL GUILTY--AS IF BEING "REALISTIC" IS GIVING UP.
OTHER TIMES, I THINK THE UNCERTAINTY IS THE WORST PART. ALIVE OR DEAD, I JUST NEED TO KNOW...
OR MAYBE THAT'S JUST A BULLSHIT RATIONALIZATION. BECAUSE I KNOW THE DAY YOU COME HERE TO TELL ME THAT SHE'S DEAD WILL BE THE WORST DAY OF MY LIFE.

146

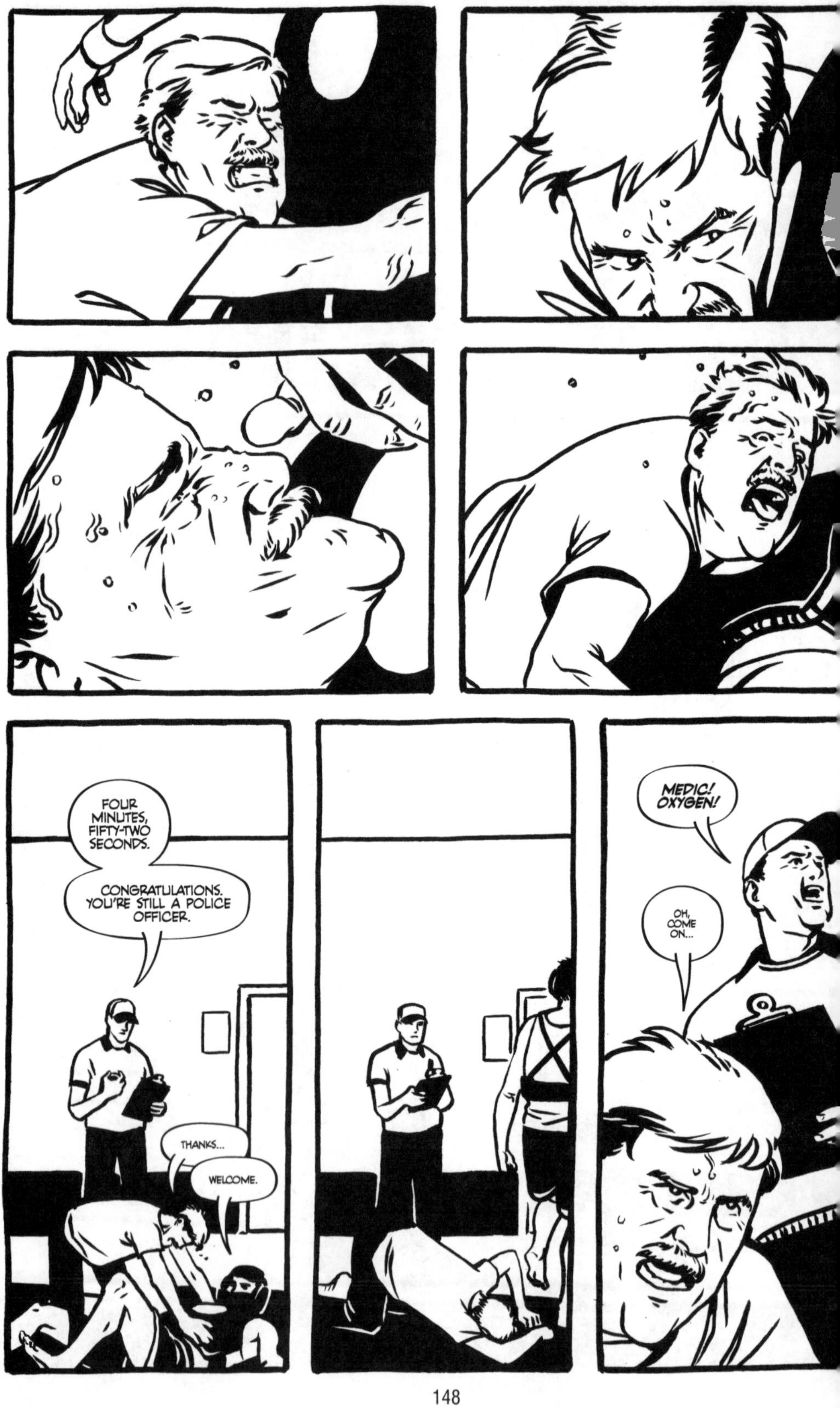
FOUR MINUTES, FIFTY-TWO SECONDS.
CONGRATULATIONS. YOU'RE STILL A POLICE OFFICER.
THANKS...
WELCOME.
MEDIC! OXYGEN!
OH, COME ON...

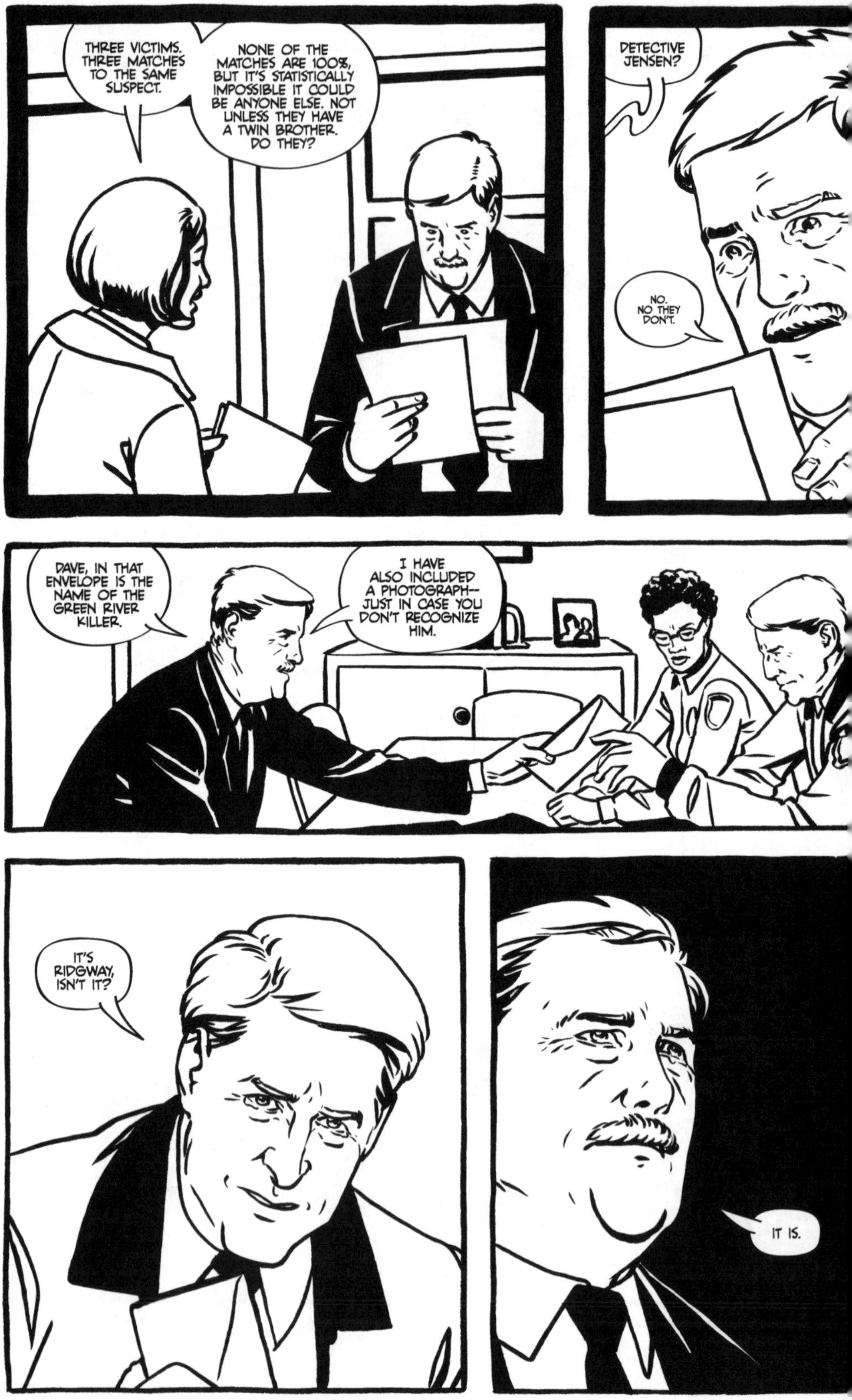
THREE VICTIMS. THREE MATCHES TO THE SAME SUSPECT.
NONE OF THE MATCHES ARE 100%, BUT IT'S STATISTICALLY IMPOSSIBLE IT COULD BE ANYONE ELSE. NOT UNLESS THEY HAVE A TWIN BROTHER. DO THEY?
DETECTIVE JENSEN?
NO. NO THEY DON'T.
DAVE, IN THAT ENVELOPE IS THE NAME OF THE GREEN RIVER KILLER.
I HAVE ALSO INCLUDED A PHOTOGRAPH-- JUST IN CASE YOU DON'T RECOGNIZE HIM.
IT'S RIDGWAY, ISN'T IT?
IT IS.

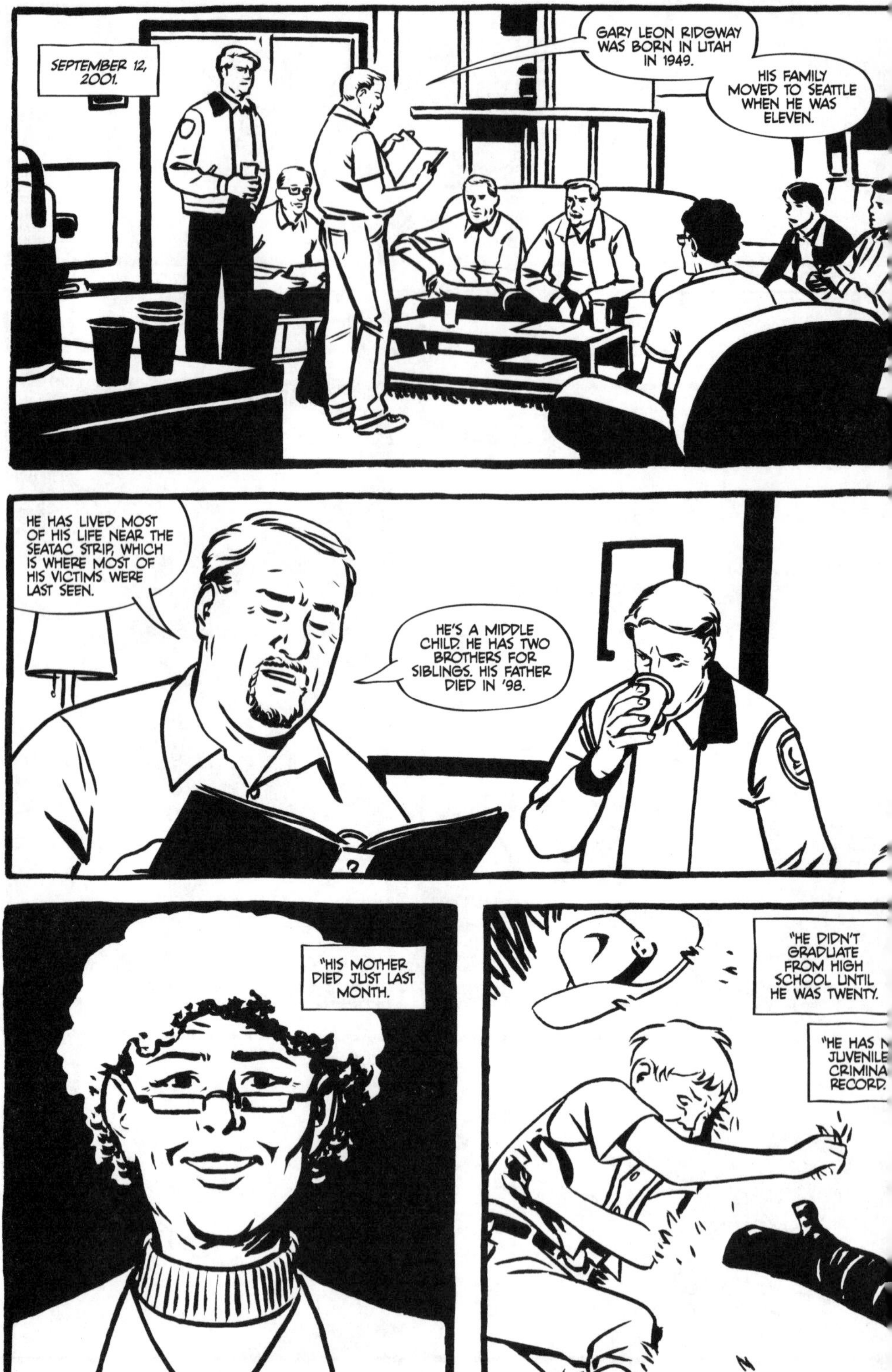
SEPTEMBER 12, 2001.
GARY LEON RIDGWAY WAS BORN IN UTAH IN 1949.
HIS FAMILY MOVED TO SEATTLE WHEN HE WAS ELEVEN.
HE HAS LIVED MOST OF HIS LIFE NEAR THE SEATAC STRIP, WHICH IS WHERE MOST OF HIS VICTIMS WERE LAST SEEN.
HE'S A MIDDLE CHILD. HE HAS TWO BROTHERS FOR SIBLINGS. HIS FATHER DIED IN '98.
"HIS MOTHER DIED JUST LAST MONTH.
"HE DIDN'T GRADUATE FROM HIGH SCHOOL UNTIL HE WAS TWENTY.
"HE HAS N JUVENILE CRIMINA RECORD.

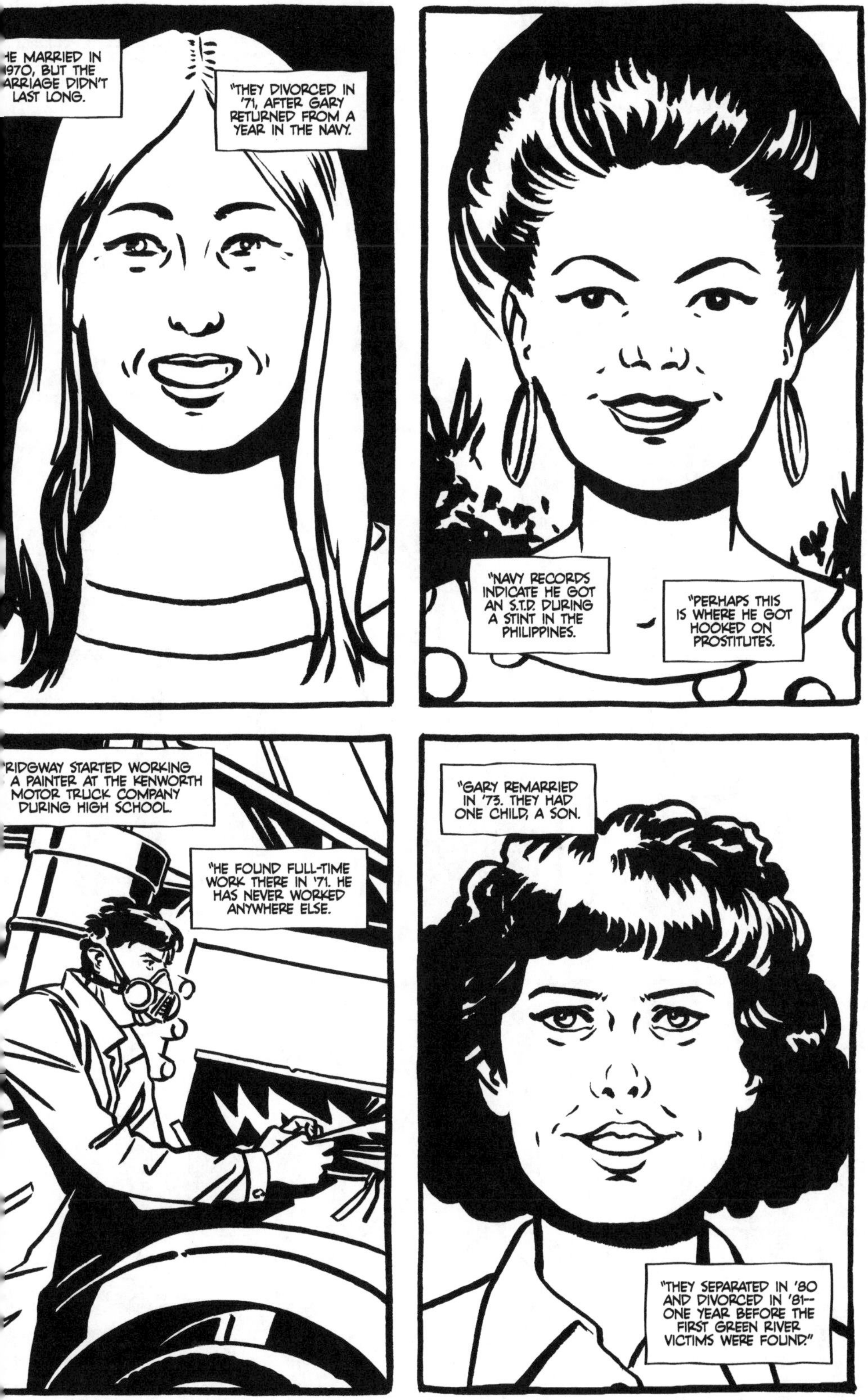
IE MARRIED IN 970, BUT THE ARRIAGE DIDN'T LAST LONG.
"THEY DIVORCED IN '71, AFTER GARY RETURNED FROM A YEAR IN THE NAVY.
"NAVY RECORDS INDICATE HE GOT AN S.T.D. DURING A STINT IN THE PHILIPPINES.
"PERHAPS THIS IS WHERE HE GOT HOOKED ON PROSTITUTES.
RIDGWAY STARTED WORKING A PAINTER AT THE KENWORTH MOTOR TRUCK COMPANY DURING HIGH SCHOOL.
"HE FOUND FULL-TIME WORK THERE IN '71. HE HAS NEVER WORKED ANYWHERE ELSE.
"GARY REMARRIED IN '73. THEY HAD ONE CHILD, A SON.
"THEY SEPARATED IN '80 AND DIVORCED IN '81-- ONE YEAR BEFORE THE FIRST GREEN RIVER VICTIMS WERE FOUND."

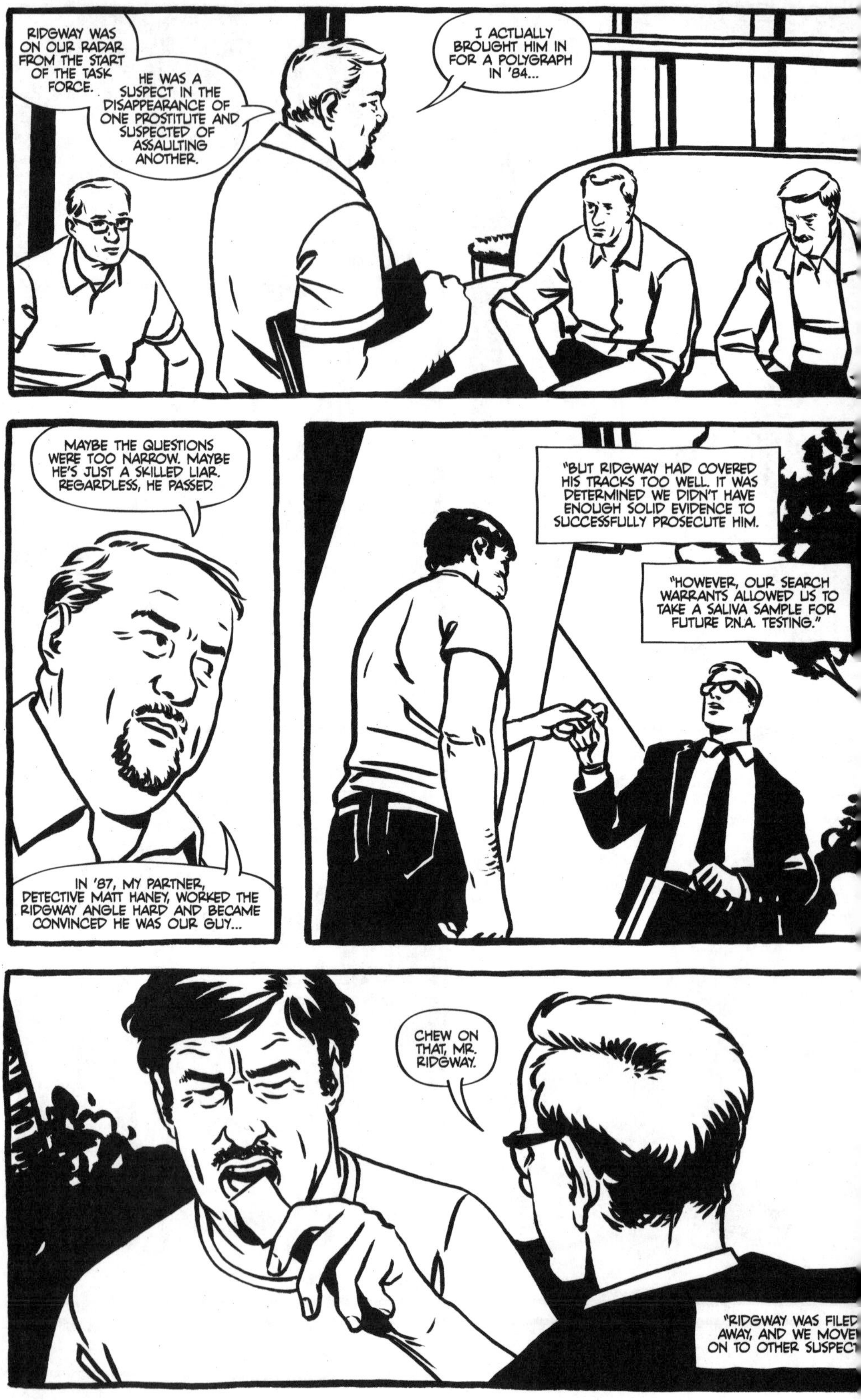
RIDGWAY WAS ON OUR RADAR FROM THE START OF THE TASK FORCE.
HE WAS A SUSPECT IN THE DISAPPEARANCE OF ONE PROSTITUTE AND SUSPECTED OF ASSAULTING ANOTHER.
I ACTUALLY BROUGHT HIM IN FOR A POLYGRAPH IN '84...
MAYBE THE QUESTIONS WERE TOO NARROW. MAYBE HE'S JUST A SKILLED LIAR. REGARDLESS, HE PASSED.
IN '87, MY PARTNER, DETECTIVE MATT HANEY, WORKED THE RIDGWAY ANGLE HARD AND BECAME CONVINCED HE WAS OUR GUY...
"BUT RIDGWAY HAD COVERED HIS TRACKS TOO WELL. IT WAS DETERMINED WE DIDN'T HAVE ENOUGH SOLID EVIDENCE TO SUCCESSFULLY PROSECUTE HIM.
"HOWEVER, OUR SEARCH WARRANTS ALLOWED US TO TAKE A SALIVA SAMPLE FOR FUTURE D.N.A. TESTING."
CHEW ON THAT, MR. RIDGWAY.
"RIDGWAY WAS FILED AWAY, AND WE MOVE ON TO OTHER SUSPECT

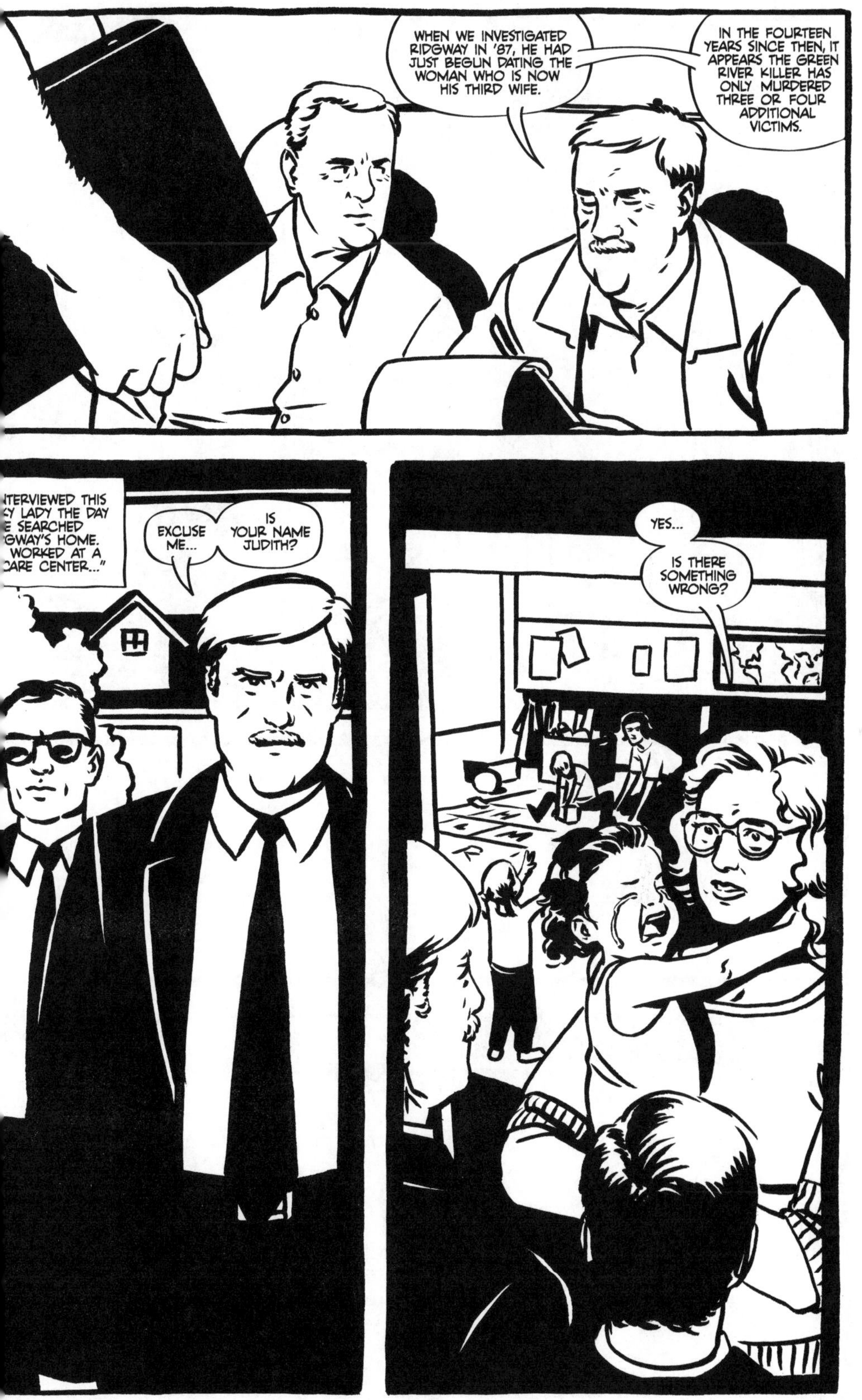
WHEN WE INVESTIGATED RIDGWAY IN '87, HE HAD JUST BEGUN DATING THE WOMAN WHO IS NOW HIS THIRD WIFE.
IN THE FOURTEEN YEARS SINCE THEN, IT APPEARS THE GREEN RIVER KILLER HAS ONLY MURDERED THREE OR FOUR ADDITIONAL VICTIMS.
NTERVIEWED THIS Y LADY THE DAY E SEARCHED GWAY'S HOME. WORKED AT A CARE CENTER..."
EXCUSE ME...
IS YOUR NAME JUDITH?
YES...
IS THERE SOMETHING WRONG?

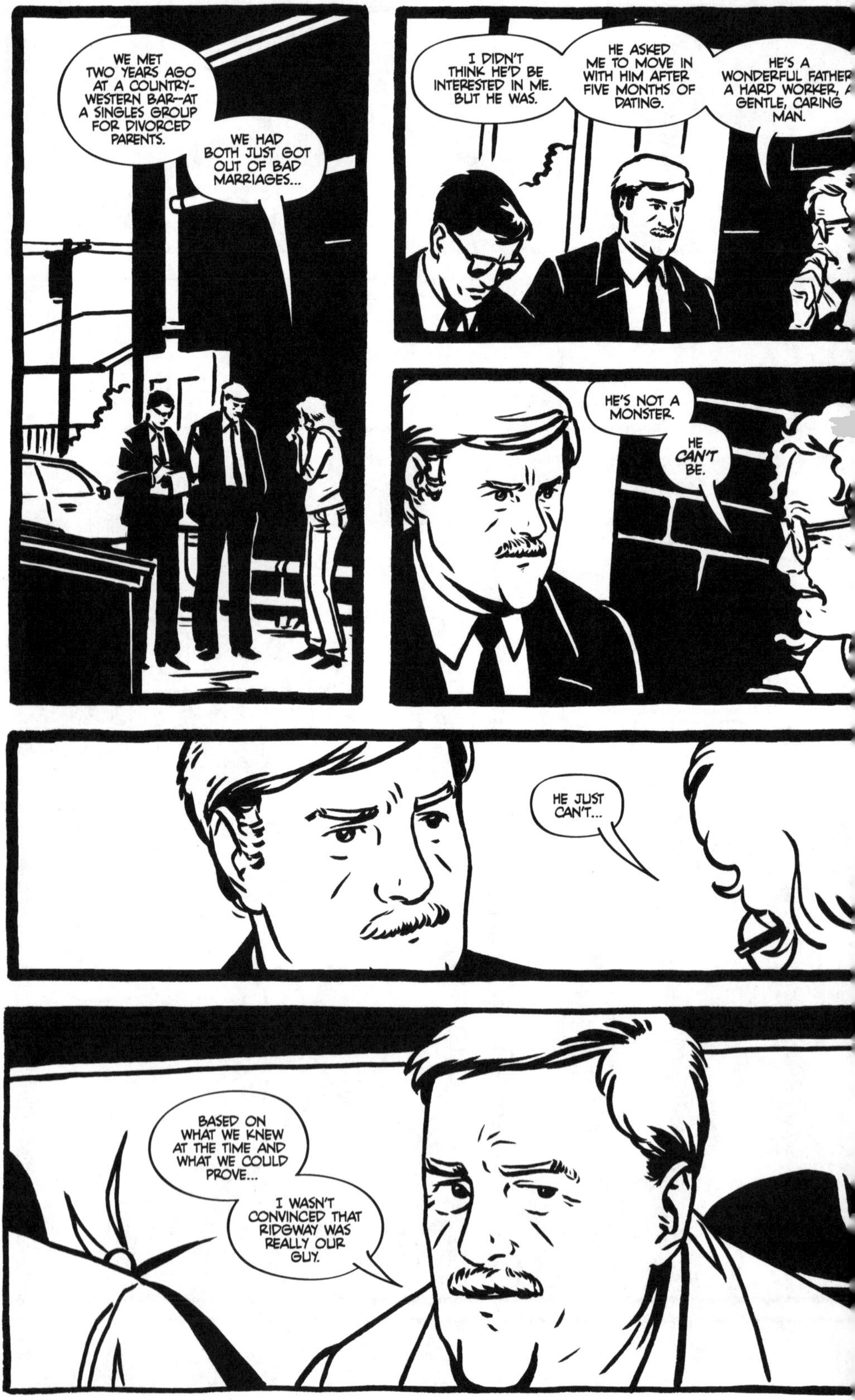
WE MET TWO YEARS AGO AT A COUNTRY-WESTERN BAR--AT A SINGLES GROUP FOR DIVORCED PARENTS.
WE HAD BOTH JUST GOT OUT OF BAD MARRIAGES...
I DIDN'T THINK HE'D BE INTERESTED IN ME. BUT HE WAS.
HE ASKED ME TO MOVE IN WITH HIM AFTER FIVE MONTHS OF DATING.
HE'S A WONDERFUL FATHER, A HARD WORKER, A GENTLE, CARING MAN.
HE'S NOT A MONSTER.
HE *CAN'T* BE.
HE JUST CAN'T...
BASED ON WHAT WE KNEW AT THE TIME AND WHAT WE COULD PROVE...
I WASN'T CONVINCED THAT RIDGWAY WAS REALLY OUR GUY.

SERGEANT GRADDON WILL SERVE AS COMMANDING OFFICER OF THIS NEW TASK FORCE.

THE TIMETABLE FOR AN ARREST IS STILL T.B.D....

"GIVEN WHAT HAPPENED IN NEW YORK YESTERDAY, I'M NOT SURE WHAT OUR PRIORITIES WILL BE IN THE COMING DAYS.

"STILL, WE WANT RIDGWAY UNDER SURVEILLANCE, BEGINNING IMMEDIATELY.

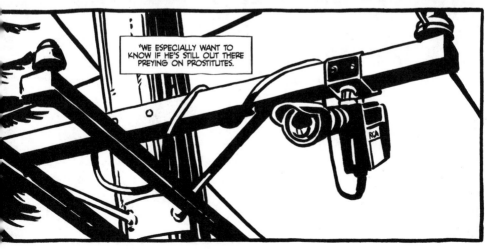

"WE ESPECIALLY WANT TO KNOW IF HE'S STILL OUT THERE PREYING ON PROSTITUTES.

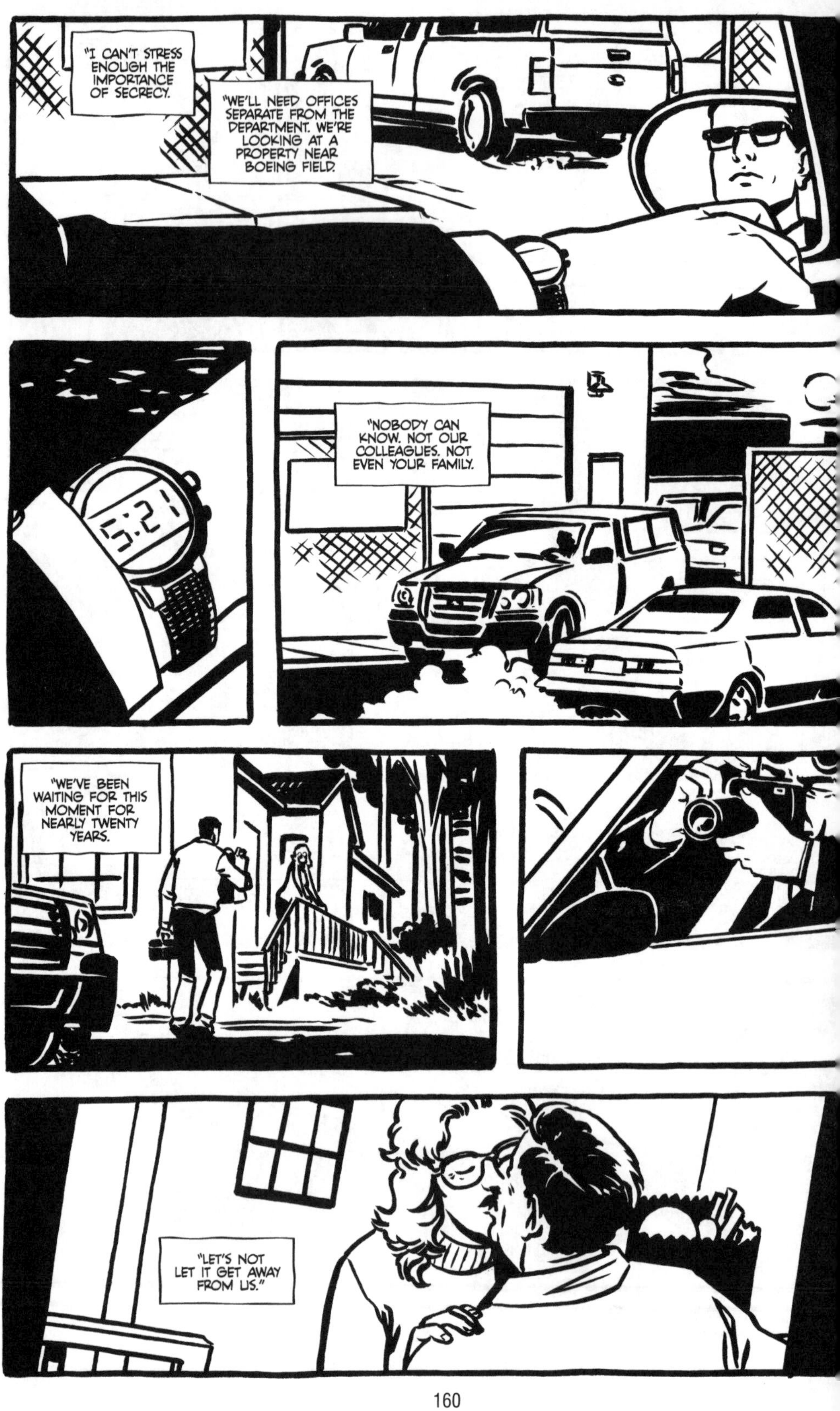
"I CAN'T STRESS ENOUGH THE IMPORTANCE OF SECRECY.
"WE'LL NEED OFFICES SEPARATE FROM THE DEPARTMENT. WE'RE LOOKING AT A PROPERTY NEAR BOEING FIELD.
5:21
"NOBODY CAN KNOW. NOT OUR COLLEAGUES. NOT EVEN YOUR FAMILY.
"WE'VE BEEN WAITING FOR THIS MOMENT FOR NEARLY TWENTY YEARS.
"LET'S NOT LET IT GET AWAY FROM US."

THANKSGIVING 2001.
[LO]NG BEACH, CALIFORNIA.

CAN YOU KEEP A SECRET, JEFF?

I'M AN ENTERTAINMENT JOURNALIST, DAD. OF COURSE I CAN KEEP A SECRET.

WE'RE GOING TO ARREST THE GREEN RIVER KILLER.

WHAT? WHEN? I MEAN-- YOU ACTUALLY *CAUGHT HIM?!* HOW?

D.N.A. WE'RE MAKING THE ARREST ON DECEMBER TENTH.

[I] CAN'T [BELIE]VE YOU'RE [TELL]ING ME [T]HIS.

I'M NOT *SUPPOSED* TO BE TELLING YOU THIS. HENCE--KEEP YOUR MOUTH SHUT.

YOU TOO, BEN.

PLEASE DON'T THROW UP ON ME.

DAD, I'M SO HAPPY FOR YOU. YOU MUST BE THRILLED.

I AM PLEASED, YES.

"PLEASED." COME ON! YOU'VE ONLY BEEN WORKING ON THIS FOR SEVENTEEN YEARS!

DIDN'T YOU EVER FEEL IT WAS ALL HOPELESS?

NO, NOT REALLY...

THIS IS PROBABLY GOING TO SOUND CORNBALL, BUT...

REMEMBER WHEN YOU W IN "MAN OF MANCHA" I HIGH SCHOO

"THE STORY OF A SILLY OLD KNIGHT WITH AN IMPOSSIBLE DREAM...

"WELL, THAT MEANT A LOT TO ME.

"I HAVE A MEMENTO OF YOUR PERFORMANCE THAT I KEEP IN MY DESK.

"IT'S THERE FOR INSPIRATION, WHENEVER I NEED IT..."

TO REMIND ME OF THE QUEST.

"THE QUEST"?

YES. THAT'S WHAT I CALLED IT. TO MYSELF. NOT OUT LOUD OR ANYTHING.

AND WHAT DID THAT MEAN TO YOU? A "QUEST" FOR JUSTICE?

ANSWERS

ANSWE TO ALL QUESTIO

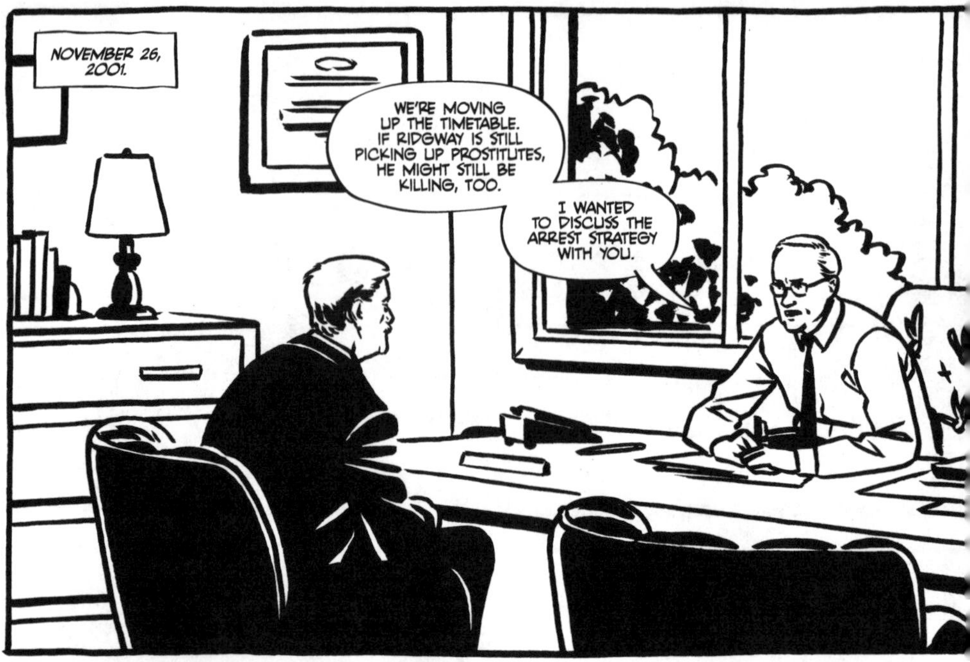
NOVEMBER 26, 2001.
WE'RE MOVING UP THE TIMETABLE. IF RIDGWAY IS STILL PICKING UP PROSTITUTES, HE MIGHT STILL BE KILLING, TOO.
I WANTED TO DISCUSS THE ARREST STRATEGY WITH YOU.

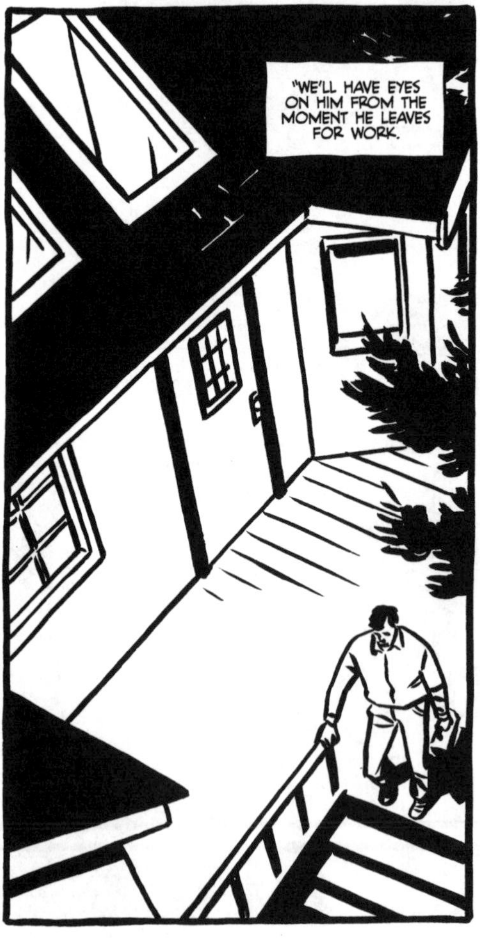
"WE'LL HAVE EYES ON HIM FROM THE MOMENT HE LEAVES FOR WORK.

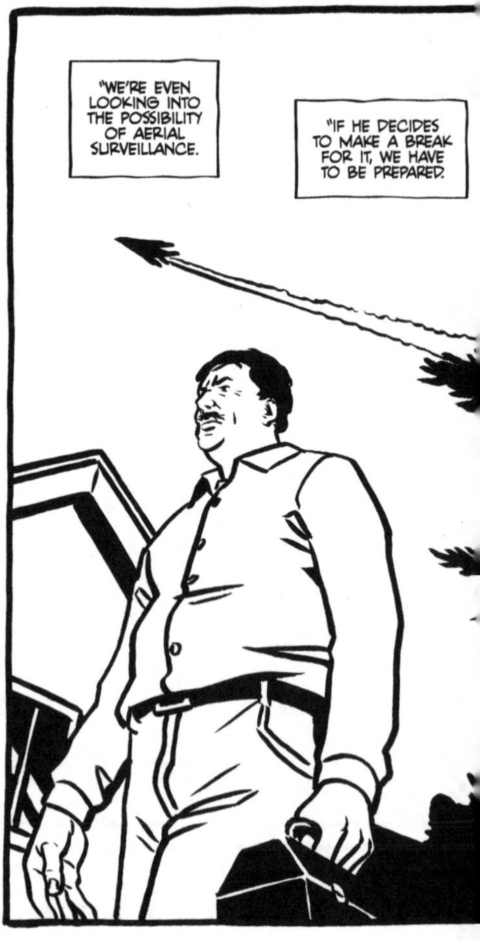
"WE'RE EVEN LOOKING INTO THE POSSIBILITY OF AERIAL SURVEILLANCE.
"IF HE DECIDES TO MAKE A BREAK FOR IT, WE HAVE TO BE PREPARED.

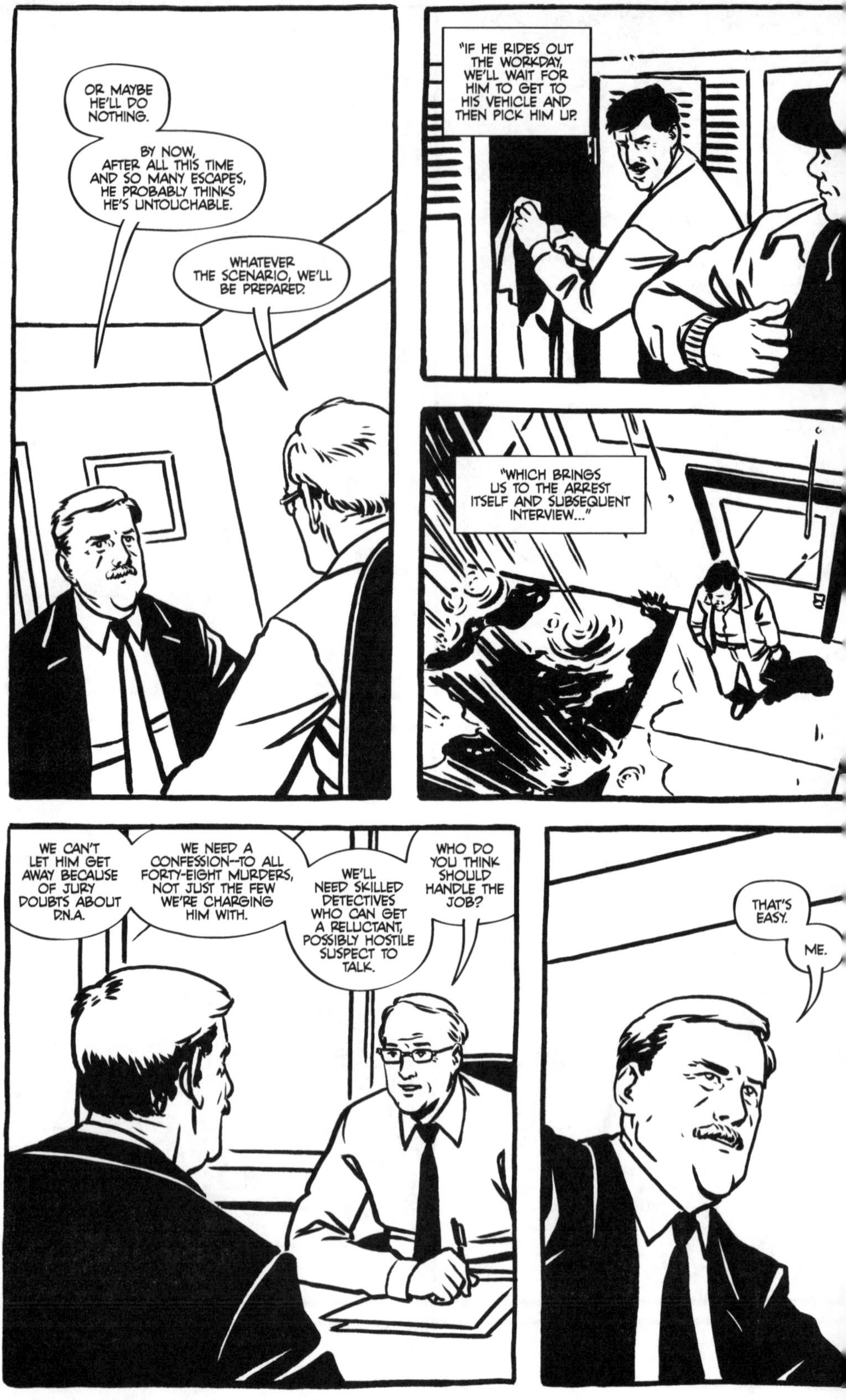

OR MAYBE HE'LL DO NOTHING.
BY NOW, AFTER ALL THIS TIME AND SO MANY ESCAPES, HE PROBABLY THINKS HE'S UNTOUCHABLE.
WHATEVER THE SCENARIO, WE'LL BE PREPARED.
"IF HE RIDES OUT THE WORKDAY, WE'LL WAIT FOR HIM TO GET TO HIS VEHICLE AND THEN PICK HIM UP.
"WHICH BRINGS US TO THE ARREST ITSELF AND SUBSEQUENT INTERVIEW..."
WE CAN'T LET HIM GET AWAY BECAUSE OF JURY DOUBTS ABOUT D.N.A.
WE NEED A CONFESSION--TO ALL FORTY-EIGHT MURDERS, NOT JUST THE FEW WE'RE CHARGING HIM WITH.
WE'LL NEED SKILLED DETECTIVES WHO CAN GET A RELUCTANT, POSSIBLY HOSTILE SUSPECT TO TALK.
WHO DO YOU THINK SHOULD HANDLE THE JOB?
THAT'S EASY.
ME.

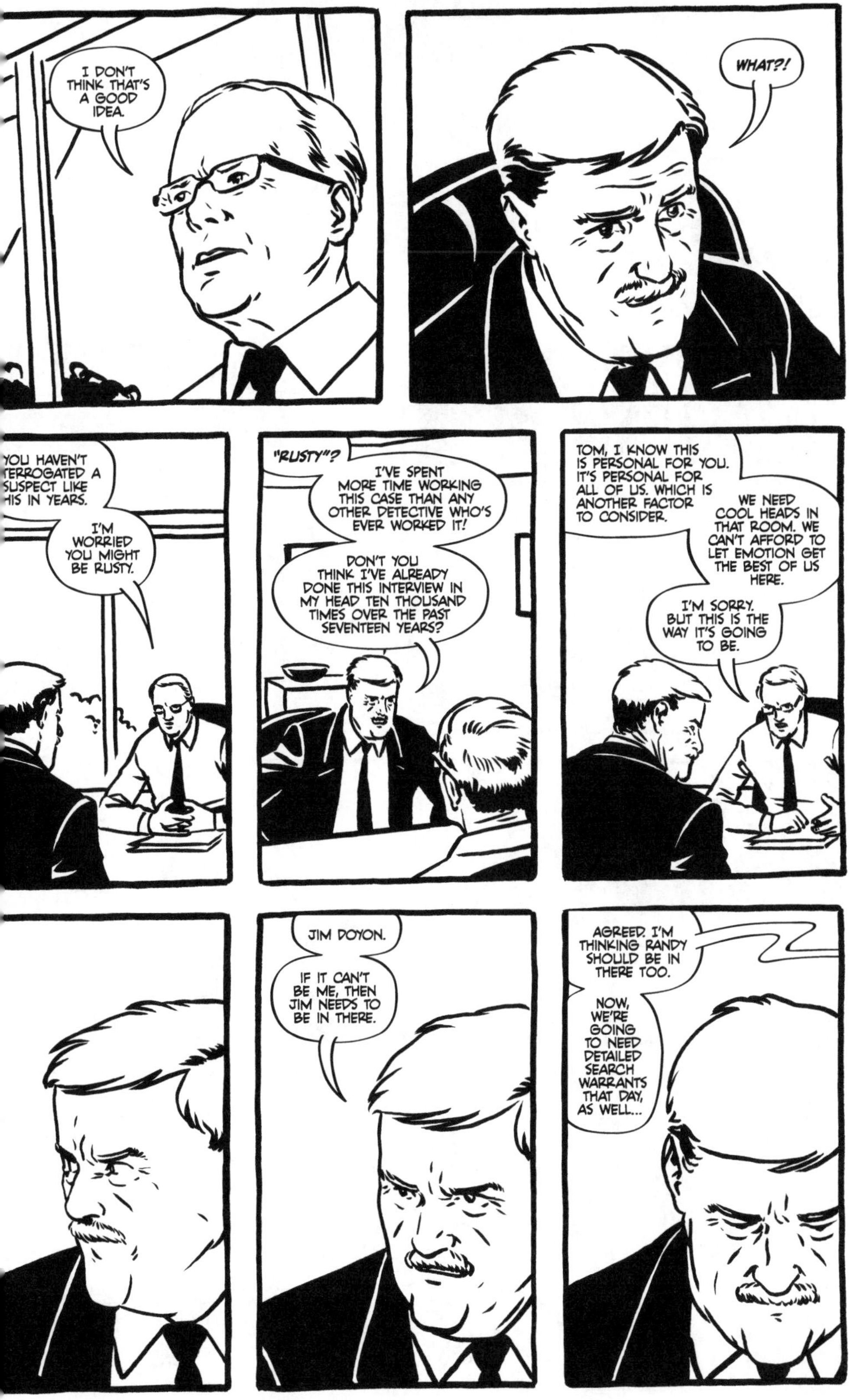
I DON'T THINK THAT'S A GOOD IDEA.
WHAT?!
YOU HAVEN'T TERROGATED A SUSPECT LIKE HIS IN YEARS.
I'M WORRIED YOU MIGHT BE RUSTY.
"RUSTY"?
I'VE SPENT MORE TIME WORKING THIS CASE THAN ANY OTHER DETECTIVE WHO'S EVER WORKED IT!
DON'T YOU THINK I'VE ALREADY DONE THIS INTERVIEW IN MY HEAD TEN THOUSAND TIMES OVER THE PAST SEVENTEEN YEARS?
TOM, I KNOW THIS IS PERSONAL FOR YOU. IT'S PERSONAL FOR ALL OF US. WHICH IS ANOTHER FACTOR TO CONSIDER.
WE NEED COOL HEADS IN THAT ROOM. WE CAN'T AFFORD TO LET EMOTION GET THE BEST OF US HERE.
I'M SORRY. BUT THIS IS THE WAY IT'S GOING TO BE.
JIM DOYON.
IF IT CAN'T BE ME, THEN JIM NEEDS TO BE IN THERE.
AGREED. I'M THINKING RANDY SHOULD BE IN THERE TOO.
NOW, WE'RE GOING TO NEED DETAILED SEARCH WARRANTS THAT DAY, AS WELL...

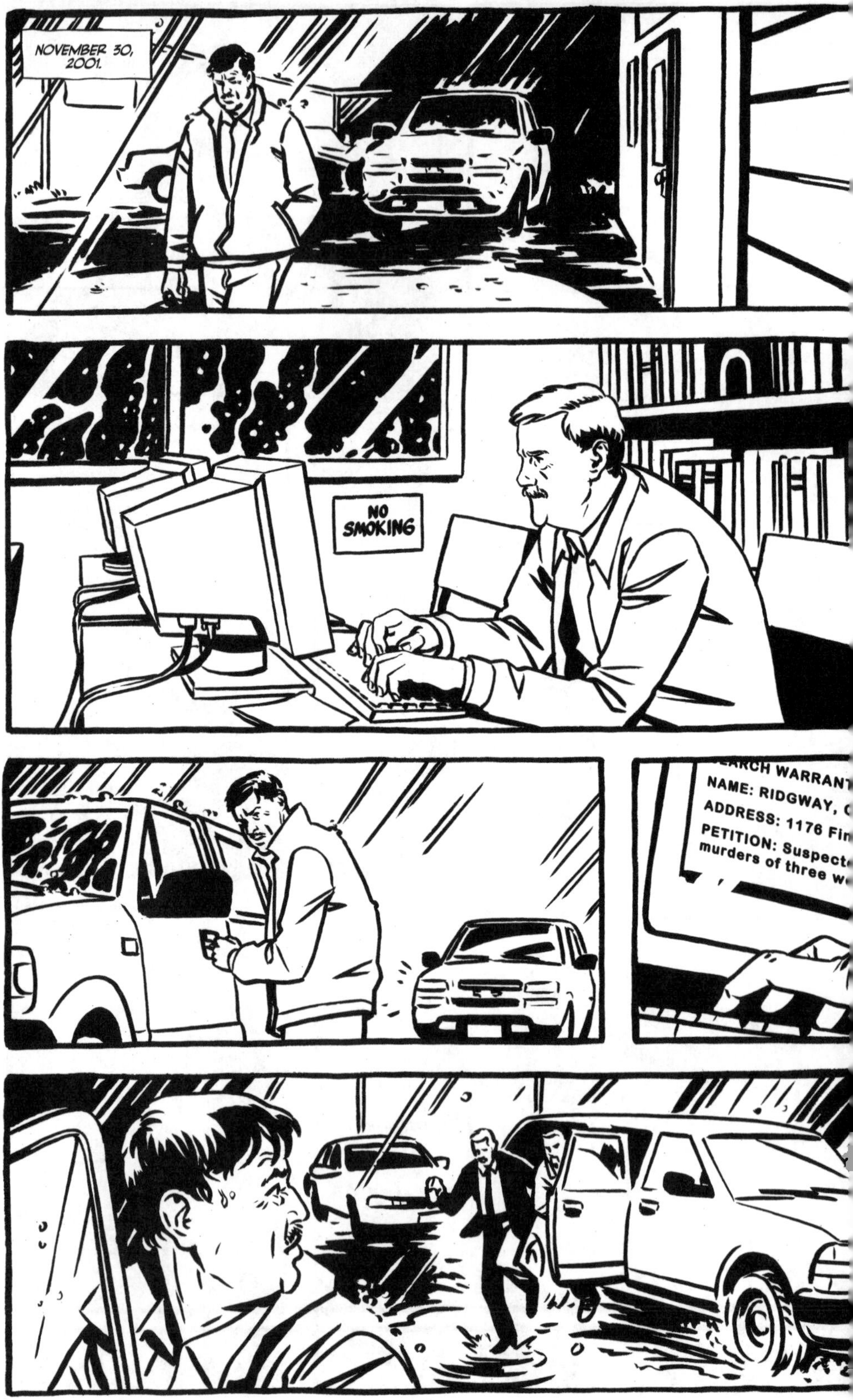
NOVEMBER 30, 2001.
NO SMOKING
WARRANT
NAME: RIDGWAY,
ADDRESS: 1176
PETITION: Suspect
murders of three

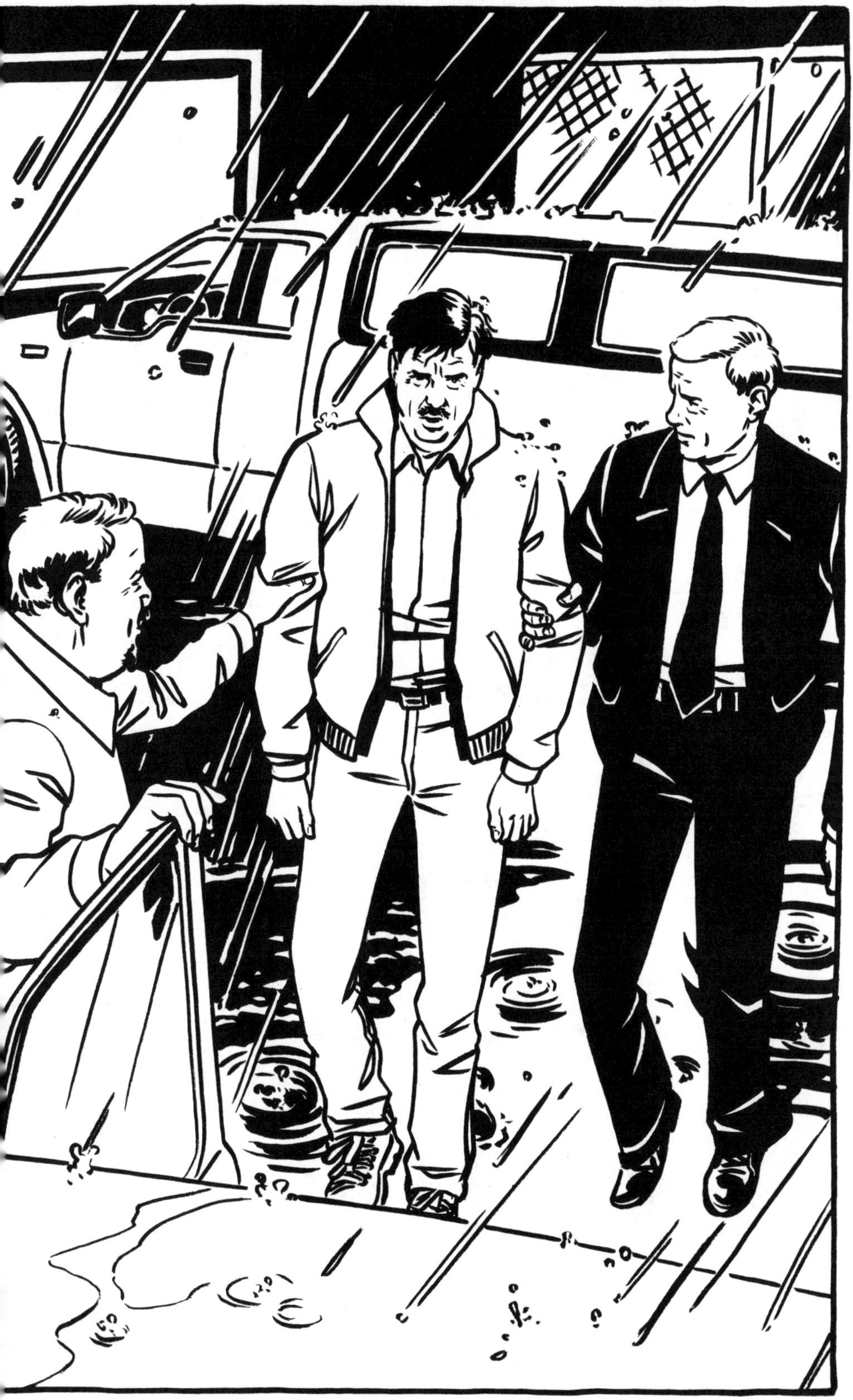

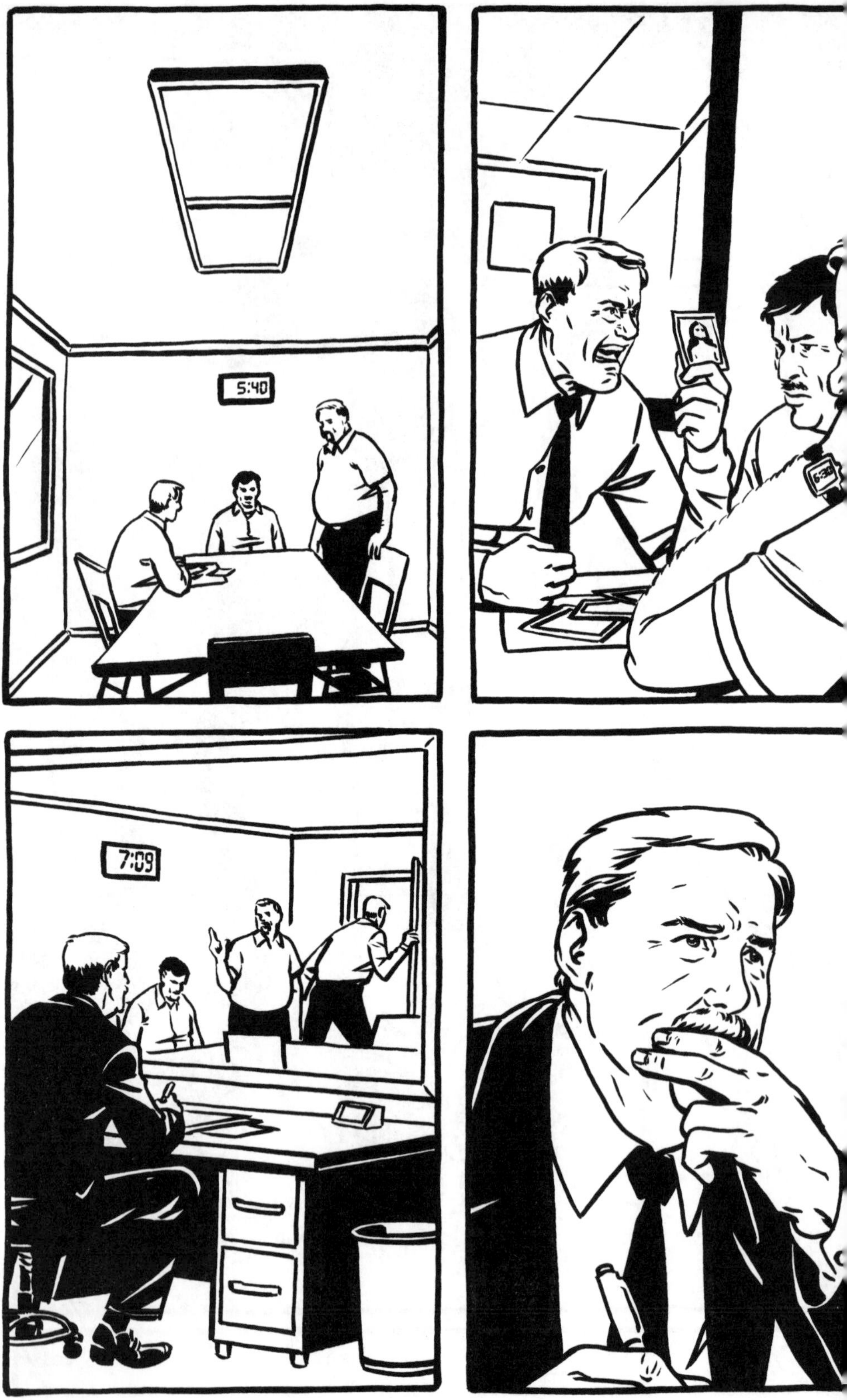
5:40
7:09

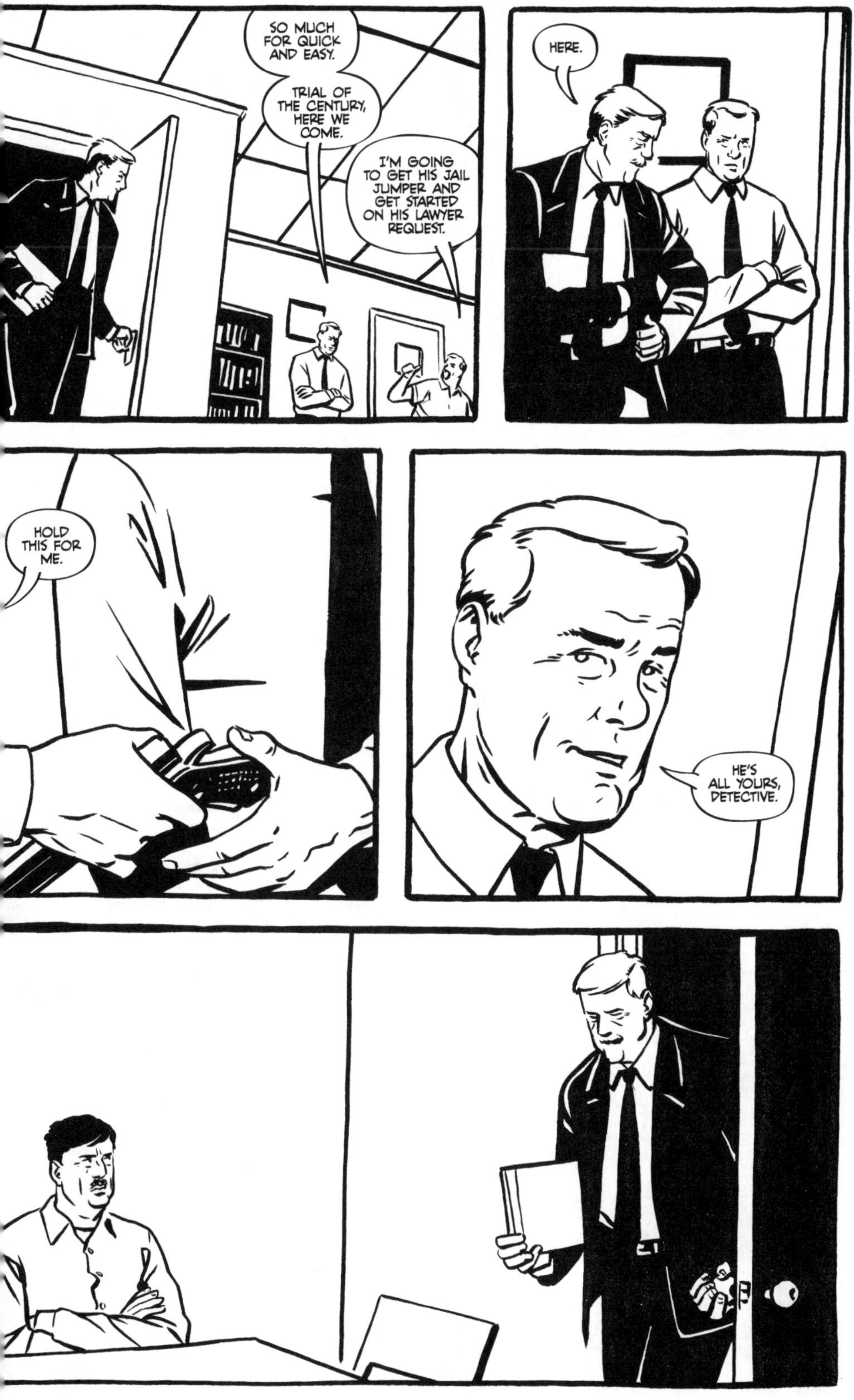
SO MUCH FOR QUICK AND EASY.
TRIAL OF THE CENTURY, HERE WE COME.
I'M GOING TO GET HIS JAIL JUMPER AND GET STARTED ON HIS LAWYER REQUEST.
HERE.
HOLD THIS FOR ME.
HE'S ALL YOURS, DETECTIVE.

DO YOU KNOW WHO I AM?

YES, I DO.

YOU'RE THE MAN LOOKING FOR THE GREEN RIVER KILLER.

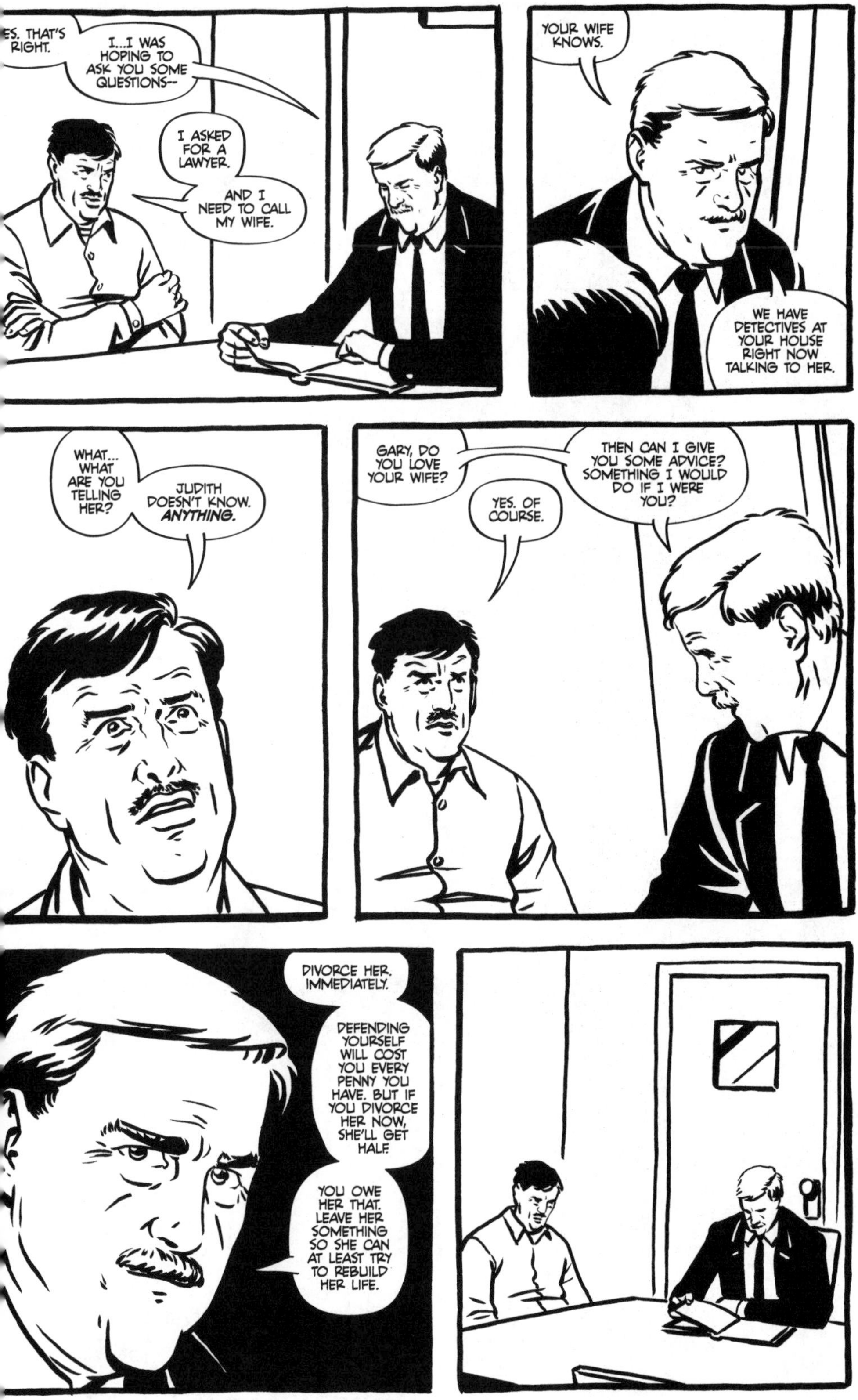

ES. THAT'S RIGHT.
I...I WAS HOPING TO ASK YOU SOME QUESTIONS--
I ASKED FOR A LAWYER.
AND I NEED TO CALL MY WIFE.
YOUR WIFE KNOWS.
WE HAVE DETECTIVES AT YOUR HOUSE RIGHT NOW TALKING TO HER.
WHAT... WHAT ARE YOU TELLING HER?
JUDITH DOESN'T KNOW. *ANYTHING.*
GARY, DO YOU LOVE YOUR WIFE?
YES. OF COURSE.
THEN CAN I GIVE YOU SOME ADVICE? SOMETHING I WOULD DO IF I WERE YOU?
DIVORCE HER. IMMEDIATELY.
DEFENDING YOURSELF WILL COST YOU EVERY PENNY YOU HAVE. BUT IF YOU DIVORCE HER NOW, SHE'LL GET HALF.
YOU OWE HER THAT. LEAVE HER SOMETHING SO SHE CAN AT LEAST TRY TO REBUILD HER LIFE.

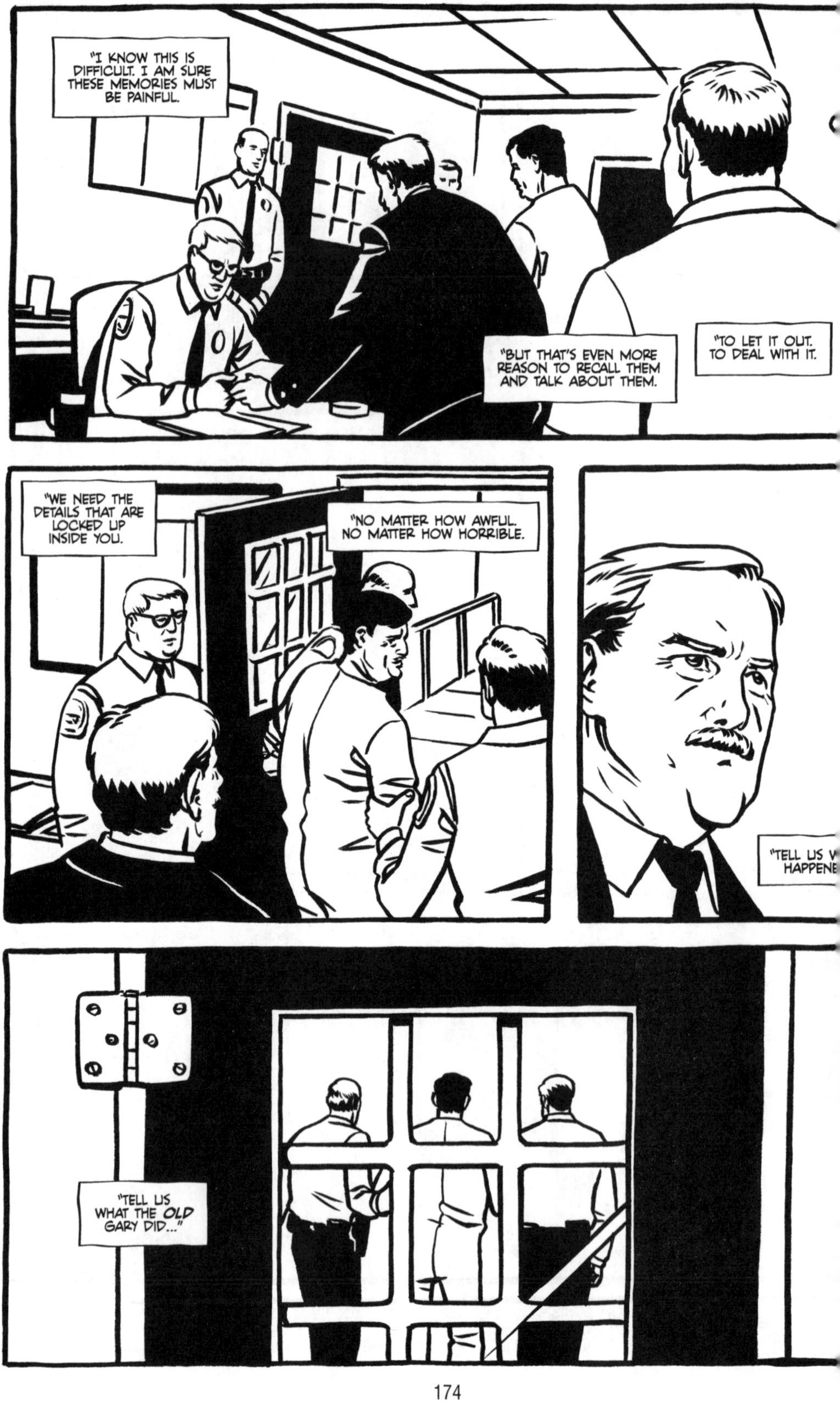
"I KNOW THIS IS DIFFICULT. I AM SURE THESE MEMORIES MUST BE PAINFUL.
"BUT THAT'S EVEN MORE REASON TO RECALL THEM AND TALK ABOUT THEM.
"TO LET IT OUT. TO DEAL WITH IT.
"WE NEED THE DETAILS THAT ARE LOCKED UP INSIDE YOU.
"NO MATTER HOW AWFUL. NO MATTER HOW HORRIBLE.
"TELL US W HAPPENE
"TELL US WHAT THE *OLD* GARY DID..."

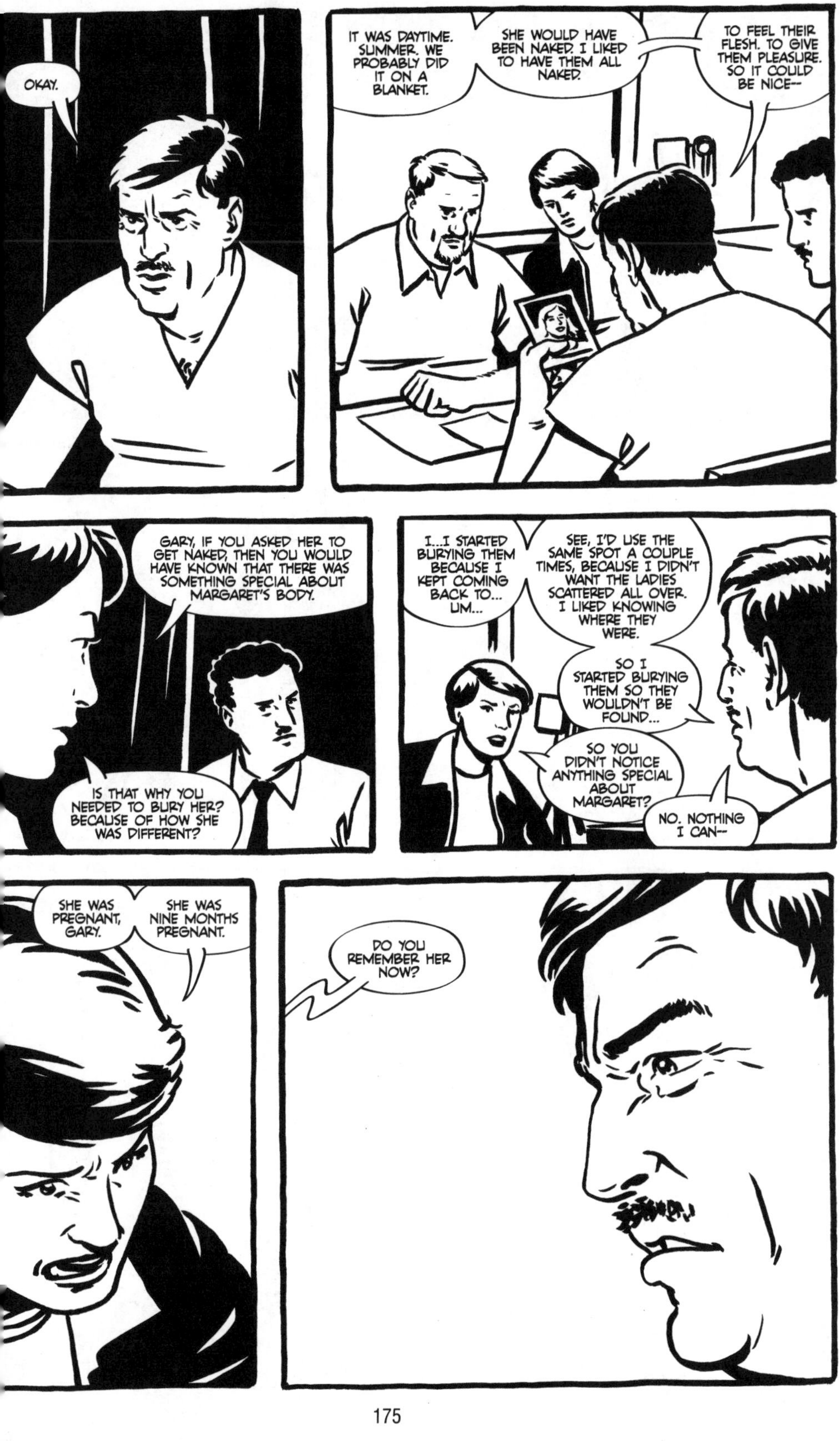
OKAY.
IT WAS DAYTIME. SUMMER. WE PROBABLY DID IT ON A BLANKET.
SHE WOULD HAVE BEEN NAKED. I LIKED TO HAVE THEM ALL NAKED.
TO FEEL THEIR FLESH. TO GIVE THEM PLEASURE. SO IT COULD BE NICE--
GARY, IF YOU ASKED HER TO GET NAKED, THEN YOU WOULD HAVE KNOWN THAT THERE WAS SOMETHING SPECIAL ABOUT MARGARET'S BODY.
IS THAT WHY YOU NEEDED TO BURY HER? BECAUSE OF HOW SHE WAS DIFFERENT?
I...I STARTED BURYING THEM BECAUSE I KEPT COMING BACK TO... UM...
SEE, I'D USE THE SAME SPOT A COUPLE TIMES, BECAUSE I DIDN'T WANT THE LADIES SCATTERED ALL OVER. I LIKED KNOWING WHERE THEY WERE.
SO I STARTED BURYING THEM SO THEY WOULDN'T BE FOUND...
SO YOU DIDN'T NOTICE ANYTHING SPECIAL ABOUT MARGARET?
NO. NOTHING I CAN--
SHE WAS PREGNANT, GARY.
SHE WAS NINE MONTHS PREGNANT.
DO YOU REMEMBER HER NOW?

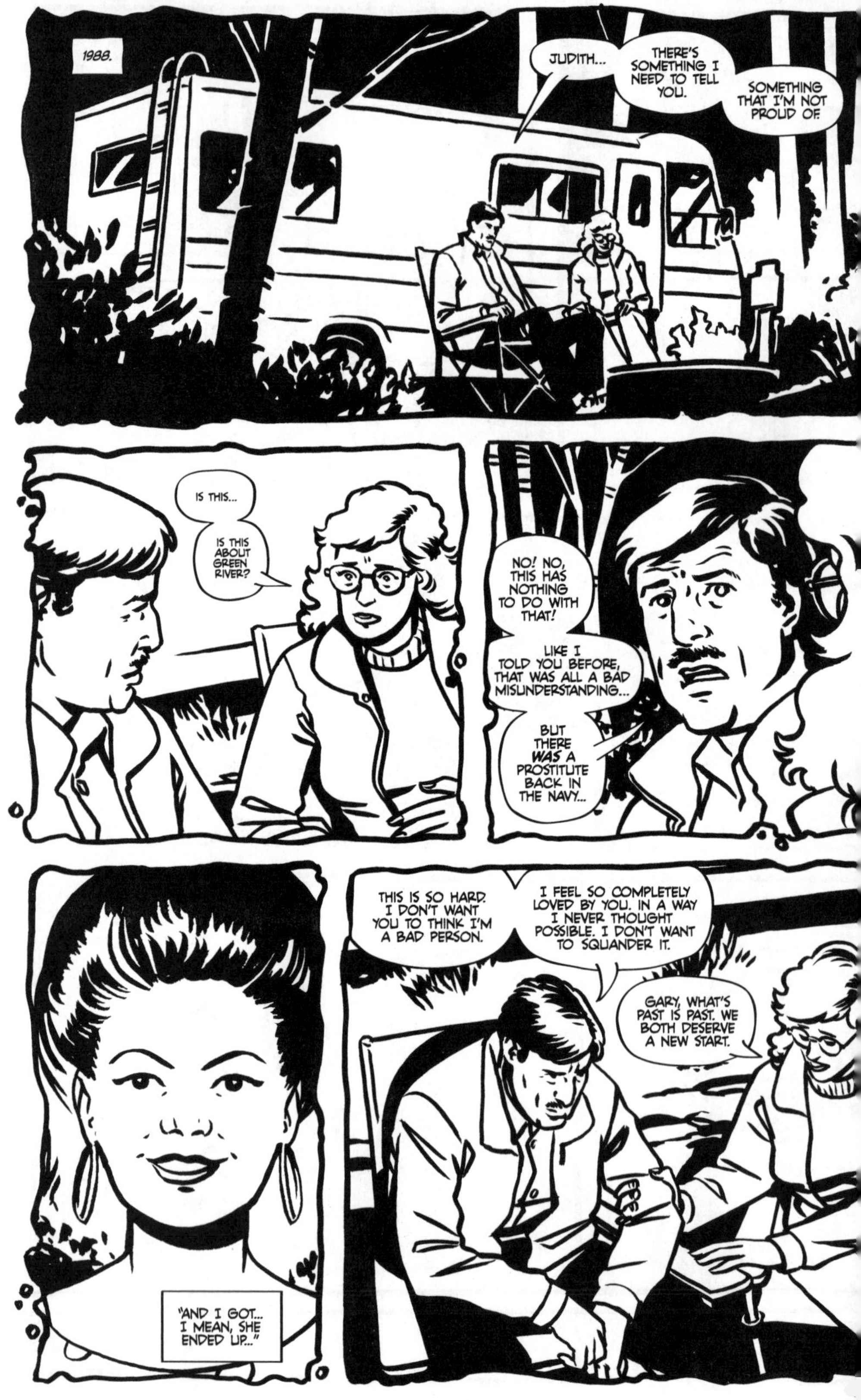
1988.
JUDITH...
THERE'S SOMETHING I NEED TO TELL YOU.
SOMETHING THAT I'M NOT PROUD OF.
IS THIS...
IS THIS ABOUT GREEN RIVER?
NO! NO, THIS HAS NOTHING TO DO WITH THAT!
LIKE I TOLD YOU BEFORE, THAT WAS ALL A BAD MISUNDERSTANDING...
BUT THERE WAS A PROSTITUTE BACK IN THE NAVY...
"AND I GOT... I MEAN, SHE ENDED UP..."
THIS IS SO HARD. I DON'T WANT YOU TO THINK I'M A BAD PERSON.
I FEEL SO COMPLETELY LOVED BY YOU. IN A WAY I NEVER THOUGHT POSSIBLE. I DON'T WANT TO SQUANDER IT.
GARY, WHAT'S PAST IS PAST. WE BOTH DESERVE A NEW START.

177

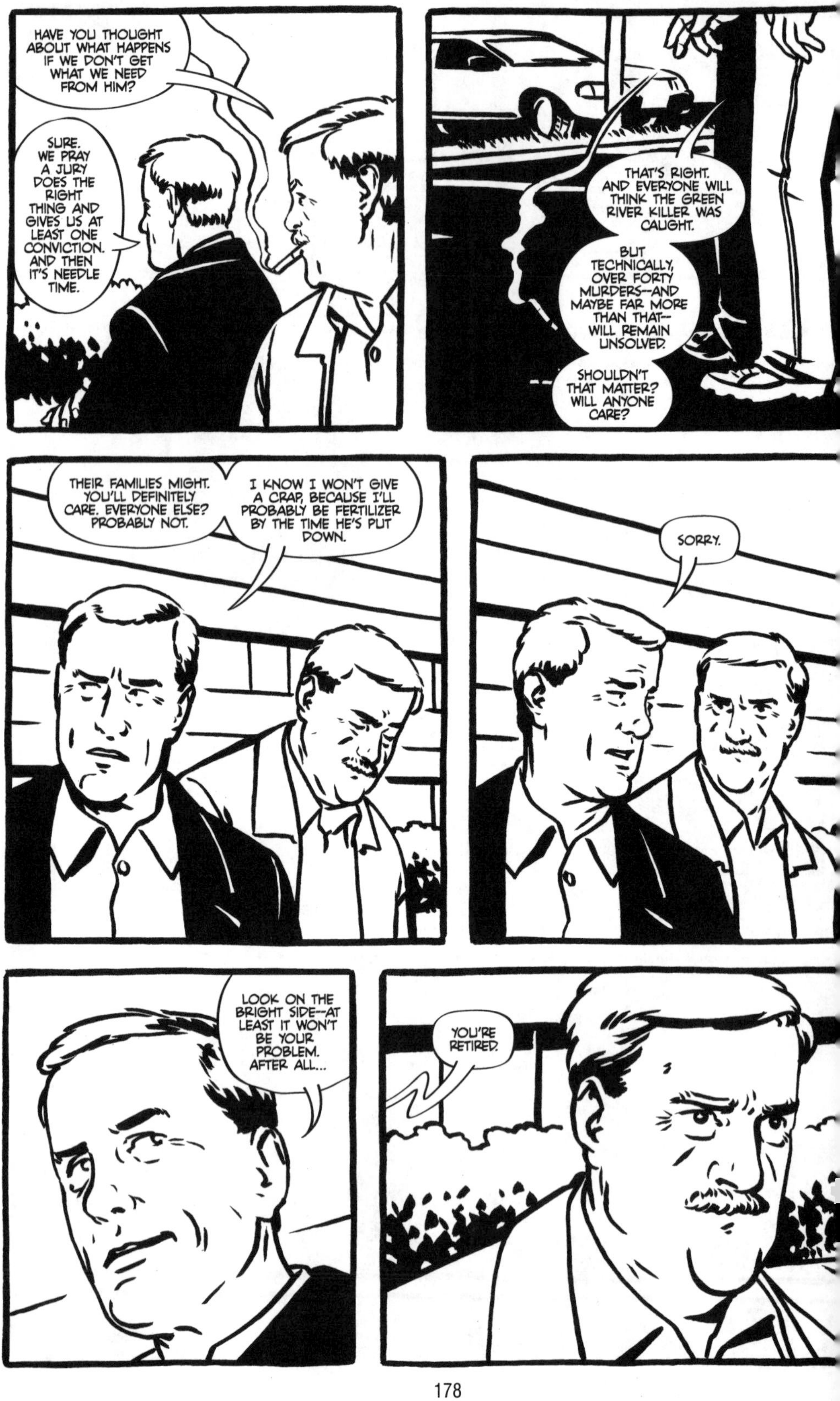
HAVE YOU THOUGHT ABOUT WHAT HAPPENS IF WE DON'T GET WHAT WE NEED FROM HIM?
SURE. WE PRAY A JURY DOES THE RIGHT THING AND GIVES US AT LEAST ONE CONVICTION. AND THEN IT'S NEEDLE TIME.
THAT'S RIGHT. AND EVERYONE WILL THINK THE GREEN RIVER KILLER WAS CAUGHT.
BUT TECHNICALLY, OVER FORTY MURDERS--AND MAYBE FAR MORE THAN THAT--WILL REMAIN UNSOLVED.
SHOULDN'T THAT MATTER? WILL ANYONE CARE?
THEIR FAMILIES MIGHT. YOU'LL DEFINITELY CARE. EVERYONE ELSE? PROBABLY NOT.
I KNOW I WON'T GIVE A CRAP, BECAUSE I'LL PROBABLY BE FERTILIZER BY THE TIME HE'S PUT DOWN.
SORRY.
LOOK ON THE BRIGHT SIDE--AT LEAST IT WON'T BE YOUR PROBLEM. AFTER ALL...
YOU'RE RETIRED.

DAY FIVE: THE DETECTIVE

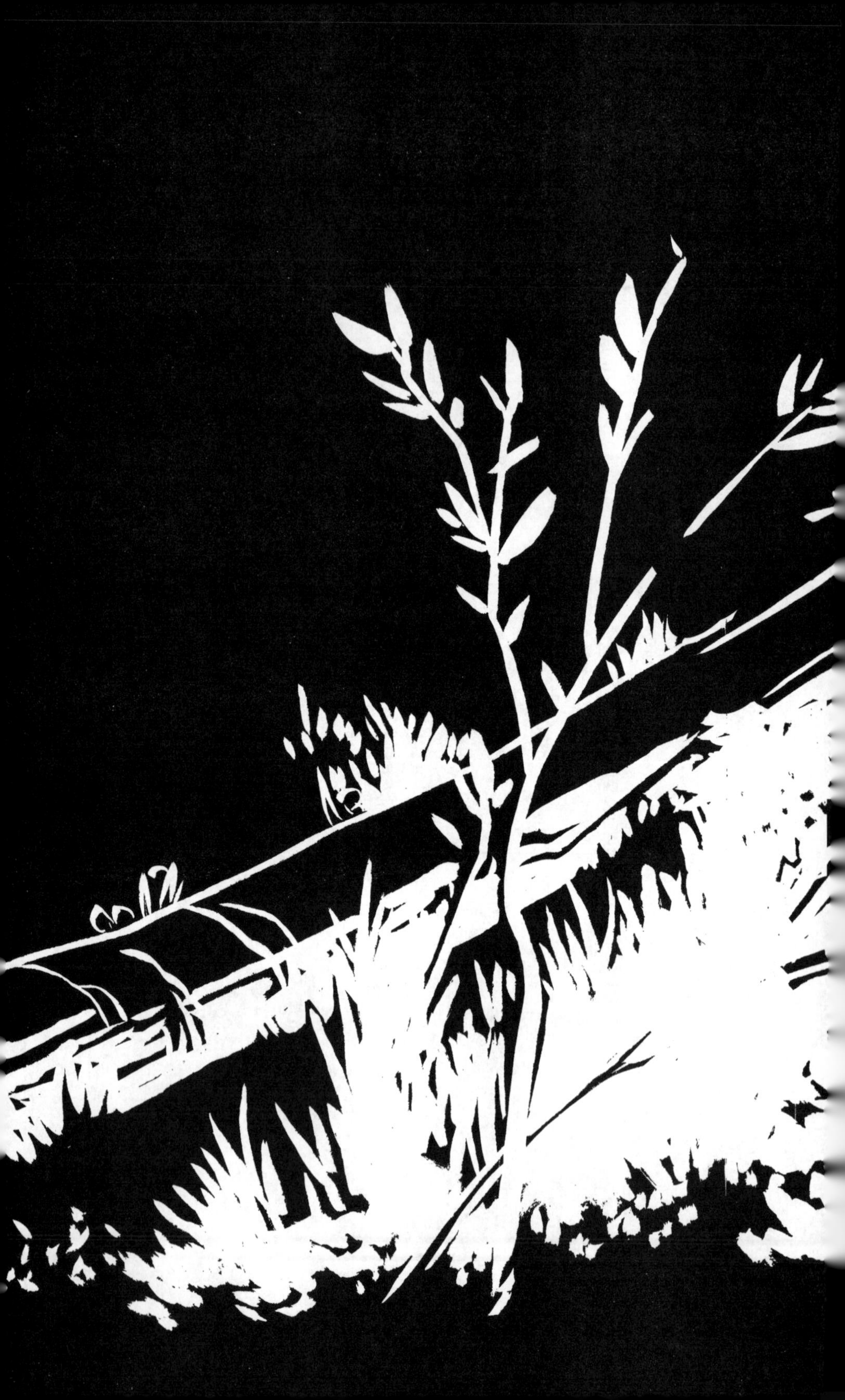

FORE WE
... DETECTIVE,
ME JUST
SAY...

I
APPRECIATE
THAT...

CONGRATULATIONS
ON CATCHING THE
GREEN RIVER KILLER.

REQUEST FOR RETIREMENT
Date: MARCH 25, 2003
Name: Thomas Richard Jensen

BUT TECHNICALLY
SPEAKING, IT WAS
SCIENCE THAT
CAUGHT GARY
RIDGWAY.

I MERELY
HELPED THE
PROCESS.

REQUEST FOR RETIREMENT
Date: MARCH 25, 2003
Name: Thomas Richard Jensen

WHATEVER
YOU'RE CALLING IT—
CONGRATULATIONS.

I NEED
YOUR BADGE
AND YOUR
GUN.

THOMAS
RICHARD JENSEN,
YOU ARE HEREBY
RELIEVED OF DUTY.
THE KING COUNTY
SHERIFF'S DEPARTMENT
THANKS YOU FOR
THIRTY YEARS OF
DISTINGUISHED
SERVICE.

NOW,
REGARDING
YOUR APPLICATION
FOR CIVILIAN
EMPLOYMENT...

...TOAST TO A [KI]NDA-SORTA [A]CTIVE ON HIS [KI]NDA-SORTA [R]ETIREMENT.

YOU HAVE A LOT OF TO BE THANKFUL FOR IN YOUR OLD AGE...

A WIFE AND KIDS WHO STILL LIKE YOU.

GRANDCHILDREN WHO DON'T THINK YOUR MOUSTACHE IS SCARY.

A SMOKING HABIT THAT SOMEHOW, SOMEWAY HASN'T KILLED YOU. *YET.*

AND OF COURSE, THE WHOLE CATCHING-A-SERIAL-KILLER, SENSE-OF-ACCOMPLISHMENT THING.

L'CHAIM. OR SOMETHING.

OR SOMETHING.

The Seattle Examiner

Prosecutors Charge Green River Suspect With More Murders

New evidence links Gary Leon Ridgway to three additional

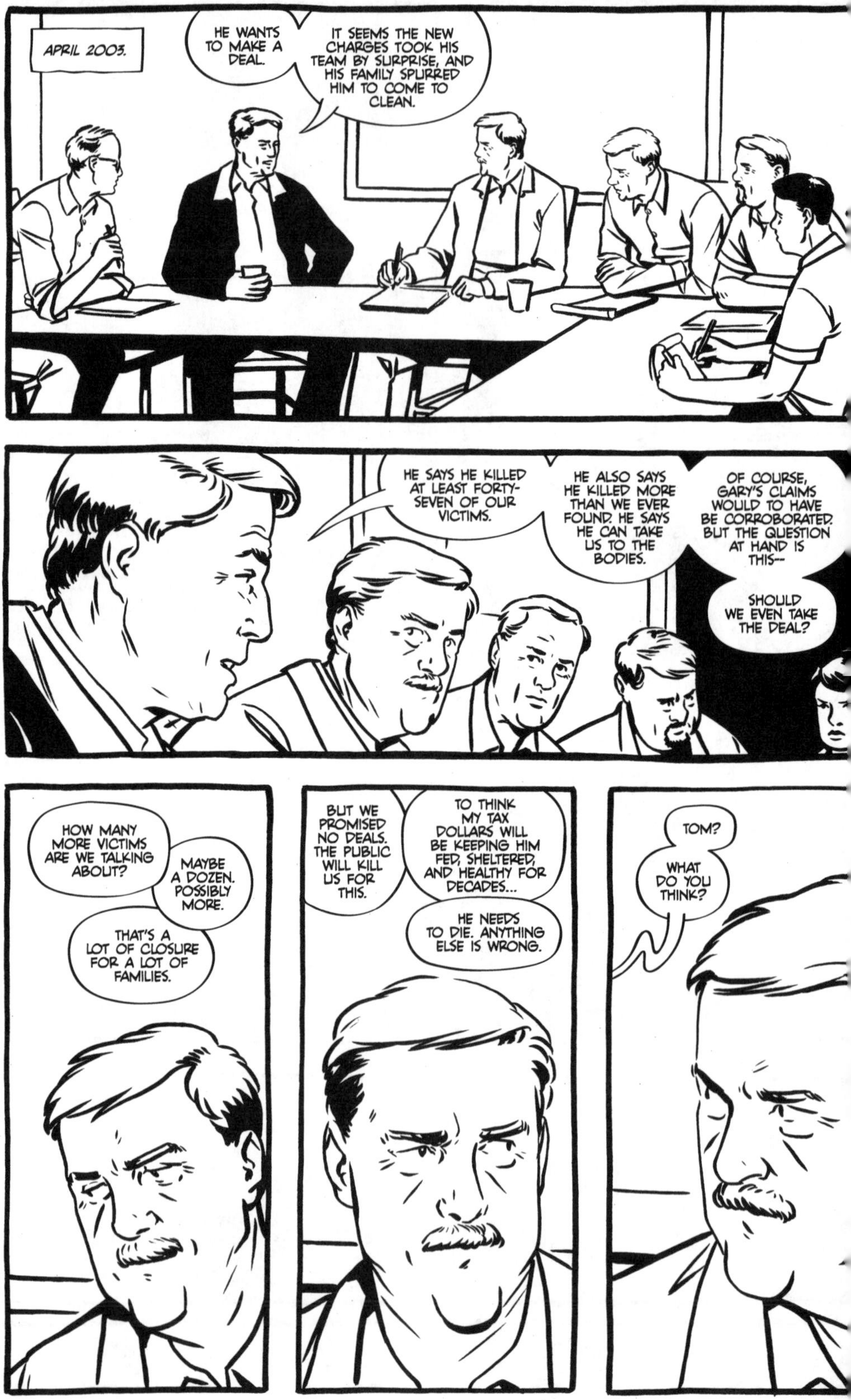
APRIL 2003.
HE WANTS TO MAKE A DEAL.
IT SEEMS THE NEW CHARGES TOOK HIS TEAM BY SURPRISE, AND HIS FAMILY SPURRED HIM TO COME TO CLEAN.
HE SAYS HE KILLED AT LEAST FORTY-SEVEN OF OUR VICTIMS.
HE ALSO SAYS HE KILLED MORE THAN WE EVER FOUND. HE SAYS HE CAN TAKE US TO THE BODIES.
OF COURSE, GARY'S CLAIMS WOULD TO HAVE BE CORROBORATED. BUT THE QUESTION AT HAND IS THIS--
SHOULD WE EVEN TAKE THE DEAL?
HOW MANY MORE VICTIMS ARE WE TALKING ABOUT?
MAYBE A DOZEN. POSSIBLY MORE.
THAT'S A LOT OF CLOSURE FOR A LOT OF FAMILIES.
BUT WE PROMISED NO DEALS. THE PUBLIC WILL KILL US FOR THIS.
TO THINK MY TAX DOLLARS WILL BE KEEPING HIM FED, SHELTERED, AND HEALTHY FOR DECADES...
HE NEEDS TO DIE. ANYTHING ELSE IS WRONG.
TOM?
WHAT DO YOU THINK?

DO YOU KNOW HOW MANY SUSPECTS I HAVE IN THAT DATABASE ON MY DESK?

ALMOST *TEN THOUSAND.*

TEN THOUSAND FALSELY ACCUSED PEOPLE. NAMED BY TEN THOUSAND OTHER PEOPLE WHO BELIEVED THEM CAPABLE OF MURDER.

EVERYONE WHO'S BEEN TOUCHED BY THIS MADNESS DESERVES ANSWERS.

AND THE ONLY WAY WE'LL GET IT IS IF EVERY SINGLE VICTIM IS ACCOUNTED FOR.

POSSIBLY SIXTY VICTIMS?

JESUS.

185

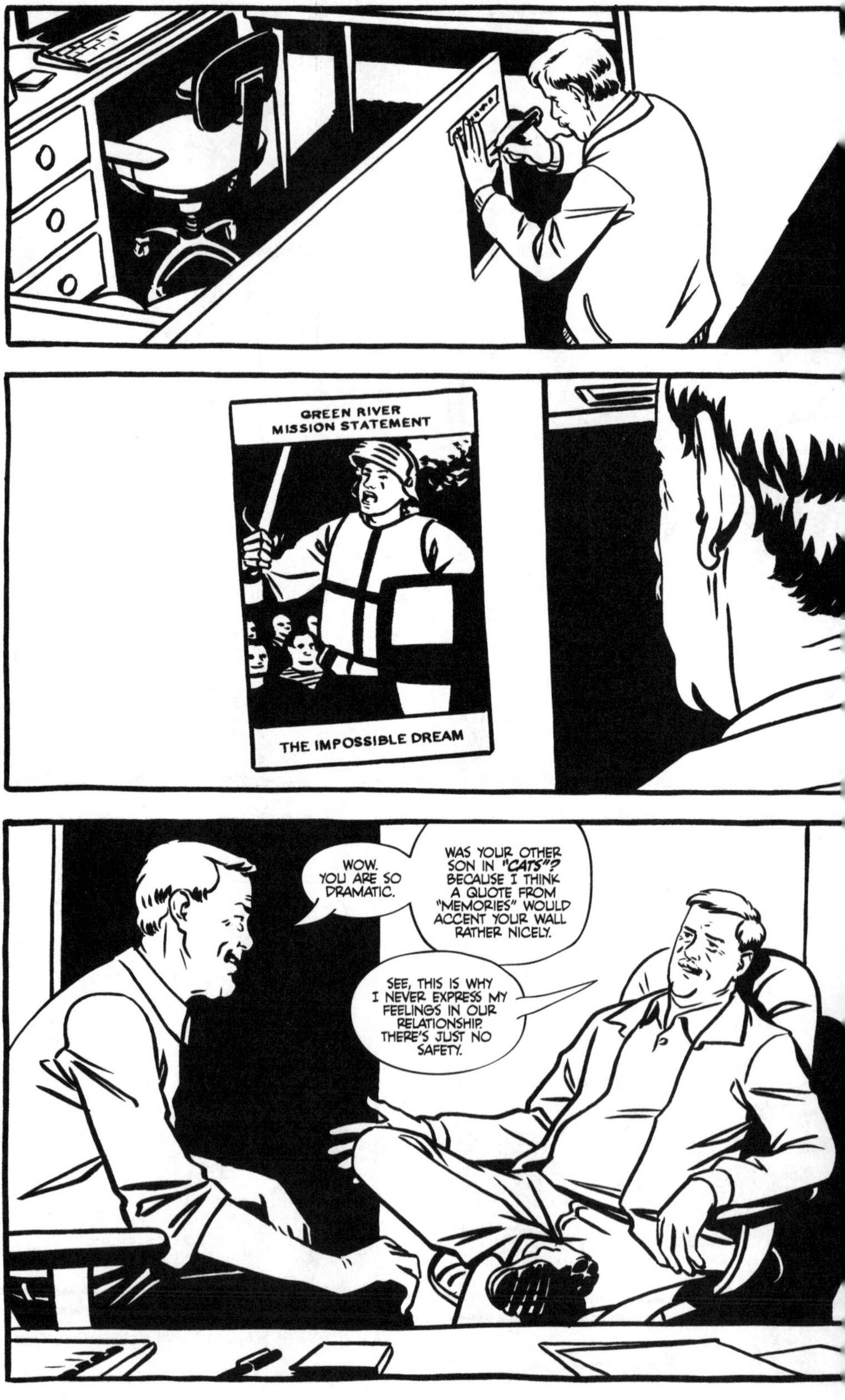
GREEN RIVER
MISSION STATEMENT
THE IMPOSSIBLE DREAM
WOW. YOU ARE SO DRAMATIC.
WAS YOUR OTHER SON IN "CATS"? BECAUSE I THINK A QUOTE FROM "MEMORIES" WOULD ACCENT YOUR WALL RATHER NICELY.
SEE, THIS IS WHY I NEVER EXPRESS MY FEELINGS IN OUR RELATIONSHIP. THERE'S JUST NO SAFETY.

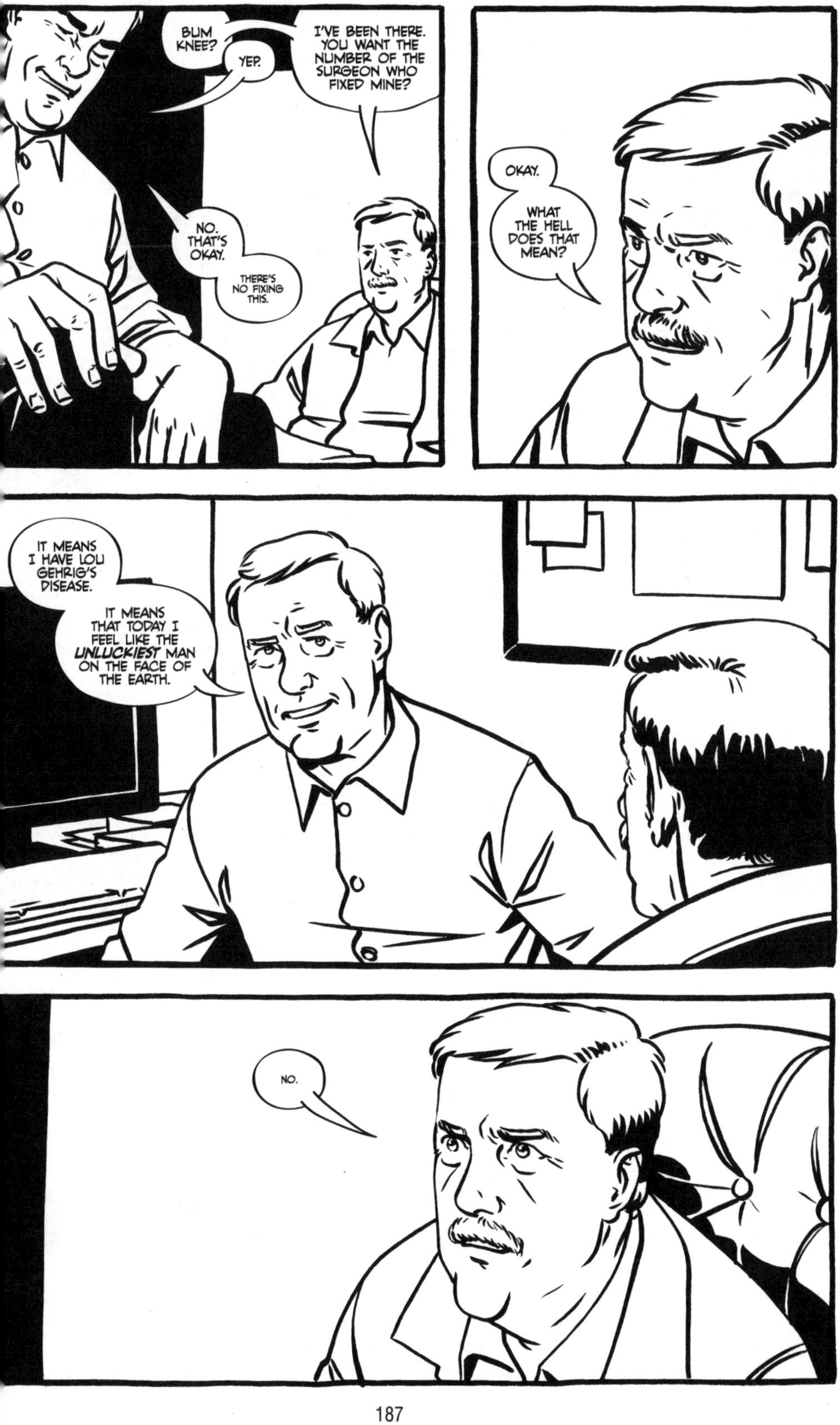
BUM KNEE?
YEP.
I'VE BEEN THERE. YOU WANT THE NUMBER OF THE SURGEON WHO FIXED MINE?
NO. THAT'S OKAY.
THERE'S NO FIXING THIS.
OKAY.
WHAT THE HELL DOES THAT MEAN?
IT MEANS I HAVE LOU GEHRIG'S DISEASE.
IT MEANS THAT TODAY I FEEL LIKE THE UNLUCKIEST MAN ON THE FACE OF THE EARTH.
NO.

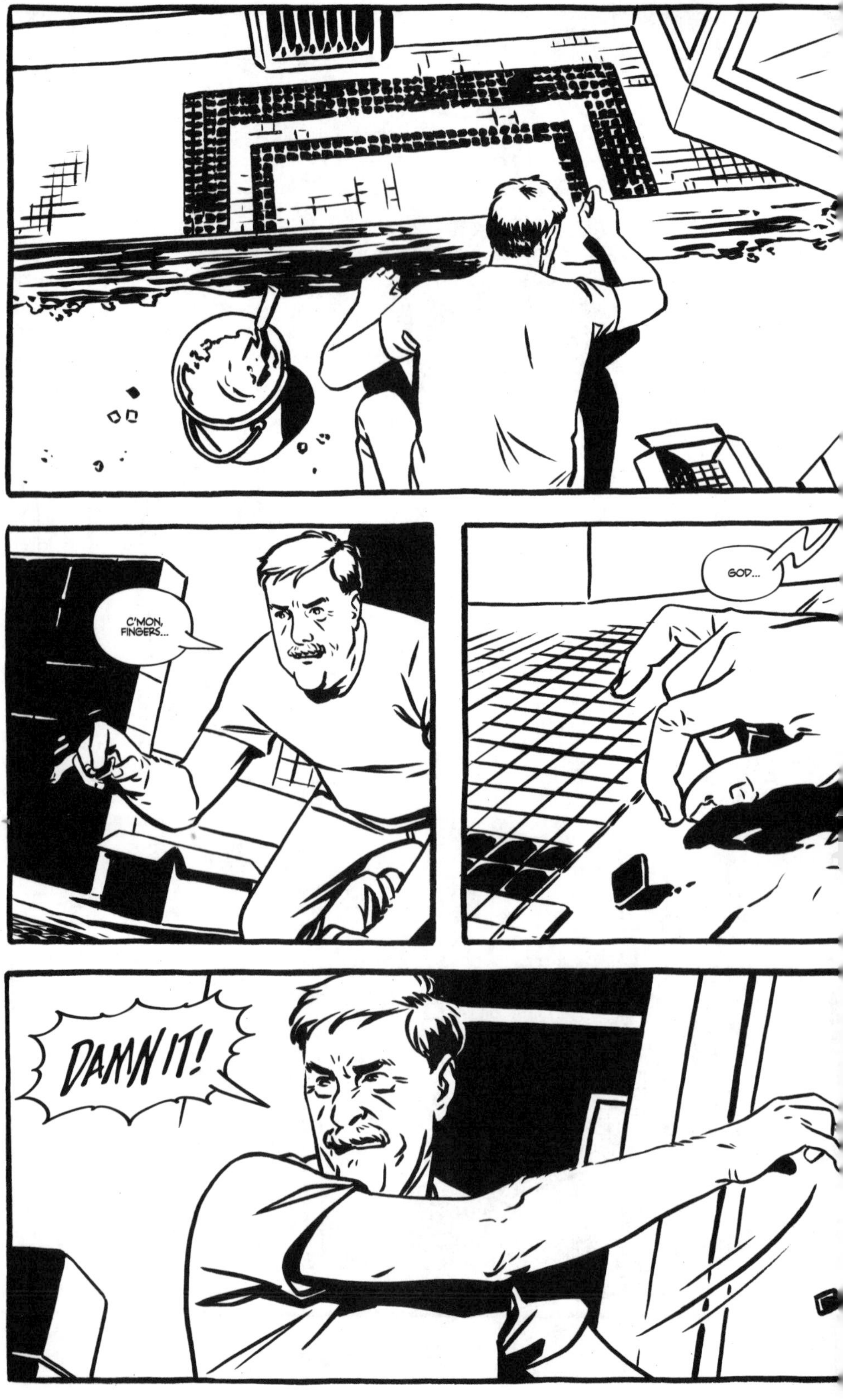
C'MON, FINGERS...
GOD...
DAMN IT!

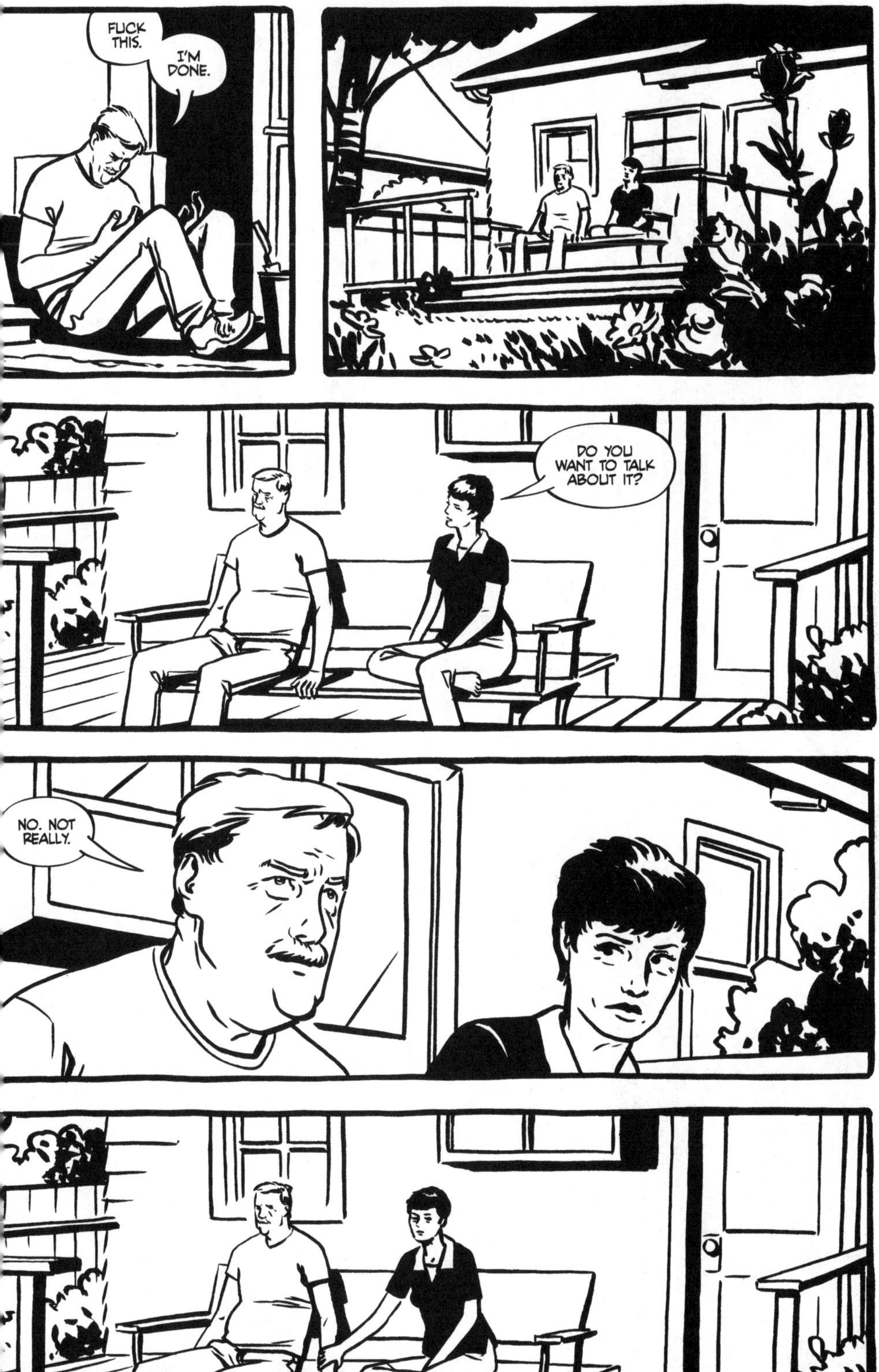
FUCK THIS.
I'M DONE.
DO YOU WANT TO TALK ABOUT IT?
NO. NOT REALLY.

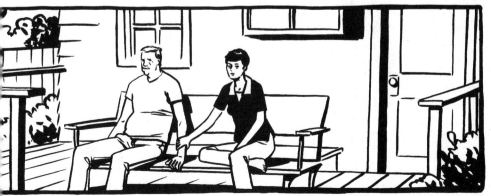

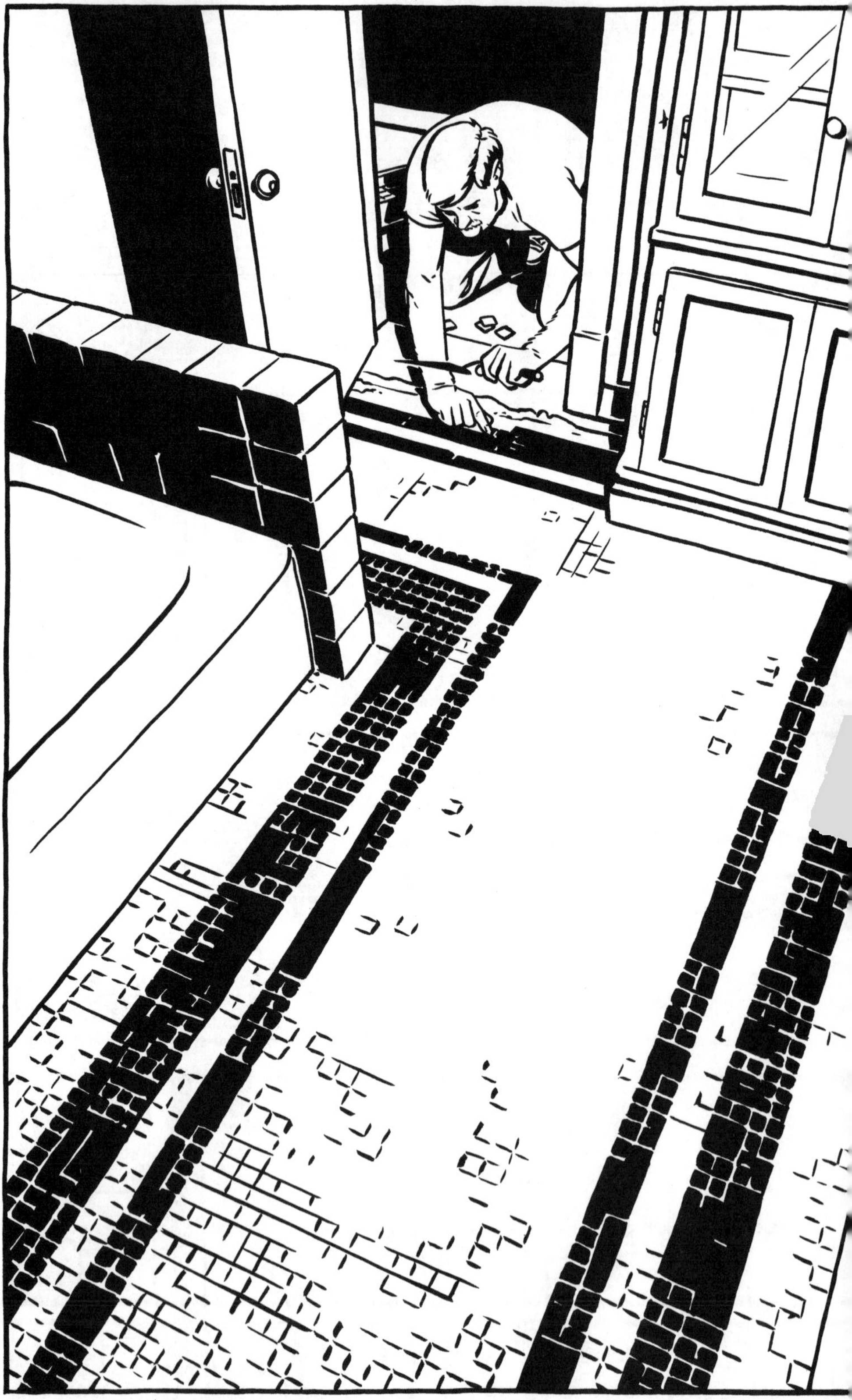

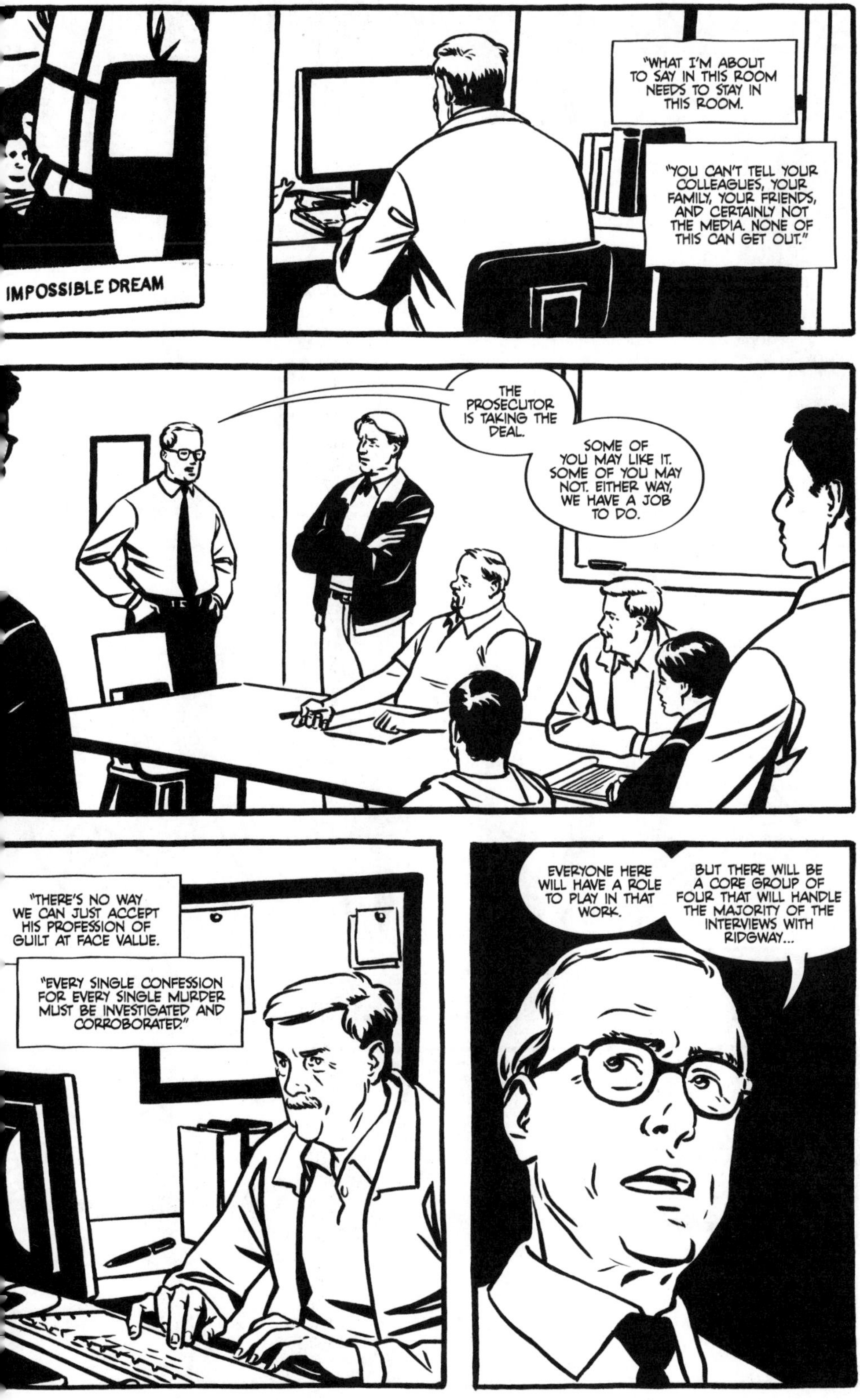
IMPOSSIBLE DREAM
"WHAT I'M ABOUT TO SAY IN THIS ROOM NEEDS TO STAY IN THIS ROOM.
"YOU CAN'T TELL YOUR COLLEAGUES, YOUR FAMILY, YOUR FRIENDS, AND CERTAINLY NOT THE MEDIA. NONE OF THIS CAN GET OUT."
THE PROSECUTOR IS TAKING THE DEAL.
SOME OF YOU MAY LIKE IT. SOME OF YOU MAY NOT. EITHER WAY, WE HAVE A JOB TO DO.
"THERE'S NO WAY WE CAN JUST ACCEPT HIS PROFESSION OF GUILT AT FACE VALUE.
"EVERY SINGLE CONFESSION FOR EVERY SINGLE MURDER MUST BE INVESTIGATED AND CORROBORATED."
EVERYONE HERE WILL HAVE A ROLE TO PLAY IN THAT WORK.
BUT THERE WILL BE A CORE GROUP OF FOUR THAT WILL HANDLE THE MAJORITY OF THE INTERVIEWS WITH RIDGWAY...

196

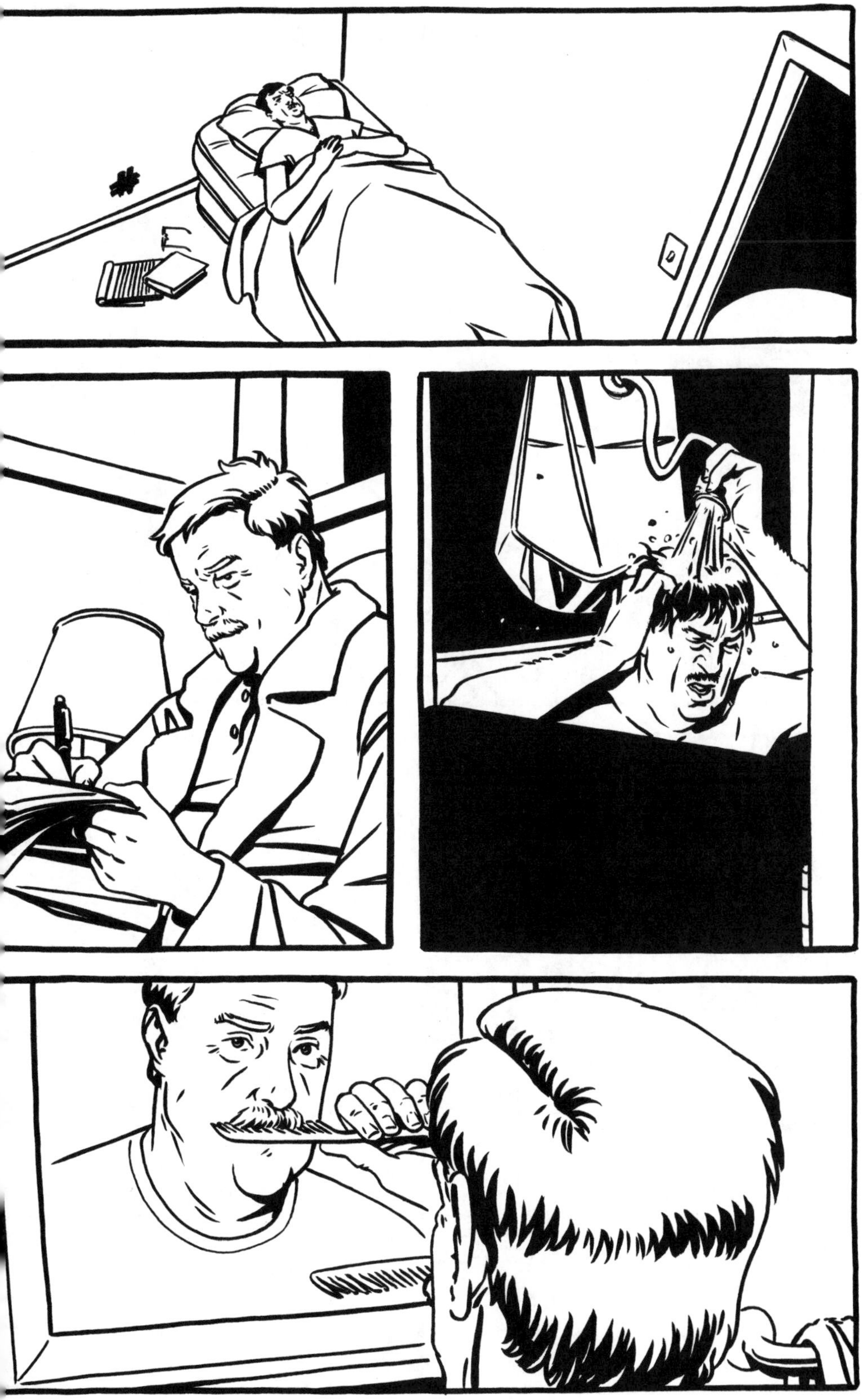

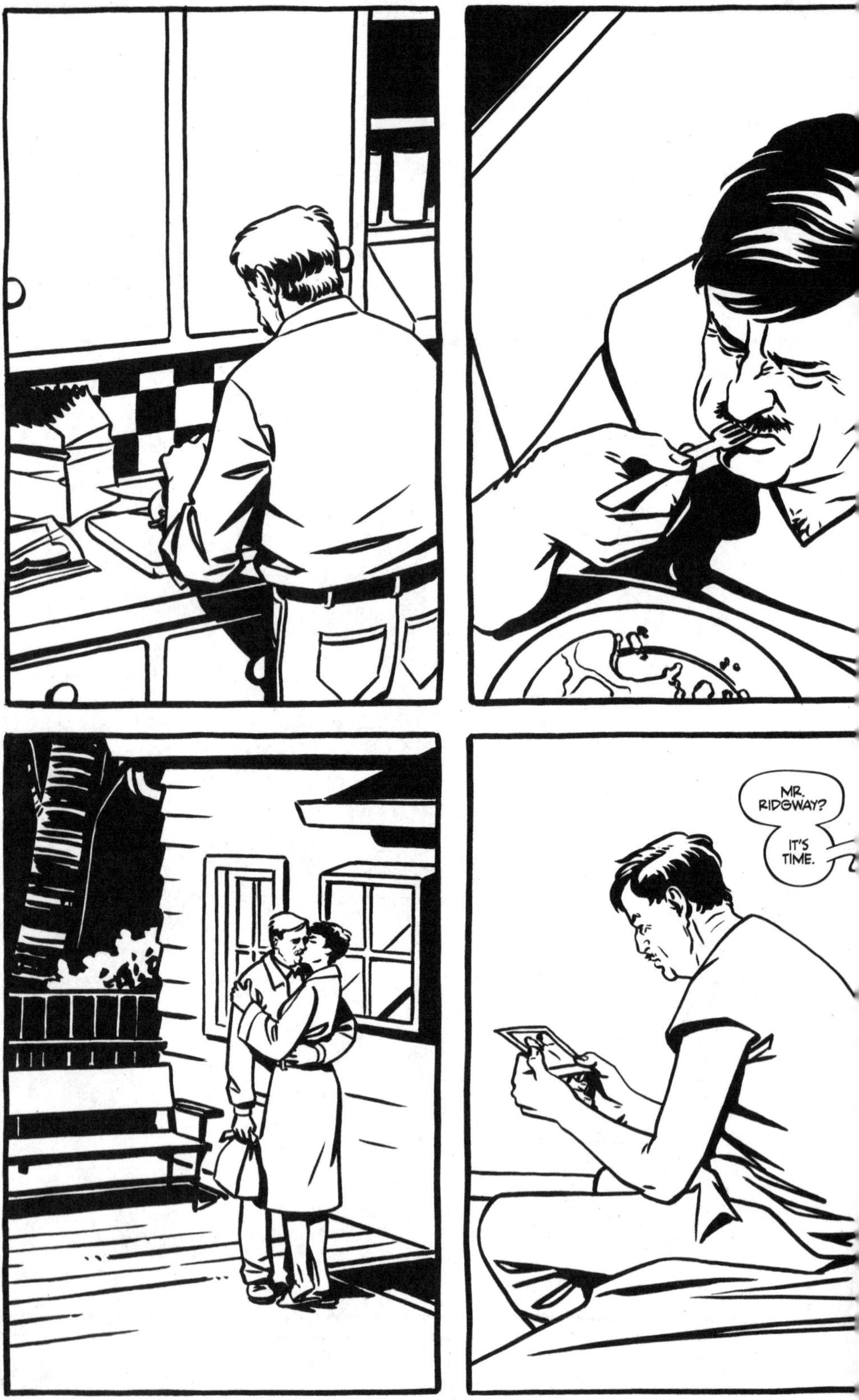
MR. RIDGWAY?
IT'S TIME.

GARY'S ON THE MOVE.

READY TO ROLL?

I AM NOW.

OKAY.

WHAT'S THE DEAL WITH THE SHERLOCK HOLMES QUOTES?

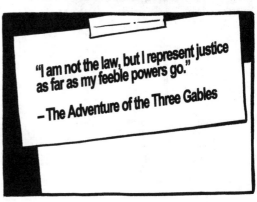

"I am not the law, but I represent justice as far as my feeble powers go."

– The Adventure of the Three Gables

...OT INTO HOLMES ...N AFTER JOINING ...SHERIFF'S ...RTMENT--WHILE ...S STUDYING ...ECOME A ...CTIVE.

I FIGURED IF I WANTED TO BE A GOOD ONE, I BETTER LEARN FROM THE BEST.

IT ALSO HELPED PASS THE TIME DURING SOME SERIOUSLY DULL GRAVEYARD SHIFTS.

GOD, I HATED PATROL...

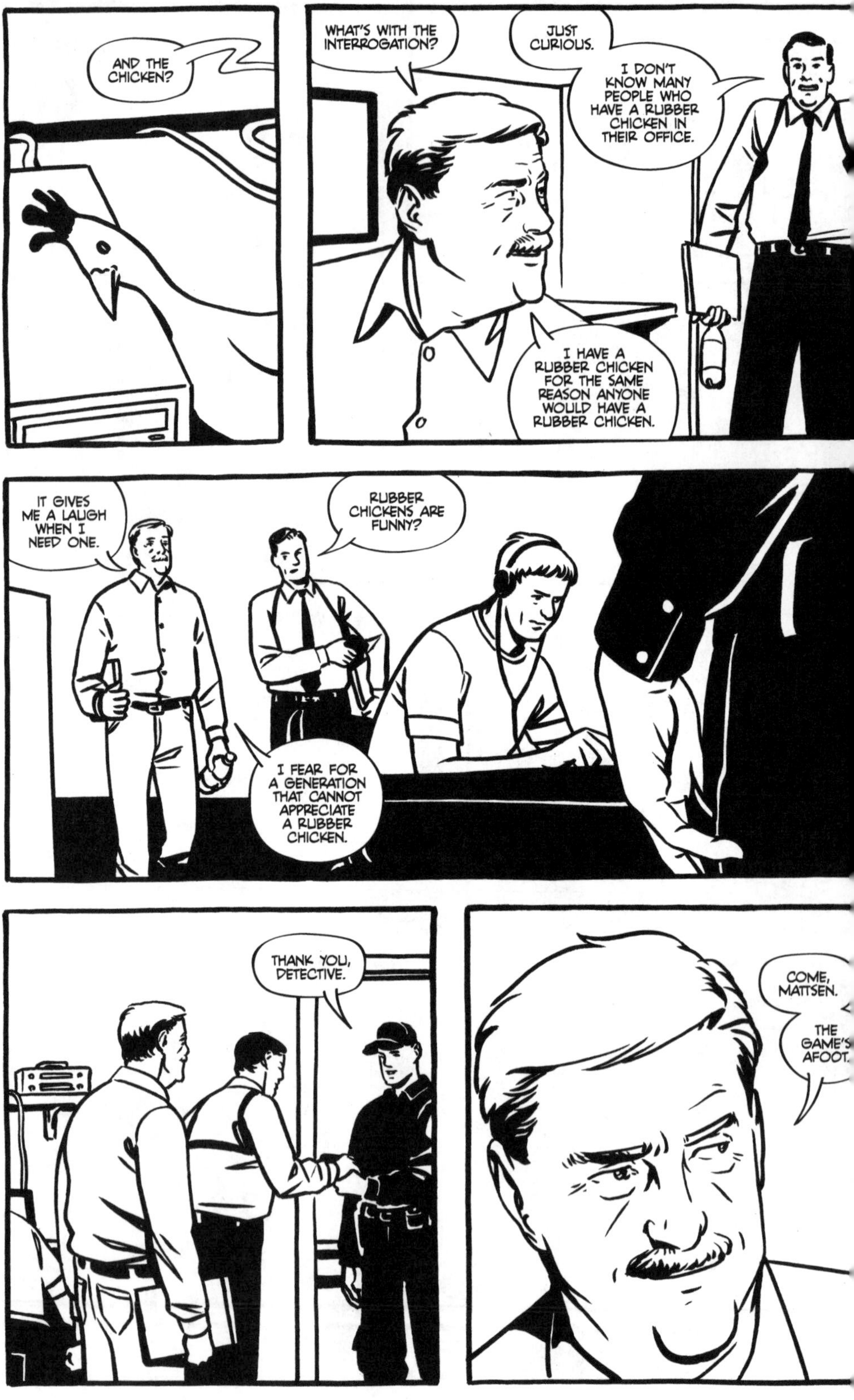
AND THE CHICKEN?
WHAT'S WITH THE INTERROGATION?
JUST CURIOUS.
I DON'T KNOW MANY PEOPLE WHO HAVE A RUBBER CHICKEN IN THEIR OFFICE.
I HAVE A RUBBER CHICKEN FOR THE SAME REASON ANYONE WOULD HAVE A RUBBER CHICKEN.
IT GIVES ME A LAUGH WHEN I NEED ONE.
RUBBER CHICKENS ARE FUNNY?
I FEAR FOR A GENERATION THAT CANNOT APPRECIATE A RUBBER CHICKEN.
THANK YOU, DETECTIVE.
COME, MATTSEN.
THE GAME'S AFOOT.

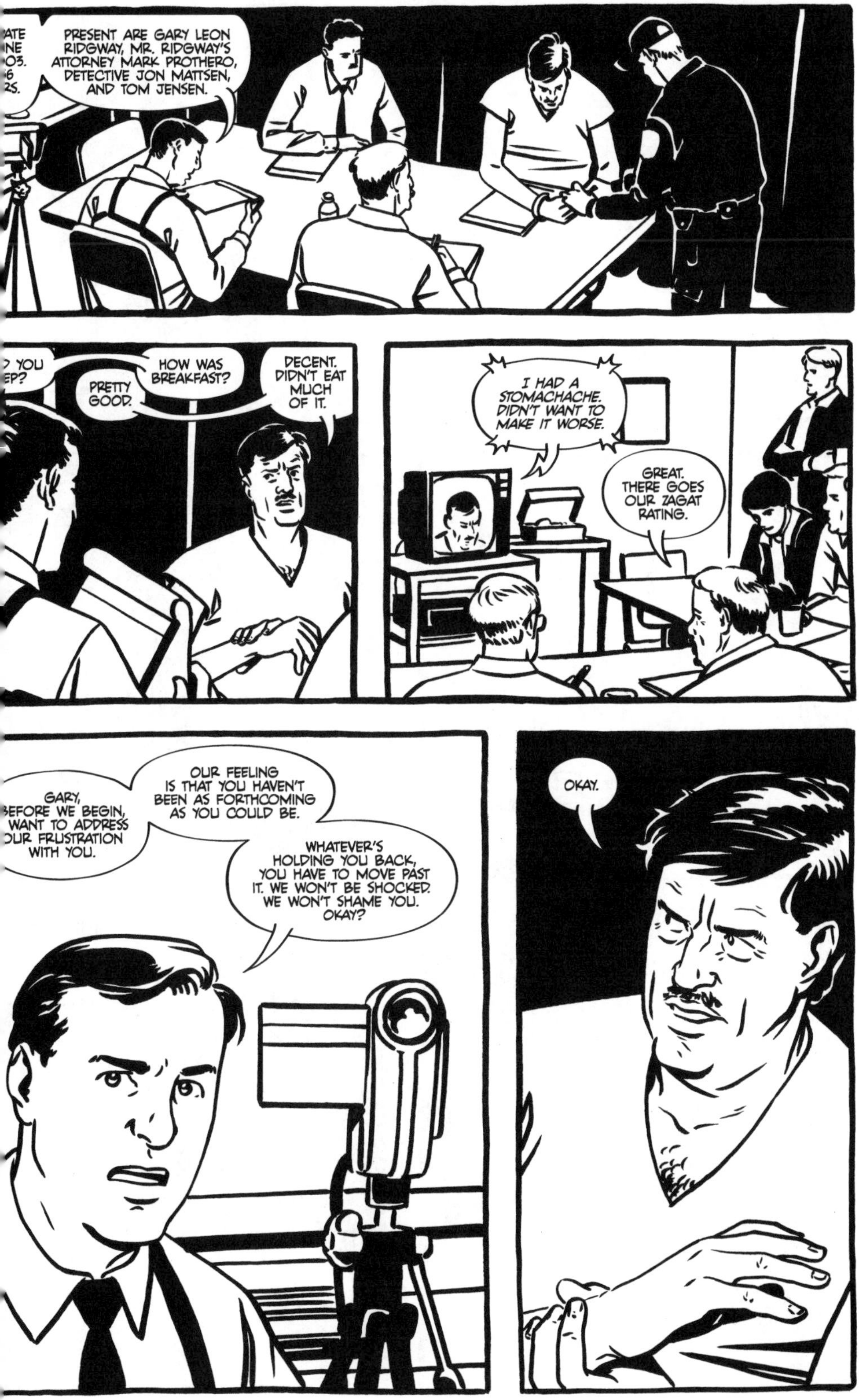
PRESENT ARE GARY LEON RIDGWAY, MR. RIDGWAY'S ATTORNEY MARK PROTHERO, DETECTIVE JON MATTSEN, AND TOM JENSEN.
HOW WAS BREAKFAST?
PRETTY GOOD.
DECENT. DIDN'T EAT MUCH OF IT.
I HAD A STOMACHACHE. DIDN'T WANT TO MAKE IT WORSE.
GREAT. THERE GOES OUR ZAGAT RATING.
GARY, EFORE WE BEGIN, WANT TO ADDRESS UR FRUSTRATION WITH YOU.
OUR FEELING IS THAT YOU HAVEN'T BEEN AS FORTHCOMING AS YOU COULD BE.
WHATEVER'S HOLDING YOU BACK, YOU HAVE TO MOVE PAST IT. WE WON'T BE SHOCKED. WE WON'T SHAME YOU. OKAY?
OKAY.

202

WHAT YOU'RE SAYING IS THAT YOU WANTED TO RETURN TO THE BODIES AND HAVE SEX WITH THEM. RIGHT?

THAT'S AN IMPORTANT DETAIL, GARY. BECAUSE WE KNOW SOMETHING WAS DONE TO THE VICTIMS AFTER--

IT WAS JUST AN URGE. I DIDN'T ACTUALLY DO IT, THOUGH. THAT'S WHY I BURIED THEM.

TO STOP MYSELF.

GARY...

DID YOU GO BACK TO THE BODIES?

IDN'T NT TO ACK...

GARY, WE NEED TO KNOW THIS.

IT KEPT GETTING WORSE. THE URGE.

IT'S OKAY IF YOU DID THIS THING. OKAY?

THOUSANDS OF PEOPLE HAVE DONE THIS BEFORE YOU. YOU'RE NOT THE FIRST.

THIS...

THIS WAS THE GARY I WAS BEFORE...

YOU WANT TO TELL US THIS, GARY. YOU NEED TO LET IT OUT. IT'S...

IT'S LIKE A BAD CHEESEBURGER. IT'S MESSING WITH YOU, AND...

AND YOU NEED TO TAKE A SHIT.

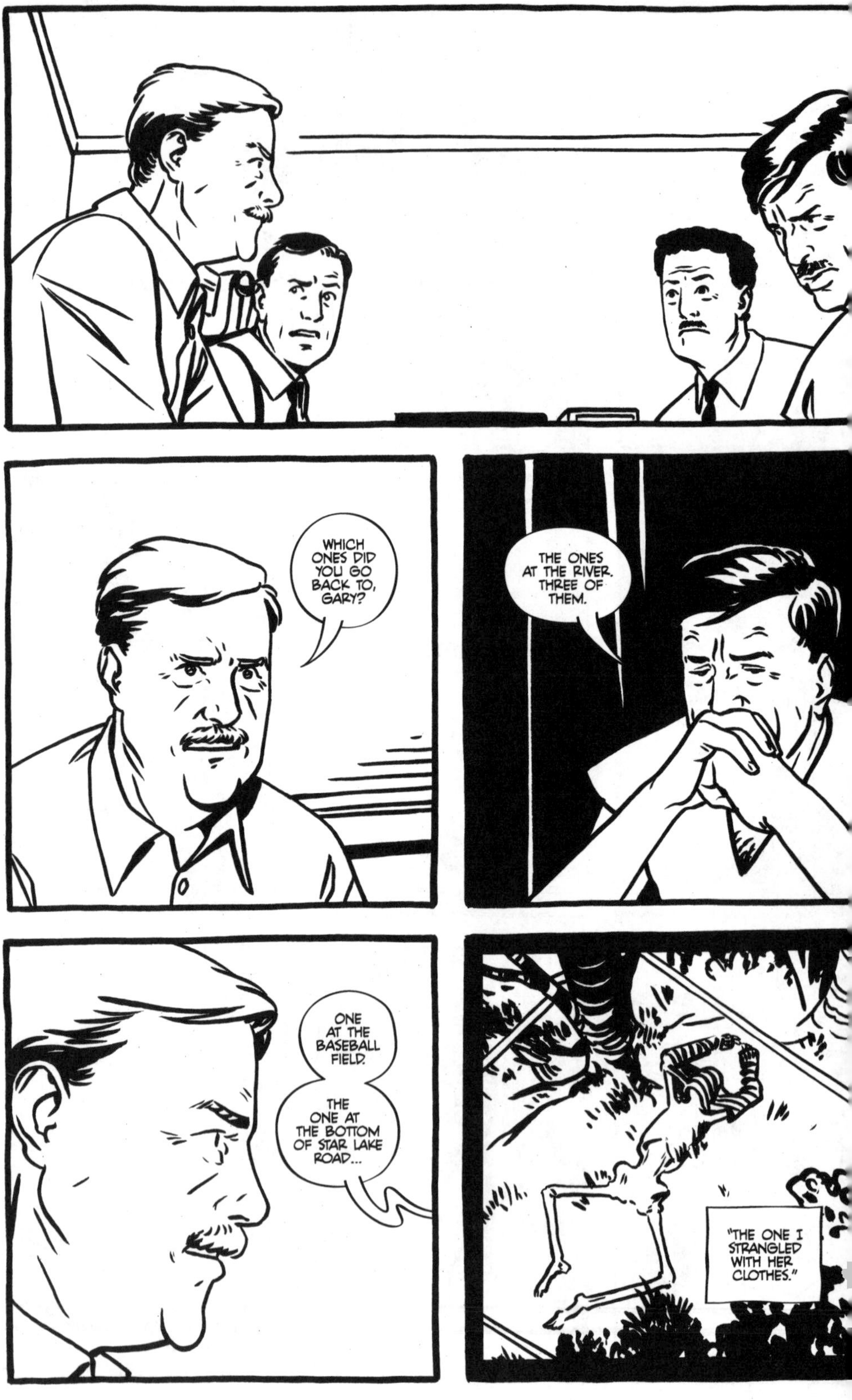
WHICH ONES DID YOU GO BACK TO, GARY?
THE ONES AT THE RIVER. THREE OF THEM.
ONE AT THE BASEBALL FIELD.
THE ONE AT THE BOTTOM OF STAR LAKE ROAD...
"THE ONE I STRANGLED WITH HER CLOTHES."

205

206

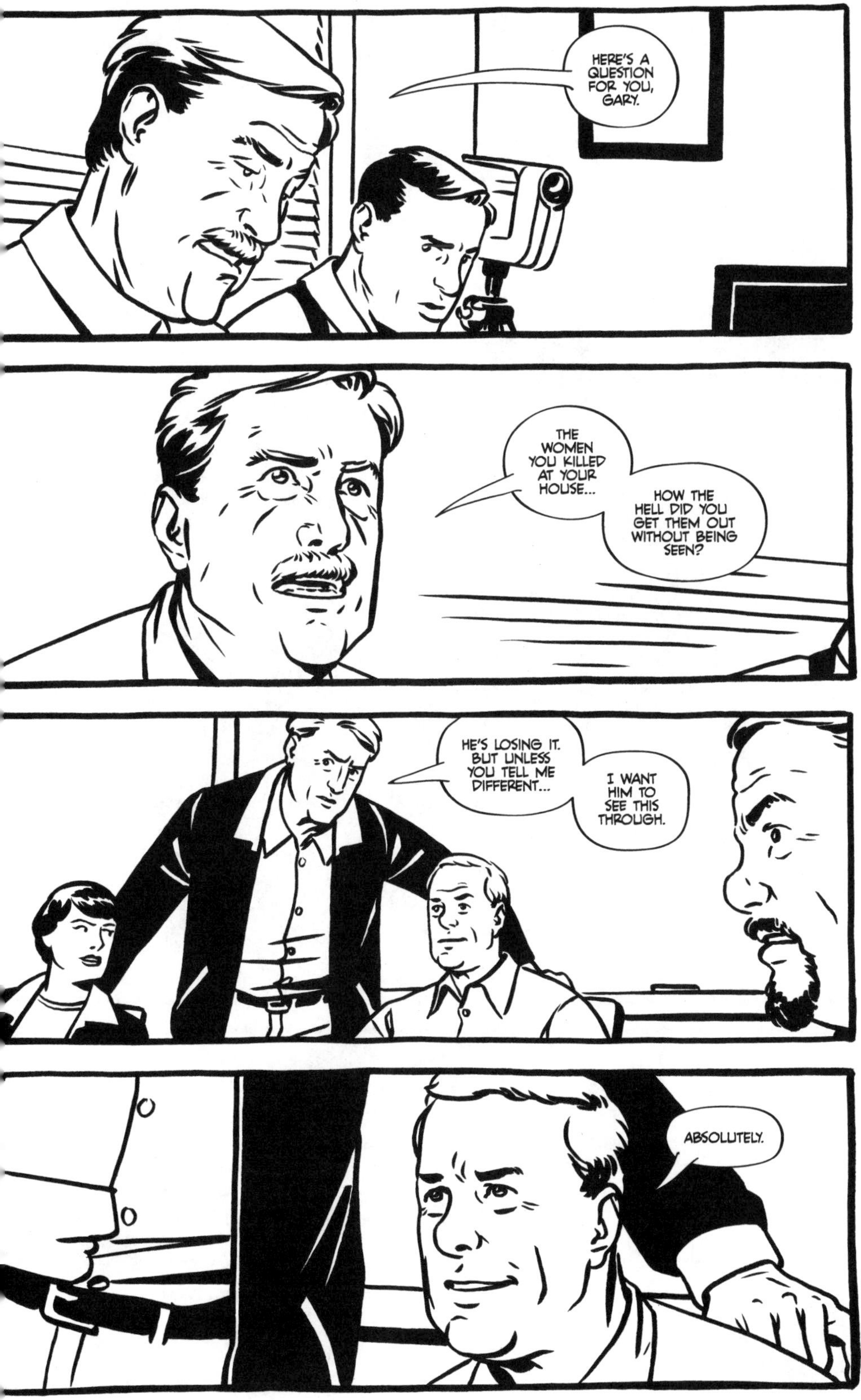
HERE'S A QUESTION FOR YOU, GARY.
THE WOMEN YOU KILLED AT YOUR HOUSE...
HOW THE HELL DID YOU GET THEM OUT WITHOUT BEING SEEN?
HE'S LOSING IT. BUT UNLESS YOU TELL ME DIFFERENT...
I WANT HIM TO SEE THIS THROUGH.
ABSOLUTELY.

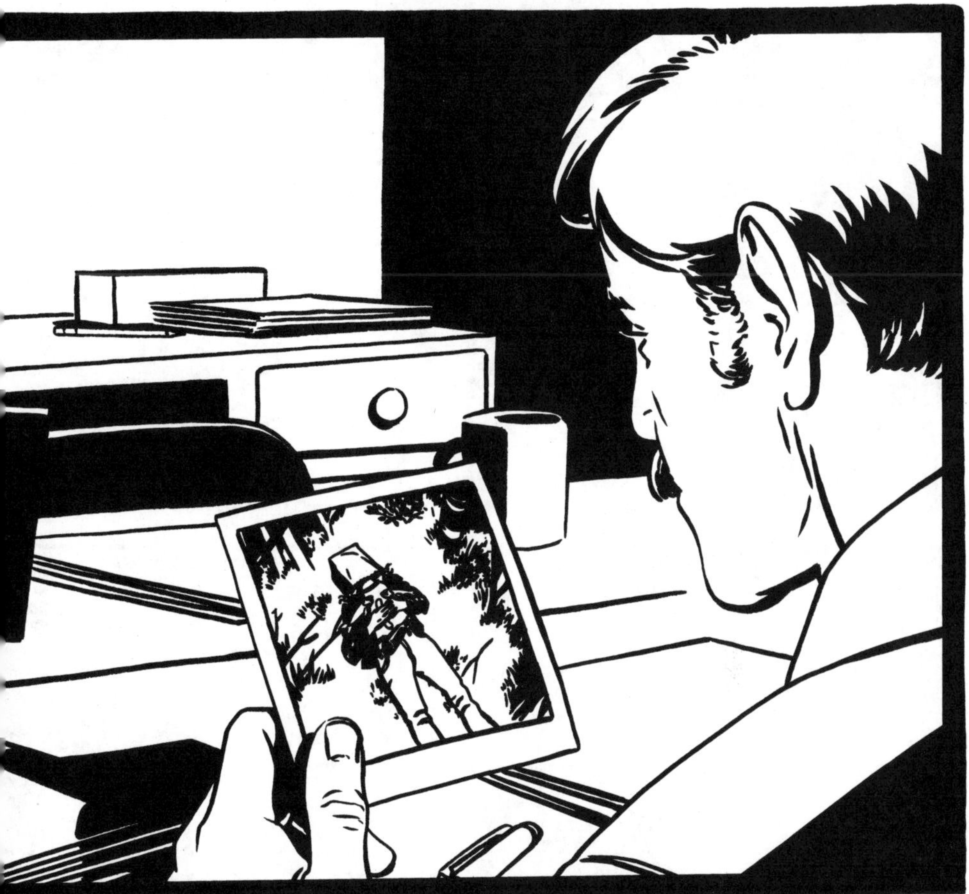

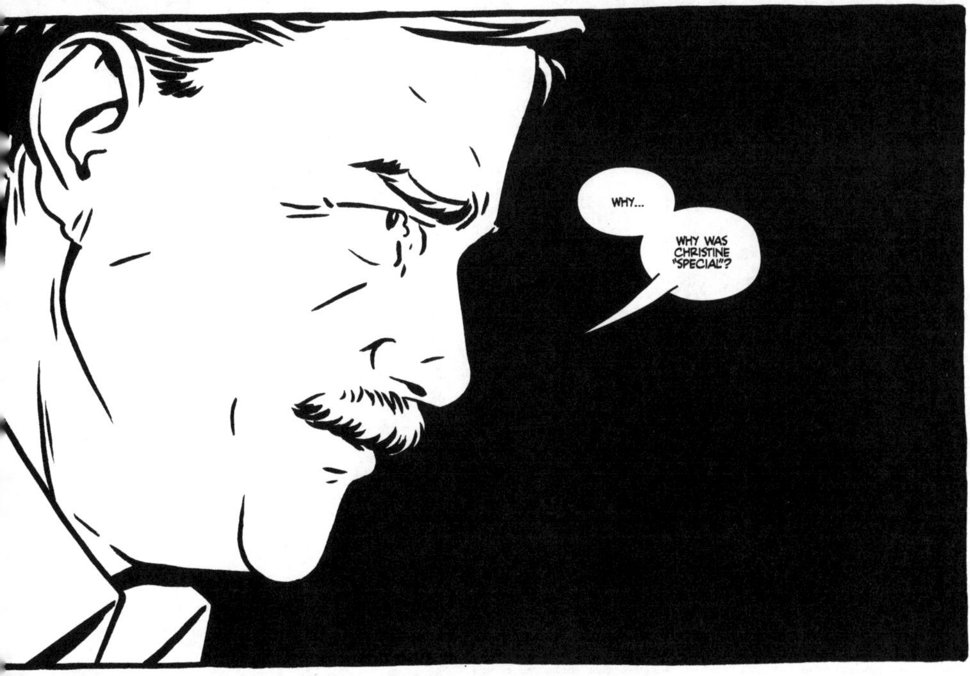
WHY...
WHY WAS CHRISTINE "SPECIAL"?

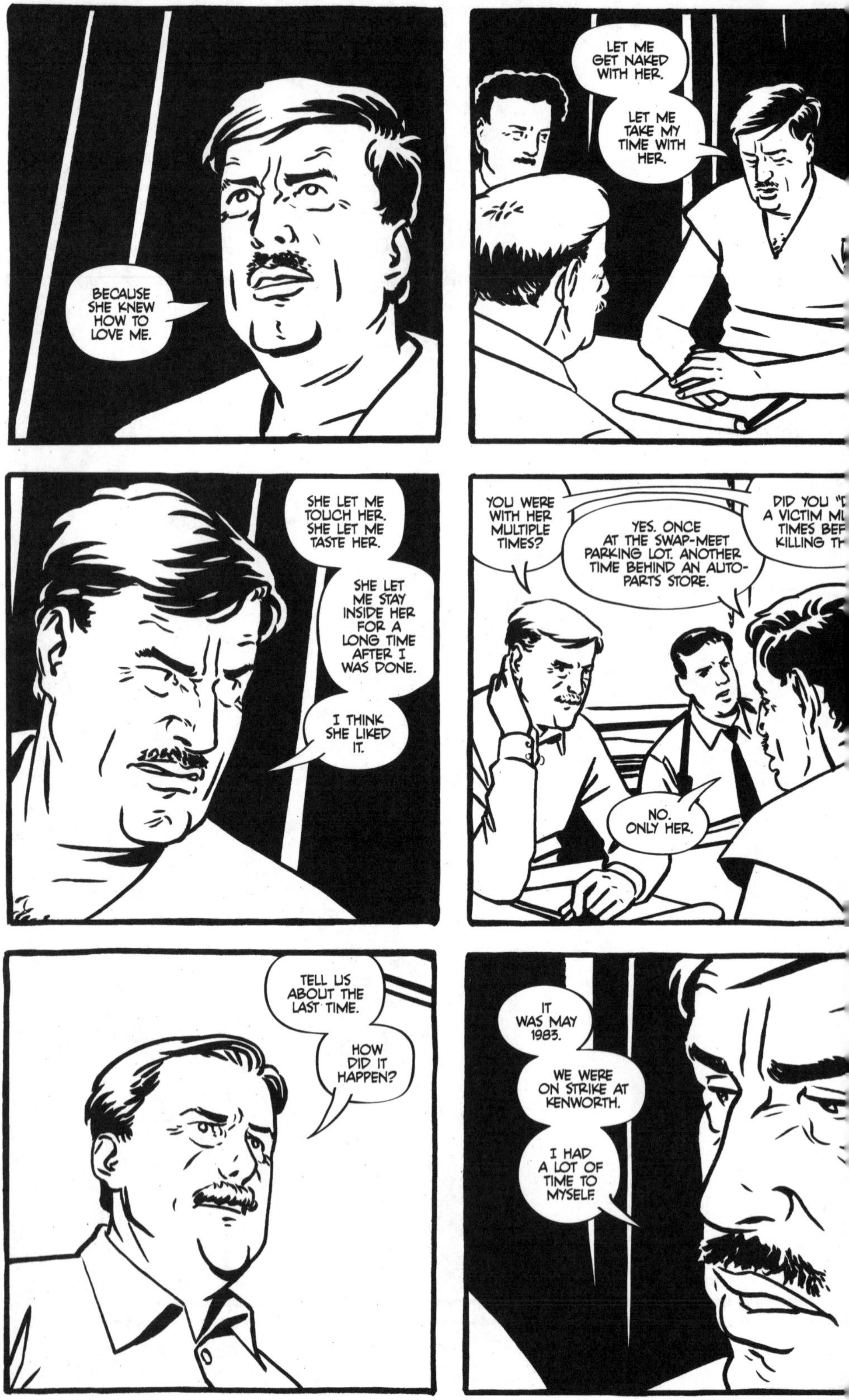
BECAUSE SHE KNEW HOW TO LOVE ME.
LET ME GET NAKED WITH HER.
LET ME TAKE MY TIME WITH HER.
SHE LET ME TOUCH HER. SHE LET ME TASTE HER.
SHE LET ME STAY INSIDE HER FOR A LONG TIME AFTER I WAS DONE.
I THINK SHE LIKED IT.
YOU WERE WITH HER MULTIPLE TIMES?
DID YOU
A VICTIM
TIMES
KILLING
YES. ONCE AT THE SWAP-MEET PARKING LOT. ANOTHER TIME BEHIND AN AUTO-PARTS STORE.
NO. ONLY HER.
TELL US ABOUT THE LAST TIME.
HOW DID IT HAPPEN?
IT WAS MAY 1983.
WE WERE ON STRIKE AT KENWORTH.
I HAD A LOT OF TIME TO MYSELF.

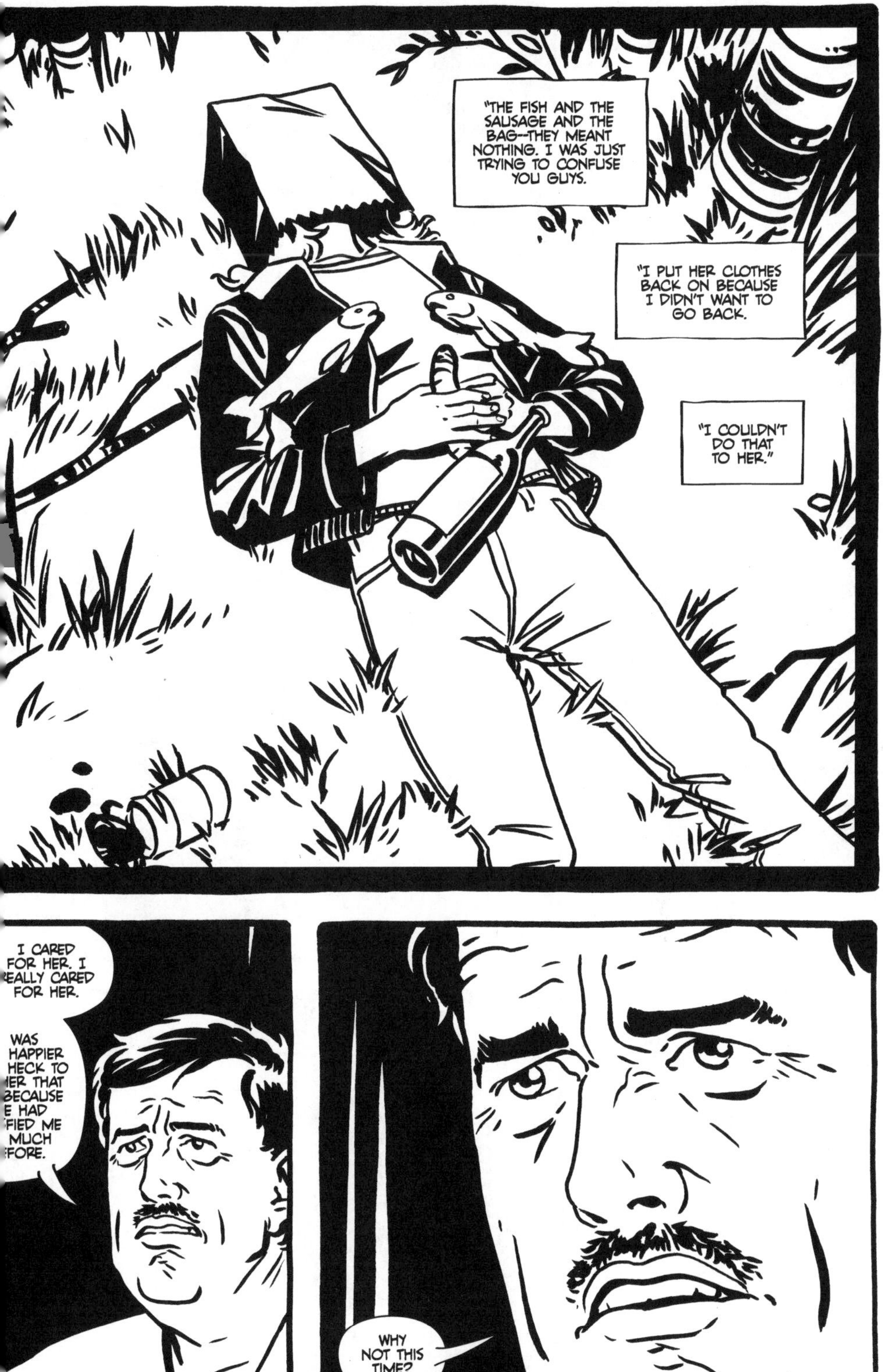
"THE FISH AND THE SAUSAGE AND THE BAG--THEY MEANT NOTHING. I WAS JUST TRYING TO CONFUSE YOU GUYS.
"I PUT HER CLOTHES BACK ON BECAUSE I DIDN'T WANT TO GO BACK.
"I COULDN'T DO THAT TO HER."
I CARED FOR HER. I EALLY CARED FOR HER.
WAS HAPPIER HECK TO ER THAT BECAUSE E HAD FIED ME MUCH FORE.
WHY NOT THIS TIME?

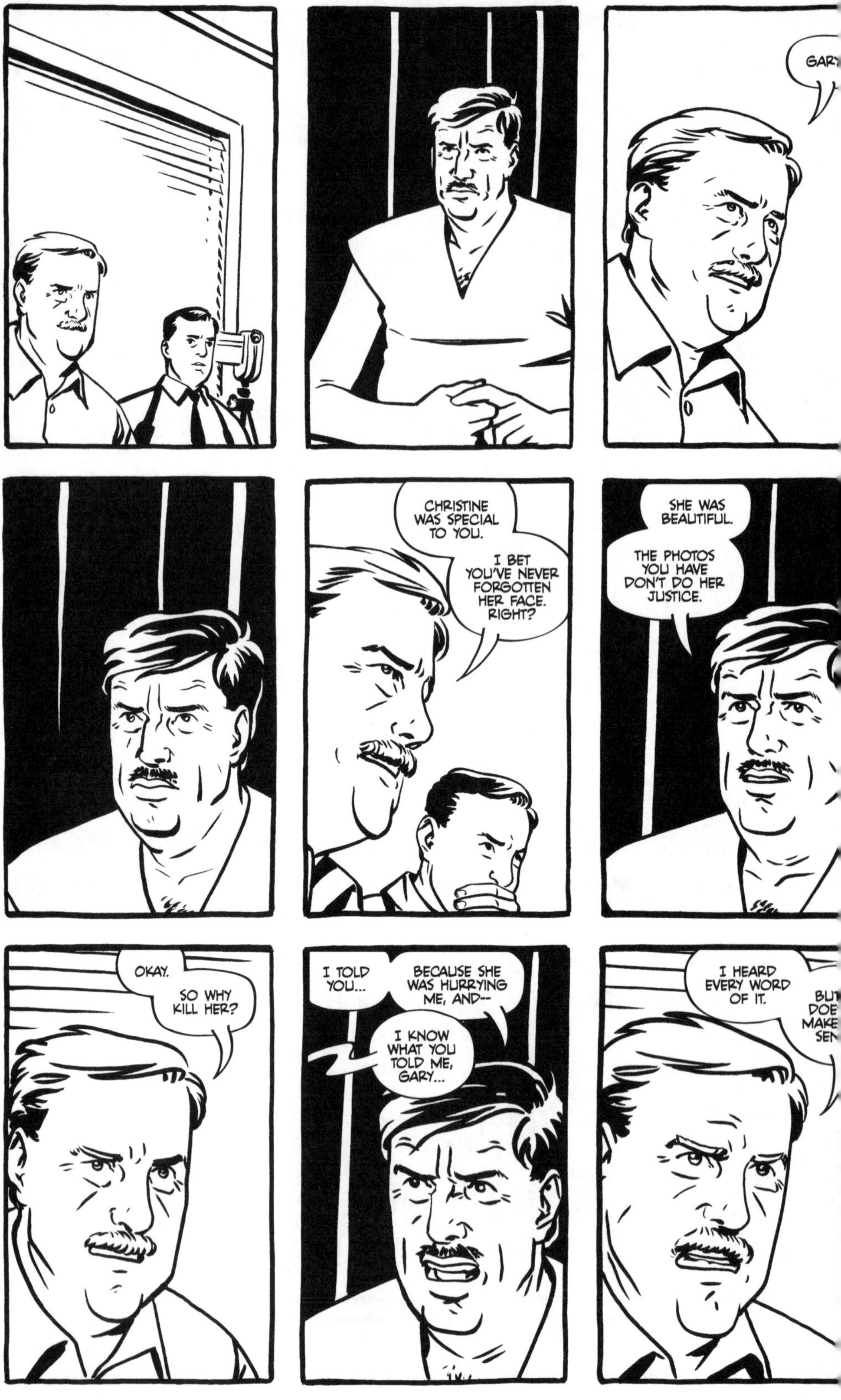
GARY
CHRISTINE WAS SPECIAL TO YOU.
I BET YOU'VE NEVER FORGOTTEN HER FACE. RIGHT?
SHE WAS BEAUTIFUL.
THE PHOTOS YOU HAVE DON'T DO HER JUSTICE.
OKAY.
SO WHY KILL HER?
I TOLD YOU...
BECAUSE SHE WAS HURRYING ME, AND--
I KNOW WHAT YOU TOLD ME, GARY...
I HEARD EVERY WORD OF IT.

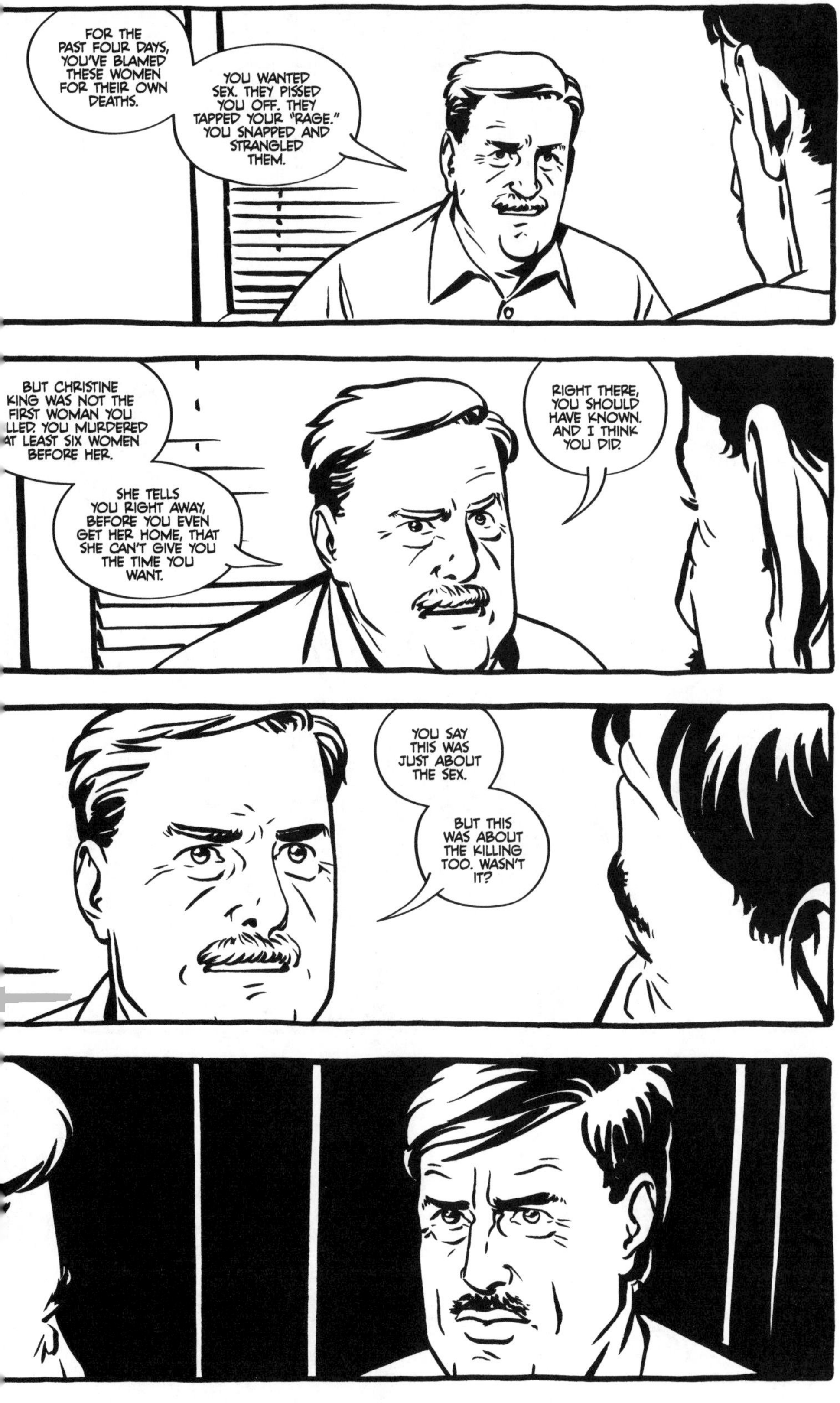
FOR THE PAST FOUR DAYS, YOU'VE BLAMED THESE WOMEN FOR THEIR OWN DEATHS.
YOU WANTED SEX. THEY PISSED YOU OFF. THEY TAPPED YOUR "RAGE." YOU SNAPPED AND STRANGLED THEM.
BUT CHRISTINE KING WAS NOT THE FIRST WOMAN YOU
LLED. YOU MURDERED
AT LEAST SIX WOMEN BEFORE HER.
SHE TELLS YOU RIGHT AWAY, BEFORE YOU EVEN GET HER HOME, THAT SHE CAN'T GIVE YOU THE TIME YOU WANT.
RIGHT THERE, YOU SHOULD HAVE KNOWN. AND I THINK YOU DID.
YOU SAY THIS WAS JUST ABOUT THE SEX.
BUT THIS WAS ABOUT THE KILLING TOO. WASN'T IT?

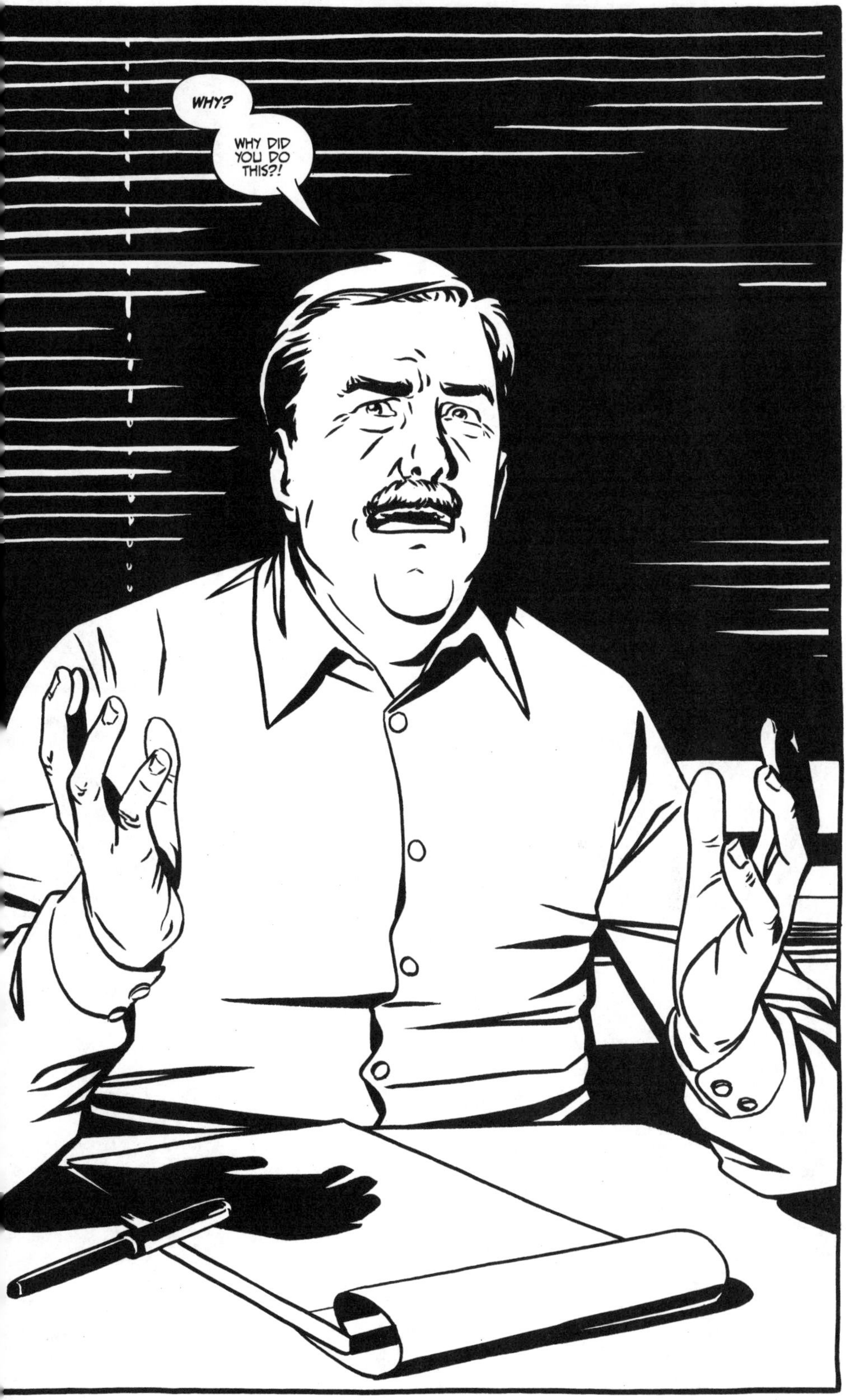
WHY?
WHY DID YOU DO THIS?!

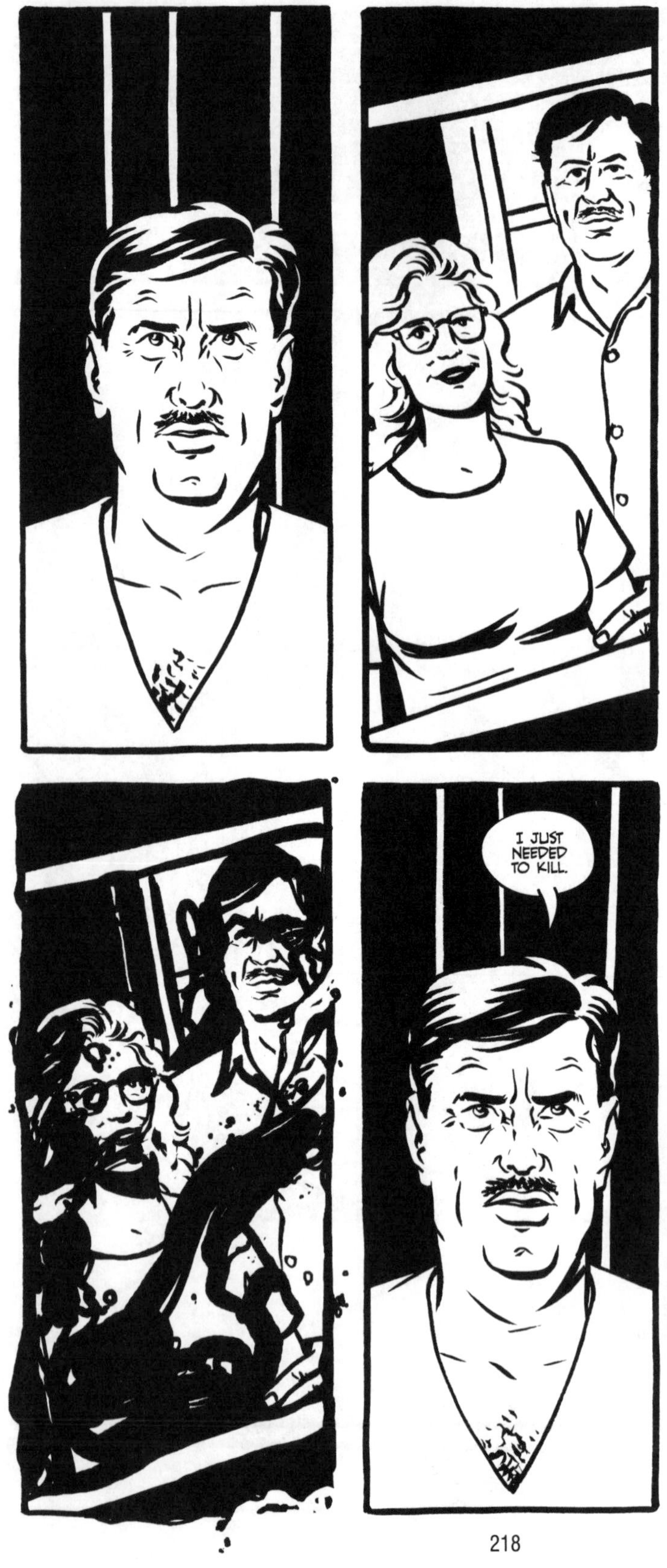
I JUST NEEDED TO KILL.

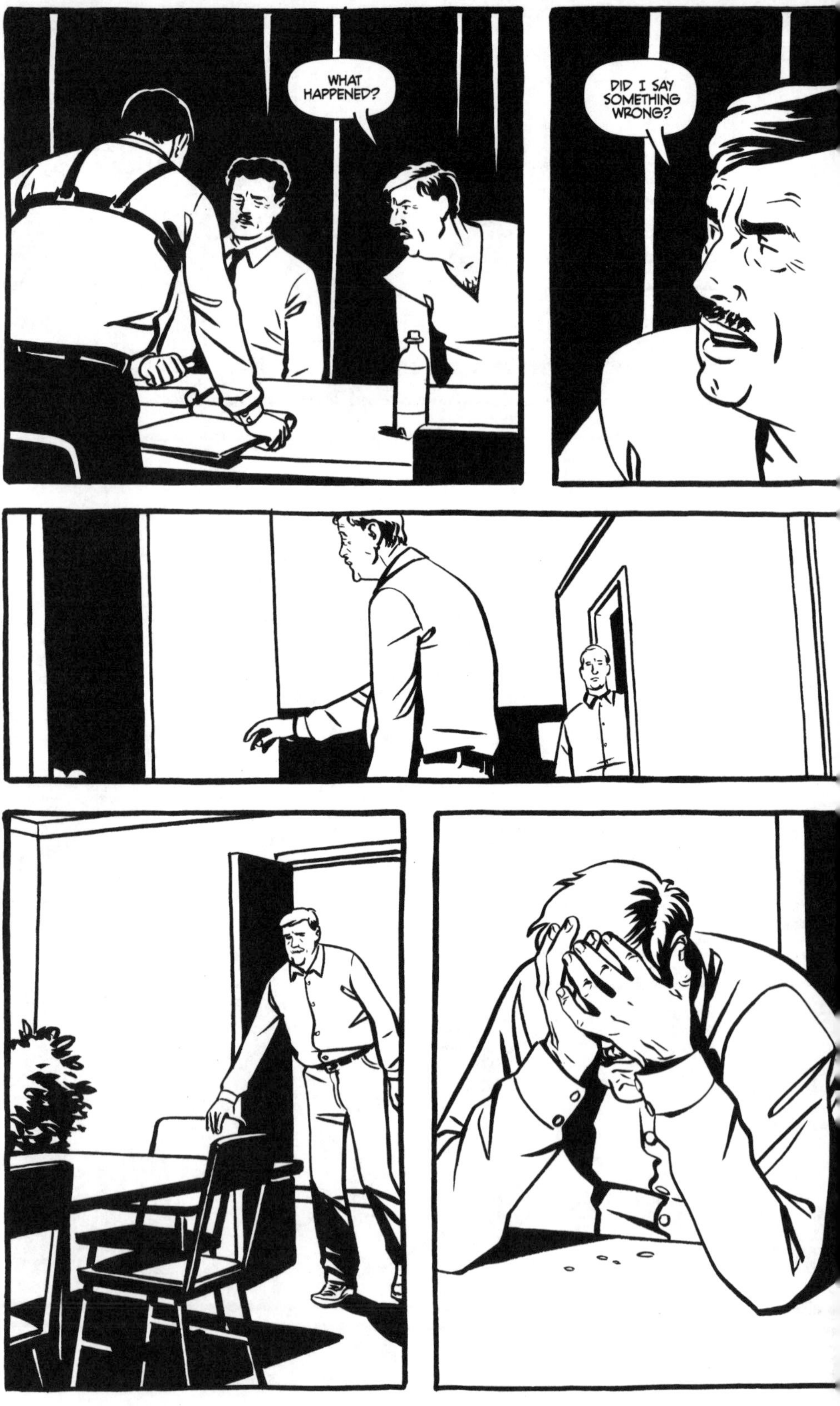
WHAT HAPPENED?
DID I SAY SOMETHING WRONG?

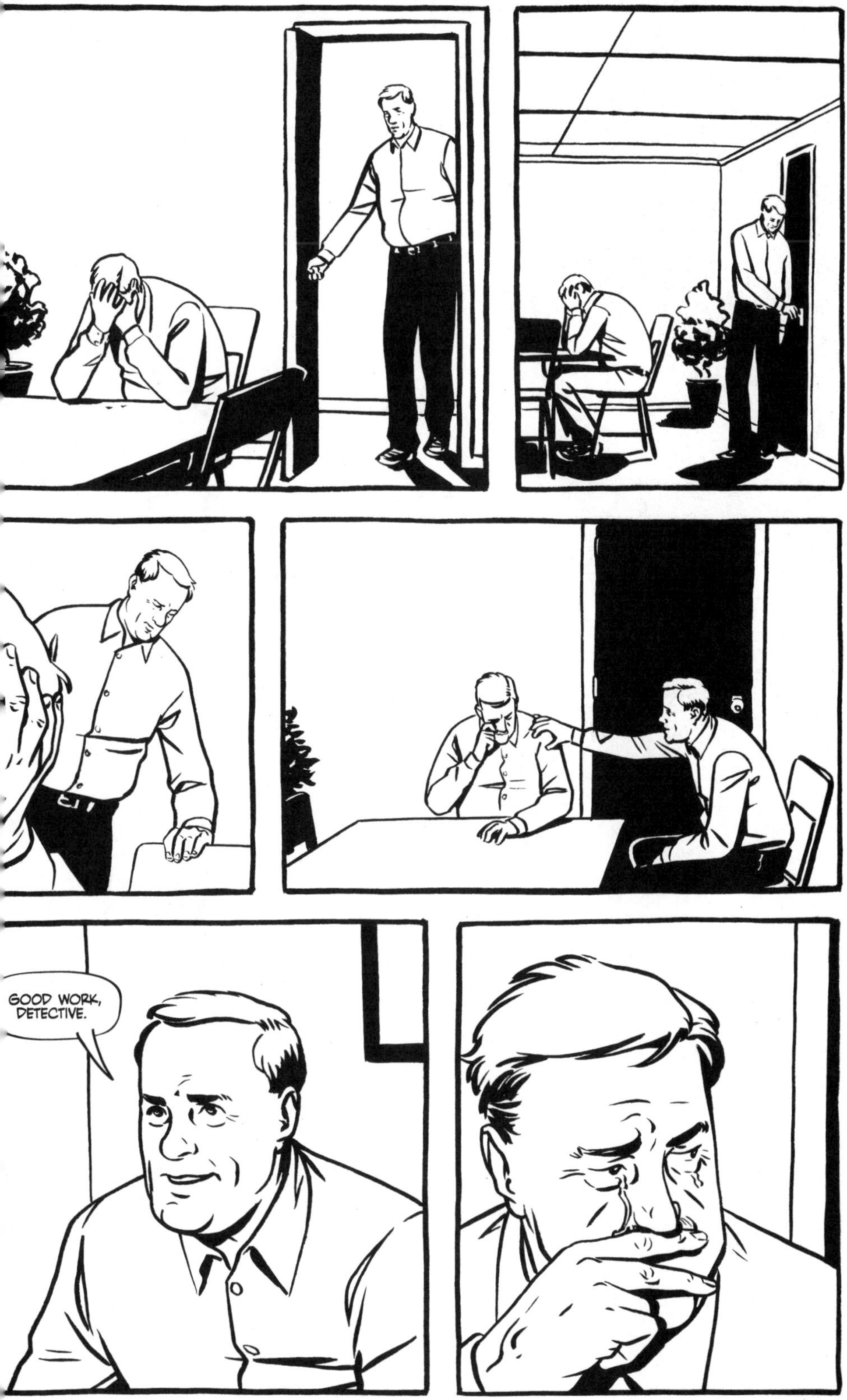
GOOD WORK, DETECTIVE.

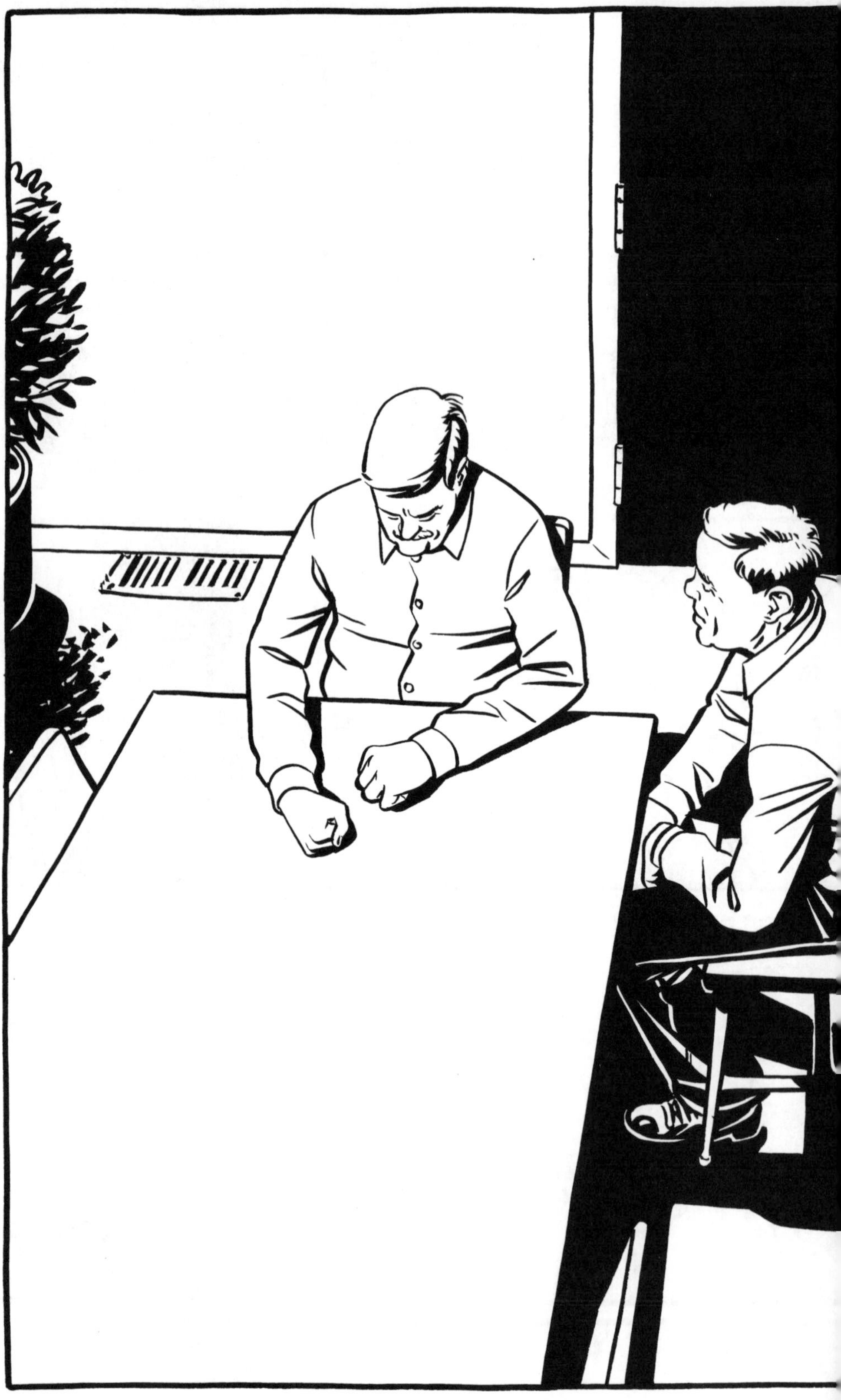

EPILOGUE

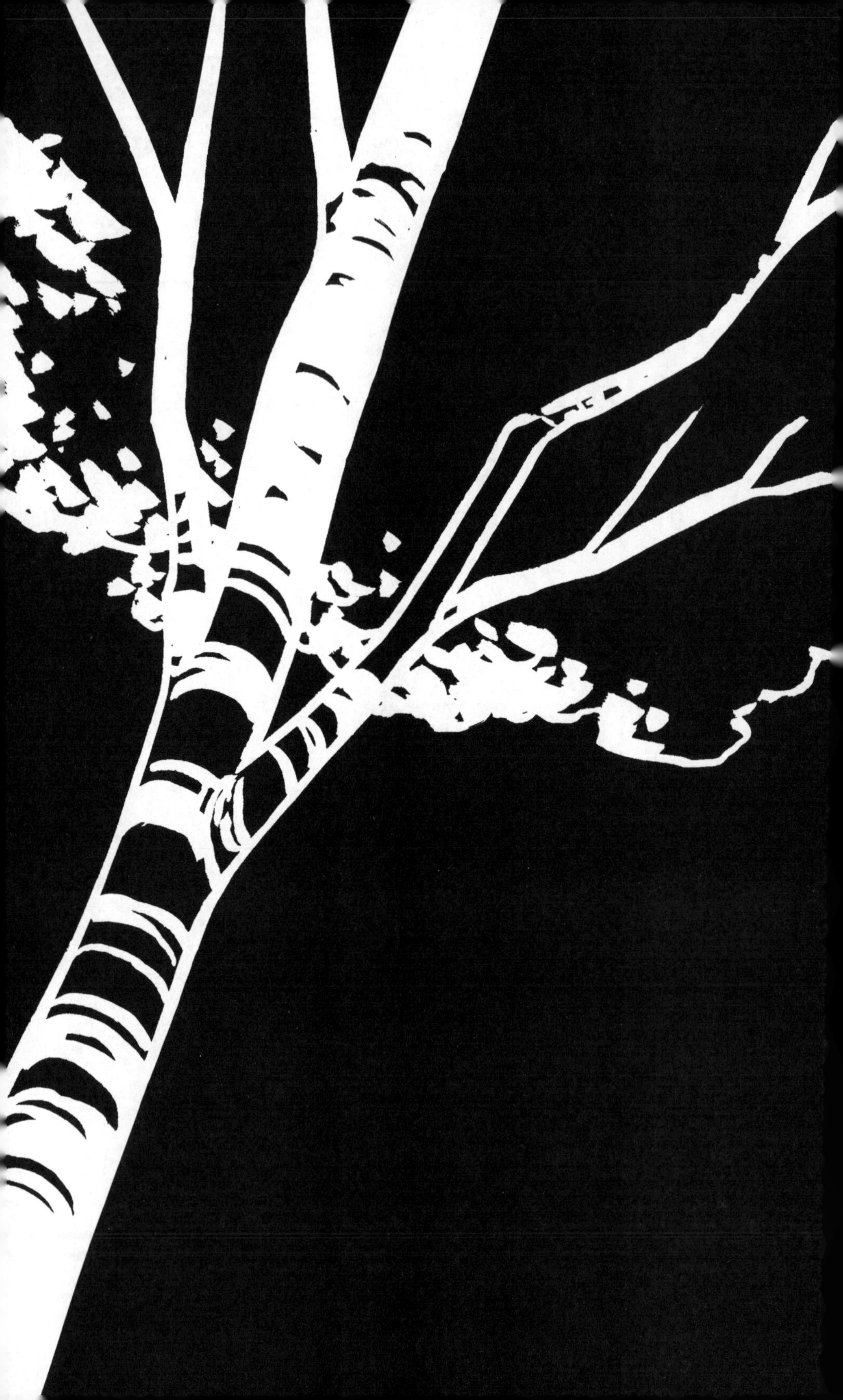

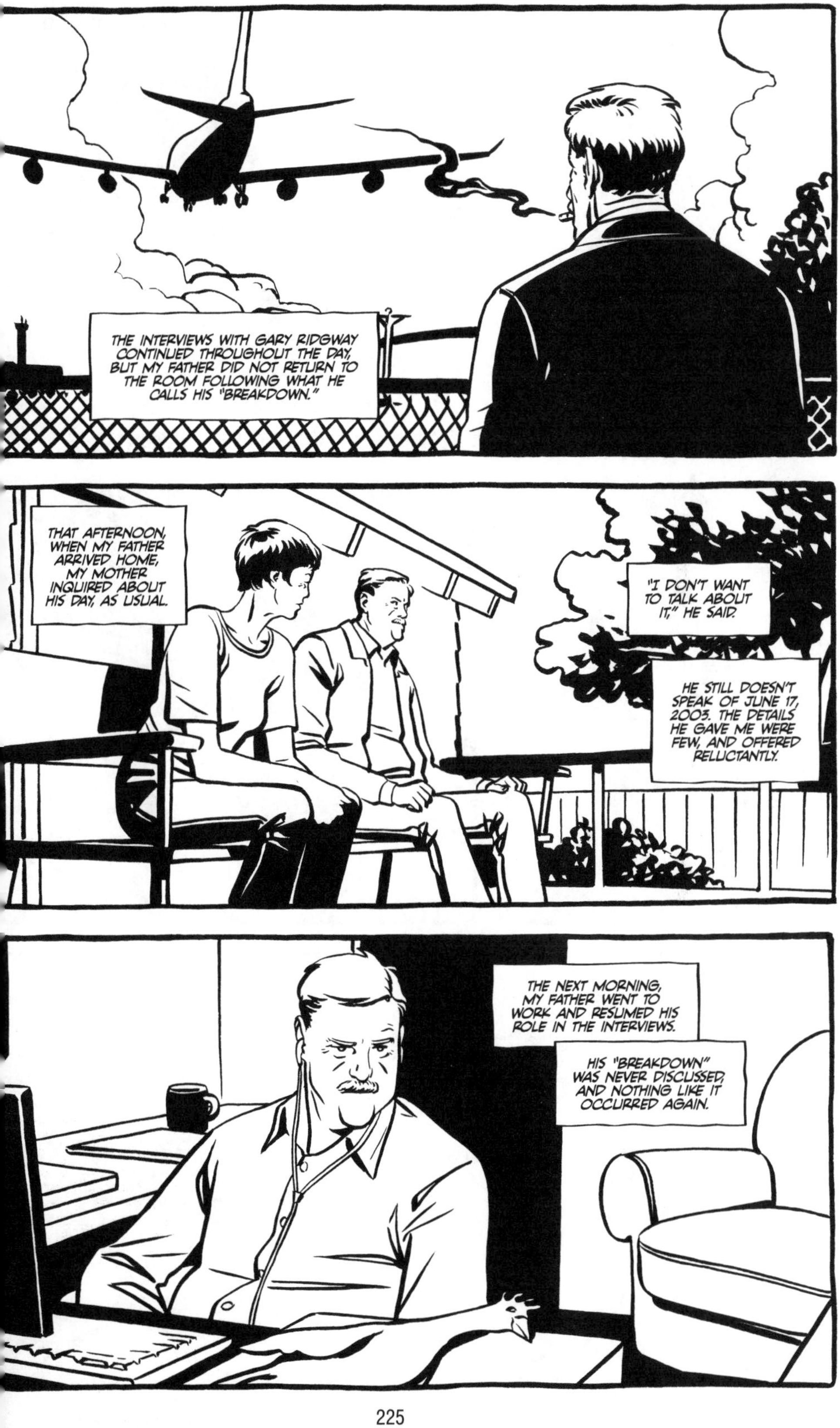
THE INTERVIEWS WITH GARY RIDGWAY CONTINUED THROUGHOUT THE DAY, BUT MY FATHER DID NOT RETURN TO THE ROOM FOLLOWING WHAT HE CALLS HIS "BREAKDOWN."
THAT AFTERNOON, WHEN MY FATHER ARRIVED HOME, MY MOTHER INQUIRED ABOUT HIS DAY, AS USUAL.
"I DON'T WANT TO TALK ABOUT IT," HE SAID.
HE STILL DOESN'T SPEAK OF JUNE 17, 2003. THE DETAILS HE GAVE ME WERE FEW, AND OFFERED RELUCTANTLY.
THE NEXT MORNING, MY FATHER WENT TO WORK AND RESUMED HIS ROLE IN THE INTERVIEWS.
HIS "BREAKDOWN" WAS NEVER DISCUSSED, AND NOTHING LIKE IT OCCURRED AGAIN.

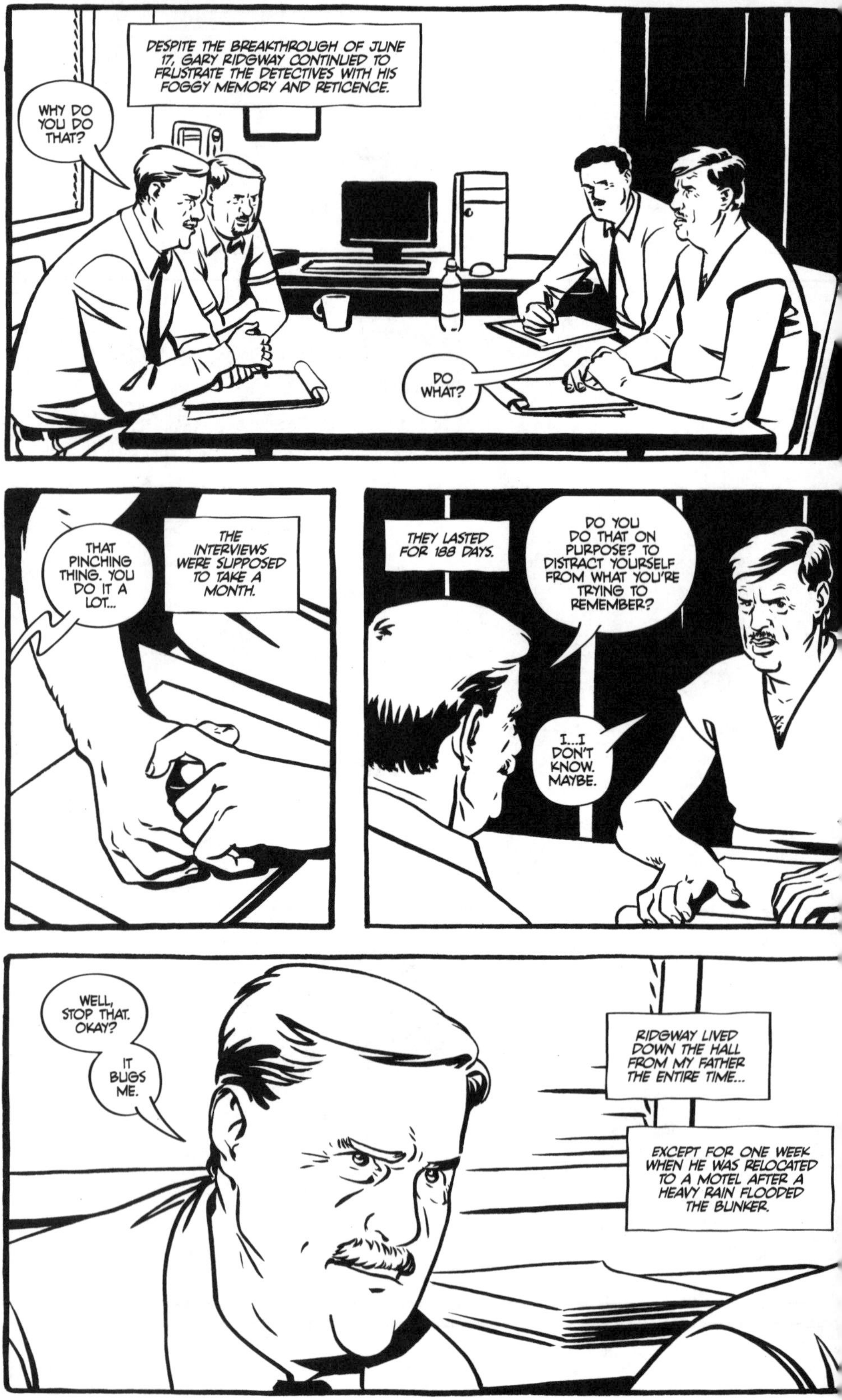

DESPITE THE BREAKTHROUGH OF JUNE 17, GARY RIDGWAY CONTINUED TO FRUSTRATE THE DETECTIVES WITH HIS FOGGY MEMORY AND RETICENCE.
WHY DO YOU DO THAT?
DO WHAT?
THAT PINCHING THING. YOU DO IT A LOT...
THE INTERVIEWS WERE SUPPOSED TO TAKE A MONTH.
THEY LASTED FOR 188 DAYS.
DO YOU DO THAT ON PURPOSE? TO DISTRACT YOURSELF FROM WHAT YOU'RE TRYING TO REMEMBER?
I...I DON'T KNOW. MAYBE.
WELL, STOP THAT. OKAY?
IT BUGS ME.
RIDGWAY LIVED DOWN THE HALL FROM MY FATHER THE ENTIRE TIME...
EXCEPT FOR ONE WEEK WHEN HE WAS RELOCATED TO A MOTEL AFTER A HEAVY RAIN FLOODED THE BUNKER.

GARY'S RIDGWAY'S CHILDHOOD INCLUDES ALL THE MARKERS OF A DEVELOPING SERIAL KILLER. ANIMAL CRUELTY. SEXUALLY PRECOCIOUS BEHAVIOR. DARK FANTASIES ABOUT HIS MOTHER. MORE.

WHEN HE WAS SIXTEEN, RIDGWAY HAPPENED UPON A CHILD DRESSED AS A COWBOY PLAYING ALONE NEAR A PARK. HE LURED HIM INTO THE WOODS AND STABBED HIM.

THE BOY--WHO SURVIVED THE ATTACK--REPORTED THAT HIS ASSAILANT EXPLAINED, "I WANTED TO KNOW WHAT IT FELT LIKE TO KILL SOMEONE."

RIDGWAY WAS NEVER CAUGHT OR EVEN SUSPECTED.

DURING THE INTERVIEWS WITH DETECTIVES, RIDGWAY CLAIMED HE BEGAN MURDERING PROSTITUTES AFTER HIS SECOND WIFE DECIDED SHE DIDN'T LOVE HIM ANYMORE AND LEFT HIM.

HE TARGETED PROSTITUTES BECAUSE THEY WERE EASY PREY--"CANDY IN A DISH." HE THOUGHT HE WAS DOING SEATTLE A FAVOR BY GETTING RID OF THEM. HE CALLED THEM "TRASH." HE DIDN'T THINK ANYONE WOULD EVER MISS THEM.

STILL, MY FATHER NEVER GOT A SATISFACTORY ANSWER TO THE "WHY" OF THE GREEN RIVER KILLER. PERHAPS RIDGWAY WAS INCAPABLE OF GIVING ONE.

RIDGWAY BELIEVED THE FUNDAMENTAL DIFFERENCE BETWEEN HIMSELF AND OTHER PEOPLE WAS A LACK OF "CARING."

ASKED TO RATE HIS EVIL ON A SCALE OF ONE TO FIVE...

RIDGWAY GAVE HIMSELF A THREE.

227

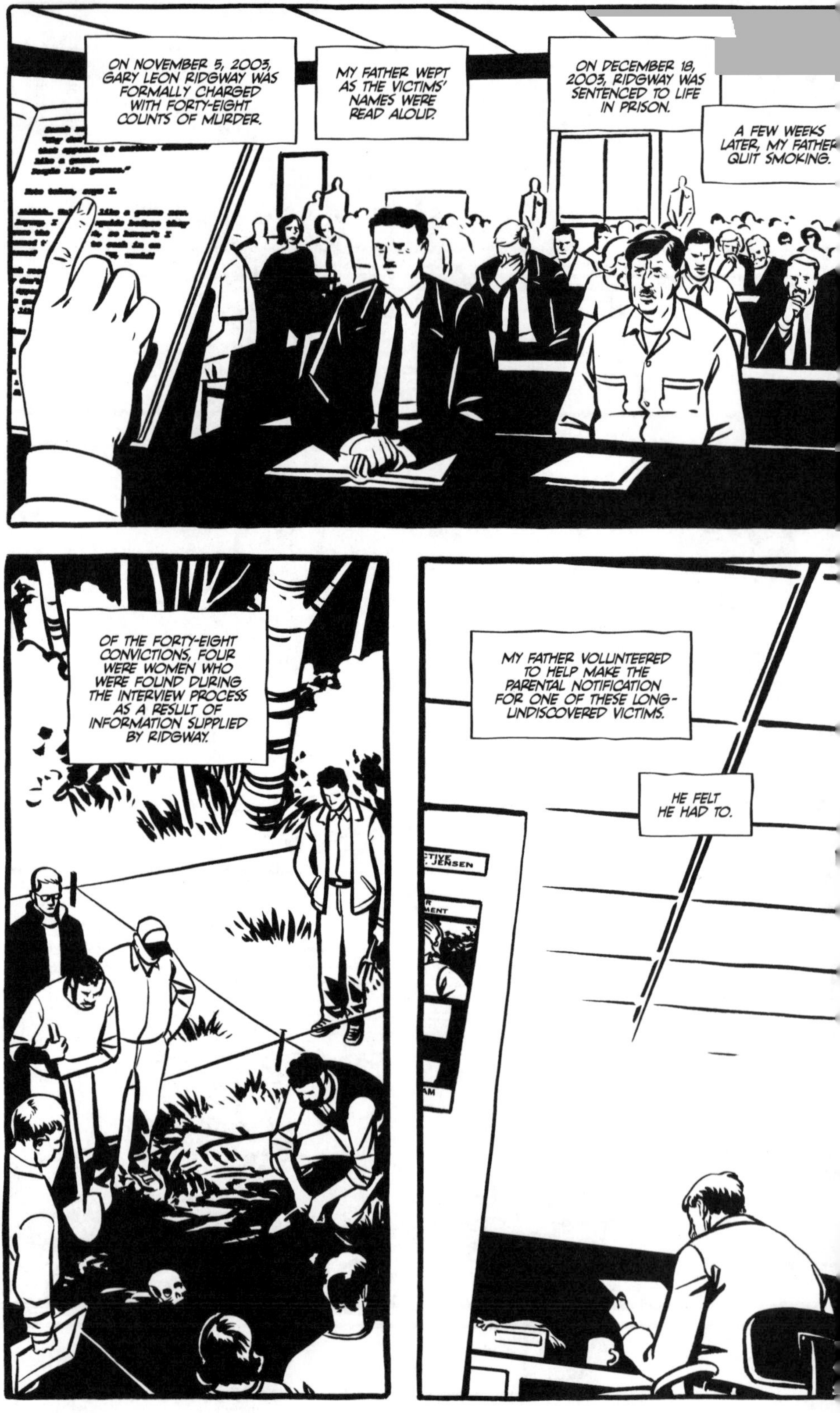
ON NOVEMBER 5, 2003, GARY LEON RIDGWAY WAS FORMALLY CHARGED WITH FORTY-EIGHT COUNTS OF MURDER.
MY FATHER WEPT AS THE VICTIMS' NAMES WERE READ ALOUD.
ON DECEMBER 18, 2003, RIDGWAY WAS SENTENCED TO LIFE IN PRISON.
A FEW WEEKS LATER, MY FATHER QUIT SMOKING.
OF THE FORTY-EIGHT CONVICTIONS, FOUR WERE WOMEN WHO WERE FOUND DURING THE INTERVIEW PROCESS AS A RESULT OF INFORMATION SUPPLIED BY RIDGWAY.
MY FATHER VOLUNTEERED TO HELP MAKE THE PARENTAL NOTIFICATION FOR ONE OF THESE LONG-UNDISCOVERED VICTIMS.
HE FELT HE HAD TO.

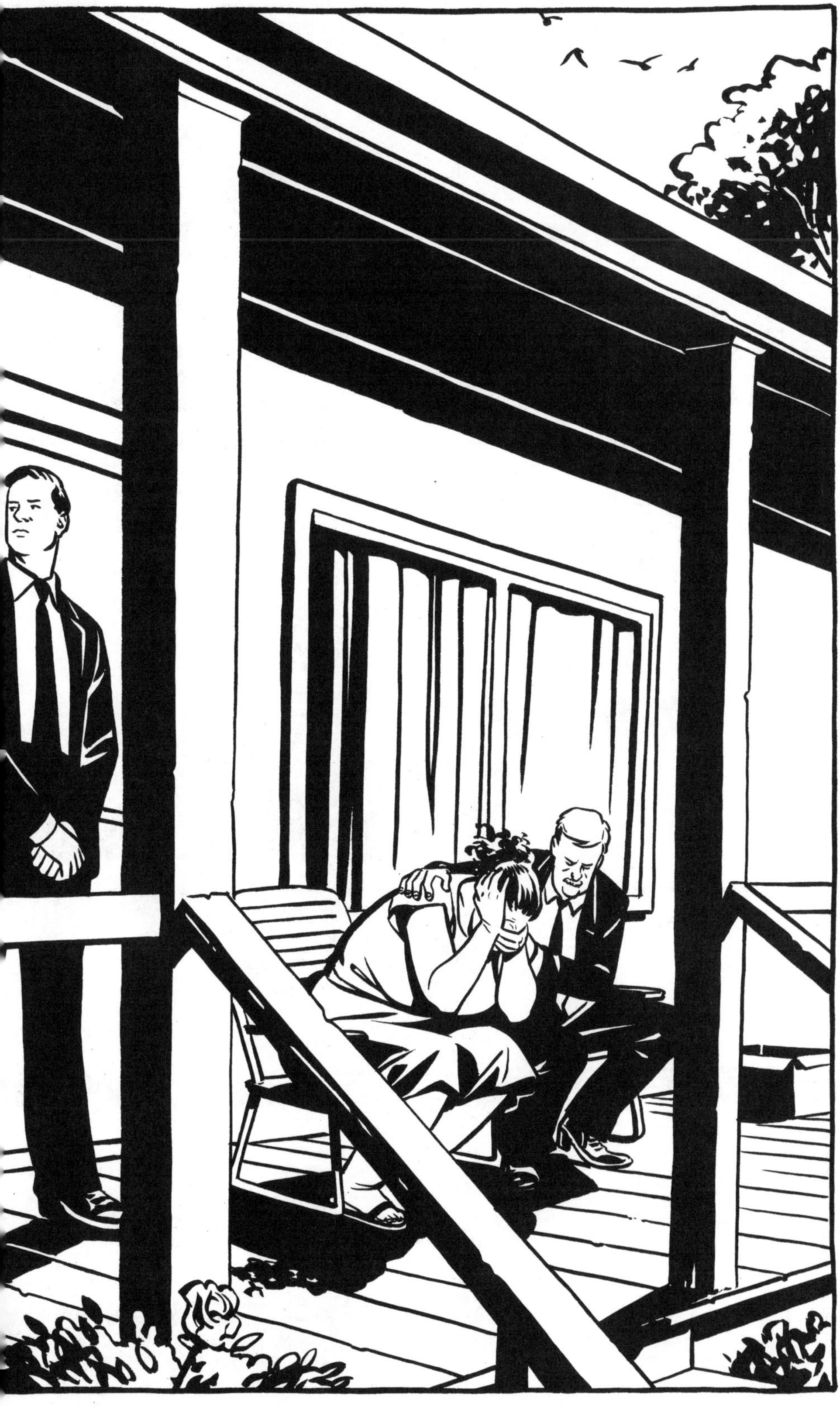

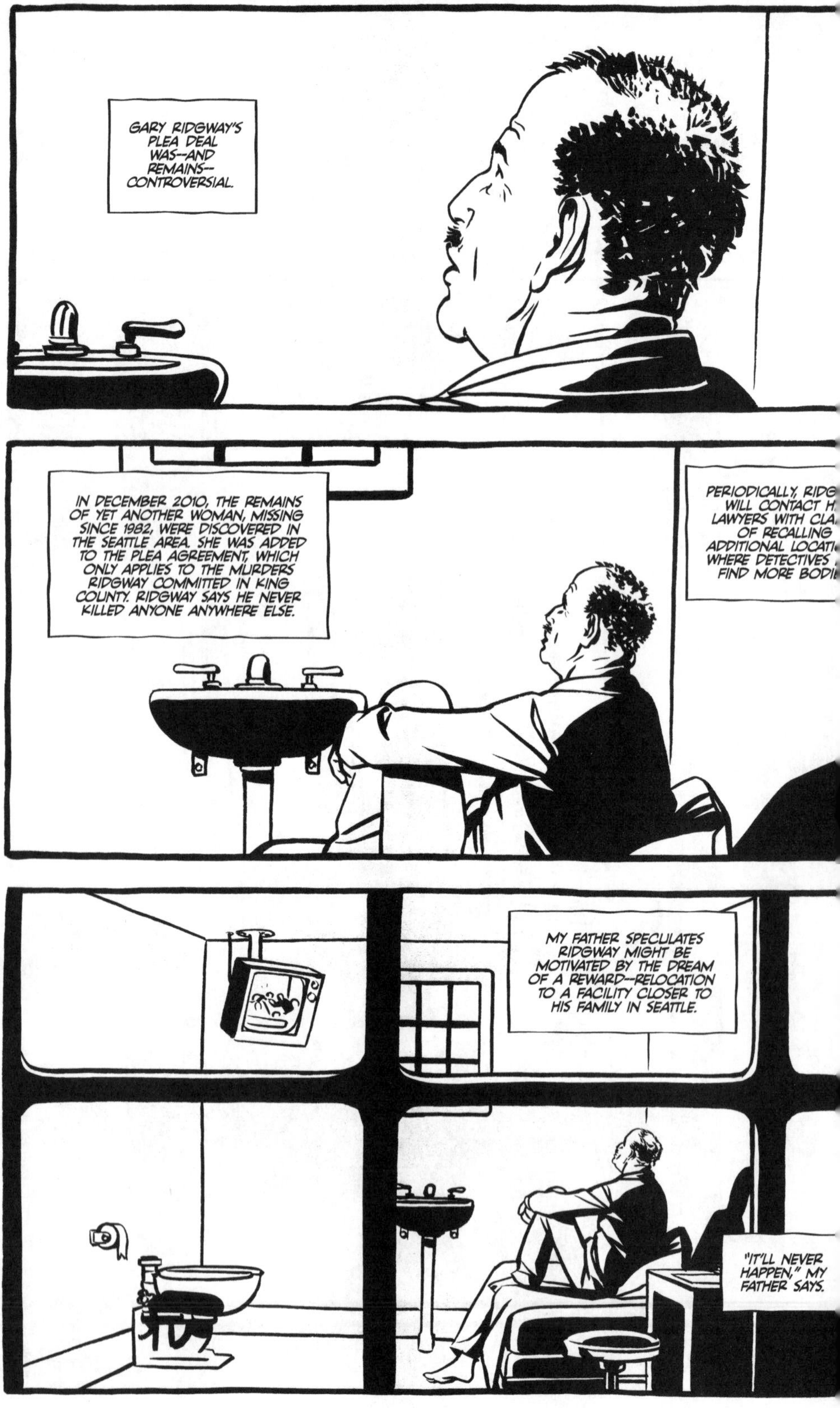
GARY RIDGWAY'S PLEA DEAL WAS--AND REMAINS--CONTROVERSIAL.
IN DECEMBER 2010, THE REMAINS OF YET ANOTHER WOMAN, MISSING SINCE 1982, WERE DISCOVERED IN THE SEATTLE AREA. SHE WAS ADDED TO THE PLEA AGREEMENT, WHICH ONLY APPLIES TO THE MURDERS RIDGWAY COMMITTED IN KING COUNTY. RIDGWAY SAYS HE NEVER KILLED ANYONE ANYWHERE ELSE.
PERIODICALLY, RIDG WILL CONTACT H LAWYERS WITH CLA OF RECALLING ADDITIONAL LOCATI WHERE DETECTIVES FIND MORE BODI
MY FATHER SPECULATES RIDGWAY MIGHT BE MOTIVATED BY THE DREAM OF A REWARD--RELOCATION TO A FACILITY CLOSER TO HIS FAMILY IN SEATTLE.
"IT'LL NEVER HAPPEN," MY FATHER SAYS.

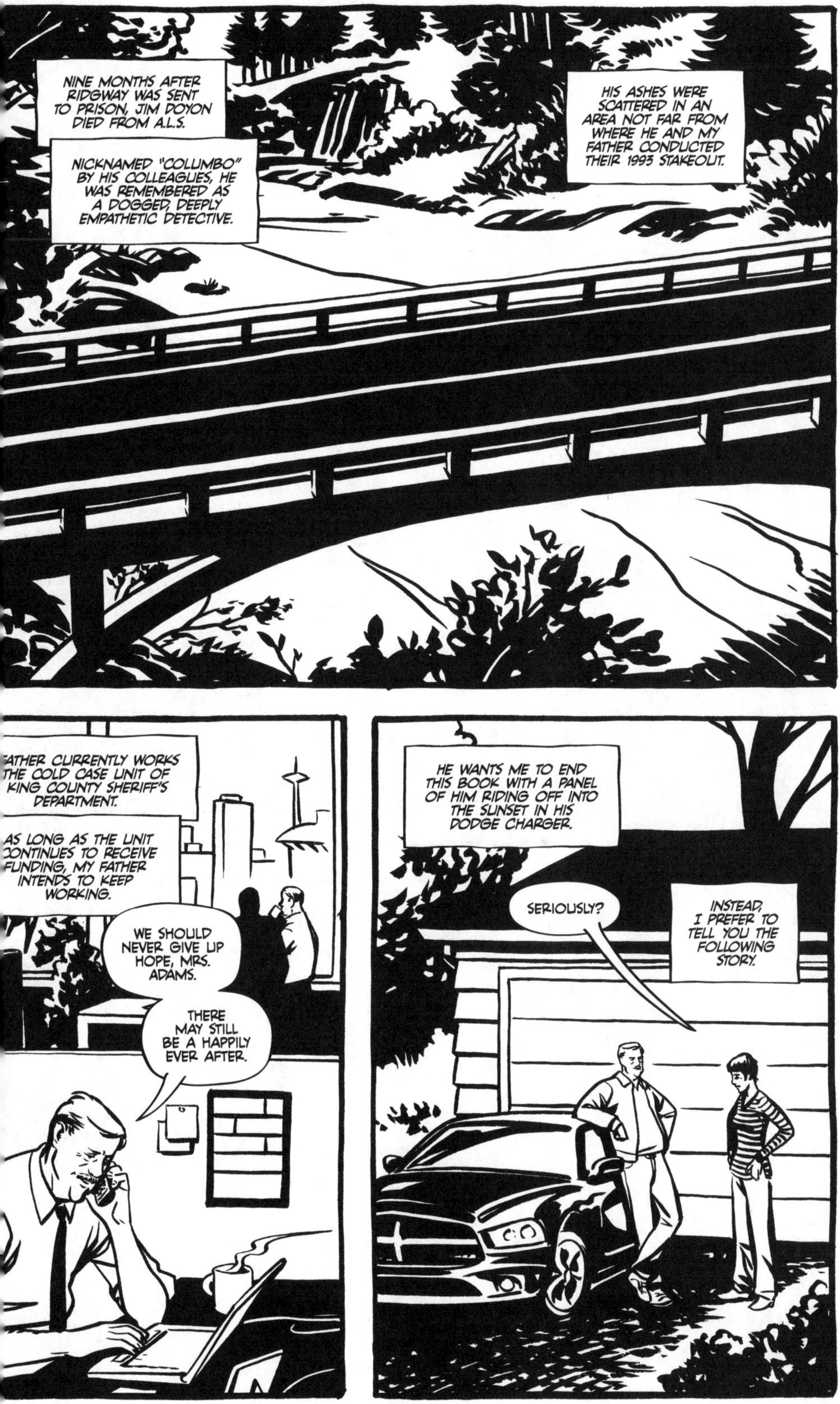
NINE MONTHS AFTER RIDGWAY WAS SENT TO PRISON, JIM DOYON DIED FROM A.L.S.
NICKNAMED "COLUMBO" BY HIS COLLEAGUES, HE WAS REMEMBERED AS A DOGGED, DEEPLY EMPATHETIC DETECTIVE.
HIS ASHES WERE SCATTERED IN AN AREA NOT FAR FROM WHERE HE AND MY FATHER CONDUCTED THEIR 1993 STAKEOUT.
FATHER CURRENTLY WORKS THE COLD CASE UNIT OF KING COUNTY SHERIFF'S DEPARTMENT.
AS LONG AS THE UNIT CONTINUES TO RECEIVE FUNDING, MY FATHER INTENDS TO KEEP WORKING.
WE SHOULD NEVER GIVE UP HOPE, MRS. ADAMS.
THERE MAY STILL BE A HAPPILY EVER AFTER.
HE WANTS ME TO END THIS BOOK WITH A PANEL OF HIM RIDING OFF INTO THE SUNSET IN HIS DODGE CHARGER.
SERIOUSLY?
INSTEAD, I PREFER TO TELL YOU THE FOLLOWING STORY.

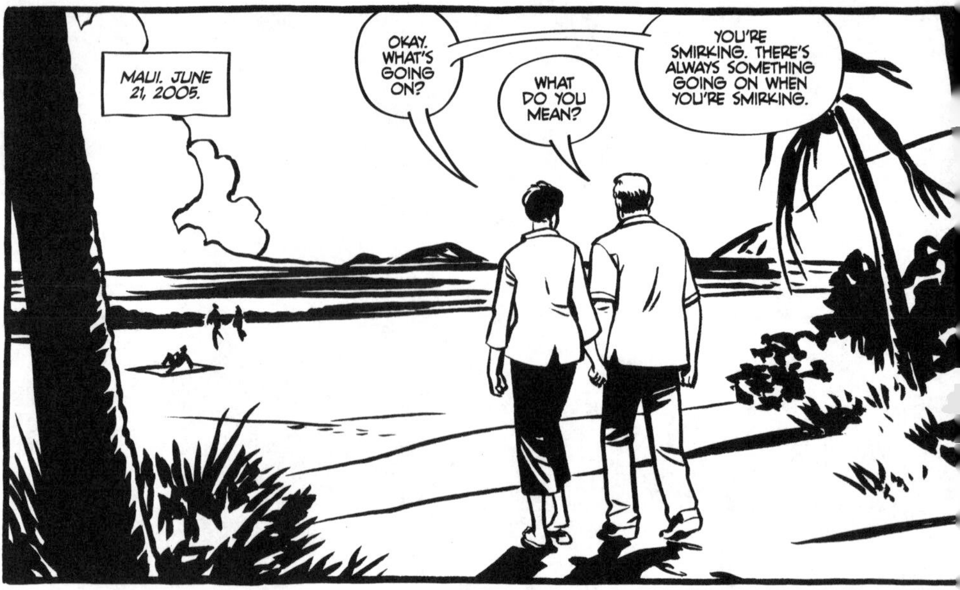
MAUI. JUNE 21, 2005.
OKAY. WHAT'S GOING ON?
WHAT DO YOU MEAN?
YOU'RE SMIRKING. THERE'S ALWAYS SOMETHING GOING ON WHEN YOU'RE SMIRKING.

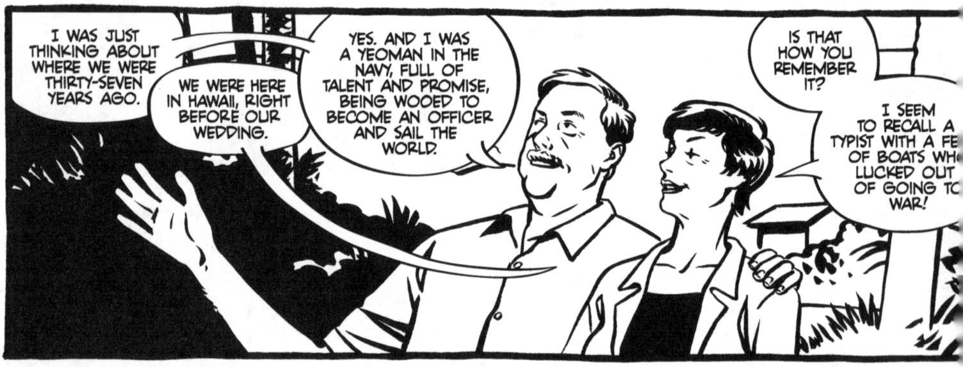
I WAS JUST THINKING ABOUT WHERE WE WERE THIRTY-SEVEN YEARS AGO.
WE WERE HERE IN HAWAII, RIGHT BEFORE OUR WEDDING.
YES. AND I WAS A YEOMAN IN THE NAVY, FULL OF TALENT AND PROMISE, BEING WOOED TO BECOME AN OFFICER AND SAIL THE WORLD.
IS THAT HOW YOU REMEMBER IT?
I SEEM TO RECALL A TYPIST WITH A FE OF BOATS WH LUCKED OUT OF GOING TO WAR!

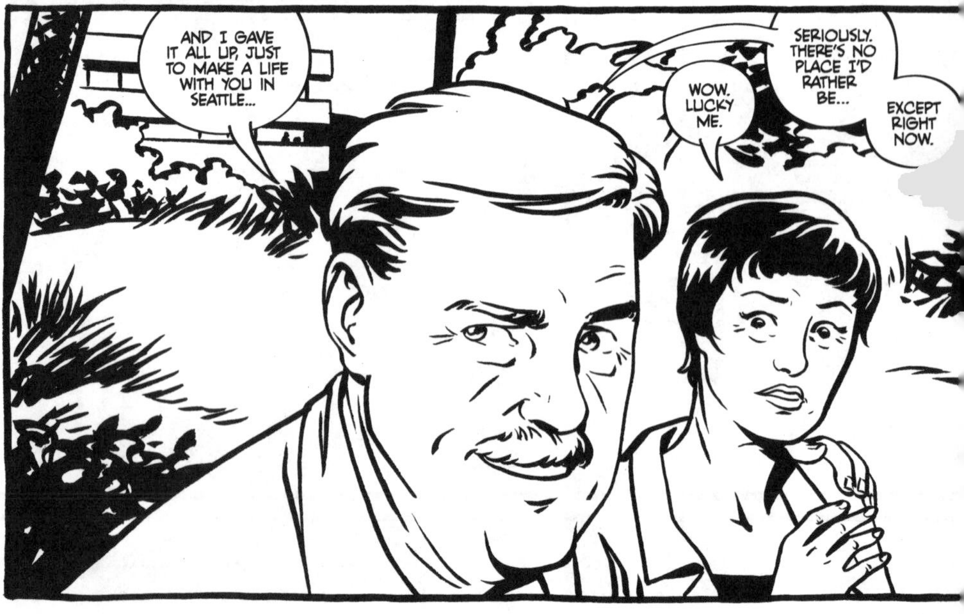
AND I GAVE IT ALL UP, JUST TO MAKE A LIFE WITH YOU IN SEATTLE...
WOW. LUCKY ME.
SERIOUSLY. THERE'S NO PLACE I'D RATHER BE...
EXCEPT RIGHT NOW.

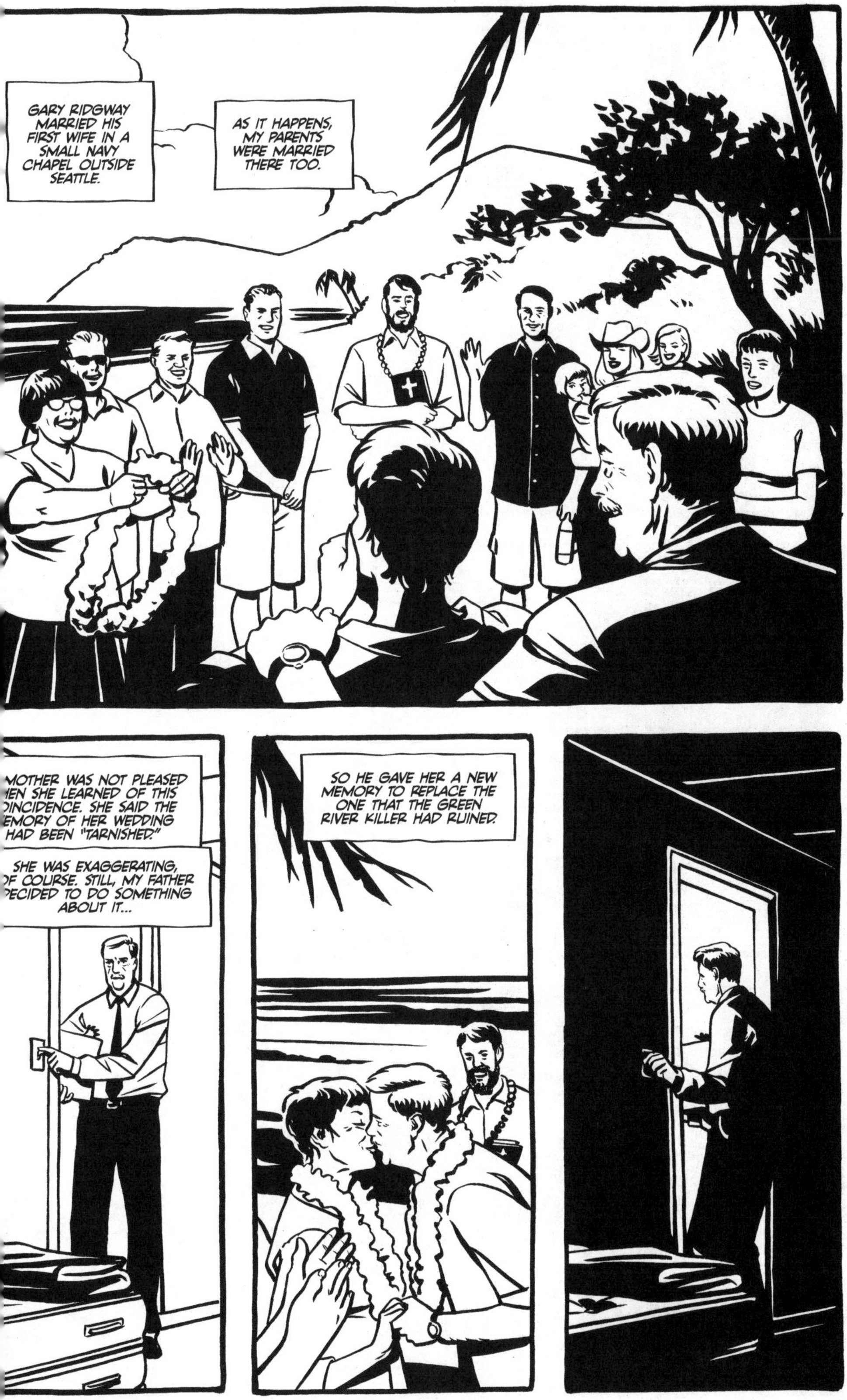
GARY RIDGWAY MARRIED HIS FIRST WIFE IN A SMALL NAVY CHAPEL OUTSIDE SEATTLE.
AS IT HAPPENS, MY PARENTS WERE MARRIED THERE TOO.
MOTHER WAS NOT PLEASED IEN SHE LEARNED OF THIS OINCIDENCE. SHE SAID THE EMORY OF HER WEDDING HAD BEEN "TARNISHED."
SHE WAS EXAGGERATING, OF COURSE. STILL, MY FATHER ECIDED TO DO SOMETHING ABOUT IT...
SO HE GAVE HER A NEW MEMORY TO REPLACE THE ONE THAT THE GREEN RIVER KILLER HAD RUINED.

ACKNOWLEDGMENTS

JEFF JENSEN

I wrote this book to gain a better understanding of my father and to express my love for him. I am grateful to the following, who offered insight and encouragement in pursuit of those goals: My wife, Amy Jensen; my mother, Charlaine Jensen; my brother and his wife, Mike and Stephanie Jensen; Phil Jimenez; Dave Reichert, Randy Mullinax, Jon Mattsen, and Mark Prothero; my Seattle family; my community of friends (Pine Tree; Small Group; Grace Brethren Church of Long Beach); my colleagues at *Entertainment Weekly*; Dan Snierson; Ken Tucker; Damon Lindelof, Carlton Cuse, and Jack Bender; Andy Ward and Dan Fierman; Ramon Perez; Marc Bernardin; Craig Thompson; Jonathan Case; Mike Richardson, Scott Allie, Brendan Wright, and everyone at Dark Horse, but especially my editor, Sierra Hahn, whose faith, nurturing, and deep humanity were not only blessings to this book but to my life and my family. Thank you.

JONATHAN CASE

Thanks to Sierra and Jeff for bringing this story to me, and especially to Tom, for seeing it through. A big thanks to my studio mates at Periscope, who helped keep a smile on my face. And to Sarah, for her support and love.

LEARN MORE

Green River Killer: A True Detective Story is a graphic novel inspired by true events. It is not intended as history or memoir. The names and some biographical details of the victims and their families have been changed. For the record, Gary Ridgway was represented by a team of lawyers, not just Mark Prothero. Other characters, like Jim Graddon, are composites representing multiple individuals.

The Green River Killer's victims were prostitutes, but to their families they were daughters, sisters, and mothers. They stand for a larger group of women and children victimized through sex and labor exploitation, brought into prostitution by force, fraud, and coercion. To learn more and discover how you can help, please check out the following resources:

- The Polaris Project (PolarisProject.org) runs the National Human Trafficking Resource Center, a nonprofit, nongovernmental organization.

- The Nest Foundation (PlaygroundProject.com) raises public awareness of commercial sexual exploitation of children through their documentary *Playground*, executive produced by George Clooney and Steven Soderbergh, among others.

- The FBI (FBI.gov) provides a wealth of information on human trafficking and the US government's efforts against it.

- Your local nonprofits and law-enforcement offices.

ABOUT THE CREATORS

JEFF JENSEN lives with his family in Southern California and is the television critic for *Entertainment Weekly*. He co-wrote the Disney film *Tomorrowland* with Damon Lindelof and Brad Bird.

JONATHAN CASE is a comics creator and illustrator living in Portland, Oregon. He's best known for his graphic novels *Dear Creature* and *The New Deal* and has collaborated on several projects, including *Batman '66* with Jeff Parker and *The Creep* with John Arcudi. Case also cowrote and illustrated the novel *Before Tomorrowland* with Jeff Jensen, Damon Lindelof, and Brad Bird.

President and Publisher **MIKE RICHARDSON**

Editor **SIERRA HAHN**

Assistant Editor **BRENDAN WRIGHT**

Collection Designer **AMY ARENDTS**

Neil Hankerson *Executive Vice President* · Tom Weddle *Chief Financial Officer* · Randy Stradley *Vice President of Publishing* · Michael Martens *Vice President of Book Trade Sales* · Scott Allie *Editor in Chief* Matt Parkinson *Vice President of Marketing* · David Scroggy *Vice President of Product Development* Dale LaFountain *Vice President of Information Technology* · Ken Lizzi *General Counsel* · Davey Estrada *Editorial Director* · Chris Warner *Senior Books Editor* · Cary Grazzini *Director of Print and Development* Lia Ribacchi *Art Director* · Cara Niece *Director of Scheduling* · Mark Bernardi *Director of Digital Publishing*

Published by Dark Horse Books
A division of Dark Horse Comics, Inc.
10956 SE Main Street
Milwaukie, OR 97222

DarkHorse.com

International Licensing: (503) 905-2377

First paperback edition: October 2015
ISBN 978-1-61655-812-3

1 2 3 4 5 6 7 8 9 10
Printed in the United States of America

More great

NOIR AND ESPIONAGE

from Dark Horse Books

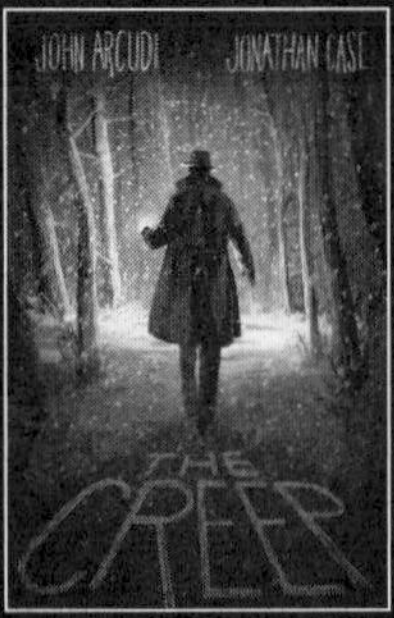
JOHN ARCUDI
JONATHAN CASE
THE CREEP

THE CREEP

JOHN ARCUDI, JONATHAN CASE, AND TONCI ZONJIC

A young boy puts a gun in his mouth and pulls the trigger. The police don't care—not about his death or the death of his best friend two months earlier. The dead boy's mom seeks help from an old flame that's employed as a detective. Will the detective's freakish appearance get in the way of uncovering the terrible secrets of these two teenagers?

ISBN 978-1-61655-061-5
$19.99

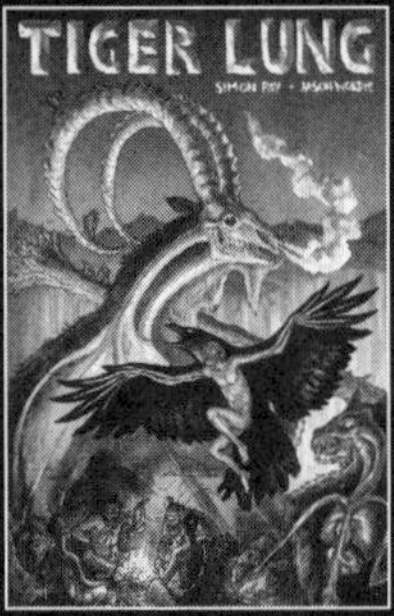
TIGER LUNG

TIGER LUNG

SIMON ROY AND JASON WORDIE

Thirty-five thousand years ago, the world was ruled by strange beasts and ancient gods! For some Paleolithic tribes, hope lay in the shaman warriors who stood between them and the unknown. *Tiger Lung* follows the struggle of one of these shamans to keep his people alive in a vast, hostile universe!

ISBN 978-1-61655-543-6
$15.99

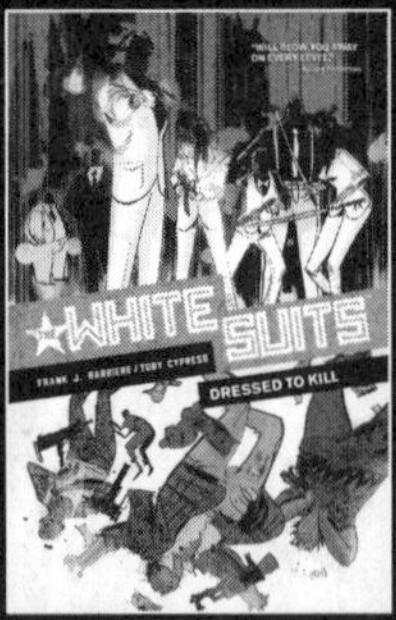
WHITE SUITS
FRANK J. BARBIERE / TOBY CYPRESS
DRESSED TO KILL

THE WHITE SUITS

FRANK BARBIERE AND TOBY CYPRESS

They savaged the Cold War Russian underworld—then disappeared. When they resurface, leaving a trail of dead mobsters in their wake, an amnesiac and an FBI agent seek to answer a single question: Who are the White Suits?

ISBN 978-1-61655-493-4
$17.99

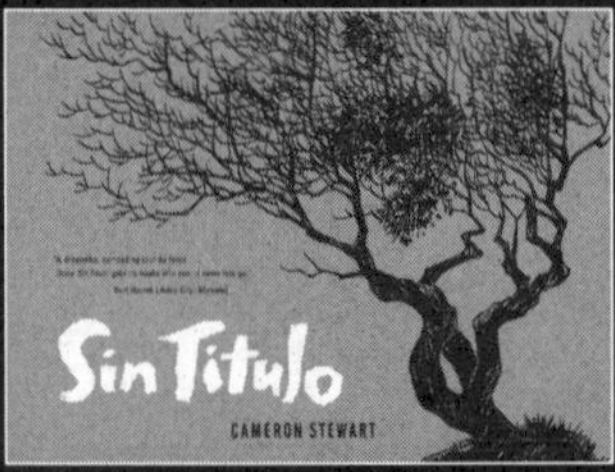
Sin Titulo
CAMERON STEWART

SIN TITULO

CAMERON STEWART

The Eisner Award–winning webcomic! Following the death of his grandfather, young Alex Mackay discovers a mysterious photograph in the old man's belongings that sets him on an adventure like no other—where dreams and reality merge, family secrets are laid bare, and lives are irrevocably altered.

ISBN 978-1-61655-248-0
$19.99

DARK HORSE BOOKS
DarkHorse.com

AVAILABLE AT YOUR LOCAL COMICS SHOP OR BOOKSTORE • TO FIND A COMICS SHOP IN YOUR AREA, CALL 1-888-266-4226

For more information or to order direct: • On the web: DarkHorse.com • E-mail: mailorder@darkhorse.com • Phone: 1-800-862-0052 Mon.–Fri. 9 AM to 5 PM Pacific Time.